Maristella Agosti   Fabio Crestani
Gabriella Pasi (Eds.)

Lectures on Information Retrieval

Third European Summer-School, ESSIR 2000
Varenna, Italy, September 11-15, 2000
Revised Lectures

Springer

Series Editors

Gerhard Goos, Karlsruhe University, Germany
Juris Hartmanis, Cornell University, NY, USA
Jan van Leeuwen, Utrecht University, The Netherlands

Volume Editors

Maristella Agosti
Universitá di Padova, Dipartimento di Elettronica e Informatica
Via Ognissanti, 72, 35131 Padova
E-mail: agosti@dei.unipd.it

Fabio Crestani
University of Strathclyde, Department of Computer Science
Glasgow G1 1XH, Scotland, UK
E-mail: fabioc@cs.strath.ac.uk

Gabriella Pasi
ITIM, Consiglio Nazionale delle Ricerche
Via Ampere, 56, 20131 Milano, Italy
E-mail: gabriella.pasi@itim.mi.cnr.it

Cataloging-in-Publication Data applied for

Die Deutsche Bibliothek - CIP-Einheitsaufnahme

Lectures on information retrieval : third European summerschool ;
revised lectures / ESSIR 2000, Varenna, Italy, September 11 - 15,
2000. Maristella Agosti ... (ed.). - Berlin ; Heidelberg ; New York ;
Barcelona ; Hong Kong ; London ; Milan ; Paris ; Singapore ; Tokyo :
Springer, 2001
  (Lecture notes in computer science ; Vol. 1980)
  ISBN 3-540-41933-0

CR Subject Classification (1998): H.3, H.4, H.5, C.2.4, I.2,1

ISSN 0302-9743
ISBN 3-540-41933-0 Springer-Verlag Berlin Heidelberg New York

Springer-Verlag Berlin Heidelberg New York
a member of BertelsmannSpringer Science+Business Media GmbH

http://www.springer.de

© Springer-Verlag Berlin Heidelberg 2001
Printed in Germany

Typesetting: Camera-ready by author, data conversion by Christian Grosche, Hamburg
Printed on acid-free paper   SPIN 10781284   06/3142   5 4 3 2 1 0

Preface

Information retrieval (IR) is concerned with the effective and efficient retrieval of information based on its semantic content. The central problem in IR is the quest to find the set of relevant documents, among a large collection, containing the information sought, thereby satisfying a user's information need usually expressed in a natural language query. Documents may be objects or items in any medium: text, image, audio, or indeed a mixture of all three.

This book contains the proceedings of the *Third European Summer School in Information Retrieval (ESSIR 2000)*, held on 11–15 September 2000, in Villa Monastero, Varenna, Italy.

The event was jointly organised by the Institute of Multimedia Technologies of the CNR (National Council of Research) based in Milan (Italy), the Department of Electronics and Computer Science of the University of Padova (Italy), and the Department of Computer Science of the University of Strathclyde, Glasgow (UK). Administrative support was provided by Milano Ricerche, a consortium of industries, research institutions and the University of Milano, whose purpose is to provide administrative and technical support for the research and development activities of its members.

This third edition of the European Summer School in Information Retrieval is part of the ESSIR series which began in 1990. The first was organised by Maristella Agosti of the University of Padova and was held in Bressanone (Italy) in 1990. The second ESSIR was organised by Keith van Rijsbergen of the University of Glasgow (UK) and held in Glasgow in 1995, in the context of the IR Festival.

At the time of the first ESSIR, the Internet did not exist, so there is no website available for this event, but from its second edition a web presentation has been made available: the URL for ESSIR'95 is: `http://www.dcs.gla.ac.uk/essir/`, and the URL for ESSIR 2000 is: `http://www.itim.mi.cnr.it/Eventi/ essir2000/index.htm`. These websites contain useful material. In particular, the ESSIR 2000 website contains copies of the material distributed at the school (presentation, notes, etc.).

The aim of ESSIR 2000 was to give participants a grounding in the core subjects of IR, including methods and techniques for designing and developing IR systems, web search engines, and tools for information storing and querying in digital libraries. To achieve these aims, the program of ESSIR 2000 was organised into a series of lectures divided into foundations and advanced parts as reported in the next section. The lecturers were leading European researchers (with only one non-European exception), their course subjects strongly reflecting the research work for which they are all well known.

ESSIR 2000 was intended for researchers starting out in IR, for industrialists who wish to know more about this increasingly important topic and for people working on topics related to the management of information on the Internet. This book, distributed at the school in draft form to incorporate in the final version useful participants' comments, contains 12 chapters written by the school's lecturers, providing surveys of the state of the art of IR and related areas.

Book Structure

The ESSIR 2000 programme of lectures and this book are divided into in two parts: one part on the foundations of IR and related areas (e.g. digital libraries), and one on advanced topics.

The part on foundations contains seven papers/chapters. In Chap. 1, Keith van Rijsbergen introduces some underlying concepts and ideas essential for understanding IR research and techniques. He also highlights some related hot areas of research, emphasising the role of IR in each. In Chap. 2, Norbert Fuhr presents the main mathematical models of IR. This paper provides the theoretical basis for representing the informative content of documents and for estimating the relevance of a document to a query. In Chap. 3, Páraic Sheridan and Carol Peters detail the issues and proposed solutions for multilingual information access in digital archives. Chapter 4, by Stephen Robertson, addresses the topic of evaluation, a very important aspect of IR. In Chap. 5 and 6, Alan Smeaton and John Eakins address issues and techniques related to indexing, browsing and searching multimedia information (audio, image, or digital video). Finally, in Chap. 7 Ingeborg Solvberg covers the basics and the challenges of digital libraries.

The part on advanced topics contains five papers/chapters. In Chap. 8, Peter Ingwersen concentrates on user issues and the usability of interactive IR. Chap. 9, by Fabio Crestani and Mounia Lalmas addresses the use of logic and uncertainty theories in IR. Closely related is Chap. 10, by Gabriella Pasi and Gloria Bordogna, which presents the area of research that aims at modelling the vagueness and imprecision involved in the IR process. In Chap. 11, Maristella Agosti and Massimo Melucci address the use of IR techniques on the Web for searching and browsing. Finally, in Chap. 12, Yves Chiaramella addresses the issues related to indexing and retrieval of structured documents.

Acknowledgements

The editors would like to thank all the participants of ESSIR 2000 for making the event a success. ESSIR 2000 was a success not just for the quality of the lectures, the authority of the lecturers, and the beautiful surroundings, it was a success because it was informal and interactive. For the best part of a week, more than 60 participants and 12 lecturers exchanged ideas and inspirations on where IR is at and where it should go. Many attendants (not just school participants, but some of the lecturers too) returned home with renewed encouragement and motivation.

We thank the sponsoring and supporting institutions for making it possible, financially, to hold the event. Also, we thank the Local Organising Committee, the student volunteers and the personnel of Villa Monastero (Rino Venturini) for their invaluable help.

A special thanks to all the lecturers for their contributions, encouragement, and support. The quality of this book is mostly due to their work.

Finally, we would like to thank the Board of the Special Interest Network on Information Retrieval of the Council of European Professional Informatics Societies (CEPIS-IR), which includes Keith van Rijsbergen, Norbert Fuhr and Alan Smeaton, for their scientific support and invaluable advice on the school content and program.

September 2000

Maristella Agosti
Fabio Crestani
Gabriella Pasi

Organisation and Support

Scientific Program and Organising Committee

ESSIR 2000 was jointly organised by:

- Maristella Agosti, Department of Electronics and Computer Science, University of Padova, Padova, Italy;
- Fabio Crestani, Department of Computer Science, University of Strathclyde, Glasgow, UK;
- Gabriella Pasi, Institute of Multimedia Technologies, National Council of Research (CNR), Milan, Italy.

Local Organising Committee

ESSIR 2000 was locally organised by the Institute of Multimedia Technologies of CNR in Milan, Italy. In particular by: Gabriella Pasi, Gloria Bordogna, Paola Carrara, Alba L'Astorina, Luciana Onorato and Bruna Zonta.

Sponsoring Institutions

The main sponsoring and supporting organisation was the Special Interest Network on Information Retrieval of the Council of European Professional Informatics Societies (CEPIS-IR). CEPIS-IR provided a running grant, which made it possible to award a number of bursaries to support young students and researchers to attend the school. CEPIS-IR also provided invaluable advice on the school program.
The other sponsors were:

- Arnoldo Mondadori Editore, Verona, Italy;
- Microsoft Italia, Milan, Italy;
- Oracle Italia, Milan, Italy;
- Sharp Laboratories of Europe, Oxford, UK;
- 3D Informatica, San Lazzaro di Savena (Bologna), Italy.

Supporting Institutions

ESSIR 2000 benefited from the support of the following organisations:

- CEPIS-IR (Special Interest Network on Information Retrieval of the Council of European Professional Informatics Societies);
- AEI (Gruppo Specialistico Tecnologie e Applicazioni Informatiche);
- EUREL (Convention of National Societies of Electrical Engineers of Europe).

Contents

Getting into Information Retrieval

C.J. "Keith" van Rijsbergen

Department of Computing Science, University of Glasgow
Glasgow G12 8QQ, Scotland
keith@dcs.gla.ac.uk

Abstract This is a general introduction to Information Retrieval concentrating on some specific topics. I will begin by setting the scene for IR research and introduce its extensive experimental evaluation methodology. I will highlight some of the related areas of research which are currently in fashion emphasising the role of IR in each. For each introductory topic I will illustrate its relevance to IR in the context of a multimedia and multi-lingual environment where appropriate. I will also try and relate these topics to the other papers contained in this volume. My main purpose will be to introduce some underlying concepts and ideas essential for the understanding of IR research and techniques.

1 Introduction

As one who has been involved in information retrieval research since about 1969 it is wonderful to see how some of our work has been absorbed and adopted by a number of technologies. In particular it is fascinating to see how the development of the Web has spawned a number of exciting and unique IR research problems. In this paper I hope to touch on some of these but always from the perspective of an IR researcher who is looking to make connections between the IR research methodology and the interests of those focused on other technologies. For example, it is clear to us in the IR community that the web represents an emerging technology which encompasses much more than information retrieval, nevertheless, some of its important problems relate specifically to IR.

The history of IR is long and fraught [42]. For many years it was unclear whether it was a subject at all, then when it became a subject, it was claimed by both Information Science and Computer Science. Although in the early days during the 50's and 60's this difficulty was responsible for a number of frustrations, for example the unwillingness of librarians to accept hard experimental results, it now is also one of its strengths. We interact fruitfully, the information science community guarding us against technological, or system-based excesses, the computer science community representing a hard-nosed approach to experimental designs and being forced into taking user-interface issues seriously. A marriage made in heaven!

For years I have advocated the interplay of theory, practice, and experiment. My first serious attempt to talk about this was probably in a seminar presentation I gave in 1977 where I quoted the following from Freud:

M. Agosti, F. Crestani, and G. Pasi (Eds.): ESSIR 2000, LNCS 1980, pp. 1–20, 2000.
© Springer-Verlag Berlin Heidelberg 2000

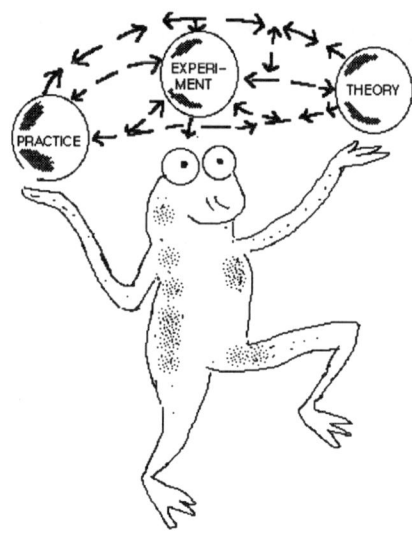

(During my 1977 talk, Robert Fairthorne[1], one the pioneers of IR was in the audience, and clearly taken with my three way balancing act drew the above cartoon.)

> ..., I think ... that the great problems of the universe and of science have the first claim on our interest. But it is as a rule of very little use to form an express intention of devoting oneself to research into this or that great problem. One is then often at a loss to know the first step to take. It is more promising in scientific work to attack whatever is immediately before one and offers an opportunity for research. If one does so really thoroughly and without prejudice or preconception, and if one has luck, then since everything is related to everything, including small things to great, one may gain access even from such unpretentious work to a study of the great problems

I still largely agree with this slogan, or motto. Curiously I would claim that considerable progress in IR has been made precisely because IR researchers took seriously the solving of "whatever is immediately before" us. The theoretical models and breakthroughs largely arose out of detailed experimentation, and new models sometimes arose out of the failure of existing models to deliver the anticipated experimental performance. For example the failure of probabilistically based term dependence models to show improvement in effectiveness over simpler independence models has lead to a number of alternative approaches.

2 Some Meta-thoughts on IR

It seems to me that it is possible to characterise the IR viewpoint in a number of ways. To begin with no a priori assumptions are made about structure or

---

[1] Sadly Fairthorne has recently died, he was fondly known to some as the "frog-prince."

process, unless given by the raw data or some external constraints. This is most obvious when it comes to classifications; these are intended to reflect the inherent structure in the data and are not imposed. When it comes to features/attributes, relevance, or aboutness a categorical view is not always taken, that is, a document is not either relevant or not-relevant, a document is not either about X or not about X, etc. Processes in IR are usually adaptive making them user-driven and context dependent, this is particular evident in relevance feedback. The semantics of objects are defined by the data, in other words, it is the distribution both within a document and across documents that give the "meaning" of terms. IR on the whole makes no claims about Knowledge we tend to work with notions of Information and as such consider the probability of propositions to be indefinitely revisable in the light of the weight of evidence. (This is an issue in the Bayesian context when $P(X) = 1$; as an exercise the reader might like to do a Bayesian revision of a proposition X whose probability is one in the light of some new evidence.). Following from this we tend to work with contingent truths rather than necessary truth, and of course this effects the kind of logics we are interested in. Finally, a trend that has emerged in the last few years is that interactions with IR systems can be based on ostensive manipulation and definition, that is, systems react to what a user does, or points to, not only to what the user says or writes.

3 Practice, Experiments, and Theory

Let me say a little more about these three disparate activities in IR.

Practice. A huge amount of operational retrieval using the web takes place, and a lot of it is woeful. A major practical challenge for IR is to influence the design of search engines so that retrieval performance goes beyond what you get by just submitting a 2.4 word query. In electronic publishing, as pursued by the large publishers for example, much multimedia data is conveniently made available but unfortunately the search capabilities are mostly inadequate. Commerce seems have discovered the knowledge economy and so data mining and knowledge discovery are the flavour of the month. Of course there is a long history in IR using statistical techniques to model significance and dependence. If one thinks about the provision of materials for distance learning whether they be text, image or graphics, then once large repositories of such information becomes available a major issue will be its retrieval. Many of these issues, especially those concerned with standards, are now addressed in the context of Digital Libraries (see Sølvberg, this volume).

Experiments. There is a long and honourable tradition of experimental work in IR. Cyril Cleverdon one of the pioneers, together with Jack Mills and Michael Keen produced a series of reports, initially the Cranfield I (1960) study followed by a more substantial study in 1966 [10], "Factors determining the performance of indexing systems." These projects can claim to be responsible for founding the experimental approach that is now know as the "Cranfield Paradigm," it to this day continues in the extremely successful series of experiments known as TREC (see http://trec.nist.gov). To understand the difficulties associated with designing test collections for IR one may read the report by Sparck Jones and Van Rijsbergen [41]. Future experimenters are encouraged to examine the approach to experimentation in IR thoroughly. A classic summary of the IR approach can be found in the collection of papers edited by Sparck Jones, "Information retrieval experiment" in 1981.

Theory. Much theory in IR has come about through "knob twiddling," this generally means adjusting a set of parameters for a given retrieval model and observing the effect on retrieval performance. Of course this can lead to mindless experimentation but it has also led to new variants of statistical models. Dissatisfaction with a given model, often because of poor retrieval, has led to proposals for new models embodying such disparate approaches as Bayesian Inference, Clustering, Non-classical Logic, Dempster Shafer Theory of Evidence, etc. Considerable theoretical work has also gone into the design of evaluation measures, that is, ways to mathematically, represent retrieval effectiveness, to average it, and to establish statistical significance. Two recent papers worth looking at demonstrating that the debate over effectiveness measures continues are [21] and [58]. Ever since the time of Cleverdon, Precision and Recall have been favoured. Unfortunately recall is not always readily available, think of retrieval from the Web, nor is precision always appropriate in dynamic task-oriented environments. To pursue this problem I recommend a look at [17].

4   IR System Architecture

Figure 2 shows a traditional view of an IR system. I believe that since the early seventies we have displayed it this way, and it has been used regularly ever since in papers on IR, just like I am doing now. It highlights one of the central concerns of IR, namely, Relevance Feedback. Of all the techniques invented to enhance retrieval effectiveness, relevance feedback is perhaps the most consistently successful. For a detailed overview see the survey article by [43]. A side-effect of this success has been to concentrate on system's development to improve and generalise relevance feedback perhaps to the detriment of actual user studies. It is common knowledge that many users do not understand relevance feedback and are not good at using it. Furthermore, when the initial input to the feedback cycle is poor, as it often is in Web searches, a sophisticated feedback mechanism is not much use: telling the IR system that all the retrieved documents are non-relevant is not helpful, the prior probability of such a retrieval is already very high.

5   The Twelve Dimensions of IR

I originally [50] designed the table in Table 1 as a way of comparing databases with information retrieval, however over time this comparison has become more generic. The differences between DB and IR have become less marked. I now

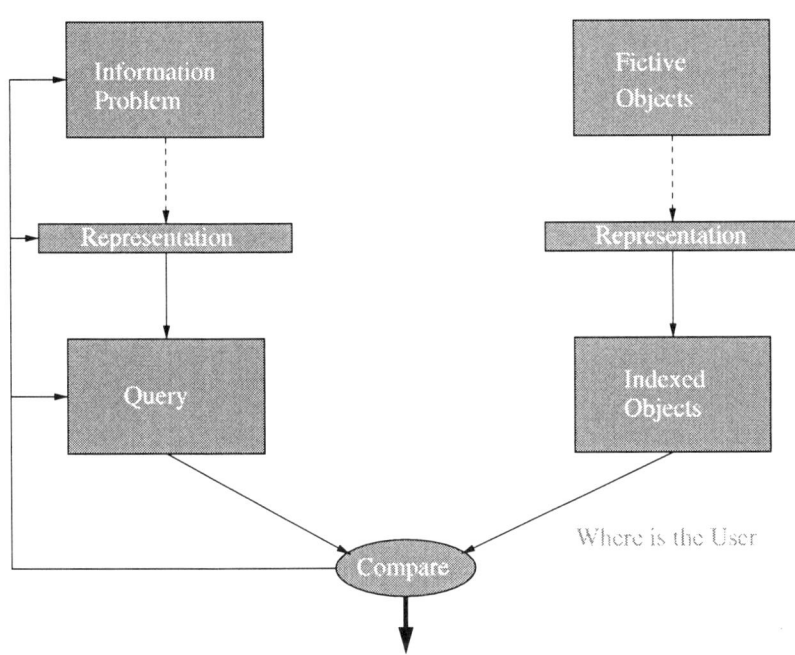

view this table as a way of focussing attention on a number of salient dimensions that span research in areas such as IR, databases, data-mining, knowledge discovery etc. It enables me to discuss IR research in a limited and constrained way without taking on the whole subject. In what follows I will address each one of these dimensions and describe where we are with research in that area. For a more recent discussion of this table in terms of data and document retrieval I recommend David Blair's book, Language and Representation in Information Retrieval, Elsevier, 1990.

6   Matching

Fundamental to any retrieval operation is the notion of matching. One can track progress in IR in terms of the increased sophistication of the matching function. Typically these functions are the consequence of a model of retrieval. For example the Boolean matching, and the Logical Uncertainty Principle (LUP) (see the paper by Crestani and Lalmas, this volume) both presuppose an elementary model and proof theory from formal logic. In the case of the LUP an assumption is made about how to measure partial entailment. There are four major IR models[2], vector-space, probabilistic, logical, and Bayesian net. Each has its corresponding matching function, for example the vector-space model predominantly uses the cosine correlation or one of its variants. Optimality criteria come

---

[2] A fifth model based on the ASK (Anomolous State of Knowledge) hypothesis does not really fit into this scheme, I will return to it in the section on models.

Table 1.

Matching	Exact Match	Partial (best) Match
Inference	Deduction	Induction
Model	Deterministic	Probabilistic
Classification	Monothetic	Polythetic
Query language	Artificial	Natural
Query definition	Complete	Incomplete
Query dependence	Yes	No
Items wanted	Matching	Relevant
Error response	Sensitive	Insensitive
Logic	Classical	Non-classical
Representation	A priori	A posteriori
Language Models	Logical	Statistical

into play in deriving these functions, sometimes related to performance as in the case of the Probability Ranking Principle [32], sometimes related to minimal change as in LUP (see Crestani and Lalmas, this volume). In the case of the Bayesian net there is a strict adherence to Bayes' Theorem to control the propagation of probabilities. These functions do not necessarily presuppose a representation mechanism, so objects may be represented by absence/presence of index terms, or indeed may involve frequency data related to index term distributions within a document or over the entire collection. Each one of these models has led to a significant working IR system, for example,

Table 2.

Vector-space →	SMART	Salton, 1971
Probabilistic →	Okapi	Robertson, 1997
Logical →	Hyspirit	Rölleke, 1999
Bayesian net →	INQUERY	Callan et al, 1992

One of the difficulties in extending this type of matching to web data is that frequency data may not be available—we operate in an open world rather than a closed one. Another problem is associated with extending these functions to image matching. Right now it is fashionable to invent ontologies for representing and describing web documents, it is difficult to see how to combine the results of "ontology matching" or inference with the standard IR forms of matching. Of course different search engines use different matching functions and combining the results of those is a problem in its own right.

7   Inference

The major kind of inference that is used in IR is inductive (and sometimes abductive), that is a weight of evidence calculation is done to support a hypothesis or its alternative. One could characterise this by saying that what is important here is to be able to execute intelligent guessing. So for example, modus ponens is usually subject to degrees of uncertainty, where A and $A \to B$ is known only with a probability and we "guess" at the probability of B [54]. The kind of inference common in ontology based reasoning does not allow for uncertainty. This raises the spectre of the debate about controlled versus uncontrolled vocabularies that took place in IR many years ago.

Some of the inductive inferences in IR are based on assumptions about the associations between descriptors/attributes used to represent objects. A frequent assumption is that attributes are probabilistically independent. This means that one attribute does not contain any information about another. The reverse assumption can be made, that is, that knowing something about one attribute, for example it features prominently in relevant documents, then a closely associated attribute may also be a good indicator of relevance. IR has found a number of ways of exploiting this. In the past it has been difficult to do so because of the small data sets available to estimate importance of attributes. Within the context of the web this is not a problem. This approach could be extremely useful if users only type very short queries and techniques are needed to extend (automatically) such queries.

A longstanding inductive hypothesis is the Cluster Hypothesis. This was originally formulated to justify the use of automatic classification, or clustering, of documents, as; closely associated documents tend to be relevant to the same requests [55]. A more appropriate and alternative way to formulate it would be:

If document X is closely associated with document Y, then over the population of potential queries the probability of relevance for X will be approximately the same as the probability of relevance for Y, or in symbols

$$P(\text{relevance}|X) \sim P(\text{relevance}|Y)$$

Much experimentation has since gone into establishing empirical evidence for and against it. There is a long tradition of clustering in IR; some of the earliest work was done by Salton's students, especially Murray and Rocchio (see [13, 37, 39, 46, 56]). This work lay unexploited until recently when the development in the web caused people to rethink the issue of data reduction and representation techniques.

Another inductive hypothesis, the Association Hypothesis, is concerned with index terms: If one index term is good at discriminating relevant from non-relevant documents, then any closely associated index term is also likely to be good at this. This seems to be a possible flip-side of the Cluster Hypothesis. In this hypothesis one is looking for dependence between attributes. It is a well known fact that the set of documents and the set of index terms can be viewed as dual spaces of each other. Thus in principle given enough information about the index term space and the document space one can model retrieval in one or the other. A quantitative development of this is the discrimination gain hypothesis.

Under the hypothesis of conditional independence the statistical information contained in one index term about another is less than the information contained in either index term about relevance. That is,

$$P(X,Y|W) = P(X|W) \times P(Y|W) \Rightarrow I(X,Y) < I(X,W) \text{ or } I(Y,W),$$

where X and Y are index terms, W is relevance, P a probability measure, and I a measure of information. A detailed discussion of this result can be found in [52].

One comment worth making is that given the tendency of users searching the web to generate short queries, often a single term, one can see how a hypothesis like this might be exploited to help improve the query through a form of query expansion. Interest in research in this area has recently been rekindled by Wong and Butz [57] continuing a development initiated by Van Rijsbergen [48], Harper [16] and Yu, et al [59].

8   Models

One of the interesting aspects of current search technology for the WWW is that it is almost model free, although one could claim that many search engines approximate some of the IR models more or less. This is not necessarily a bad thing to ensure that these engines work reliably and scaleably. Unfortunately to improve the effectiveness of such search engines one will need to pay more attention to models of the process so that one can reason about it and make predictions. In IR there has been a steady development of such models.

I have already alluded to these models when describing different matching functions. The Vector-Space model is very dependent on the choice of inter document similarity/dissimilarity, that is, it takes its structure from the 'metric' on the document space. There is a large literature on the choice of appropriate 'metrics', or equivalently similarity, dissimilarity, or association measures, some guidance is given in Chapter 3 of [50]. Some of the practical aspects of the computation of such measures is given in [14], and more theoretical detail independent of IR applications are best found in [38]. Although there is this a large variety of measures to represent structure there is little evidence to suggest that one measure is preferred over another, and so researchers have tended to work with the standard ones such as cosine correlation, Jaccard and Dice coefficients, the Expected Mutual Information Measure, and more recently the Kullback-Leibler divergence.

The Probabilistic Model comes in various flavours, one is determined by the probability with which a term occurs in a relevant document as compared with its probability of occcurrence in a non-relevant document (see Chapter 6 of [50] for a tutorial). A second version is based on an estimate of the probability with which a user would use a term to ask for a particular document [23]. And then of course one could combine these [34]. It is curious that the difference between Objective and Subjective probability is reflected here: 'objective because the probability is based on counting terms, 'subjective' because the probability is based on user judgment. A further development of the probabilistic model is achieved through the use of probability kinematics (Jeffrey, 1983) [19] and its application to generalising Bayesian conditioning [53] leading to a new form of conditionalisation known as imaging (see [11], and, Crestani and Lalmas, this volume).

The Logical Model, as it has now become know, is less well developed and has been tested less extensively than the vector-space and probabilistic one. Its basis is a form of plausible inference. The model starts by assuming that IR can be regarded as uncertain inference. A specific model then arises by specifying an underlying logic to handle implications and by deciding how uncertainty for such implications is to be handled, further details are given by Fuhr in his chapter in this volume. The model was originally formulated in 1986, the paper describing it has been reprinted in [12] together with a number of related papers presenting modifications, improvements, generalisations, critiques of the original model.

The Probabilistic Net approach created by Croft and his co-workers also rely on a form of plausible inference. However, this time no particular logic is assumed and the propagation of uncertainty through the net is constrained by the operation of Bayes' Theorem. A discussion of this model can be found in [45].

The four major retrieval models described thus far have been based on a particular formal and mathematical formalism. There is a well known model that does not fall under this theme, it is the ASK model. ASK stands for anomolous state of knowledge and takes a cognitive perspective of the retrieval process. The underlying idea is that a user's information need is generated by a user's state of knowledge, in particular the sense that, his or her state of knowledge is incomplete, or in need of revision. The retrieval of a relevant document is then one that completes or revises the state of knowledge, to generate a new state which then gives rise to a new information need, etc. This is a simplified description of ASK, interested readers can consult [2]. A further development of this cognitive approach to IR is given by Ingwersen in this volume.

The models described above are mostly concerned with the structure of document sets considering documents largely as atomic units. There are new models concerned with the internal structure of documents. One of these is described by Chiaramella in this volume, another involving the use of uncertainty is documented in [20]. Both arose out of the original work on the FERMI project [8].

Finally, I should mention language models which constitute an active area of research, see for example [30]. Until recently statistical information about the occurrence of terms (tokens) in a document or over a collection of documents has been largely used in a heuristic manner. In the last few years elaborate stochastic process models have been proposed to represent the tokens within a document: retrieval is then determined by the probability with which a query is generated. In my view this is a development of the logical framework which attempts to give a semantics for $P(d \rightarrow q)$.

9 Partial Models

All this talk of models and modelling often leaves one lost in levels of abstraction. Let me try and describe in a general way how models arise in IR. We make the assumption that at any moment in time, there are relevant documents (white) to be found amongst the set of documents (green). Let us assume that by some

Partial Models

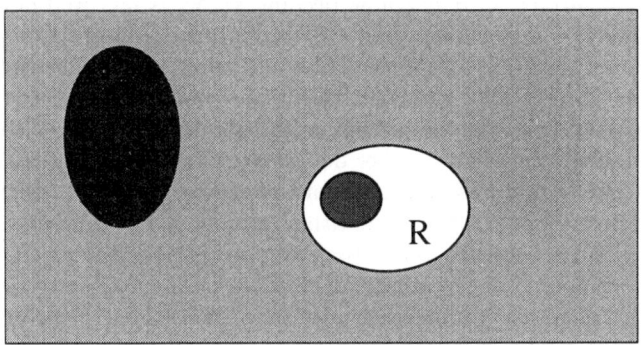

means one can identify some of the relevant ones (red) and non-relevant ones (blue). This means that one has devised a way, maybe a decision function, to separate at least partially the relevant from the non-relevant ones. Most of the retrieval models are able to make this initial separation. Also, mostly this initial separation is not good enough. The grand challenge is to use the 'sample' information to adapt the separation to reflect the user's orientation so that the remaining relevant documents can be found. To this end the full strength of all the modelling: metrics, logics, stochastic processes, inference, etc come into play. This is similarly the case when the green set is the entire web.

10   Classification

The use of automatic classification (or clustering) techniques in IR goes back a long way. It may be of interest to give a little history about the use and development of these techniques for IR, especially since recently these techniques have found favour again for supporting browsing (see the paper by Agosti amd Melucci, this volume) and for the generation of thesaurus classes.

One of the earliest people to use clustering in IR was Roger Needham in Cambridge. Both he an Karen Sparck Jones worked in the Cambridge Language Research Unit, and of course Sparck Jones continued to work in classification publishing a book and a number of papers on the subject [39]. Salton and his students [37] did extensive work on document clustering followed by extensive work in the late seventies by Bruce Croft [13] and Peter Willett [56]. Much of this early work was influenced by the theoretical work carried out in Numerical Taxonomy (see [38]). The recent return of interest in clustering does not seem to have picked up on the extensive theoretical work that was done in the sixties and seventies. This is particularly noticeable in the work that is proposing the Kullback-Leibler information as an asymmetric measure of similarity. For example, [18] contains an extensive account of how to construct dissimilarity measures based on information-theoretic considerations. Similarly many of the theoretical properties of clustering methods, such as order independence, continuity, go unnoticed, which from a scientific point of view: reproducibility and reliability of experiments, are important.

A simple introduction to Automatic Classification can be found in [49] where further historical references are given, more advanced details are available in Chapter 3 of [50]. A recent collection of papers on clustering and classification can be found in a special issue edited by Murtagh [25], it also contains some papers specifically dealing with IR.

In IR, classification has always been seen as "classification for a purpose." The idea that one could define classification independent of other considerations has never been attractive. A quote from Borges [4, p. 108] shows wonderfully how extreme these purposes might be.

> "On those remote pages it is written that animals are divided into (a) those that belong to the Emporer, (b) embalmed ones, (c) those that are trained, (d) suckling pigs, (e) mermaids, (f) fabulous ones, (g) stray dogs, (h) those that are included into this classification, (i) those that tremble as if they were mad, (j) innumerable ones, (k) those drawn with a very fine camel's hair brush, (l) others, (m) those that have just broken a flower vase, (n) those that resemble flies from a distance." Taken from the Celestial Emporium of Benevolent Knowledge.

In the world of Ontologies there is an inclination to perceive classification as defined in absolute terms, for example one might write down the necessary and sufficient conditions, following [31], for class membership to arrive at "natural kinds," this would be an example of a monothetic classification, a polythetic approach would be less strict about class membership, in the latter case membership might depend on the number of shared attributes. IR, pattern recognition, and numerical taxonomy have tended to follow the second approach. Thus the similarity measures mentioned before mostly represent a polythetic approach to classification.

11   Queries Language, Definition, and Dependence

One of the main thrusts of IR research has been to concentrate on natural language queries. This is in contrast to the work in databases which has been mostly concerned with artificial query construction such as SQL and QBE, although that has changed recently. This concentration on natural language has led to a reasonable amount of work being devoted to processes that can take pieces of text, normalise them so that they can enter into a computational comparison/matching calculation leading to a score which indicates degree of relevance. This is well illustrated in Figure 2. (See any introductory text on IR, such as, [1], or the book by Manning and Schutze [22] for more details.) Furthermore, this quantitative approach scales and has worked effectively in IR (e.g. Porter stemmer). More recently this naove approach to the semantics of NL has made it relatively easy to address multi- and cross- lingual approaches to IR, especially the problem of retrieving from a foreign language collection by means of the formulation of a query in a different language, that is, say by retrieving from French documents, by putting an English query. The paper by Peters and Sheridan in this volume illustrates well the extent of the research in this area.

The "mathematico-statistical semantics" for text has to some extent transferred with obvious limitations to the retrieval of images, although there are no visual keywords (yet). The feedback loop kicked off by an initial query, transfers quite happily to the retrieval of images. What is especially interesting is the way one medium (text) can assist another (image), or vice versa, in retrieval (Smeaton, this volume). The querying of time-based media is still in its infancy. Eakins, in his chapter in this volume shows clearly the stage we are at with content-based (still) image retrieval. It may be that interaction with time-based, and still images will come to depend more heavily on an ostensive approach, since the formulation of queries in this context is inherently more difficult than in the textual domain. The ostensive approach dispenses with queries altogether (see [7]). This latter approach should also be natural for browsing the web, where users are inclined to submit very small queries indeed and so there is a need to support tools which will enhance retrieval through interaction without requiring a user to formulate query terms.

An assumption made in IR is that a query is always an incomplete specification of an information need, moreover, it is also assumed that at any one stage in a search a user's information need has only partially emerged and may change. So although the very precise mathematical approach to representing a query leads one to think that information needs are mapped down onto mathematical structures once and for all, this is not so. The difficulty of eliciting information needs has led to a number of ways for overcoming it (see Ingwersen's paper this volume for details).

One of the versions of the probabilistic model, assumes that the index terms are distributed independently, this is obviously not so, models have been created that attempt to capture arbitrary dependence between terms thereby representing information needs more accurately (Van Rijsbergen, 1977, and Yu, et al, 1983. These techniques for capturing the implied relationships between index terms have been exploited in a number of contexts. At another level statistical counting is used to increase the precision with which a query describes the information need. Although I do not know with any detail how the various search engines process queries, it is my impression that they do it very coarsely.

Although most of the search engines would have one think that retrieval is a matter of formulating a query and then doing a search looking for matching documents, there is a welter of other techniques that do not depend on a query except perhaps for starting things off. I have alread mentioned the ostensive approach [7], here the retrieval process and visualisation is entirely driven by pointing and by user actions. More obvious ones come about through the linking of objects which is well known. The use of citation links has a venerable history in IR, for example, in 1980, Belver Griffiths published a collection of "Key Papers in Information Science" which emphasised the importance of citation linkage. Some of the early IR models were based on decision theory and did not presuppose a query but took as their starting point that the objects to be retrieved were separable in at least two classes and went on to use, what are now called, machine learning or vector support machines to generate a decision function separating the classes [9,29]. Early versions of this decision-theoretic approach can be found in [50].

More recently the design of recommender systems has given rise to filters that are not based on content at all but use the actions of a user and his or her friends to construct appropriate filters. Some of the above techniques are of course used in the current Google implementation but to the best of my knowledge very little probabilistic or frequency information is used: there is scope for generalising these techniques incorporating some of the probabilistic approaches to IR. As always it is easier to model things either deterministically or stochastically but mixing the models is hard.

12   Items Wanted

The nature of what is wanted by a user is a matter for debate. In IR the approach is to assume that a user has an information need which will reveal itself through interaction with a system, this may involve query formulation and reformulation. It is not enough to say that what is wanted is a matching item, matching items may be irrelevant or useless. Thus the specification of what is wanted may be left to unfold through interaction and the "passage of experience." Indeed it may be the case that it is not possible to come up with a propositonal form of what is wanted, of course, SQL-like systems assume that it always is! Furthermore, in the end, users seek information that may or may not be contained in what are apparently relevant documents. It is a convenience to conflate relevance with aboutness, but now especially in the context of web searching it may be necessary to begin separating these. Recently there has been a thorough re-examination of the notions of relevance, see for example the papers by Mizzaro [24] and Spink, et al [44].

Also, increasingly searches are done within a context of performing a task; the nature of the task could have a significant effect on what is worth retrieving [35]. To date IR has concentrated on modelling content to support retrieval, but increasingly it is other factors that play a significant role, some of these may only appear as a consequence of iterating a search. Take for example the average query that is put to a search engine which will contain 2.4 query terms, it cannot be assumed that 2.4 terms is a good representation of a user's information need, so what to do? IR offers obvious techniques like relevance feedback, query expansion and a host of other techniques for going beyond a simple query.

13   Error Response (or Effectiveness)

The evaluation methodology in IR has been extremely strong, and I would say that the continuing success of the subject as a discipline owes much to that strength. It is also a good example of something that research, concerned with the web, as a source of information for utilisation and discovery, would do well to look at. Much IR research is subject to extensive testing and experimentation, which has led to very modest, claims being made about the success of IR. On the other hand such claims generally have stood the test of time. The basis of much evaluation has been the two well known parameters precision and recall (see Robertson, this volume, for a definition) used in conjunction with each other. Their use has been backed by extensive statistical analysis and indeed a theory of measurement [47].

The approach arising out of the Cranfield Paradigm via the ideal collection [41] culminating in TREC has been to design data for experimentation so that the evaluation of these parameters make sense, thus the implied trade-off between the two parameters is taken seriously, quoting one without the other makes little sense. Unfortunately the data available on the web does not fall within this paradigm although the retrieval performance is still subject to the trade-off. Hence it would seem important to extend the IR evaluation approach to web data, but to do this, problems will have to be solved, for example, how to deal with the lack of recall.

Retrieval performance, or its lack of performance, is not sensitive to small errors in the retrieval process. This is due to a number of factors. Firstly, retrieval output is typically ranked, thus ensuring that small changes in the matching function will not cause large changes in the ranking. Secondly, the performance measures, such as precision and recall, are robust estimators of the corresponding error probabilities. And, thirdly, the results are usual averaged over a large set of queries, again ensuring that small changes in the data do not impact the average very much. Typically, this allows for the use of statistical significance tests, such as the t-test or the sign test to determine significant differences in retrieval effectiveness between retrieval strategies.

14   Logic

One of the active areas of research in IR is the search for appropriate logics to support the reasoning about objects [28]. What has become increasingly clear is that classical Boolean logic is not appropriate in IR, and it is my guess, that the same is true for the use of ontologies. This can be illustrated by a simple rule of inference,

$$A \to B, \ B \to C \text{ infer } A \to C,$$

which requires that the following inference goes through,

> "If Mark were to lose his job, he would work less. If mark were to work less, he would be less tense. Therefore, if Mark were to lose his job, he would be less tense."

Nie, et al. [27] gives a number of other examples of rules of inference, like this, which one would like to see blocked. Much of this boils down to representing the aggregation of objects into subsets or subspaces, and showing what the relationship between an object and a subset might be. For example in Boolean Logic when the aggregation is simply subset formation and the relationships are given by inclusion, union, intersection etc, things are relatively straightforward. For example, the distribution law,

$$M \cap (N^c \cup N) = (M \cap N^c) \cup (M \cap N) = M,$$

holds (where N^c is the complement of N).

But in IR we have more structure than just the naming of objects, we have a notion of similarity/dissimilarity on the information space, and we aggregate objects algebraically through something akin to subspace formation. The logic that comes with the increased space structure is typically non-classical; for example it fails to meet the distribution law. Thus,

$$M \otimes (N^c \oplus N) = M, \text{ but}$$
$$(N \otimes N^c) \oplus (M \otimes N) = \varnothing \neq M,$$

$\otimes$, and $\oplus$ are subspace intersection and union, and $\varnothing$, is the empty space.

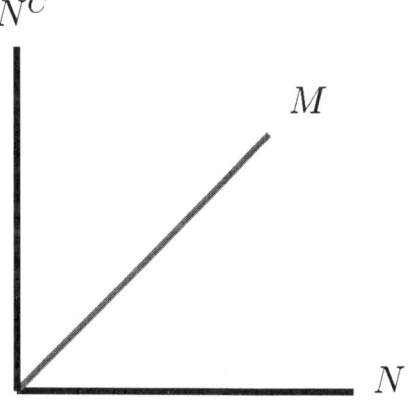

I have illustrated this failure in a two-dimensional vector space in Fig. 4, where $N^c \oplus N$ is the entire space, and M, N, N^c, are one-dimensional rays. Thus if one uses the subspace structure, and looks at the logics generated by insisting that the semantics conforms to the usual operation with subspaces, then one ends up with a non-classical logic which in general will block the counter-intuitive inferences given above.

This is not the end of the story, we require the generation of an appropriate probability measure on the space, this in itself is non-trivial.

15   Representation of Information

There are two conflicting ways of looking at the problem of characterising documents for retrieval. One is to characterise a document through a representation of its contents, regardless of the way in which other documents may be described;

this might be called representation without discrimination. The other way is to insist that in characterising a document one is discriminating it from all, or potentially all, other documents in the collection, this we might call discrimination without representation. Naturally neither of these extreme positions is assumed in practice, although identifying the two is useful when thinking about the problem of characterisation. In reality there is a trade-off between the two. Traditionally this is described as the trade-off between exhaustivity and specificity of indexing. To the best of my knowledge in IR this has been inescapable, in fact the balance between within document term frequency (tf) and inverse document frequency (idf) can be seen as an attempt to control this balance. Clearly one can adopt either a representation orientation that would emphasise the modelling of documents, for example through a language model. Or one could adopt a discrimination orientation that would emphasise the query, leading to query expansion techniques. But whichever one emphasises it is generally at the loss of the other. The implication of these considerations (and others) is that perfect retrieval is impossible, this is by way of The Second Law of Retrieval [50]. This is a statistical statement, namely, it applies for sets of queries and documents, clearly if there was only one document then perfect retrieval would be easy.

Chiaramella, in his chapter in this volume, gives a logical version of this trade-off between exhaustivity and specificity drawing on the original formulation by [26]. Exhaustivy is measured by the extent to which $D \to Q$, and specificity by the extent to which $Q \to D$. The strength of the match between D and Q is then given by a combination function, combining these two measures. This is a direct extension of the Logical Uncertainty Principle. The best choice of logic, that is, the implication connective, and measure of uncertainty is still a matter of research.

One of the hallmarks of IR to date is that within the interaction between the user and a document, the document is seen as a passive object. I would like to suggest that perhaps we should consider a document as being active. The model I have in mind for that is somewhat akin to the "expectation catalogue" idea Schrodinger had for the state, or wave function in Quantum Mechanics. According to this view a document is a stochastic object and it is only through interaction with it that we uncover its meaning. The result of an interaction, or the application of an observable, is a measurement which is inherently uncertain. Thus relevance and aboutness are seen as observables which are represented by Operators, the documents are state functions. To apply an operator is to elicit a measurement with a certain probability. For example, a document is seen to be about ducks or rabbits, but what it is actually about will depend on who is looking with what probability. Looking at things this way opens up a duality between the document and the query space. Documents can be seen as probability measures on the space of operators. There is a direct parallel between this model and the Von Neumann model for QM, this is not accidental. In fact some of the Quantum Logics are the same as some of the non-classical logics for IR. I would suggest that if we pursue the development of a framework such as this, then the ontological approach would integrate nicely with the statistical, or probabilistic, approach of IR.

Viewing interaction in IR as above corresponds nicely to the cognitive viewpoint in IR. Let me quote a representative view [5],

> "That is, the relevance or irrelevance of a given retrieved document may affect the user's current state of knowledge resulting in a change of the user's information need, which may lead to a change of the user's perception/interpretation of the subsequent retrieved documents ... " [5]

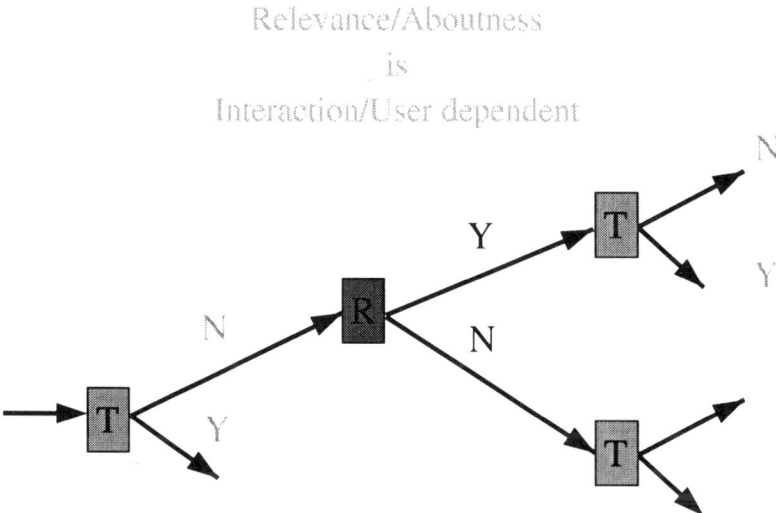

In Figure 5, I give an illustration of how this might work. Perceiving that a document is not about T, followed by an interpretation of relevance, a subsequent perception of that document may result in a user perceiving that it is about T. Given that we model queries as operators on state space, then it becomes possible to model the dependence between observables such as relevance and aboutness.. It has always struck me as absurd, that in classical IR models relevance and aboutness do not interact. For example, observing that a document is not about banks, followed by an observation that it is, say relevant should affect a subsequent observation about its "bankness"; in current IR it does not. I am sure the reader can think of a host of examples where such an interaction should be expected and not blocked. Thinking of documents as dynamic objects, and modelling them in relation to operators in the way I have described should open the door to such dependence between attributes. Of course developing a non-classical logic, such as Quantum Logic, for IR will give us a formalism to reason about such things—one of the grand challenges in IR!

16   Conclusions

I have tried to give an overview of a number essential characteristics of the discipline of what is loosely described as Information Retrieval. This overview is by no means complete nor is it exhaustive. It is meant as a framework to support the subsequent chapters in this book. On the way I have tried to highlight a few special topics where research is particularly exciting from my point of view, thus making this overview a rather personal perspective of the subject of IR. Nevertheless I hope it will serve as an introduction to the uninitiated and the not so uninitiated.

Acknowledgments

I would like to thank the organisors of the ESSIR 2000 summer school in Information Retrieval at Varenna, Italy for inviting me to present an earlier version of this paper and thereby giving me the opportunity to elaborate on some of these ideas. Also, I wish to express my gratitude to all my past and present graduate students for forcing me to clarify some of these ideas, however inadequately.

References

1. Belew, R., *Finding out about About*, Cambridge University press, 2000.
2. Belkin, N.J., Oddy, R.N., and Brooks, H.M., ASK for information retrieval. Part I. Background and Theory. *Journal of Documentation*, 38:61–71, 1982.
3. Blair, D. C., *Language and Representation in Information Retrieval, Elsevier*, Amsterdam, 1990.
4. Borges, J.L., *Other Inquisitions*, Washington Square Press: New York, 1966.
5. Borlund, P., Private communication, 2000.
6. Callan, J., Croft, W.B., and Harding, S., The INQUERY retrieval system. In: *Proceedings of the 3rd international Conference on Databases and Expert Systems Applications*, 78–83, Springer Verlag, Berlin, 1992.
7. Campbell, I., Interactive Evaluation of the Ostensive Model Using a New Test Collection of Images with Multiple Relevance Assesments, *Information Retrieval*, 2:87–114, 2000.
8. Chiaramella, Y., Mulhem, Ph., and Fourel, F., A model for Multimedia Information Retrieval. Technical Report of ESPRIT project 8134 "FERMI". Technical Report, University of Glasgow, No. 4/96, 1996.
9. Christianini, N., and Shawe-Taylor, J., *An introduction to Support Vector Machines and other kernel-based learning methods*, Cambridge University Press, 2000.
10. Cleverdon, C., Mills, J., and Keen, M., Factors Determining the Performance of Indexing Systems, *ASLIB*, Cranfield, 1966.
11. Crestani, F., and Van Rijsbergen, C.J., A study of probability kinematics in information retrieval, *ACM Transactions in Information Systems*, 16, 225–255, 1998.
12. Crestani, F., Lalmas, M., and Van Rijsbergen, C.J., Information Retrieval: *Information Retrieval: Uncertainty and Logics*. Kluwer Academic Publisher, Norwell, MA, USA, 1998.
13. Croft, W.B., *Organizing and Searching Large Files of Document Descriptions*, PhD Thesis, University of Cambridge, 1978
14. Frakes, W.B., Baeza-Yates, R.: *Information Retrieval: Data Structures and Algorithms*, Prentice-Hall, 1992
15. Griffiths, B.V. (ed), Key Papers in Information Science, *ASIS*, Washington DC., 1980.

16. Harper, D.J., *Relevance Feedback in Document Retrieval Systems: an Evaluation of Probabilistic Strategies*, PhD Thesis, University of Cambridge, 1980.
17. Heine, M.H. Reassessing and Extending the Precision and Recall Concepts, In http://www.ewic.org.uk/ewic, http://www.ewic.org.uk/ewic (revised 18Jan 2000). Revised version of 'Time to dump '*P* and *R*'? Proceedings of Mira 99: *Final Mira Conference on Information Retrieval Evaluation*, Glasgow, April 1999.
18. Jardine, N.,and Sibson, R., *Mathematical Taxonomy*, Wiley, London, 1971.
19. Jeffrey, R.C. *The logic of decision*. McGraw-Hill, New York, USA, 1965.
20. Lalmas, M., A model for representing and retrieving heterogeneous structured documents based on evidential reasoning, *The Computer Journal*, 42:547–568, 1999.
21. Losee, R.M. When Information Retrieval Measures Agree About the Relative Quality of Document Rankings, *Journal of the American Society for Information Science*, 51:834–840, 2000.
22. Manning, C.D., and Schutze, H., *Foundations of Statistical Natural Language Processing*, MIT press, 1999.
23. M. Maron and J. Kuhns. On relevance, probabilistic indexing, and information retrieval. *Journal of the ACM*, 7:216–244, 1960.
24. Mizzaro, S., How many relevances in information retrieval? *Interacting with Computers*, 10:303–320, 1998.
25. F. Murtagh Guest editor Special issue on Clustering and Classification, *The Computer Journal*, 41:(8), 1998
26. Nie, J.-Y, An information retrieval model based on modal logic, *Information Processing & Management*, 25:477–491, 1990.
27. Nie, J.-Y, Brisebois, M., and Lepage, F., Information retrieval as counterfactual, *The Computer Journal*, 38, 643–657, 1995.
28. Nie, J.-Yand Lepage, F., Toward a broader logical model for information retrieval, In: [12], 17–38, 1998.
29. Nilsson, N.J., *Learning Machines: Foundations of Trainable Pattern-Classifying Systems*, McGraw-Hill: New York, 1965.
30. Ponte, J.M., The language modelling approach to IR, In: *Advances in Information retrieval: Recent Research from the Center for Intelligent Information Retrieval*, W.B. Croft (Ed.), 73–95, Kluwer:Boston, 2000.
31. Quine, W.V., *Ontological Relativity & other essays*, Columbia University Press: New York, 1969.
32. Robertson, S.E., The probability ranking principle, *Journal of Documentation*, 33:294–304, 1977.
33. Robertson, S.E. (ed.), Special issue on Okapi, *Journal of Documentation*, 53, 1997.
34. Robertson, S.E., Maron, M.E., and Cooper, W.S., Probability of Relevance: A Unification of Two Competing Models for Document retrieval, *Information Technology: Research and Development*, 1:1–21, 1982.
35. Reid, J., A task-oriented non-interactive evaluation methodology for information retrieval, *Information Retrieval*, 2:115–129, 2000.
36. Rölleke, T., *POOL: probabilistics Object-Oriented Logical Representation and Retrieval of Complex Objects; A model for hypermedia retrieval*, PhD Thesis, University of Dortmund, Springer Verlag, 1999.
37. Salton, G. (ed), *The SMART Retrieval System: Experiments in Automatic Document Processing*, Prentice Hall, Englewood Cliffs, 1971.
38. Sneath, P. H.A, and Sokal, R.R., *Numerical Taxonomy: The Principles and Practice of Numerical Classification*, W.H. Freeman, San Francisco, 1973.
39. Sparck Jones, K., *Automatic Keyword Classification for Information retrieval*, Butterworths, London, 1971.

40. Sparck Jones, K. (ed) *Information Retrieval Experiment*, Butterworths, London, 1981.
41. Sparck Jones, K., and Van Rijsbergen, C.J., Report on the need for and provision of an 'ideal' information retrieval test collection, Computer Laboratory, University of Cambridge, 1975. A more accessible version can be found in *Journal of Documentation*, 32:59–75, 1976
42. Sparck Jones, K., and Willett, P., *Readings in Information Retrieval, Morgan Kaufmann*, SanFrancisco, 1997.
43. Spink, A., Feedback in information retrieval, In Williams, M., ed., *Annual review of Information Science and Technology*, 31:33–78, 1996.
44. Spink, A., Greisdorf, H., and Bateman, J., From highly relevant to not relevant: examining different regions of relevance, *Information Processing & Management*, 43:599–621, 1998.
45. Turtle, H., and Croft, W.B., Inference networks for document retrieval. In J.L. Viddick (Ed.), *Proceedings of the 13th International Conference on Research and Development in Information Retrieval*, 1–24, ACM, New York, 1990.
46. Van Rijsbergen, C.J., *Automatic Information Structuring and Retrieval*, PhD Thesis, University of Cambridge, 1972.
47. Van Riisbergen, C.J., Foundation of Evaluation, *Journal of Documentation*, 30:365–373, 1974.
48. Van Riisbergen, C.J., A theoretical basis for the use of cooccurrence data in information retrieval, *Journal of Documentation*, 33:30–48, 1977.
49. Van Rijsbergen, C.J., Automatic Classification in Information Retrieval, In: Special issue on Theory and Foundations of Information Retrieval, M.E. Maron (Ed.), *Drexel Library Quaterly*, 14:75–89, 1978.
50. Van Rijsbergen, C.J., *Information Retrieval*, Second Edition, Butterworths, London, 1979.
51. Van Rijsbergen, C.J., Retrieval Effectiveness, In: *Progress in Communication Sciences*, Voigt, M.J., and Hanneman, G.J. editors, 91–118, 1979.
52. Van Rijsbergen, C.J., A discrimination gain hypothesis, *Proceedings of the 6th Annual ACM SIGIR conference*, 101–105, 1983.
53. Van Rijsbergen, C.J., Probabilistic Retrieval Revisited, *The Computer Journal*, 35:291–298, 1992.
54. Van Rijsbergen, C.J., Another Look at the Logical Uncertainty, *Information Retrieval*, 2:15–24, 2000
55. Van Rijsbergen, C.J., and Sparck Jones, K., A test for the separation of relevant and non-relevant documents in experimental retrieval collections, *Journal of Documentation*, 29:251–257, 1973.
56. Willett, P., Recent trends in hierarchic document clustering: a critical review, *Information Processing & Management*, 24:577–97, 1988.
57. Wong, S.K.M.and Butz, C.J., A Bayesian approach to User Profiling in Information retrieval, *Technology Letters*, 4:50–56, 2000.
58. Yeh, A. More acurate tests for the statistical significance of result differences, *COLING 2000*, 947–953, 2000.
59. Yu, C. T., Buckley, D., Lam, K., and Salton. G., A generalised term dependence model in information retrieval, *Information technology: Research and Development*, 2:129–154, 1983.

Models in Information Retrieval

Norbert Fuhr

Informatik VI
University of Dortmund, Germany
fuhr@cs.uni-dortmund.de

Abstract Retrieval models form the theoretical basis for computing the answer to a query. They differ not only in the syntax and expressiveness of the query language, but also in the representation of the documents. Following Rijsbergen's approach of regarding IR as uncertain inference, we can distinguish models according to the expressiveness of the underlying logic and the way uncertainty is handled.

Classical retrieval models are based on propositional logic. In the vector space model, documents and queries are represented as vectors in a vector space spanned by the index terms, and uncertainty is modelled by considering geometric similarity. Probabilistic models make assumptions about the distribution of terms in relevant and nonrelevant documents in order to estimate the probability of relevance of a document for a query. Language models compute the probability that the query is generated from a document. All these models can be interpreted within a framework that is based on a probabilistic concept space.

For IR applications dealing not only with texts, but also with multimedia or factual data, propositional logic is not sufficient. Therefore, advanced IR models use restricted forms of predicate logic as basis. Terminological/description logics are rooted in semantic networks and terminological languages like e.g. KL-ONE. Datalog uses function-free horn clauses. Probabilistic versions of both approaches are able to cope with the intrinsic uncertainty of IR.

1 Introduction

The major task in information retrieval is to find relevant documents for a given query. Very early in the history of information retrieval, it has become clear that simple models based on Boolean logic are not appropriate for this task. Instead, a wide variety of so-called best-match methods has been developed. Whereas many approaches from the 60s and 70s were based on some plausibility assumptions and heuristics, theoretical models became more popular over the years.

In this paper, we will give a survey on major retrieval models. By taking the logical view on information retrieval systems, we first will show that most classical models are based on propositional logic, in combination with uncertain inference.

For multimedia retrieval, propositional logic is not sufficient. Thus, we will look at models based on predicate logic suited for this task. Again, uncertain

M. Agosti, F. Crestani, and G. Pasi (Eds.): ESSIR 2000, LNCS 1980, pp. 21–50, 2000.
© Springer-Verlag Berlin Heidelberg 2000

inference is required in order to deal with the intrinsic uncertainty and vagueness of information retrieval.

The structure of this paper is as follows: First, we will introduce some basic concepts for IR models. Then we will present a number of classical models (based on propositional logic), followed by a section on models for multimedia retrieval (using predicate logic). Finally, we will give an outlook on some open research problems.

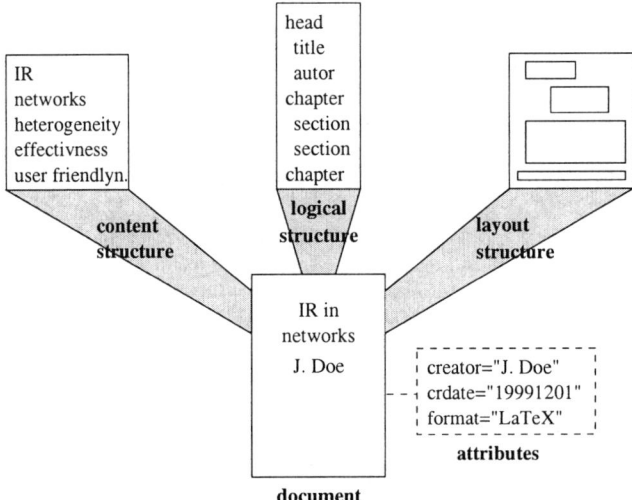

Figure 1. Views on Documents

2   Basic Concepts of IR Models

2.1   A Conceptual Model of IR

When dealing with text or multimedia documents, one should distinguish different views on these documents. Several subfields of computer science and related fields deal with documents, where most of the fields focus on one or two views and ignore the others. Here we try to present an integration of the different perspectives. For this purpose, we propose to distinguish four different views, as illustrated in Fig. 1

External attributes comprise data that is not contained within the document, i.e. a user looking at the document only may not see these values. External attributes contain information that is needed for certain types of processing the document, e.g. the name of the creator of the document, access rights, or publication information. In digital libraries, this type of data often is called metadata.

Logical Structure: The media data that is contained within the document, and its internal structure comprise the logical structure of a document. Usually, documents have a hierarchical structure (e.g. a book divided into chapters, chapters containing sections, consisting of subsections, which comprise paragraphs, images and tables). In this tree structure, the data is located in the leaves, where a leaf contains single media data only (e.g. text, graphics, images, audio, video, animation, 3D). Hypermedia links allow for non-hierarchical structures.

Layout Structure: In order to show a document to a user, it must be presented at some kind of output media (e.g. when a document is printed, we have a sequence of pages). Based on a so-called style sheet, the layout process maps the logical structure onto the output media. The layout structure describes the spatial distribution of the data over the output media, e.g. the sequence of pages, which in turn are subdivided into rectangular areas (e.g. page header, footer, columns). This concept can be extended to time-dependent media (e.g. audio, video), where the layout structure describes the temporal and spatial distribution on an appropriate output device (see e.g. the SMIL[1] or HyTime [13] standards).

Content deals with the meaning of a document (e.g.: What is the document about? What does it deal with?). The content is derived from the logical structure, in most cases by an automatic process. The content representation may have an internal structure, too, but often rather simple schemes are used. For example, in text retrieval, content mostly is represented as a set of concepts.

When we want to perform information retrieval on multimedia documents, we have to consider all these views, in order to allow for queries addressing each of these views separately, as well as queries for combinations. Examples of queries with respect to (w.r.t.) to the different views are: Give me all documents published last month (attributes). Show me all books that have the string 'XML' in the title and contain more than 10 chapters (logical structure). Show me all articles that are typeset in two columns, with a length of more than 15 pages (layout). Find all documents about image retrieval (content). Since IR focusses on content, we also will prefer this view throughout this paper. However, since real applications typically involve more than one view, there is a need for retrieval mechanisms that are not restricted to a single view.

2.2 IR as Inference

In the logical view on database systems, retrieval can be interpreted as implication: Let o denote a database object (represented as a logical formula) and q denote a query, then query processing deals with the task of finding all objects in the database for which the implication $o \rightarrow q$ is true. As Rijsbergen has shown in [21], IR can be interpreted in the same way: Let d denote a document and q again a query, then retrieval deals with the task of finding those documents which imply the query, i.e. for which the formula $d \rightarrow q$ is true. As a simple

---

[1] http://www.w3.org/AudioVideo/

example using Boolean retrieval, assume that we have a document represented as a set of terms, e.g. $d_T = \{t_1, t_2, t_3\}$ and a query represented in the same way, e.g. $q_T = \{t_1, t_3\}$. In the logical view, both documents and queries are mapped onto logical formulas, i.e. $d = t_1 \wedge t_2 \wedge t_3$ and $q = t_1 \wedge t_3$. Obviously, $d \rightarrow q$ holds, so d is an answer to q. The advantages of the logical approach become apparent when we want to consider additional knowledge (e.g. a thesaurus) in retrieval. For example, assume that we have a query q containing the term 'multimedia', whereas a document d contains only the terms 'audio' and 'video.' Obviously, d would not be retrieved in response to q, since $d \not\rightarrow q$. By adding additional knowledge, we can make the inference go through, e.g. by adding the rule 'audio $\wedge$ video $\rightarrow$ multimedia.'

However, Boolean logic does not address the issue of uncertainty and vagueness in information retrieval: query formulations typically are vague, due to the fact that users have problems in specifying their information need. Vice versa, document representations are imprecise, since an IR system has only limited means for representing the content of a document. In text documents, language processing methods can represent the semantics of a text only to a limited extent. As discussed before, non-textual media pose even more difficult problems. In order to cope with is problem, we have to switch to uncertain inference, as proposed by Rijsbergen. Here we have the problem of defining the meaning of uncertain implication.

Assume that we have a probability space where terms represent disjoint events, as shown in Fig. 2. Taking the classical logical approach, one would compute $P(d \rightarrow q)$ as $P(\neg d \vee q)$. Assuming an equal probability distribution over the terms, this would give us $P(d \vee \neg) = 5/6$ for the left-hand side of Fig. 2. However, the result would be the same when we either would add the term t_1 to the document or t_4 to the query. Since this is not reasonable, classical logic seems to be inappropriate for this task. Thus, Rijsbergen proposed to define $P(d \rightarrow q)$ as conditional probability $P(q|d)$, yielding the value $2/3$ in this example.

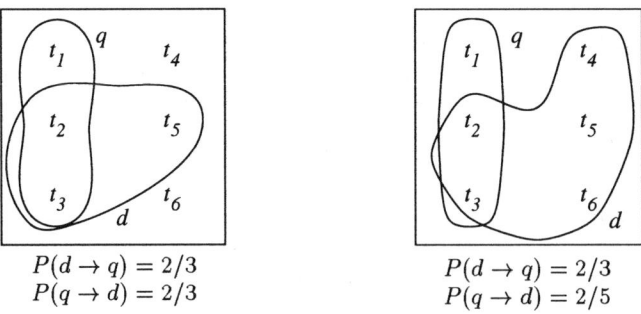

$$P(d \rightarrow q) = 2/3$$
$$P(q \rightarrow d) = 2/3$$

$$P(d \rightarrow q) = 2/3$$
$$P(q \rightarrow d) = 2/5$$

Figure 2. $P(d \rightarrow q)$ vs. $P(q \rightarrow d)$

Some years later, Nie has shown [14] that in some cases, it also may be reasonable to consider also the implication $P(q \rightarrow d)$, which should be defined according to Rijsbergen as $P(d|q)$. Whereas the first implication measures the exhaustivity of a document w.r.t. a query, the latter can be used as a measure of specifity. As an extreme example, assume that we have an encyclopedia among other documents in our collection. Obviously, many queries can be answered by the encyclopedia, since $P(d \to q)$ is high due to the large number of terms contained in the encyclopedia. However, only a small part of this large document will be relevant in most cases; this feature can be measured by $P(q \to d)$. Figure 2 gives another example for this problem.

In general, we are looking for documents relevant to a query. Following the probabilistic approach, we would search for documents that have a high probability of being relevant. In [17], it is shown that ranking documents according to decreasing probability of relevance will yield optimum retrieval quality.

Here we briefly describe the decision-theoretic justification of the probability ranking principle (PRP). Let C $(\bar{C})$ denote the costs for retrieving a relevant (nonrelevant) document, respectively. Since a user prefers relevant documents, we assume that $\bar{C} > C$. Then the *expected costs* for retrieving a document d are computed as

$$EC(d) = C \cdot P(R|q, d) + \bar{C} \cdot (1 - P(R|q, d))$$

In response to a query, a user looks at output documents in the ranked order and stops at an arbitrary point. In order to minimize the sum of expected costs at any cutoff point, documents have to be ranked according to increasing expected costs, i.e. for any two documents d, d', rank d ahead of d', if $EC(d) < EC(d')$. Due to $\bar{C} > C$, this condition is equivalent to $P(R|q, d) > P(R|q, d')$; that is, documents should be ranked according to decreasing probability of relevance, in order to minimize expected costs of retrieval. So probabilistic retrieval models are directly related to retrieval quality.

Now there is the question about the relationship between probability of inference and probability of relevance. This is still an open issue: At the moment, we only know that the probability of relevance $P(R|q, d)$ is a function of the two implication probabilities.

3   Models Based on Propositional Logic

In this section, we will show that based on the concept of uncertain inference, most classical retrieval models can be given a probabilistic interpretation. Most of the material presented here is based on the paper [22], which the reader should consult for further details. Surveys on probabilistic IR models are given in [4] and [6].

3.1   A Probabilistic Inference Model

Most text retrieval models represent documents as sets of (weighted) propositions. In order to set up a basic framework for these models, we assume a concept space U consisting of a set of elementary, disjoint concepts c_i (see Fig. 3).

Any proposition p is a set of concepts, i.e. a subset of the concept space $(p \subseteq U)$. Boolean combinations of propositions can be expressed as set operations

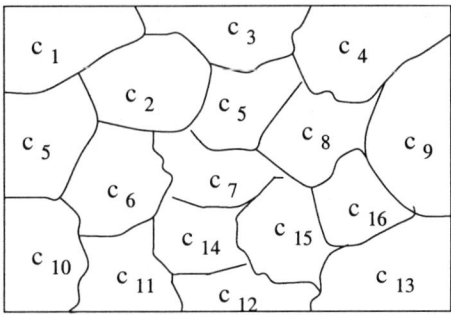

Figure 3. Concept Space

on this concept space. Let e.g. $p_1 = \{c_1, c_2, c_3\}$ and $p_2 = \{c_2, c_4\}$, then $p_1 \cap p_2 = \{c_2\}$.

In order to support probabilistic inference, we define a probability function $P(.)$ over U, i.e.

$$\sum_{c_i \in U} P(c_i) = 1$$

Now queries and documents are treated as propositions as well, Considering the probability function, we have

$$P(d) = \sum_{c_i \in d} P(c_i)$$

$$P(q \cap d) = \sum_{c_i \in q \cap d} P(c_i)$$

$$P(d \to q) = P(q|d) = \frac{P(q \cap d)}{P(d)}$$

3.2   Classical IR Models

Now we will describe a number of classical IR models and show how they can be interpreted in terms of probabilistic inference. Whereas text retrieval is based on terms, our basic model uses concepts as elementary propositions; thus, we have to define the relationship between terms and concepts. A straightforward approach identifies each term with a concept. Alternatively, one can assume that terms are overlapping, so we need a different mapping from terms onto concepts. We will consider both possibilities in the following. Figure 4 gives a systematic survey of the classical IR models described here.

Disjoint Basic Concepts. Here we assume that terms $\{t_1 \ldots t_n\}$ correspond to disjoint basic concepts: $t_i \cap t_j = \emptyset$ for $i \neq j$. Furthermore, let us assume that

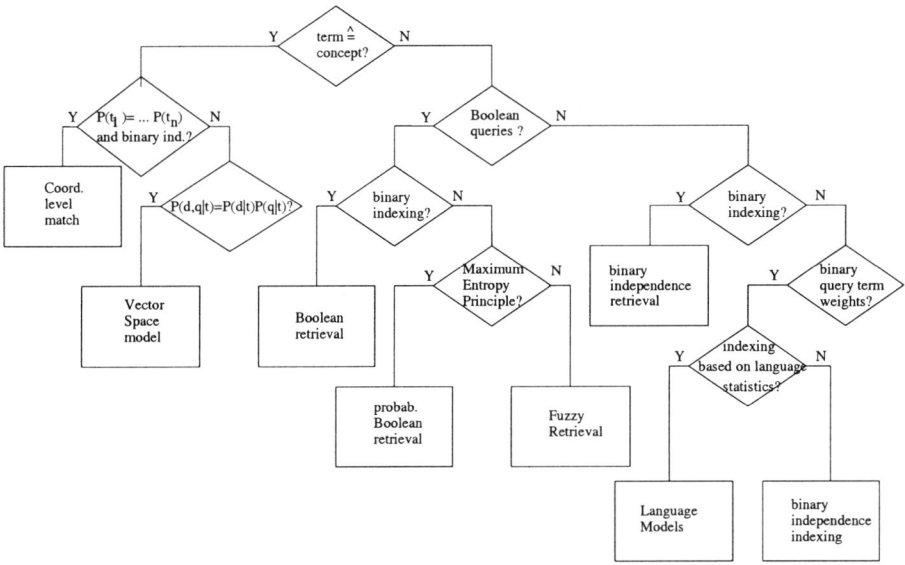

Figure 4. Classification of Classical IR Models

the terms for a complete cover of the concept space: $U = t_1 \cup t_2 \cup \cdots \cup t_n$. So the terms form a dissection of U. This property can be used for computing the probability of the implication $P(d \rightarrow q)$:

$$
\begin{aligned}
P(d \rightarrow q) &= P(q|d) \\
&= \frac{P(d \cap q)}{P(d)} \\
&= \frac{\sum_t P(d \cap q \cap t)}{P(d)} \\
&= \frac{\sum_t P(d \cap q|t)P(t)}{P(d)}
\end{aligned}
\tag{1}
$$

With the exception of the normalizing factor $P(d)$, the last equation defines the probability $P(d \rightarrow q)$ as sum of the probabilities of w.r.t. single terms $P(d \cap q|t)$. Each of these probabilities describes the relationship between the query q and the document d w.r.t. a single term t. In order to estimate these probabilities, we need additional assumptions.

As a straightforward approach, one can assume a uniform distribution over the set of terms, i.e. $P(t_1) = \cdots = P(t_n)$. Treating documents and queries as sets of terms, we get a variant of the *coordination level match* where only the number of terms common to query and document is considered.

Vector Space Model. Now we show that a variant of the popular vector space model [19] can be explained in terms of our basic model. Here only the probabilities $P(d|t)$ and $P(q|t)$ are known. By applying the maximum entropy principle, we get the following independence assumption:

$$P(d \cap q|t) = P(d|t)P(q|t)$$

By combining this assumption with (1), we get

$$P(d \rightarrow q) = \frac{\sum_t P(d \cap q|t)P(t)}{P(d)}$$

$$= \frac{\sum_t P(d|t)P(q|t)P(t)}{P(d)}$$

$$= \sum_t P(t|d)P(q|t)$$

$$= \sum_t P(d \rightarrow t)P(t \rightarrow q) \tag{2}$$

The two parameters in the last equation can be interpreted as follows:

$P(d \rightarrow t)$ describes the representation of a document d as the probability that document d implies term t. This kind of representation usually is called document indexing.

$P(t \rightarrow q)$ stands for the representation of a query q in terms of the probability that term t implies query q. These parameters often are called query indexing or query term weighting.

In order to show the analogy to the vector space model, we define document vectors $\mathbf{d} = (P(d \rightarrow t_1), \ldots, P(d \rightarrow t_n))^T$ and query vectors $\mathbf{q} = (P(t_1 \rightarrow q), \ldots, P(t_n \rightarrow q))^T$. Then, (2) can be rewritten as vector (dot) product:

$$P(d \rightarrow q) = \mathbf{d}^T \cdot \mathbf{q}$$

As an example, assume the following document vectors:

$$\mathbf{d_1} = (0, 1/3, 2/3) \qquad \mathbf{d_2} = (1/3, 2/3, 0)$$
$$\mathbf{d_3} = (1/2, 0, 1/2) \qquad \mathbf{d_4} = (3/4, 1/4, 0)$$

Given the query vector $\mathbf{q} = (1/5, 0, 2/3)^T$ we can compute the probability of implication for document d_1 as follows:

$$P(d_1 \rightarrow q_1) = \sum_t P(d \rightarrow t)P(t \rightarrow q) = \mathbf{d} \cdot \mathbf{q}$$

$$= 0 \cdot \frac{1}{5} + \frac{1}{3} \cdot 0 + \frac{2}{3} \cdot \frac{2}{3} = \frac{4}{9}$$

For the other documents in our example, we get $P(d_2 \rightarrow q_1) = 1/15$, $P(d_3 \rightarrow q_1) = 11/30$ and $P(d_4 \rightarrow q_1) = 3/20$. Thus, we arrive at the following ranking: $\{d_1\}, \{d_3\}, \{d_4\}, \{d_2\}$.

For practical applications, a number of heuristic weighting formulas has been developed for the vector space model as well as for related probabilistic models. According to the two major factors in these formulas, they are called tf×idf weights. Here we briefly describe a formula that is widely used at the moment.

First, we introduce a number of parameters:

$T(d)$ set of terms occurring in d,
$l(d)$ length of document d,
al average length of a document in the collection,
$df(t)$ document frequency of t (# docs containing t),
$tf(t, d)$ within-document frequency of term t in document d,
N_d number of documents in the collection.

Now the inverse document frequency of term t w.r.t. a collection is defined as follows

$$idf(t) = \frac{\log \frac{N_d}{df(t)}}{N_d + 1}.$$

In addition, we need the normalized term frequency of term t w.r.t. document d:

$$ntf(t, d) = \frac{tf(t, d)}{tf(t, d) + 0.5 + 1.5\frac{l(d)}{al}}$$

Then the document indexing weight of term t w.r.t. d is defined as

$$tfidf(t, d) = ntf(t, d) \cdot idf(t).$$

In order to fit into our model, an additional normalization would be required such that $\sum_{t \in d} tfidf(t, d) = 1$.

Nondisjoint Basic Concepts. Now we consider the case where terms represent nondisjoint concepts, i.e. there are terms t_i, t_j with $t_i \cap t_j \neq \emptyset$. However, we still assume that the terms form a complete cover of the concept space U.

In order to apply our framework model, we map terms onto disjoint atomic concepts in the following way: We form complete conjuncts (or minterms) of all terms t, in which each term occurs either positively or negated, i.e.

$$m_0 = \bar{t}_1 \cap \bar{t}_2 \cap \bar{t}_3 \cap \cdots \bar{t}_{n-1} \cap \bar{t}_n$$
$$m_1 = t_1 \cap \bar{t}_2 \cap \bar{t}_3 \cap \cdots \bar{t}_{n-1} \cap \bar{t}_n$$
$$m_2 = \bar{t}_1 \cap t_2 \cap \bar{t}_3 \cap \cdots \bar{t}_{n-1} \cap \bar{t}_n$$
$$m_3 = \bar{t}_1 \cap \bar{t}_2 \cap t_3 \cap \cdots \bar{t}_{n-1} \cap \bar{t}_n$$
$$\vdots$$
$$m_{2^n-2} = \bar{t}_1 \cap t_2 \cap t_3 \cap \cdots t_{n-1} \cap t_n$$
$$m_{2^n-1} = t_1 \cap t_2 \cap t_3 \cap \cdots t_{n-1} \cap t_n$$

Figure 5 illustrates this approach for the case of three terms. Based on this type of disjoint concepts, Boolean, fuzzy and probabilistic retrieval models can be explained.

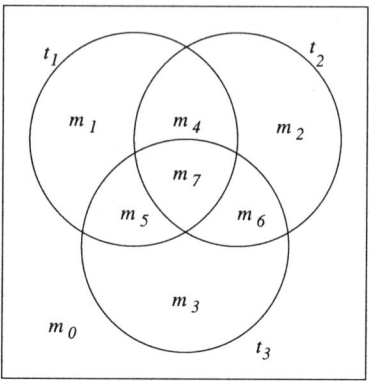

Figure 5. Construction of Disjoint Concepts for the Case of Three Terms

Boolean Retrieval. For Boolean retrieval, we assume binary indexing of documents, where each document is represented as a single atomic concept:

$$d = m_d = t_1^{\alpha_1} \cap \cdots \cap t_n^{\alpha_n} \qquad \text{with} \qquad t_i^{\alpha_i} = \begin{cases} t_i & \text{if} \ \alpha_i = 1, \\ \bar{t}_i & \text{if} \ \alpha_i = 0. \end{cases}$$

Here assume a close world, that is, all terms not occurring within a document d are assumed to be negated, e.g.

$$d_1 = \{t_1, t_3, t_4\}$$
$$\hat{=} \ t_1 \cap \bar{t}_2 \cap t_3 \cap t_4 \cap \bar{t}_5 \cap \cdots \cap \bar{t}_n$$

By mapping terms onto disjoint concepts, we can represent terms as union of the corresponding basic concepts:

$$t_i = m_{i_1} \cup \cdots \cup m_{i_r},$$

For example, term t_1 can be expressed as $t_1 = m_1 \cup m_4 \cup m_5 \cup m_7$ (see Fig. 5).

For a given Boolean query, we construct the corresponding disjunctive normal form, thus giving us a set of minterms. Thus, any query is mapped onto a set of minterms:

$$q = \bigcup m_{q_i}$$

Based on these assumptions, we can compute the probability of implication as follows:

$$\begin{aligned} P(d \to q) &= \frac{P(q \cap d)}{P(d)} \\ &= \frac{P(q \cap m_d)}{P(m_d)} \\ &= \begin{cases} 1 & \text{if} \ m_d \subseteq q, \\ 0 & \text{if} \ m_d \not\subseteq q. \end{cases} \end{aligned}$$

Boolean retrieval always yields a set of documents as result, without any further ranking; this feature is due to the fact that each document corresponds to a minterm, and a query is a set of minterms. From a theoretical point of view, a Boolean retrieval system only has to decide whether or not a document belongs to the minterms as specified by the query.

$$
\begin{array}{c|ccc}
 & t_1\ t_2\ t_3 \\
\hline
d_1 & 0\ \ 1\ \ 1 \\
d_2 & 1\ \ 1\ \ 0 \\
d_3 & 1\ \ 0\ \ 1 \\
d_4 & 1\ \ 1\ \ 0
\end{array}
\qquad
\begin{aligned}
d_1 &= m_6 = \bar{t}_1 \cap t_2 \cap t_3 \\
d_2 &= m_3 = t_1 \cap t_2 \cap \bar{t}_3 \\
d_3 &= m_5 = t_1 \cap \bar{t}_2 \cap t_3 \\
d_4 &= m_3 = \bar{t}_1 \cap \bar{t}_2 \cap t_3
\end{aligned}
$$

Figure 6. Example: Document Representations for Boolean Retrieval

Let us consider an example with three terms, thus leading to eight minterms depicted in Fig. 5. For the (binary) document-term matrix shown in Fig. 6, we get the representation as minterms shown in the same figure. The query

$$
\begin{aligned}
q_2 &= (t_1 \cup t_2) \cap t_3 \\
&= (t_1 \cap t_2 \cap t_3) \cup (t_1 \cap \bar{t}_2 \cap t_3) \cup (\bar{t}_1 \cap t_2 \cap t_3) \\
&= m_7 \cup m_5 \cup m_6
\end{aligned}
$$

leads to the answer set $\{d_1, d_3\}$, due to the fact that their minterms are contained within the query.

Fuzzy Retrieval. Whereas Boolean retrieval is restricted to binary indexing of documents, fuzzy retrieval also can cope with weighted indexing (in the presence of Boolean queries). For single-term queries, we have

$$
P(d \to q) = \frac{P(q \cap d)}{P(d)} = \frac{P(t \cap d)}{P(d)} = P(t|d) = P(d \to t)
$$

When we have a Boolean combination of query terms, then there are different possibilities for computing the resulting weights. Following a probabilistic approach, one can assume the index weights to be independent of each other, thus leading to the following definitions:

$$
P(d \to \bar{q}) = \frac{P(\bar{q} \cap d)}{P(d)} = \frac{P(\bar{q} \cap d)}{P(d)} = 1 - P(q|d) = 1 - P(d \to q)
$$
$$
P(d \to q \cap q') = P(q \cap q'|d) \approx P(q|d)P(q'|d) = P(d \to q)P(d \to q')
$$
$$
P(d \to q \cup q') = P(q \cup q'|d) \approx P(q|d) + P(q'|d) - P(q|d)P(q'|d)
$$
$$
= P(d \to q) + P(d \to q') - P(d \to q)P(d \to q')
$$

Whereas this interpretation is based on the maximum entropy principle, the standard fuzzy interpretation is based on the principle of minimum entropy, thus leading to the following definitions for conjunction and disjunction:

$$P(d \to q \cap q') = P(q \cap q'|d) \approx \min(P(q|d), P(q'|d)) = \min(P(d \to q), P(d \to q'))$$
$$P(d \to q \cup q') = P(q \cup q'|d) \approx \max(P(q|d), P(q'|d)) = \max(P(d \to q), P(d \to q'))$$

Probabilistic Retrieval.
As the most important representative of a number of probabilistic IR models, we describe the binary independence retrieval (BIR) model [18] here.

Like in Boolean retrieval, the BIR model is based on binary document indexing, thus representing a document as a single atomic concept:

$$d = m_d = t_1^{\alpha_1} \cap \cdots \cap t_n^{\alpha_n}$$

Instead of the probability of implication $P(d \to q)$, we consider a monotone transformation of this parameter, namely the logg-odds transformation. Furthermore, we apply Bayes' theorem:

$$
\begin{aligned}
\log \frac{P(d \to q)}{1 - P(d \to q)} &= \log \frac{P(q|d)}{P(\bar{q}|d)} \\
&= \log \frac{P(d|q)}{P(d|\bar{q})} + \log \frac{P(q)}{P(\bar{q})} \\
&= \log \frac{P(t_1^{\alpha_1} \cap \cdots \cap t_n^{\alpha_n}|q)}{P(t_1^{\alpha_1} \cap \cdots \cap t_n^{\alpha_n}|\bar{q})} + \log \frac{P(q)}{P(\bar{q})}
\end{aligned}
\tag{3}
$$

For the distribution of terms within relevant and nonrelevant documents, we assume linked dependence [3]:

$$\frac{P(t_1^{\alpha_1} \cap \cdots \cap t_n^{\alpha_n}|q)}{P(t_1^{\alpha_1} \cap \cdots \cap t_n^{\alpha_n}|\bar{q})} = \frac{\prod_{i=1}^n P(t_i^{\alpha_i}|q)}{\prod_{i=1}^n P(t_i^{\alpha_i}|\bar{q})}$$

This assumption is less strict than the independence assumption mentioned in [22]. Combining the linked dependence with (3), we get:

$$
\begin{aligned}
\log \frac{P(d \to q)}{1 - P(d \to q)} &= \log \frac{\prod_{i=1}^n P(t_i^{\alpha_i}|q)}{\prod_{i=1}^n P(t_i^{\alpha_i}|\bar{q})} + \log \frac{P(q)}{P(\bar{q})} \\
&= \sum_{i=1}^n \log \frac{P(t_i^{\alpha_i}|q)}{P(t_i^{\alpha_i}|\bar{q})} + \log \frac{P(q)}{P(\bar{q})}
\end{aligned}
\tag{4}
$$

Figure 7 shows a simple example for the last formula. Here our vocabulary consists of two terms only, thus leading to four basic concepts which are represented as small squares in this figure. A document representation also corresponds to a basic concept, thus any document in the collection belongs to one of the four basic concepts here. In contrast, queries can be arbitrary subsets of the concept space.

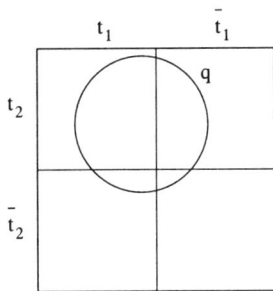

Figure 7. Example of BIR Model with Two Terms

In order to apply (4), we have to estimate $P(t_i^{\alpha_i}|q)$ and $P(t_i^{\alpha_i}|\bar{q})$ for each term (in addition to $P(q)$ and $P(\bar{q})$). For example, with $\alpha_i = 1$, the probability $P(t_i|q)$ corresponds to the fraction of q that is covered by $t_i \cap q$ in the concept space; vice versa, for $\alpha_i = 0$ the probability $P(\bar{t}_i|\bar{q})$ denotes the ratio between $P(\bar{t}_i \cap \bar{q})$ and $P(\bar{q})$. Subsequently, we use the notations $u_i = P(t_i|q)$ and $v_i = P(t_i|\bar{q})$.

For $\alpha_i = 0$, the corresponding parameters can be computed as counter probabilities, i.e. $P(\bar{t}_i|q) = 1 - u_i$ and $P(\bar{t}_i|\bar{q}) = 1 - v_i$. Now we use a trick for expressing the probabilities $P(t_i^{\alpha_i}|q)$ (and analogously for $\bar{q}$) in a closed formula:

$$P(t_i^{\alpha_i}|q) = u_i^{\alpha_i}(1 - u_i)^{1-\alpha_i} \quad \text{and} \quad P(t_i^{\alpha_i}|\bar{q}) = v_i^{\alpha_i}(1 - v_i)^{1-\alpha_i}$$

By substituting these parameters in (4), we get

$$\log \frac{P(d \to q)}{1 - P(d \to q)} = \sum_{i=1}^{n} \log \frac{u_i^{\alpha_i}(1 - u_i)^{1-\alpha_i}}{v_i^{\alpha_i}(1 - v_i)^{1-\alpha_i}} + \log \frac{P(q)}{P(\bar{q})}$$

$$= \sum_{i=1}^{n} \alpha_i \log \frac{u_i(1 - v_i)}{(1 - u_i)v_i} + \sum_{i=1}^{n} \log \frac{(1 - u_i)}{(1 - v_i)} + \log \frac{P(q)}{P(\bar{q})} \quad (5)$$

In the last equation, only the first sum depends on the specific document, whereas the other addends are constant for a query. In most practical applications, one is only interested in the ranking of documents. Thus we only consider the first sum, for which we need the parameters u_i and v_i for all terms. In addition, one usually assumes that $u_i = v_i$ for all terms not included in the query formulation, thus restricting the evaluation of this sum to the query terms.

Table 1 shows an example for the application of the BIR model. Here we have relevance judgements from 20 documents, from which we can estimate the following parameters:

$$u_1 = P(t_1|q) = 8/12 \qquad u_2 = P(t_2|q) = 7/12$$
$$v_1 = P(t_1|\bar{q}) = 3/8 \qquad v_2 = P(t_1|\bar{q}) = 3/8$$

Table 1. Example Parameter Estimation for the BIR Model

d_i	1 2 3 4 5	6 7 8 9 10 11	12 13 14 15 16 17	18 19 20
x_1	1 1 1 1 1	1 1 1 1 1 1	0 0 0 0 0 0	0 0 0
x_2	1 1 1 1 1	0 0 0 0 0 0	1 1 1 1 1 1	0 0 0
$r(q, d_i)$	$R\ R\ R\ R\ \bar{R}$	$R\ R\ R\ R\ \bar{R}\ \bar{R}$	$R\ R\ R\ \bar{R}\ \bar{R}\ \bar{R}$	$R\ \bar{R}\ \bar{R}$
BIR	0.76	0.69	0.48	0.40
$P(d \to q)$	0.80	0.67	0.50	0.33

Substituting these estimates in (5) (in addition, we have $P(q) = 12/20$ here), we get the values shown in the row titled "BIR" in Table 1. These estimates can be compared with the values that could be derived directly for the four possible document representations in this example (row "$P(d \to q)$"). Obviously, the values in the two rows are different, but the ranking between the four classes of documents remains unchanged. The difference is due to the linked dependence assumption employed in the BIR model, which is only an approximation to reality.

The major advantage of the BIR model over a direct estimation of the probabilities $P(d \to q)$ does not become apparent in this example: When we have a larger number n of query terms, then the BIR model requires the estimation of $2n$ parameters. In contrast, we would have 2^n different representations, each requiring its won parameter. Furthermore, there is a big difference in the basis from which these parameters have to be derived: The BIR model subdivides the feedback set into relevant and nonrelevant documents only, from which the conditional probabilities have to be estimated for each term considered. In contrast, direct estimation would form 2^n disjoint subsets of the feedback set; thus, direct estimation is not applicable in practice.

The Probabilistic Indexing Model. The second probabilistic model we want to consider here is the binary independence indexing (BII) [8], which is a variant of the very first probabilistic IR model, namely the indexing model of Maron and Kuhns [11]. Whereas the BIR model regards a single query w.r.t. a number of documents, the BII model observes one document in relation to a number of queries submitted to the system. As a consequence, now a query is represented as a single atomic concept

$$q = m_q = t_1^{\beta_1} \cap \cdots \cap t_n^{\beta_n}$$

with

$$t_i^{\beta_i} = \begin{cases} t_i & \text{if} \quad \beta_i = 1, \\ \bar{t}_i & \text{if} \quad \beta_i = 0. \end{cases}$$

In addition, we consider the implication in the opposite direction $(q \to d)$; like with the BIR model, we apply the log-odds transformation:

$$\log \frac{P(q \to d)}{1 - P(q \to d)} = \log \frac{P(q|d)}{P(q|\bar{d})} + \log \frac{P(d)}{P(\bar{d})}$$

$$= \log \frac{P(t_1^{\beta_1} \cap \cdots \cap t_n^{\beta_n}|d)}{P(t_1^{\beta_1} \cap \cdots \cap t_n^{\beta_n}|\bar{d})} \tag{6}$$

$$+ \log \frac{P(d)}{P(\bar{d})} \tag{7}$$

Our linked dependence assumption in this case can be formulated as follows:

$$\frac{P(t_1^{\beta_1} \cap \cdots \cap t_n^{\beta_n}|d)}{P(t_1^{\beta_1} \cap \cdots \cap t_n^{\beta_n}|\bar{d})} = \frac{\prod_{i=1}^{n} P(t_i^{\beta_i}|d)}{\prod_{i=1}^{n} P(t_i^{\beta_i}|\bar{d})}$$

Combining this assumption with (7), we get

$$\log \frac{P(q \to d)}{1 - P(q \to d)} = \log \frac{P(t_1^{\beta_1} \cap \cdots \cap t_n^{\beta_n}|d)}{P(t_1^{\beta_1} \cap \cdots \cap t_n^{\beta_n}|\bar{d})} + \log \frac{P(d)}{P(\bar{d})}$$

$$= \log \frac{\prod_{i=1}^{n} P(t_i^{\beta_i}|d)}{\prod_{i=1}^{n} P(t_i^{\beta_i}|\bar{d})} + \log \frac{P(d)}{P(\bar{d})}$$

$$= \sum_{i=1}^{n} \log \frac{P(t_i^{\beta_i}|d)}{P(t_i^{\beta_i}|\bar{d})} + \log \frac{P(d)}{P(\bar{d})} \tag{8}$$

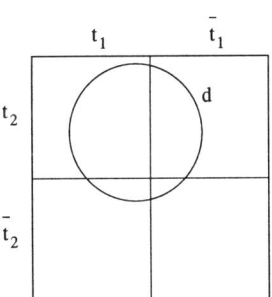

Figure 8. Example of BII Model with Two Terms

Figure 8 shows a simple example for the last formula. Here our vocabulary consists of two terms only, thus leading to four basic concepts which are represented as small squares in this figure. A query representation also corresponds to a basic concept, thus any document in the collection belongs to one of the four basic concepts here. In contrast, documents can be arbitrary subsets of the concept space.

In order to apply (8), we have to estimate $P(t_i^{\beta_i}|d)$ and $P(t_i^{\beta_i}|\bar{d})$ for each term (in addition to $P(d)$ and $P(\bar{d})$). For example, for $\beta_i = 1$, the probability $P(t_i|d)$ corresponds to the fraction of d that is covered by $t_i \cap d$ in the concept space; vice versa, for $\beta_i = 0$ the probability $P(\bar{t}_i|\bar{d})$ denotes the ratio between $P(\bar{t}_i \cap \bar{d})$ and $P(\bar{d})$. Subsequently, we use the notations $r_i = P(t_i|d)$ and $s_i = P(t_i|\bar{d})$ for these parameters:

$$P(t_i^{\beta_i}|d) = r_i^{\beta_i}(1 - r_i)^{1-\beta_i} \quad \text{and} \quad P(t_i^{\beta_i}|\bar{d}) = s_i^{\beta_i}(1 - s_i)^{1-\beta_i}$$

For $\beta_i = 0$, the corresponding parameters can be computed as counter probabilities, i.e. $P(\bar{t}_i|d) = 1 - r_i$ and $P(\bar{t}_i|\bar{q}) = 1 - s_i$. Now we use a trick for expressing the probabilities $P(t_i^{\beta_i}|d)$ (and analogously for $\bar{d}$) in a closed formula:

$$\log \frac{P(q \to d)}{1 - P(q \to d)} = \sum_{i=1}^{n} \log \frac{P(t_i^{\beta_i}|d)}{P(t_i^{\beta_i}|\bar{d})} + \log \frac{P(d)}{P(\bar{d})}$$

$$= \sum_{i=1}^{n} \log \frac{r_i^{\beta_i}(1 - r_i)^{1-\beta_i}}{s_i^{\beta_i}(1 - s_i)^{1-\beta_i}} + \log \frac{P(d)}{P(\bar{d})}$$

$$= \sum_{i=1}^{n} \beta_i \log \frac{r_i(1 - s_i)}{(1 - r_i)s_i}$$

$$+ \sum_{i=1}^{n} \log \frac{(1 - r_i)}{(1 - s_i)} + \log \frac{P(d)}{P(\bar{d})}$$

In order to apply the BII model according to the last formula, one would have to collect feedback data for each document in a collection. Only when we have enough relevance judgements for a document, we can apply this model. Obviously, this approach is not appropriate: new documents in a collection would have to wait too long before the model could be applied; in many applications, the number of documents outranges the number of queries submitted, so there would be hardly enough relevance judgements per document.

For overcoming this problem, we first reformulate the required parameters, and then we apply the concept of abstraction in order to facilitate the estimation process.

For the estimation of the parameters $r_i = P(t_i|d)$ and $s_i = P(t_i|\bar{d})$, we now consider all possible documents in the collection, and rephrase these parameters as follows:

$P(t_i|d_m) = P(t_i|I, d_m)$ is the probability that query contains term t_i, given that document d_m is implied by the query.

$P(t_i|\bar{d}_m) = P(t_i|\bar{I}, d_m)$ denotes the probability that query contains term t_i, given that document d_m is not implied by the query.

Now we apply Bayesian inversion again

$$\frac{P(t_i|I, d_m)}{P(t_i|\bar{I}, d_m)} = \frac{P(I|t_i, d_m)P(t|d_m)}{P(I|d_m)} \cdot \frac{P(\bar{I}|d_m)}{P(\bar{I}|t_i, d_m)P(t|d_m)}$$

$$= \frac{P(I|t_i, d_m)}{P(\bar{I}|t_i, d_m)} \cdot \frac{P(I|d_m)}{P(\bar{I}|d_m)} \tag{9}$$

Thus, we need two different parameters now (plus their counter probabilities):

$P(I|t_i, d_m)$ is the probability that document d_m is implied by the query, given that the query contains term t_i

$P(I|d_m)$ denotes the probability that document d_m is implied by random query

In the following, we will assume that $P(I|d_m)$ is the same for all documents; so we only have to estimate the parameters $P(I|t_i, d_m)$. A direct estimation of these parameters would suffer from the same problems as described before. Instead, we apply the so-called description-oriented approach [5]. Here the basic idea is the abstraction from specific terms and documents. Instead, we regard feature vectors $x(t_i, d_m)$ of term-document pairs, and we estimate probabilities $P(I|x(t_i, d_m))$ referring to these vectors.

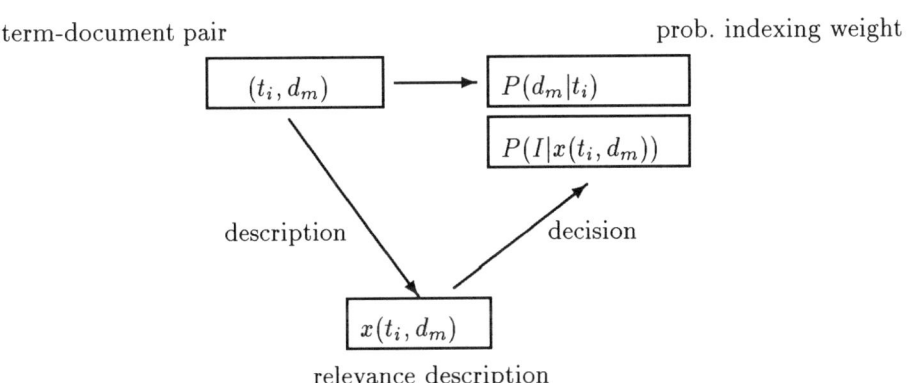

Figure 9. Direct Estimation vs. Description-Oriented Approach

The differences between the two strategies are illustrated in Fig. 9. A direct estimation would map each document-term pair (t_i, d_m) onto its probability $P(d_m|t_i)$. In the description-oriented approach, the indexing task is subdivided in a description step and a decision step.

In the description step, feature vectors for term-document pairs (t_i, d_m) are formed, where a vector $x(t_i, d_m)$ contains values of attributes of the term t_i, the document d_m and their relationship. Since this approach makes no additional assumptions about the choice of the attributes and the structure of x, the actual definition of the feature vector can be adapted to the specific application context, namely the representation of documents and the amount of learning data available.

In the decision step, a probabilistic index term weight based on this data is assigned. This means that we estimate instead of $P(I|t_i, d_m)$ the probability $P(I|x(t_i, d_m))$. In the former case, we would have to regard a single document d_m with respect to all queries containing t_i in order to estimate $P(I|t_i, d_m)$. But we replace this document-related learning strategy by a description-related one.

For that, we regard the set of all query-document pairs in which the same feature vector x occurs. Let Q denote the set of queries, $\underline{D}$ the set of documents and $\mathcal{R}$ the relevance scale; then the probabilistic index term weights $P(I|x(t_i, d_m))$ are derived from a learning example $L \subset Q \times \underline{D} \times \mathcal{R}$ of query-document pairs for which we have relevance judgements, so $L = \{(q_k, d_m, r_{km})\}$. By forming feature vectors for the terms common to query and document for every query-document pair in L, we get a multi-set (bag) of feature vectors with relevance judgements. Figure 10 illustrates this procedure for the case of a feature vector with two elements (e.g. $x_1 = 1$ if term occurs in the title, and $x_1 = 0$ otherwise; $x_2 = 1$ is term occurs exactly once in the document, and $x_2 = 2$ otherwise).

query	doc.	$q \to d?$	term	x
q_1	d_1	$+$	t_1	$(1,1)$
			t_2	$(0,1)$
			t_3	$(1,2)$
q_1	d_2	$-$	t_1	$(0,2)$
			t_3	$(1,1)$
			t_4	$(0,1)$
q_2	d_1	$+$	t_2	$(0,2)$
			t_5	$(0,2)$
			t_6	$(1,1)$
			t_7	$(1,2)$
q_2	d_3	$-$	t_5	$(0,1)$
			t_7	$(0,1)$

x	$P(I|x(t,d))$
$(0,1)$	$1/4$
$(0,2)$	$2/3$
$(1,1)$	$2/3$
$(1,2)$	1

Figure 10. Example: Learning Sample and Parameter Estimation for the BII Model

Language Models. In the models discussed so far, the issue of document indexing has not been addressed; all these models assume that e.g. the probabilities $P(d|t)$ or $P(t|d)$ are given, without specifying the4 mapping from a given document text onto these parameters. The BII model in combination with the description-oriented approach presented above may be a slight exception to that, but this approach only gives a framework for estimating the required probabilities.

During the past few years, a new class of probabilistic models has been developed which addresses the issue of document indexing: *Language models* are based on statistical models of natural language; they derive the parameters required for retrieval from the statistical properties of the document and the underlying collection.

Here we present one of these models, namely the model presented by Hiemstra [10]. The basic assumption is similar to the probabilistic models presented before, in that terms are nondisjoint concepts. Like the BII model, we regard the probability of the implication $q \rightarrow d$:

$$P(q \rightarrow d) \approx \sum_m P(q \rightarrow m)P(m \rightarrow d) \tag{10}$$

Also like the BII model, a query is assumed to be a single atomic concept $q = m_q = t_1^{\beta_1} \cap \cdots \cap t_n^{\beta_n}$.

Thus, we get for the probability of implication:

$$\begin{aligned} P(q \rightarrow d) &\approx P(q \rightarrow m_q)P(m_q \rightarrow d) \\ &= P(m_q|q)P(d|m_q) \\ &= P(d|m_q) \end{aligned}$$

Applying Bayesian inversion leads to

$$P(d|m_q) = P(d)\frac{P(m_q|d)}{P(m_q)} \tag{11}$$

Next we assume independence of terms.

$$P(t_1^{\beta_1} \cap \cdots \cap t_n^{\beta_n}|d) = \prod_{i=1}^n P(t_i^{\beta_i}|d) \tag{12}$$

In contrast to the probabilistic models discussed before, relevance of documents is not considered here; thus, this assumption seems to be stronger than the linked dependence assumptions employed for the BII and the BIR models.

Combining this assumption with 11, we get

$$P(d|m_q) = P(d)\frac{\prod_{i=1}^n P(t_i^{\beta_i}|d)}{P(m_q)} \tag{13}$$

$$= C \cdot P(d) \cdot \prod_{i=1}^n P(t_i^{\beta_i}|d) \tag{14}$$

where $1/C = P(m_q) = \sum_{d'} P(d', m_q)$. As additional assumption, we assume that the relevance of a document is only affected by those terms of the document occurring in the query. Thus, we can restrict the product to the query terms:

$$P(d|q) \approx C \cdot P(d) \cdot \prod_{t_i \subseteq q} P(t_i|d) \tag{15}$$

Since C is constant for a given query, its value is not needed for computing a ranking w.r.t. a query. So only the parameters $P(d)$ and $P(t|d)$ have to be estimated. For $P(t|d)$, there is the problem of sparse data - especially for those terms not occurring within the document d. In order to solve this problem, this parameter is estimated from a mixture of the maximum likelihood estimates of $P(t)$ and $P(t|d)$; the former denotes the probability of the term occurring in a random document of the collection, whereas the latter is the probability for the specific document. As mixture formula, Hiemstra proposes a weighted sum:

$$P(t_i|d) = \alpha_1 P(t_i) + \alpha_2 P(t_i|d) \tag{16}$$
$$\text{with } 0 < \alpha_1, \alpha_2 < 1 \text{ and } \alpha_1 + \alpha_2 = 1$$

(The language model presented in [16] proposes a risk function based on a geometric distribution for this purpose.) The estimation of these parameters is similar to the tf×idf weighting formula: Let

N_d number of documents in the collection,
$tf(t, d)$ within-document frequency of term t in document d,
$df(t)$ document frequency of t (# docs containing t).

The we can estimate

$$P(d) = \frac{1}{N_d} \tag{17}$$

$$P(t_i|d) = \alpha_1 \frac{df(t_i)}{\sum_t df(t)} + \alpha_2 \frac{tf(t_i, d)}{\sum_t tf(t, d)} \tag{18}$$

4 Models Based on Predicate Logic

4.1 Propositional vs. Predicate Logic

The text retrieval models presented above are based on proposition logic: Terms occurring in a document correspond to propositions, and the logical formula representing the document is the conjunction of these propositions. However, this approach does not allow for dealing with spatial or temporal relationships. For example, in an image containing a tree and a house, proposition logic can only represent the fact that there is a tree and a house, but it is not possible to represent their spatial position in an adequate form. Thus, queries referring to the spatial position cannot be answered correctly. Obviously, one needs at least binary predicates in order to deal with spatial and temporal relationships. Unary predicates are required for representing the values of specific properties of the multimedia content (e.g. the number of different colors in an image, the coarseness of a texture) as well as for most of the external attributes (e.g. the publication date); for comparing these values, one needs vague binary predicates (e.g. search for images where the coarseness of the texture is similar to a given one, or for documents published around 1990).

In the following, we will describe two major approaches for IR models based on predicate logic, namely terminological logic and Datalog. For the latter, we also will present a probabilistic variant.

4.2 Terminological Logic

Thesauri. If we look at classical thesauri, then we see that their structure still can be expressed in propositional logic. For example, the fact that a square is a subconcept of both a quadrangle and a regular polygon can be expressed by means of the logical formula

`square ⇔ quadrangle ∧ regular-polygon.`

Terminological logics are based originally on semantic networks (like e.g. KL-ONE), but their semantics is clearer defined. In comparison to thesauri, terminological logics offer two major advantages in terms of expressiveness:

1. Since terminological logics are based on predicate logic, it is possible to name also instances of concepts in the description of a documents, like e.g. in the image example from above. Thus, we are able to distinguish between identical and different instances of concepts. In addition to monadic predicates representing concepts, dyadic predicates describe relationships between objects, e.g. that tree `t1` is left of house `h1`.

2. For describing the relationships between different concepts terminological logics offer a more powerful machinery than thesauri. For example, we can define a student as a person who is enrolled at a university.

Elements of Terminological Logic. The basic elements of terminological logic are concepts and roles. *Concepts* are monadic predicates like e.g. `person` and `document`. *Roles* are dyadic predicates like e.g. `author` (denoting authorship of a book) and `refers-to` (for referential links between two documents).

The relationships between concepts and roles are described by means of *terminological axioms*. An axiom can be either a connotation or a definition. A *connotation* gives only necessary conditions for a concept, e.g.

`man <· person`

only states that a man is a person, whereas a *definition* names necessary and sufficient conditions, like e.g.

`square = (and rectangle regular-polygon)`

informs the system that each object which is both a rectangle and a regular polygon also is a square.

Instances of concepts and roles are defined by means of *assertions*, e.g.

`document[d123]. person[Smith]. author[d123,Smith].`

names a document `d123`, a person `Smith` and tells the system that `Smith` is the author of `d123`.

In the following, we will describe a specific terminological logic called MIRTL (Multimedia IR terminological logic), as presented in [12].

A MIRTL knowledge base consists of a terminological and an assertional module. The *terminological module* contains concepts and roles along with definitions and connotations. Let M and C denote concepts and D and R denote roles, then a definition is an expression of the form $M = C$ (or $D = R$, respectively), and a connotation has the form $M <· C$ (or $D <· R$, respectively).

The *assertional module* consists of assertions of the form $C[i]$ or of the form $R[i_1, i_2]$, where C is a concept, R is a role and i, i_1 and i_2 are individual constants. For example, `document[d123]` and `person[Smith]` state that d123 is a document and `Smith` is a person, and author[d123,Smith] stands for the fact that `Smith` is an author of `d123`.

The syntax for describing concepts and roles in the terminological module is as follows:

$$\begin{aligned}
\langle concept\rangle ::=\ &\langle monadic\ predicate\ symbol\rangle \\
|\ &(\textbf{top}) \\
|\ &(\textbf{bottom}) \\
|\ &(\textbf{a-not}\ \langle monadic\ predicate\ symbol\rangle) \\
|\ &(\textbf{sing}\ \langle individual\ constant\rangle) \\
|\ &(\textbf{and}\ \langle concept\rangle^{+}) \\
|\ &(\textbf{all}\ \langle role\rangle\ \langle concept\rangle) \\
|\ &(\textbf{c-some}\ \langle role\rangle\ \langle concept\rangle) \\
|\ &(\textbf{atleast}\ \langle natural\ number\rangle\ \langle role\rangle) \\
|\ &(\textbf{atmost}\ \langle natural\ number\rangle\ \langle role\rangle) \\
\langle role\rangle\quad ::=\ &\langle dyadic\ predicate\ symbol\rangle \\
|\ &(\textbf{inv}\ \langle role\rangle)
\end{aligned}$$

For explaining the meaning of these constructs, let the symbols $C, C_1, C_2, \ldots$ stand for concepts and $R, R_1, R_2, \ldots$ for roles.

(**and** $C_1\ C_2 \ldots C_n$) denotes the set of all individuals that belong at the same time to concept C_1 and C_2 and $\ldots C_n$. For example, we can state that a regular triangle is both a triangle and a regular polygon:
`regular-triangle = (and triangle regular-polygon)`.

(**c-some** $R\ C$) denotes the set of those individuals having at least one R that is a C. Assume that a German paper is a paper with at least one German author, which can be expressed as
`german-paper = (and paper (c-some author german))`

(**all** $R\ C$) denotes the set of those individuals whose R's are all C's. As an example, assume that a student paper is a paper where all authors are students:
`student-paper = (and paper (all author student))`

(**a-not** M) denotes the set of all individuals of the domain that are not denoted by the concept M. For example, a non-German is a person who is not German:
`non-german = (and person (a-not german))`

(**top**) and (**bottom**) denote the set of all individuals of the domain of discourse and the empty set, respectively.

(**sing** i) denotes the concept containing only the individual denoted by i. This allows for using a single individual for the definition of further concepts, e.g.
`unido=(sing univ-dortmund)`

(**atleast** $n\ R$) (resp. (**atmost** $n\ R$)) denotes the set of those individuals having at least (resp. at most) n R's. For example, assume that a multilingual person is a person who speaks at least two languages:
`multilingual = (and person (atleast 2 speaks-lang))`
Chinese parents are allowed to have at most 1 child:
`chinese-parent = (and (chinese (atmost 1 child)))`

Finally, (**inv** R) denotes the set containing the inverses of those pairs denoted by R, e.g.
`wrote = (inv author)`.

In addition to the basic syntax, we also use the following abbreviations:

$$(\textbf{exactly } n \ R) \doteq (\textbf{and } (\textbf{atleast } n \ R) \ (\textbf{atmost } n \ R))$$
$$(\textbf{func } R \ C) \doteq (\textbf{and } (\textbf{all } R \ C) \ (\textbf{exactly } 1 \ R))$$
$$(\textbf{no } R) \doteq (\textbf{atmost } 0 \ R)$$

For example, defining a student as a person who is enrolled at exactly one university can be expressed as follows:

```
student = (and person (atleast 1 enrolled)
                      (atmost 1 enrolled)
                      (all enrolled university))
        = (and person (exactly 1 enrolled)
                      (all enrolled university))
        = (and person (func enrolled university))
```

In a similar way, a bachelor can be defined as a man who has no spouse:

```
bachelor = (and man (no spouse))
```

Retrieval with Terminological Logic. Now we show how MIRTL can be used for IR. In [12], is proposed as a single representation language for modelling documents and terminological knowledge as well as for query formulation.

We use a running example from the original paper for illustrating this approach. First, we show how documents with external attributes, logical, layout and content structure can be modelled:

```
(and paper
     (func appears-in (sing SIGIR93))
     (all author (func affiliation (sing IEI-CNR)))
     (c-some author (sing Carlo-Meghini))
     (c-some author (sing Constantino-Thanos))
     (exactly 2 author))[paper666]

(and (func typeset-with (sing LaTeX))
     (func format (sing double-column))
     (no figure))[paper666]

(and (exactly 1 abstract)
     (exactly 5 section)
     (exactly 1 bibliography)) [paper666]

bibliography [paper666,bib666]

(and (func typeset-with (sing BibTeX))
     (func style (sing plain))
     (exactly 22 reference)) [bib666]

(and (c-some dw (sing Mirtl))
     (c-some dw (sing syn666))
     (c-some dw (sing sem666))
     (c-some dw (sing terminological-logic))) [paper666]

terminological-logic [Mirtl]
syntax [Mirtl,syn666]
semantics [Mirtl,sem666]
```

Queries in MIRTL are expressed as concepts, too. Then the inference algorithm seeks for concepts that are subsumed by the query concept and outputs all instances of these concepts. For example, the following query asks for papers authored by Thanos which deal with the semantics of terminological logics (obviously, **paper666** is an answer to this query):

(and **paper**
    (c-some **author** (sing **Costantino-Thanos**))
    (c-some **dw** (c-some (inv **semantics**) **terminological-logic**)))

Terminological logics, which are now also called description logics, have become more popular recently in the context of the development of Web standards, namely those related to *RDF (resource description framework)*. The basic concepts for RDF and especially RDF schemas are derived from description logics. RDF is targeted as content representation for internet resources, and thus will play an important role for IR in this area.

4.3   Datalog

Datalog is a logic programming language that has been developed in the database field (see e.g. [2, 20]). Like Prolog, it is based on horn logic. However, in contrast to Prolog, it does not allow for functions as terms, and the use of negation is restricted. Due to these constraints, there are sound and complete evaluation algorithms for Datalog—in contrast to Prolog, where certain programs cannot be evaluated. Here we show how document retrieval can be formulated in Datalog.

For modelling simple document retrieval, we assume that there is an extensional predicate (a database relation) `docTerm(D,T)`, where each ground fact gives for a document `D` a term `T` the document is indexed with, e.g.:
```
docTerm(d1,ir). docTerm(d2,ir).
docTerm(d1,db). docTerm(d2,oop).
```
In Datalog formulas, constants start with lowercase letters and variables with capitals. A query now can be formulated as a logical formula involving the predicate `docTerm`, e.g.
```
?- docTerm(D,ir).
?- docTerm(D,ir) & docTerm(D,db).
?- docTerm(D,ir) ; docTerm(D,db).
```
Here the first query searches for documents about IR, the second one for documents both about IR and DB, whereas the third one looks for documents dealing with IR or DB (the semicolon denotes disjunction here).

In order to allow for the more powerful inference mechanisms described in the following sections, a query should not relate directly to the extensional predicate `docTerm(D,T)`. Instead, we use a more general predicate `about(D,T)`, for which we will add new rules below. As basic rule, we define
```
about(D,T) :- docTerm(D,T).
```
Thus, the queries from above can also be formulated by replacing the predicate `docTerm` by `about`.

As a simple example for demonstrating the expressive power of Datalog, consider the retrieval of hypertext documents, where we have links between single documents (or nodes). Often, there are different types of links with different semantics. For representing links, we use a predicate `link(D1,D2)`, where a ground

fact states that there is a directed link from D1 to D2, e.g.:
```
link(d1,d2). link(d2,d3). link(d3,d1).
```
Now we assume that in retrieval, a document also deals with a certain topic if it refers to another document dealing with this topic. This can be written as
```
about(D,T) :- link(D,D1) & about(D1,T).
```
This rule makes about a recursive predicate. Thus if we want to prove about(D,T) for some document D, we look at the document itself as well as at those connected either directly or indirectly by links. Given the example link structure from above, the cyclic link structure also raises the problem of possible cycles in the inference process; however, Datalog can cope with these cycles. This way of considering hypertext links also allows for retrieval of nodes for which no index terms are given directly. For example, if we only have an automatic indexing method for text, then nodes containing multimedia data but no text can be retrieved via their links to textual nodes.

4.4 Probabilistic Datalog

As mentioned in the beginning of this article, IR should be interpreted as uncertain inference. Above, we have describe the application of Datalog to IR. Wo we will show how Datalog can be combined with uncertain inference by presenting a probabilistic version called Datalog$_P$.

Informal Description of Datalog$_P$. Probabilistic Datalog is an extension of ordinary Datalog. On the syntactical level, the only difference is that with ground facts, also a probabilistic weight may be given, e.g.

```
0.7 indterm(d1,ir).  0.8 indterm(d1,db).
```

Informally speaking, the probabilistic weight gives the probability that the following predicate is true. In our example, document d1 is with probability 0.7 about IR and with probability 0.8 about databases (DB). Retrieving documents dealing with both of these topics now can be accomplished by means of the the rule

```
q1(X) :- indterm(X,ir) & indterm (X,db).
```

Obviously, document d1 fulfills predicate q1 with a certain probability. Let us assume that index terms are stochastically independent. Then we can compute a probability of 0.56 for the probabilistic AND-combination in this example. In a similar way, the OR-combination produced by the rules

```
q2(X) :- indterm(X,ir).
q2(X) :- indterm(X,db).
```

would give us probability 0.94 for q2(d1).

With Datalog$_P$, we can refine the hypertext retrieval example from above by assigning weights to links, too:

```
0.5 link(d2,d1).  0.4 link(d3,d2).
```

These weights can be interpreted such that if we have a link from a document D1 to a document D2, and D2 is about a certain topic, then there is a certain probability that D1 is about the same topic. This probability is specified by the weight of the link predicate. Now we can formulate the rules

```
about(D,T) :- indterm(D,T).
about(D,T) :- link(D,D1) & about(D1,T).
```

Due to the recursive definition, the query

```
?- about(X,db).
```

now would return three documents, namely d1 with probability 0.8, d2 with probability $0.5 \cdot 0.8 = 0.4$ and d3 with probability $0.4 \cdot 0.5 \cdot 0.8 = 0.16$.

This example indicates that the idea of combining Datalog with probabilities yields very powerful retrieval methods. However, if we want to consequently apply probability theory, then we soon run into difficulties. Assume that in our hypertext structure, we search for documents both about IR and DB (similar to q1):

```
q4(X) :- about(X,ir) & about(X,db).
```

Then simple multiplication of the probabilistic weights involved in the inference process would give us for document d2: $0.5 \cdot 0.7 \cdot 0.5 \cdot 0.8 = 0.14$. This is not correct, since the probability for the link between d2 and d1 is considered twice; thus, the proper result would be 0.28. Besides counting the same probabilistic event twice, this simple approach also is unable to consider disjointness of complex events, for example when we search for documents either about IR or DB, but not about both:

```
q5(X) :- irnotdb(X).
q5(X) :- dbnotir(X).
irnotdb(X) :- indterm(X,ir) & not(indterm (X,db)).
dbnotir(X) :- indterm(X,db) & not(indterm (X,ir)).
```

If we would assume probabilistic independence of the subgoals of q5 (although they are disjoint events), we would compute the invalid result $1 - (1 - 0.7 \cdot 0.2) \cdot (1 - 0.8 \cdot 0.3) \approx 0.35$ instead of the correct probability 0.38 for q5(d1). The only way to overcome this problem in general is to switch from extensional semantics to intensional semantics (see e.g. [15, pp. 4–12] for the comparison of these two approaches to uncertainty reasoning). For this purpose, we must keep track of the events that contribute to a derived fact.

In Datalog, there are two classes of predicates: For extensional database (EDB) predicates only ground facts, but no rules are given, whereas for intensional database (IDB) predicates, only rules are specified. In Datalog$_P$, we assume that each fact for an EDB predicate corresponds to a basic (probabilistic) event, and assign it an unique event key. A fact derived for an IDB predicate relates to a Boolean combination of basic events of the EDB facts from which this fact was derived. Thus, we assign IDB facts additionally an event expression consisting of a Boolean combination of the event keys of the corresponding EDB facts.

Throughout the examples given in the following, we will use the first letter of the EDB predicate along with the argument constants as event keys. For IDB facts, we will denote the event expression in brackets. Thus, we have, for example,

q1(d1) [i(d1,ir) & i(d1,db)]
q4(d2) [l(d2,d1) & i(d1,ir) & l(d2,d1)& i(d1,db)]
q5(d1) [i(d1,ir) & ¬ i(d1,db) | ¬ i(d1,ir) & i(d1,db)]

(where '|' denotes disjunction and '¬' negation). Given these Boolean expressions, we can identify identical events occurring more than once or disjoint events (e.g. the complement of an event). Then the corresponding probabilities can be computed correctly by means of the sieve formula.

In the following, we first specify the syntax of Datalog$_P$, and the we describe the evaluation of Datalog$_P$ programs.

Syntax. As basic elements, we have in Datalog *variables* (starting with capital letters), *constants* (numbers or alphanumeric strings starting with lower-case letters) and *predicates* (alphanumeric strings starting with lower-case letters).

A *term* is either a constant or a variable. Note that as a major difference to Prolog, Datalog does not allow for functions in terms. Thus, a *ground term* in Datalog can only be a constant, and the *Herbrand Universe* of a Datalog program is the set of constants occurring in it.

An *atom* $p(t_1, \ldots, t_n)$ consists of an n-ary predicate symbol p and a list of arguments $(t_1, \ldots, t_n)$ such that each t_i is a term. A *literal* is an atom $p(t_1, \ldots, t_n)$ or a negated atom $\neg p(t_1, \ldots, t_n)$.

A *clause* is a finite list of literals, and a *ground clause* is a clause which does not contain any variables. Clauses containing only negative literals are called *negative clauses*, while *positive clauses* are those with only positive literals in it. An *unit clause* is a clause with only one literal.

Horn clauses contain at most one positive literal. There are three possible types of Horn clauses, for which additional restrictions apply in Datalog:

1. *Facts* are positive unit clauses, which also have to be ground clauses.
2. *Rules* are clauses with exactly one positive literal. The positive literal is called the *head*, and the list of negative literals is called the *body* of the rule. In Datalog, rules also must be *safe*, i.e. all variables occurring in the head also must occur in the body of the rule.
3. A *goal clause* is a negative clause which represents a query to the Datalog program to be answered.

In Datalog, the set of predicates is partitioned into two disjoint sets, *EPred* and *IPred*. The elements of *EPred* denote extensionally defined predicates, i.e. predicates whose extensions are given by the facts of the Datalog program, while the elements of *IPred* denote intensionally defined predicates, where the extension is defined by means of the rules of the Datalog program. Furthermore, there are built-in predicates like e.g. $=, \neq, <$, which we do not discuss explicitly here.

If S is a set of positive unit clauses, then $E(S)$ denotes the extensional part of S, i.e. the set of all unit clauses in S whose predicates are elements of *EPred*. On the other hand, $I(S) = S - E(S)$ denotes the intensional part of S (clauses in S with at least one predicate from *IPred*).

Now we can define a *Datalog program* P as a finite set of Horn clauses such that for all $C \in P$, either $C \in EDB$ or C is a safe rule where the predicate occurring in the head of C belongs to *IPred*.

So far, we have described the syntax of pure Datalog. In order to allow also for negation, we consider an extension called *stratified Datalog*. Here negated literals in rule bodies are allowed, but with the restriction that the program must be *stratified*. For checking this property, the *dependency graph* of a Datalog program P has to be constructed. For each rule in P, there is an arc from each predicate occurring in the rule body to the head predicate. P is stratified iff whenever there is a rule with head predicate p and a negated subgoal with predicate q, then there is no path in the dependency graph from p to q.

The syntax of Datalog$_P$ is only slightly different to that of stratified Datalog. A Datalog$_P$ program P consists of two sets P_E and P_I such that $P = P_E \cup P_I$. The intensional part P_I is a set of stratified Datalog rules, with the syntax of single rules as shown in the examples above. The extensional part P_E is a set of probabilistic ground facts of the form αg, where g is a ground fact and α is a probabilistic weight with $0 < \alpha \leq 1$. A probabilistic weight of 1 can be omitted. Furthermore, ground facts must be unique, i.e. $\alpha g \in P_E \wedge \alpha' g' \in P_E \wedge g = g'$ implies that $\alpha = \alpha'$.

Evaluation of Datalog$_P$ Programs. Here we only give a brief explanation of the evaluation process for Datalog$_P$ programs (for the details, see, [9]). As described above, each fact derived by an IDB predicate or a query is accompanied by an event expression that describes the derivation of this fact from the underlying EDB facts.

In order to compute the probability for an event expression, we use the so-called inclusion-exclusion (or sieve) formula. For that, we first have to transform the event expression into disjunctive normal form (DNF), that is:

$$e = K_1 \vee \cdots \vee K_n,$$

where the K_i are event atoms or conjunctions of event atoms, and an event atom is either an event key or a negated event key (n is the number of conjuncts of the DNF). From Boolean algebra, we know that any Boolean expression can be transformed into DNF. Now we can apply the inclusion-exclusion formula:

$$P(e) = P(K_1 \vee \cdots \vee K_n)$$

$$= \sum_{i=1}^{n} (-1)^{i-1} \left(\sum_{\substack{1 \leq j_1 < \\ \cdots < j_i \leq n}} P(K_{j_1} \wedge \cdots \wedge K_{j_i}) \right). \quad (19)$$

For example, the event expression for q5(d1) from above leads to the following computation:

$P(\texttt{i(d1,ir)} \ \& \ \neg \ \texttt{i(d1,db)} \ | \ \neg \ \texttt{i(d1,ir)} \ \& \ \texttt{i(d1,db)}) =$
$P(\texttt{i(d1,ir)} \ \& \ \neg \ \texttt{i(d1,db)}) + P(\neg \ \texttt{i(d1,ir)} \ \& \ \texttt{i(d1,db)}) -$
$\qquad \qquad P(\texttt{i(d1,ir)} \ \& \ \neg \ \texttt{i(d1,db)} \ \& \ \neg \ \texttt{i(d1,ir)} \ \& \ \texttt{i(d1,db)}) =$
$P(\texttt{i(d1,ir)} \ \& \ \neg \ \texttt{i(d1,db)}) + P(\neg \ \texttt{i(d1,ir)} \ \& \ \texttt{i(d1,db)})$

For computing the final probability, we need additional information about the (in)dependence of events[2]. Here we discuss the most simple case only, namely that all events relating to EDB facts are stochastically independent.

That is, for any two different events with keys e_1, e_2, we have

$$P(e_1 \wedge e_2) = P(e_1) \cdot P(e_2).$$

This assumption is suitable for most IR applications. With respect to (19), this means that we can compute the probability of a conjunct of event atoms as the product of the probabilities of the single event atoms. If the event atom is an event key, then we take the probability given with the corresponding probabilistic ground fact, and in the case of a negated event key, the complement probability is to be taken. Thus, we get for the event expression from our last example:

$P(\texttt{i(d1,ir)} \ \& \ \neg \ \texttt{i(d1,db)}) + \ P(\neg \ \texttt{i(d1,ir)} \ \& \ \texttt{i(d1,db)}) =$
$\quad P(\texttt{i(d1,ir)}) \cdot (1 - P(\texttt{i(d1,db)})) + (1 - P(\texttt{i(d1,ir)} \ )) \cdot P(\texttt{i(d1,db)}).$

5   Conclusions and Outlook

In this paper, we have described some basic IR models. Classical models restricted to text retrieval are based on propositional logic, and we have outlined that most of these models can be explained within a framework of uncertain inference in concept space. For multimedia retrieval, some form or predicate logic is required; as examples, we have described two approaches, one using description logics, the other based on Datalog. In [7], some further issues of models for multimedia retrieval are discussed.

Although IR models are at the core of IR systems, the models discussed here (as well as most models published) are restricted to a rather simple view of retrieval, and they cover only a small fraction of the whole retrieval process. As illustrated with the conceptual model, IR should not only deal with the content, but also the logical structure, the layout and the external attributes of documents; furthermore, a good IR model also should address the issue of result computation, i.e. the logical structure and the layout of the result. However, the most important facet missing is the user involvement: First of all, retrieval is an interactive process—and a user should have many more interaction possibilities besides plain relevance feedback. In [1], a taxonomy of higher-level functions of IR systems is presented. Combining this approach with the possibilities of today's multimedia IR systems would lead to an appropriate model of user involvement in the IR process.

References

1. M. J. Bates. Where should the person stop and the information search interface start? *Information Processing & Management*, 26(5):575–591, 1990.
2. S. Ceri, G. Gottlob, and L. Tanca. *Logic Programming and Databases*. Springer, Berlin et al., 1990.

---

[2] Otherwise, only probability intervals could be given as result, which would hardly allow for any meaningful ranking of retrieval results.

3. W.S. Cooper. Some inconsistencies and misidentified modeling assumptions in probabilistic information retrieval. *ACM Transactions on Information Systems*, 13(1):100–111, Jan 1995.

4. Fabio Crestani, Mounia Lalmas, Cornelis J. van Rijsbergen, and Iain Campbell. "Is this document relevant? ... probably": a survey of probabilistic models in information retrieval. *ACM Computer Surveys*, 30(4):528–552, 1998.

5. N. Fuhr. Models for retrieval with probabilistic indexing. *Information Processing & Management*, 25(1):55–72, 1989.

6. N. Fuhr. Probabilistic models in information retrieval. *The Computer Journal*, 35(3):243–255, 1992.

7. N. Fuhr. Information retrieval methods for multimedia objects. To appear in: Proceedings Dagstuhl WS Content-Based Image and Video Retrieval, 2000.

8. N. Fuhr and C. Buckley. A probabilistic learning approach for document indexing. *ACM Transactions on Information Systems*, 9(3):223–248, 1991.

9. Norbert Fuhr. Probabilistic Datalog: Implementing logical information retrieval for advanced applications. *Journal of the American Society for Information Science*, 51(2):95–110, 2000.

10. Djoerd Hiemstra. A linguistically motivated probabilistic model of information retrieval. In C. Nikolaou and C. Stephanidis, editors, *Lecture Notes In Computer Science - Research and Advanced Technology for Digital Libraries - Proceedings of the second European Conference on Research and Advanced Technology for Digital Libraries: ECDL'98*, pages 569–584. Springer Verlag, 1998.

11. M.E. Maron and J.L. Kuhns. On relevance, probabilistic indexing, and information retrieval. *Journal of the ACM*, 7:216–244, 1960.

12. C. Meghini, F. Sebastiani, U. Straccia, and C. Thanos. A model of information retrieval based on a terminological logic. In *Proceedings of the Sixteenth Annual International ACM SIGIR Conference on Research and Development in Information Retrieval*, pages 298–308, New York, 1993. ACM.

13. S. R. Newcomb, N. A. Kipp, and V. T. Newcomb. The "HyTime" hypermedia/time-based document structuring language. *Communications of the ACM*, 34(11):67–83, November 1991.

14. Jianyun Nie. An information retrieval model based on modal logic. *Information processing & management.*, 25(5):477–491, 1989.

15. J. Pearl. *Probabilistic Reasoning in Intelligent Systems: Networks of Plausible Inference*. Morgan Kaufman, San Mateo, California, 1988.

16. J.M. Ponte and W.B. Croft. A language modeling approach to information retrieval. In *Proceedings of the 21st Annual International ACM SIGIR Conference on Research and Development in Information Retrieval*, pages 275–281, New York, 1998. ACM.

17. S.E. Robertson. The probability ranking principle in IR. *Journal of Documentation*, 33:294–304, 1977.

18. S.E. Robertson and K. Sparck Jones. Relevance weighting of search terms. *Journal of the American Society for Information Science*, 27:129–146, 1976.

19. G. Salton, editor. *The SMART Retrieval System - Experiments in Automatic Document Processing*. Prentice Hall, Englewood, Cliffs, New Jersey, 1971.

20. Jeffrey D. Ullman. *Principles of Database and Knowledge-Base Systems*, volume I. Computer Science Press, Rockville (Md.), 1988.

21. C. J. van Rijsbergen. A non-classical logic for information retrieval. *The Computer Journal*, 29(6):481–485, 1986.

22. S.K.M. Wong and Y.Y. Yao. On modeling information retrieval with probabilistic inference. *ACM Transactions on Information Systems*, 13(1):38–68, 1995.

Multilingual Information Access

Carol Peters[1] and Páraic Sheridan[2]

[1] Istituto di Elaborazione della Informazione, CNR, Pisa, Italy
carol@iei.pi.cnr.it
[2] MNIS-TextWise Labs, Syracuse, New York, USA
paraic@textwise.com

Abstract The global information society has radically changed the way in which know-ledge is acquired, disseminated and exchanged. Users of internationally distributed networks need to be able to find, retrieve and understand relevant information in whatever language and form it may have been stored. For this reason, much attention has been given over the past few years to the study and development of tools and technologies for multilingual information access (MLIA). This is a complex, multidisciplinary area in which methodologies and tools developed in the fields of information retrieval and natural language processing converge. Two main sectors are involved: multiple language recognition, manipulation and display; cross-language search and retrieval. The paper provides an overview of the main issues of interest in both these areas. Topics covered include: multilingual document indexing, specific requirements of particular languages and scripts, techniques for cross-language information retrieval (CLIR), resources, and system and component evaluation.

1 Introduction

1.1 Why Is MLIA Important?

The rapid expansion of the use and popularity of the World Wide Web and Internet for communication and dissemination of information throughout the world means that electronically accessible information is now available in an ever-increasing number of languages. The first Web sites were almost entirely dedicated to provision of information in English and the first search services (in about 1995) were implemented to meet the needs of an English-speaking community (e.g. Lycos, AltaVista, Yahoo!). The users of these services had mainly academic backgrounds and had sufficient English language skills to formulate meaningful queries in English and to understand the documents retrieved. However, in the last few years, the situation has changed immensely. The Web is not just used for academic purposes but for commerce, entertainment, news, tourism, banking, finance, etc. Information is increasingly published in the native language of the person or organisation providing it and searched for in the native language of the user. Many nations now have their own Web search services. It is thus far more difficult to provide a profile of the average Web user, of their needs and language skills. Recent surveys show that the number of Internet

M. Agosti, F. Crestani, and G. Pasi (Eds.): ESSIR 2000, LNCS 1980, pp. 51–80, 2000.

users who are not proficient in English is growing rapidly as is the number of non-English Web pages. The prediction is that by 2005, 78% of Internet users will be non-English speakers [39] whereas "only" 49% of Web content will be in English [103].

While the Internet is by far the largest repository for document collections in many languages, it is by no means the only one. The intranets of many large international public and private organisations also increasingly contain multilingual information as interests and activities transcend national boundaries a nd the use of a single common language is not always acceptable. Other areas where facilitating access to information in multiple languages is be coming increasingly important are, for instance: digital libraries and subject gateways, schools and school networks throughout Europe, multilingual collections of laws and regulations, multilingual collections of cultural heritage.

All this means that situations where a user is faced with the task of querying a multilingual document collection are becoming increasingly common. Many users have some foreign language knowledge, but their proficiency may not be good enough to formulate queries to appropriately express their information needs. Such users will benefit enormously if they can enter their queries in their native language, because they are able to examine relevant documents even if they are not translated. Monolingual users, on the other hand, can use translation aids to help them understand their search results in a second language.

To sum up, there is a growing need to find efficient ways to access information in whatever language it is stored and to discover and retrieve relevant information across language boundaries. This is what Multilingual Information Access is all about.

1.2 Defining the Terminology

We are talking about a new, multidisciplinary area in which the use of the terminology is not yet stable. We use the term Multilingual Information Access (MLIA) in its broadest possible sense. MLIA addresses the problem of accessing, querying and retrieving information from collections in any language at any level of specificity and includes all issues that involve the overall management of multilingual information, such as character encoding, language identification, indexing of collections in multiple languages, etc. Cross-Language (or Cross-Lingual) Information Retrieval (CLIR) technologies specifically concern the querying of a multilingual collection in one language in order to retrieve relevant documents in other languages, and address the task of filtering, selecting and ranking such documents. Peripheral but strongly related are issues concerning the presentation, summarisation and translation of the results of a query. In our use of these terms MLIA embraces and includes CLIR. Although both terms are still most frequently used to refer to the multilingual text retrieval paradigm, they also cover other media such as image, video, speech.

Other commonly found terms are Multilingual Information Retrieval and Translingual Information Retrieval. Multilingual Information Retrieval has been used to refer to various tasks ranging from monolingual IR in languages other than English (for example at TREC—Text REtrieval Conferences fo IR experiments on Spanish) to IR on single documents containing text in more than one language. However, it is generally used in a similar way to MLIA above. Translingual Information Retrieval is the term introduced by DARPA (US Defence Advanced Research Projects Agency) to describe a set of functions that include cross-language retrieval, visualisation of multilingual document collections, and other issues involving the management of multilingual information.

1.3 Brief History

Although the first experiments in cross-language text retrieval were made by Gerard Salton in 1970, only very recently has MLIA been recognised as an independent, multidisciplinary area in which methodologies and tools developed in the fields of information retrieval and natural language processing converge. Here we list some of the main milestones that have led to this recognition.

1970: Salton shows that with carefully constructed thesauri, cross-language retrieval can be nearly as effective as monolingual retrieval [43].

1978: ISO Standard 5964 for developing multilingual thesauri is first released. Revised version in 1985 [28].

1991: The Unicode Standard, Version 1.0, is first published with the aim of promoting a universal, uniform, unique, unambiguous worldwide character encoding standard [53].

1993: ISO/IEC 10646 is released as "Universal Multiple-Octet Coded Character Set" (UCS). Unicode-compatible UCS aims at eventually including all characters used in all the written languages in the world [27]. Version 3.0 of the Unicode Standard is code-for-code identical to ISO/IEC 10646–1:2000 [104].

1994: Final prototype of the European Multilingual Information Retrieval (EMIR) project—an EC ESPRIT initiative—released. EMIR was one of the first general cross-language systems to be implemented and evaluated [16].

1995: SYSTRAN Software Inc. received funding from US Government to develop a CLIR system based on NLP and MT technology [18].

1995: ALIS launches TANGO a multilingual web browser.

1996: First Workshop on "Cross-Lingual Information Retrieval" at SIGIR'96. Different approaches to CLIR are presented and a research community begins to be identified around this area [21]. From 1996 on, dedicated workshops have been held every year and aspects of the problem now routinely appear at conferences on digital libraries, information retrieval, machine translation, and computational linguistics.

1997: First Cross-Language IR track within TREC (Text REtrieval Conferences) [44].

1997: EU-NSF Working Group on Multilingual Information Access is given mandate to identify and prioritise the major open research issues and propose a short and medium term research agenda [45].

1999: The NSF/EC/DARPA report on Multilingual Information Management is released. Aim of the study is to identify how technologies developed in the areas of computational linguistics and information retrieval can be integrated to address problems of handling multilingual and multi-modal information [24].

1999: The first Japanese NTCIR Workshop on Text Retrieval System Evaluation includes a track for Cross-Lingual Information Retrieval [31]. The CLIR community for Asian languages is well established.

2000: CLEF: Cross-Language Evaluation Forum for European Languages is launched [8].

1.4   Organisation of the Paper

In this paper, our intention is to provide an overview of the major issues involved in the general area of MLIA and report on specific technologies for CLIR. The main focus will be on multilingual text access and retrieval but we will also mention some approaches now being experimented for cross-language access to spoken documents. The paper is structured as follows. In the next section, we treat issues regarding the pre-processing and indexing of documents in multiple lang uages. Section 3 will outline the best-known approaches to cross-language text retrieval whereas Sect. 4 will briefly describe strategies for retrieval from multilingual spoken documents. Section 5 will discuss the types of resources needed for all aspects of MLIA and consider the problem of acquiring these resources. The importance of evaluation in stimulating CLIR system development is discussed in Section 6 and the most relevant evaluation activities are listed. In the final section, we give some examples of experimental and commercial CLIR systems. The paper ends with a comprehensive biblio-graphy and a set of pointers to usef ul Web sites.

2   Multilingual Text Processing

For information retrieval in general, a representation of the text to be searched is usually obtained by extracting 'indexing features' from a document collection or from the text of a user's query. In a simple approach, this extraction process consists of four basic steps: conversion of characters, extraction of words (tokenisation), removal of 'stopwords', and normalisation of remaining content words. While these processing steps have been studied extensively in the context of retrieval of English texts, new challenges are presented when access to multilingual information is involved.

Since processing texts to extract indexing features often involves steps which use language-specific knowledge, it is important to first establish the language of the text, if that is not already known. To date many different approaches have been used to address the problem of language identification in general texts. In general these techniques rely on identifying particular sequences of characters which provide a unique 'signature' for a given language or which are 'suggestive' of a give language. Approaches which have been tried range from approaches relying on the presence of individual characters [59] in texts, or the presence of particular character N-grams [14] or even on the presence of given words [52]. One approach to language identification specifically for multilingual access [56] has used language-specific stopwords, which are by nature very common, to identify the language of texts. Many analytical techniques have also been employed, such as the use of Markov models [15] or task-specific modes [12]. In [50], Sibun describes an approach where the language of a text is identified based on distances of statistical distributions of N-grams occurring in the text. This system works well particularly for brief text passages.

An approach which is specifically oriented toward language identification on the World Wide Web is reported in [32]. This application also raises the issue of different document encoding schemes which may be encountered in Internet documents, especially when Asian languages are concerned. Although English and most of the Western European languages are all covered under the standard ISO–8859-1 (Latin-1) encoding scheme, multilingual access to non-Roman languages involves addressing the issue of document encoding. The language-recognition approach of Kikui first addresses the identification of the document encoding as a step toward language identification. For example if the document encoding is US-ASCII, then Korean is ruled out as a possibility for the document language.

The encoding of a language, or more specifically the encoding of the character set used to represent the alphabet of a given language's script, specifies the mapping between the written script and its binary representation. A character encoding (mapping) is therefore specific to a given alphabet and in many cases there exist multiple mappings for a given alphabet (for example the Cyrillic alphabet used in Russian). Depending on the number of characters needed in the representation of a language, an encoding scheme for that language can be based on a single byte (e.g. German) or must require a double-byte encoding (e.g. Chinese).

In an attempt to provide a single encoding scheme for mapping all of the world's languages, the UNICODE consortium (http://www.unicode.org) has designed the UNICODE standard. This provides a character encoding system designed to support the interchange, processing and display of the written texts of the diverse languages of the modern world. In addition, it supports classical and historical texts of many written languages. In its most recent version, the standard contains 38,887 distinct coded characters which cover the principal written languages of the Americas, Europe, the Middle East, Africa, India, Asia and Pacifica. In processing texts for multilingual access, it is common for UNICODE compliant systems to use standard libraries to convert the native encoding of texts (e.g. Shift-JIS for Japanese) into a UNICODE format (e.g. UTF-8) as a single standard representation.

Once the language of a text to be processed has been determined and the character encoding has been standardised if necessary, the next step is to identify the specific words being used. While in many languages this is straightforward because of the use of spaces to delimit words, many languages compound or concatenate words together to form new compound words (e.g. German: Abendnachrichtensendungen—Abend, Nachricht, Sendung). In the most difficult cases, no spaces are used between words in text (e.g. Japanese, Chinese) so that the tokenisation process must determine all word boundaries. In this case, a dictionary or lexicon of valid words in the language is typically used to determine legal words. A process is then used whereby a sentence of text is scanned in order to find the set of words from the dictionary which provides full coverage of the characters found in the text. In Japanese and Korean, further evidence is found from the fact that there is often a change in alphabet (Kanji to Hiragana) at word boundaries since content words are written in Kanji while function words typically use Hiragana. In the tokenisation stage, punctuation is also removed from words and hyphens between word segments are processed.

In order to reduce the number of indexing features to be included in the representation of a piece of text, words which have little or no value in representing the content of the text are often discarded; so-called 'stopwords'. For instance, words like *the* and *at* do not usually contribute to a representation of an English text. As single words they have little meaning, even though they may be important in context. Such stop words are usually collected together into a *stoplist* so that words from this list are not included in the index. Since between 30% and 50% of the words of a text may be included in a stoplist [54], the removal of such words can have a significant impact on the retrieval index. Stopwords in any given language are usually easily determined on the basis of either on parts-of-speech (determiners, prepositions...) or of frequency within a given sample text, being many of the most frequently occurring words. Based on frequency, it is also possible to have words that should be considered stopwords within a given collection of documents only. For example the word *'document'* might be considered a stopword if all queries ask for, *'documents related to...'*

The final step in processing text for retrieval indexing involves the normalisation of content words remaining after the tokenisation and stopword removal processes. The most common form of normalisation involves reducing words to a *stem* form by removing suffixes or inflections. In the simplest case a stemming algorithm can proceed by simply removing standard suffixes (e.g. '-s', '-es', '-ation' in English) in an iterative process until the shortest form remains. Such an algorithm, which is widely used, was developed by Porter [42] for English and similar algorithms have been developed for other languages [56]. In some cases however, suffix removal can be crude (e.g. removing 'ic' from 'organic'!) and results in mismatches between stems of words that are not related. An alternative is to perform a *morphological* analysis of the text and reduce the words to their lexical stem as it would appear in a standard dictionary.

There is a long history of experiments examining the benefits of using word normalisation or stemming algorithms as part of the indexing process (e.g. [17, 22, 23, 25, 33, 34, 36, 42]), sometimes with conflicting conclusions. Although it is sometimes claimed that experiments on stemming have proved inconclusive (e.g. [17]), Krovetz [33] has demonstrated increased performance due to stemming of between 15% and 35% on some test collections and a recent detailed study of various stemming algorithms concluded that, "Some form of stemming is almost always beneficial" [25]. While many of these experiments have focused on retrieval of English-only texts, it has been suggested that when dealing with European languages, which have a much richer inflectional morphology than English, the benefits to be obtained from the use of stemming should be even greater than with English.

In the normalisation phase of processing, or possibly in the tokenisation process, it is also common, especially in the context of multilingual access, to attempt to identify multi-word phrases as individual index features. This is helpful so that phrases can be translated as a unit rather than as individual words. In many cases, a word-by-word translation of a phrase does not render a true translation in the target language (e.g. translate *'fast food'* into French or German). Phrases can be identified in a text by matching against a dictionary or lexicon of known phrases, although it has also been shown that phrases can be effectively identified by analysing words which frequently occur together in a collection of texts.

It should be clear that the steps in text processing for information access will vary depending on the language of the text involved. It is also the case, however, that the steps or processes used for multilingual text processing will depend on the overall approach being used within a given system for multilingual information access. It is necessary that the index features which result from the text processing phase are compatible with the resource that is being used to match queries in one language to documents in possibly many other languages. It is therefore important to have an understanding of the different approaches to cross-language information retrieval and the kinds of resources used in each approach. This is presented in the following sections.

3 Approaches to Cross-Language Text Retrieval

Basically, in cross-language text retrieval the task is to develop methods which successfully match queries against documents over languages and rank the retrieved documents in order of relevance. In monolingual text retrieval, the traditional way to do this is through some kind of word matching and weighting; with cross-language text retrieval we have the additional problem of matching (and weighting) words across languages. This implies employing some kind of lexical resource in order to translate from the language of the query to that of the documents or vice versa, and addressing the problem of sense disambiguation, already present in monolingual retrieval but greatly increased when mapping over languages. Three main approaches have been experimented:

1. Machine translation techniques
2. Knowledge-based techniques
3. Corpus-based techniques

Each of these methods has given promising results but also has disadvantages associated with it. In this section, we briefly outline the main issues involved.

3.1   Machine Translation Techniques

Full machine translation (MT) is not viewed as a realistic answer to the problem of matching documents and queries over languages. The goal of an MT system is to produce a readable and reliable target language version of a source text; whereas cross-language retrieval aims at finding sufficient similarities between a source language query and a target language document in order to be able to claim that the document is more or less relevant to the information needs expressed by the query. The translating of entire collections of documents into another language (that of the query) is thus not only very expensive, but also involves a number of tasks that are redundant from the purely retrieval viewpoint, e.g. encoding of linguistic, semantic and pragmatic information.

Efforts using MT systems have thus concentrated on attempting to translate the query into the language(s) of the documents. However, MT does not represent a cost-effective solution for query translation either. Queries are usually a set of words with little or no syntactic structure. The input cannot thus be parsed by the MT system and traditional methods of word-sense disambiguation cannot be applied as there is no semantically coherent text. Accurate translation is thus possible and also not necessary. There is no need for a linearly coherent and unique output in a target language query and in fact multiple translations of query terms can provide a form of query expansion that can improve performance. It has been shown that simpler and less resource costly techniques can work just as effectively. For example, Ballesteros and Croft report that for query translation, dictionary-based techniques outperform one commercial MT system and perform as well as another [4].

3.2   Knowledge-Based Techniques

Knowledge-based approaches apply thesauri or ontologies, bi- or multilingual dictionaries to cross-language text retrieval.

Using Thesauri: The first approaches to cross-language retrieval were thesaurus-based [40, 43]. A thesaurus is an ontology specialised in organising terminology; a multilingual thesaurus organises terminology for more than one language. ISO 5964 gives specifications for the incorporation of domain knowledge in multilingual thesauri. The early experiments showed that multilingual thesauri can give acceptable results for cross-language retrieval and there are now a number of thesaurus-based systems available commercially.

A multilingual thesaurus for indexing and searching with a controlled vocabulary can be seen as a set of monolingual thesauri that all map to a common system of concepts. With a controlled vocabulary, there is a defined set of concepts used in indexing and searching. In this way, the problem of ambiguity is eliminated. The user should be able to use a term in his/her language to find the corresponding concept identifier in order to retrieve documents in another language. In the simplest system, this can be achieved through manual look-up in a thesaurus that includes for each concept corresponding terms from several languages and has an index for each language. In more sophisticated systems, the mapping from term to descriptor would be done internally [51].

With the controlled vocabulary approach, appropriate terms from the vocabulary must be assigned to each document in the collection. Traditionally this was done manually by experts in the field. This is expensive. Methods are now being developed for the (semi)automatic assignation of these indicators. The fact remains that thesauri and ontologies are expensive to build, costly to maintain and difficult to update. Furthermore, it has been found to be quite difficult to train users to effectively exploit the thesaurus relationships.

With multilingual thesauri or ontologies, language differences and cultural factors mean that it is difficult to achieve an effective mapping between lexical or conceptual equivalences in two languages; this problem is greatly exacerbated when several languages are involved. It is to be expected that the trade-off for multilinguality will be the loss of some monolingual specificity.

In any case, the current trend is away from controlled vocabulary searching in favour of free text searching even though, from many viewpoints, cross-language free-text searching is a more complex task. It requires that each term in the query be mapped to a set of search terms in the language of the texts, possibly attaching weights to each search term expressing the degree to which occurrence of a search term in a text would contribute to the relevance of the text to the query term. The greater difficulty of free-text cross-language retrieval stems from the fact that one is working with actual usage while in controlled-vocabulary retrieval usage can, to some extent, be dictated. On the other hand, the query potential is greater than with a controlled vocabulary.

Using Dictionaries: Many free-text cross-language systems use bilingual machine readable dictionaries (MRDs) as their transfer resource. Such resources are becoming increasingly available both commercially and on-line (see Sect. 5.2). As they have generally been prepared for human use, they require some kind of pre-processing before they can be used in an automatic system. This essentially implies analysing the mark-up information to identify the different lexical information: headwords, parts-of-speech, sense division, translation equivalents, etc.

It has been demonstrated that straightforward dictionary-based query translation, where each term or phrase in the query is replaced by a list of all its possible translations, represents an acceptable first pass at cross-language information retrieval although such—relatively simple—methods clearly show performance below that of monolingual retrieval. Automatic MRD query translation has been found to lead to a drop in effectiveness of 40 − 60% of monolingual retrieval [5, 26]. There are three main reasons for this: (i) general purpose dictionaries do not normally contain specialised vocabulary; (ii) failure to translate multiword terms; (iii) the problem of ambiguity.

The general purpose MRDs normally used in cross-language systems tend to have a broad coverage which does not include many domain-specific words or specialised terminology. It has been claimed that out-of-vocabulary words are responsible for up to 23% of drop in effectiveness for cross-language retrieval. Dictionaries are also frequently very poor on multiword coverage. Word by word translation and matching over languages tends to fail miserably when applied to such terms. Various researchers have shown that if phrases in a query are identified and translated as such, retrieval will be greatly improved.

Perhaps the greatest problem using MRDs is coping with ambiguity. In word-by-word dictionary translation, each word is replaced by all possible translation equivalents in the target language. When the query term is polysemous and thus in itself ambiguous, this can result in a large set of target search terms, many of which are spurious and will contribute to the retrieval of irrelevant documents. In sentence or document translation, the context provides information that can be used for disambiguation; the shortness of the average query means that there is a lack of context for this scope. Current research work is giving considerable attention to this question.

It has been shown that both syntactic and statistical methods can be applied to significantly reduce the effects of ambiguity and bring the effectiveness of cross-language retrieval near the level of monolingual retrieval. Well-formed queries can be tagged by part-of-speech taggers to eliminate grammatical homonyms and thus reduce the number of incorrect target terms generated by the dictionary. In particular, query expansion techniques have been shown to help considerably in reducing ambiguity. Basically, such techniques add new terms, selected according to a given criteria, in order to make the query more precise. Ballesteros & Croft [6] have shown that pre- and post-translation local context analysis can both significantly reduce the error associated with the dictionary by adding a set of significant co-occurring terms to the query. They also obtain terms for query expansion using relevance feedback techniques. This technique assumes that the top ranked documents initially retrieved are relevant. Terms in these documents are then added to the queries. In [1], Adriani and van Rijsbergen show that statistical term similarity measures can be used to select the best translation of a query term from a set of possible candidates; they then use a query expansion technique to further improve retrieval.

Another difficulty using MRDs is represented by the fact that for many language pairs it is not easy to find a suitable resource. One way to address this problem is suggested by Ballesteros. She describes what she calls a transitive translation approach where a third language is employed as an interlingua between source and target languages. In order to translate Spanish queries to French, she first translates from Spanish to English and then from English to French. It is clear that this strategy greatly increases translation ambiguity. In fact, her tests show that transitive translation effectiveness is 91% below that of straight bilingual translation before the application of any ambiguity reduction strategy. She manages to reduce this difference considerably by applying various techniques for disambiguation. For details, see [3].

3.3 Corpus-Based Techniques

Corpus-based approaches analyse large collections of texts on a statistical basis and automatically extract the information needed to construct application-specific translation techniques. The collections analysed may consist of parallel (translation equivalent) or comparable (domain-specific) sets of documents. The main approaches that have been experimented using corpora are vector space and probabilistic techniques.

The first tests with parallel corpora were on statistical methods for the extraction of multilingual term equivalence data which could be used as input for the lexical component of MT systems. Some of the most interesting experiments, however, are those using a matrix reduction technique known as Latent Semantic Indexing (LSI) to extract language independent terms and document representations from parallel corpora [35]. LSI is based on the vector space retrieval model but applies a singular value decomposition to a large, sparse term document co-occurrence matrix (including terms from all parallel versions of the documents) and extracts a subset of the singular vectors to form a new vector space. The underlying theory is that the dimensions of the resulting matrix are representative of "core" or "basic" concepts of discourse. When applied to a collection of documents and their translations, a bilingual indexing space is created. Thus queries in one language can retrieve documents in the other (as well as in the original language). This method has been tested with positive results on relatively small parallel text collections in English with French, Spanish, Greek and Japanese. Its effectiveness has not been demonstrated for larger collections. The problem with using parallel texts as training corpora is that test corpora are usually domain-specific and costly to acquire—it is difficult to find already existing translations of the right kind of documents and translated versions are expensive to create. For this reason, there has been a lot of interest in the potential of comparable corpora.

A comparable document collection is one in which documents are aligned on the basis of the similarity between the topics they address rather than because they are translation equivalent. The requirement is that they are similar in genre, register, and period. The basic idea underlying the use of such corpora is that the words used to describe a particular topic will be related semantically across languages.

The best known cross-language strategy using comparable corpora is the multilingual similarity thesaurus approach. Sheridan and Ballerini [48] report results using a reference corpus created by aligning news stories from the Swiss news agency (SDA) in German and Italian by topic label and date and then merging them to build the "similarity thesaurus." German queries were then tested over a large collection of Italian documents. They found that the Italian documents were retrieved with a better effectiveness than with a baseline system evaluating Italian queries against Italian documents. This is a result of the query expansion method used as the query is padded with related terms from the document collection. The results of this approach are promising, especially when used on a domain-specific collection [49].

Comparable corpora are probably easier to find or build than parallel ones. However, the difficulty lies in creating appropriate alignments between the documents in the different languages in order to extract the cross-language equivalences. The SDA collection was a special case, as each document has a number of manually assigned subject descriptors from the same classification scheme. Picchi and Peters [41] have a different approach. Their alignment is done on a context rather than a document basis and they use a bilingual MRD to establish the links between contexts over languages. To do this, they identify a vocabulary of significant co-occurring terms for a lexical item in one language, hypothesising that a similar vocabulary will be associated with lexically equivalent terms in the target language collection. They then use the bilingual dictionary to build a set of translation equivalents representing the source language vocabulary associated with a given term in the corpus and search the target collection for contexts which contain a significant number of the members of this set. This approach has been demonstrated on a special language corpus of European parliamentary texts, however, its extendability to more general-purpose texts and its scalability to larger collections has not been shown.

A strong disadvantage of corpus-based techniques is that they are tend to be very application dependent. New reference corpora are needed for new domains.

3.4   Summing Up

With the current-state-of-the-art, all the above approaches if implemented in a well-designed, tested and tuned system can be expected to achieve approximately 80% of monolingual effectiveness in the general domain. However, as can be seen from this brief overview, any single method for cross-language retrieval presents limitations. Whatever the method chosen, the resources used to provide the means for mapping between query and collection are a major factor towards successful retrieval. Already existing resources—such as electronic bilingual dictionaries—are normally inadequate for the purpose; the building of specific resources such as thesauri and training corpus is expensive and such resources are generally not fully reusable; a new multilingual application will require the construction of new resources or considerable work on the adaptation of previously built ones.

It should also be noted than most of the systems and methods we have described concentrate on pairs rather than multiples of languages. This is hardly surprising. The situation is far more complex when we attempt to achieve effective retrieval over a number of languages than over a single pair; it is necessary to study some kind of interlingual mechanism—at a more or less conceptual level—in order to permit multiple cross-language transfer. In a conceptual interlingua, terms and phrases from multiple languages which refer to the same concept are mapped into a language-independent scheme. In this way it is possible to match to equivalent terms in all languages and to achieve CLIR in any of the language combinations, not just pair-wise. However, the building of a such a resource is not an easy task and much work remains to be done before we can talk about truly multilingual retrieval systems.

4   Strategies for Cross-Language Speech Retrieval

Although we have focused primarily on text retrieval so far, it is clearly noted in our introduction that multilingual access to multimedia content is of immense interest. As the bandwidth capabilities of the global information infrastructure continue to expand the amount of multimedia content available electronically has grown exponentially. A particularly rich source of online multimedia content for example, consists of the archives of the many radio stations which currently broadcast over the Internet in many different languages. This source of information content is as legitimate a target for search-based access as the text on which we have focused so far.

While we are aware of only one study directly reporting the evaluation of a cross-language speech retrieval system [47], there has been significant growth in the research community in multimedia retrieval over the past few of years, particularly with respect to retrieval of spoken documents. Much of this work is also relevant to the task of cross-language speech retrieval since it lays the foundation for effective retrieval of spoken documents.

The central focus of research on speech retrieval has long been how to automatically identify and index information from a speech signal. This corresponds to the problems of text processing outlined in Sect. 2 above (see also [46]). Speech recognition technology has to be applied for this purpose, for example in word tokenisation and recognition. Several groups have reported experiments with word recognition based speech retrieval. In Cambridge for example, a video mail retrieval system was developed where messages were retrieved based on 35 keywords [10]. A similar approach has been taken in the Informedia digital library project at CMU, where a large vocabulary system of approximately 64,000 wordforms is being used for indexing news video [57].

A major problem inherent in the use of word-recognition based speech retrieval is the fact that the query vocabulary is fairly restricted in size and must be defined in advance. Further, less common words like proper names, companies etc., which have been found to be particularly suitable for retrieval, are likely to be missing from a vocabulary of only 64,000 wordforms (the large test collections now used in Information Retrieval research are in the order of 500,000 word *stems*).

This shortcoming has led to the notion of open vocabulary indexing. In [30], indexing based on a 20,000 word recogniser was compared to and combined with a word-spotter that performed query dependent word searches. Such word-spotting searches generally operate on some phonetical representation of the speech signal. Retrieval experiments on a 5 hour video mail collection showed a 5% improvement in effectiveness of the *open* vocabulary word-spotter compared to the restricted word recogniser. Best retrieval results were achieved by combining both search strategies (85% compared to text retrieval). Very similar work, in terms of the idea of combining word recognition with an open vocabulary word-spotter, is published in [29]. Evaluation over a 2.5 hour test collection of English news broadcasts showed similar results. A large vocabulary recogniser may improve retrieval effectiveness if combined with an open vocabulary word-spotter, though the computational expense during training and recognition is immense [11].

An alternative approach to overcoming the vocabulary problem is described in [19]. This approach was centred on the idea of defining a small set of sub-word units that would be powerful enough for retrieval while also being suitable for recognition. It turned out, however, that training and tuning the recognition system for this approach would involve substantial manual effort. The results published are therefore based on simulated experiments [20].

The most recent approach to speech indexing developed at ETH includes the open vocabulary idea [55] where indexing is based on phonemic transcriptions determined by a phoneme recogniser. The phonemic transcriptions are indexed using overlapping N-gram features. At retrieval time, an additional probabilistic matching technique may be applied, during which individual words are matched *fuzzily* against the erroneous transcriptions. This technique has proven to be effective not only in speech retrieval [55] but also in retrieval from error-prone OCR texts [2,38]. This approach has the substantial advantages of requiring only a relatively simple phoneme recogniser and having a theoretically unrestricted search vocabulary (the words of a language are composed from a closed set of phonemes).

It was in fact this open vocabulary approach which was combined with the similarity thesaurus approach to cross-language retrieval outlined in Sect. 3.3 above [47] to establish a baseline of performance for the cross-language speech retrieval task, retrieving spoken German documents from written queries entered in French. Evaluated over a collection of 30 hours of German speech, the study established a baseline whereby 20% of queries had at least one relevant document in the top 10 documents returned, compared to 44% of queries which had one relevant document in a monolingual retrieval benchmark. While this is clearly a low level of retrieval effectiveness, this study did accomplish the goal of demonstrating the feasibility of cross-language speech retrieval. This baseline is likely to be improved upon in the near future as progress continues to be made in speech recognition in various languages and more resources become available in support of the task.

5   Resources

It is clear from the previous three sections that a thorough set of well-developed resources is crucial for the development of efficient MLIA systems. In this section, we give a more systematic description of the kind of resources required. We distinguish between tools and language resources. By the former we intend independent modules that perform standard functions required for MLIA (for example, the language identification procedures or stemmers described in Sect. 2), by the latter we mean language-oriented collections that are processed by systems to extract useful data (such as the machine-readable dictionaries or corpora mentioned in Sect. 3). Here below, we list the major types and give some examples of each. This section owes much to the work done by the EU-NSF Working

Group on Multilingual Information Access which met and worked together in 1997 and 1998. A summary of the results and recommendations of this group is given in [44].

The WG identified several key problems shared by most types of resources:

1. **Availability.** There is much duplication of work; for example, new projects often develop their own lexical resources or tools rather than acquiring and adapting existing ones. There is a need to build standard collections and procedures.
2. **Extensibility.** Resources should be regularly extended to include more and new words, text, or additional functionality. Without this capability, it is unlikely that any resource will be useful in the long run. This can involve updating in either automatic, semi-automatic, or completely manual ways. Attention should be paid to this factor in the development of new resources, and in the acquisition of existing ones.
3. **Coverage.** Ideally there should be language resources and tools for all languages.
4. **Quality.** Standards and evaluation procedures are needed to measure the quality of resources.

It is not possible to provide exhaustive references to all the possible resources; there are just too many. A number of Web sites provide valuable lists of different kinds of resources and indications as to where to acquire them; we indicate some of the most useful. A very good overall reference is the Cross-Language Information Retrieval Resources web site maintained by Douglas Oard, University of Maryland, which includes pointers to many other relevant sites [61].

5.1 Multilingual Language Processing Tools

By tools we intend programs that exist as standalone modules and are available either publicly or under certain conditions. In this section, we provide a list of the type of tools that can be usefully employed as components in systems for MLIA, the functionality provided by many of these tools have already been described in Sect. 2. Two very useful Web sites for pointers to publicly available tools are those maintained by the ACL Natural Language Software Registry [60] and by the Multilingual Information Society programme [62].

Language Identification Tools. As outlined in Sect. 2, several techniques for identifying the language in which a document is written have been developed. In many cases, this capability is available within commercially available toolkits aimed at multilingual text processing. The techniques published in the literature for language identification are also such that a simple n-gram or stopword based approach can be easily implemented for many languages. Some of the toolkits which include language identification functionality include:

- **Intelliscope**: From Lernout & Hauspie, the "Intelliscope Language Recogniser" includes character set recognition character set conversion and language recognition [63].

- **LinguistX**: InXight, which is a spinoff from Xerox, includes language recognition as an option within LinguistX, a general language analysis toolkit for many European languages, plus Japanese [64].
- **Qué**: Alis Technologies includes the Qué system for the identification of language and character encoding as part of the Flores toolkit [65].

Character Set Conversion. For systems that want to support multiple languages spanning different character sets and to enable transformations between native character encoding and UNICODE, the following tools are available:

- **Flores**: A "universal character set conversion engine" is available as part of the Flores toolkit or the Bantam library from Alis Technologies [66].
- **MUTT**: The Multilingual Unicode Toolkit is a set of Unicode tools for display and conversion of text. It was developed at New Mexico State University and is freely available [67].
- **Rosette**: The Rosette C++ library for Unicode was developed by Basis Technology Corp and is available as a commercial product. Uniconv, which is a full-featured demonstration of Rosette is also available for non-commercial use [68].

Tokenisation/Word Segmentation Tools. Tokenisation is of particular interest for segmenting texts in languages that lack orthographic boundaries between words (e.g. Chinese and Japanese) and for splitting compounds in agglutinative languages (e.g. German). Given the importance of Chinese and Japanese as languages on the Internet and the specific task of tokenisation for those languages, we include here tools which are specific to each of Chinese and Japanese.

- **Flores**: The Alis Flores toolkit includes a "word extraction" capability that performs segmentation [66].
- **Ch_seg**: A segmentation algorithm for Chinese which was developed by Lei Chen at New Mexico State University [69].
- **Segmenter**: A program for segmentation of Chinese developed by Erik Peterson [70].
- **LinguistX**: The InXight LinguistX package includes compound splitting functionality for German and includes tokenisation of Japanese in its Japanese version [64].
- **CHASEN**: A Japanese morphology and segmentation package which was developed at the Nara Institute of Science and Technology in Japan [71].
- **JUMAN**: A Japanese morphology and segmentation package that was developed at Kyoto University in Japan [72].

Morphological Analysis/Stemming Tools. Normalising words to their stem forms is a standard process in text processing for information access and retrieval. Morphological analysis is crucial for heavily inflected languages like Arabic but important even for relatively uninflected languages like English. Tools include:

- **Porter's stemming algorithm** for English [42].
- **Eurospider** Information Technology has created versions of Porter's stemming algorithm in several European languages [56].
- **LinguistX**: Includes morphological analysis in each of the supported languages [64].
- **Lingsoft**: A Finnish company—provides morphological analysis for a range of European languages, including Russian [73].
- **Morphy**: A freely available system for German morphology that was developed by Wolfgang Lezius at the University of Paderborn in Germany [74].
- **RMA**: A Russian Morphology Analyser, developed by Wanying Jin for the Temple machine translation system at New Mexico State University [75].

Many of the tools for morphological analysis also assign part-of-speech tags to analysed words, identifying specific classes of Nouns, Verbs, Prepositions, etc. These part-of-speech tags can be used by systems for multilingual access during the translation phase of matching queries and documents by restricting translation candidates to appropriate parts of speech.

Other kinds of tools which may be of interest include those which are aimed at tokenisation or normalisation processes such as phrase recognition or recognition of Proper Nouns (persons, places, organisations etc.). In many cases however, it is the lexical resource associated with such a tool which primarily determines the effectiveness of the process rather than the particular approach employed.

We have not explicitly included Machine Translation systems in our review of tools, although they often have a role to play in multilingual access. Some of the better-known translation systems are offered by Lernout & Hauspie [76], Systran [77] and Alis Technologies [78].

5.2 Language Resources

With respect to the creation of language-oriented resources, much work has been done over the past decade. Non-profit distribution agencies have been set up in both Europe and the United States to provide information on the accessibility of existing resources. In Europe, the major agency in this field is ELRA (European Language Resources Association) [79]. ELRA aims to collect, market, distribute, and license European language resources, and to serve as the European repository for EU-funded language resources and interact with similar bodies in other parts of the world. A similar organisation in the US for the distribution of language resources is the LDC (Linguistic Data Consortium) [80], which creates, collects and distributes speech and text databases, lexicons, and other resources for research and development purposes. Both public and private organisations can purchase resources from these agencies; research institutions generally obtain a significant discount.

Fully commercial products are also becoming increasingly available. Electronic dictionaries, especially, can be found for a variety of languages - some at low costs, others at considerable expense and other licensing encumbrance. Unfortunately, they are usually sold as closed packets and are thus impracticable for development purposes.

We briefly consider here the following types of data resources: corpora; general-purpose dictionaries; lexicons and terminologies; thesauri and ontologies. For each type, we cite only a few examples.

Corpora. Corpora. The collection, cleanup, and appropriate annotation of multilingual parallel or comparable text in many domains is of great importance for successful MLIA. Without adequate size and coverage of the languages and domains of interest, it is difficult to build accurate retrieval engines or high-quality translation engines. Appropriate mark-up is of great importance. This can regard: word segmentation / disambiguation marks, POS tags, parse trees, semantic tags, alignments to versions in other languages (comparable orparallel documents), subject codes, etc. Corpora can be used for:

1. Automated extraction of information (e.g. multilingual lexical correspondences, term frequency, etc.)
2. Corpus-attested disambiguation (for disambiguating multiple alternatives from dictionaries)
3. Learning/training of components (e.g. automated construction of LSI term spaces, construction of similarity thesauri, training of POS taggers, of grammars, etc.)
4. Evaluation

The Web site for English Language Corpora and Corpus Resources maintained by the British National Corpus project actually includes a series of useful pointers not only to English monolingual corpora but also to parallel and multilingual collections, and to tools for corpus analysis [81]. Another important site for information on Parallel Corpora around the world can be found at [82]. Of course the best known parallel corpus for cross-language studies is the Hansard Corpus of Parallel English and French parliamentary texts [83].

Dictionaries. Many well-known and high quality printed dictionaries are now available in electronic form as machine-readable dictionaries. Sometimes these have been further processed into lexical databases. However, copyright and licensing requirements limit the computational use of many commercial dictionaries.

– **Monolingual Dictionaries:** Although bilingual and multilingual lexical resources are of most interest for MLIA applications, monolingual dictionaries can also be a useful source of information. We cite just a few examples of such dictionaries that are also available in electronic form: LDOCE (Longman's Dictionary of Contemporary English), OALDCE (Oxford Advanced Learner's Dictionary of Current English), Collins COBUILD English Language Dictionary, Webster's New Collegiate Dictionary, Garzanti Italian Dictionary, etc.

- **Bilingual Dictionaries:** As examples, we can cite the Collins series of bilingual dictionaries from English to major European languages (English-Spanish, English-Italian, English-French, etc.), or the Inso Information products, a series of bilingual dictionaries developed by LSI (Linguistic Systems, Inc.), but there are many more. Although electronic bilingual dictionaries are available for most commercially important languages, it is probably not surprising that the preponderance tend to be produced for language pairs which include English is one member. In fact, a serious problem in MLIA applications is the shortage of bilingual dictionaries for many less frequent language pairs.
- **Multilingual Dictionaries:** It is much more difficult to find examples of multilingual (rather than bilingual) dictionaries. One example is Memodata, a multilingual general language lexicon for French, Italian, Spanish, English and German; the words are associated by meaning. A conceptual level links the word-senses to world knowledge. The shortage of multilingual dictionaries seriously hampers the development of new MLIA systems.

See [84, 85].

Lexicons and Terminologies. Electronic lexicons are lists of words, represented in a format easily used by computer systems. General-purpose lexicons contain a variety of information, such as word morphology, part of speech, collocations, relative frequency of use, etc. Special purpose lexicons, e.g. for terminology, proper names, etc. include controlled or non-controlled mono- or multilingual term lists. Examples are:

- **Eurodicautom:** The Official and Technical Dictionary of the European Commission. A terminological database, containing scientific and technical terms, acronyms and abbreviations with their meaning and covering areas related with the activities of the European Commission, such as European Union, administration, insurance, trade, economics, finance, law, etc.
- The **THAMUS** set of English-Italian technical bilingual terminologies for aeronautics, law, computer science, medicine, economics, engineering.
- **Geoatlas:** A multilingual lexicon of major geographical place names for English, Italian, German, French.

See [86, 87].

Thesauri and Ontologies. In addition to lexicons, MLIA systems can benefit from information on interrelationships between words or other data items, for example for query refinement or expansion. A thesaurus is a structure that manages the complexities of terminology in a language and provides conceptual relationships, ideally through a classification/ontology [51]. A classification is a structure that organises terms into a hierarchy; an ontology is a collection of concepts (often approximated by word senses) organised according to a variety of relations, including hyponymy (is-a) and meronymy (part-of).

Many monolingual thesauri exist; multilingual ones are more scarce but their number is increasing, in particular in the European context. Probably the best known example of a multilingual classification scheme is the Universal Decimal Classification, a system for classifying bibliographic records for all kinds of information in any medium. The code itself is independent of any particular language (consisting of arabic numerals) and the accompanying class descriptions have been released in many languages (currently 23 in whole or part). See [88].

When adequately large and detailed, ontologies promise to be of use for both retrieval and the translation engines. The fact that their contents are purportedly concepts, not words, makes them language-neutral by definition. Well-known ontologies include:

- **CYC:** A general purpose, conceptual knowledge base. The CYC project attempts to construct a general "common sense" knowledge substrate to support automated reasoning. CYC might serve as a standard ontology (vocabulary of concepts and organisational scheme) for information retrieval.
- **WordNet:** A general purpose, monolingual word sense taxonomy based upon English (developed at Princeton [37]). WordNet is a publicly available on-line lexical reference system whose design is inspired by current psycholinguistic theories of human lexical memory. English nouns, verbs, adjectives and adverbs are organised into synonym sets, each representing one underlying lexical concept. Different relations link the synonym sets.
- **EuroWordNet:** A general purpose, multilingual database extracted from WordNet and extended to include other languages. A shared top ontology creates basic semantic relations between words for eight European languages. Language specific properties are maintained in the individual wordnets. The database can be obtained from ELRA [79].

5.3   Standards

For both tools and language resources, standards are very important. Only through standardisation is it possible to reuse resources easily, to employ new generations of them, and to compare alternatives. Few standards have been developed in the IR and MT communities for component tools and modules, whereas, considerable work has been done with respect to language resources. The following standards are indicative of the kind of work involved:

- **TEI (Text Encoding Initiative):** Guidelines for electronic text encoding and interchange [89].
- **EAGLES:** Expert Advisory Group on Language Engineering Standards has developed standards for very large language resources (such as test corpora, computational lexicons and speech corpora) and for computational linguistic formalisms, markup languages and various software tools [90].

6   Evaluation

Evaluation is an essential part of the system development cycle as it plays an important role in stimulating development and improving performance. The participation in an evaluation activity obliges researchers and/or developers to examine closely their goals, and permits them to check hypotheses and assess progress against an objective measuring system. However, the evaluation of MLIA systems is not easy as both the effectiveness of single components and that of overall system performance needs to be assessed. It is also necessary to distinguish methodological aspects (generic across languages) from linguistic knowledge (specific to a particular language). Ideally, an MLIA system evaluation protocol would require distinction between architecture, program and linguistic data. The validity of the system (and components) should also be evaluated from both the technology and usage perspectives. Usage evaluation demonstrates the value of a technology for a given user type, thus determining the technology thresholds that are indispensable for specific usage.

Two types of evaluation are generally recognised: different approaches to a given task can be compared; single approaches can be examined against their own objectives. These have been defined by [58] as summative evaluation (comparison of different systems, approaches, etc.) and formative evaluation (development against objectives).

The most commonly used type of evaluation at the moment is probably comparative evaluation. Comparative evaluation consists of deciding on a control task, which may correspond to the function of a complete system (e.g. a CLIR system), or of a component (such as a tagger or parser), of gathering system or component developers interested in participating, organising an evaluation campaign which includes the distribution of data for training and testing the systems, and of defining the protocol and metrics to be used [7]. A corpus-based, automatic scoring approach is normally used (such as that developed by the TREC—Text REtrieval Conference series). This enables an objective comparison between systems and approaches. However, this method is not always appropriate. For example, in machine translation and summarisation there is no one 'right' answer. In these areas, judgements tend to be subjective and very much task-dependent.

6.1 Evaluation Initiatives

Over the past fifteen years, there have been a number of evaluation programmes and competitive evaluation campaigns directed at measuring the effectiveness of diverse technologies belonging to the MLIA area of interest, e.g. speech recognition, information extraction, machine translation, information retrieval and text summarisation.

We list here some of the currently active initiatives most relevant for MLIA system development:

– **TIDES:** Translingual Information Detection, Extraction and Summarisation. TIDES sponsors the TREC (Text Retrieval Conference) and TDT (Topic Detection and Tracking) evaluation activities. Both include cross-language tracks this year for English—Mandarin Chinese. TIDES currently plans Evaluations for Summarisation and Quick Machine Translation activities [91].

- **CLEF:** Cross language Evaluation Forum. CLEF sponsored by the European Commission as part of the DELOS Network of Excellence for Digital Libraries is an evaluation activity for European languages and represents the continuation of the CLIR track begun at TREC in 1997. CLEF 2000 has four tasks for multilingual, bilingual, domain-specific and monolingual (non-English) text retrieval evaluation. This year's multilingual document collection has comparable newspaper corpora for four languages (English, French, German, Italian) and topics in 8 European languages [92].
- **NTCIR:** NACSIS Test Collection for Information Retrieval hosted by the National Institute for Informatics, Tokyo. NTCIR adopts a methodology very similar to that used by TREC and CLEF. The first campaign concluded in September 1999. The second campaign is now underway and hosts three tasks: Chinese IR (including English-Chinese CLIR) which is hosted by National Taiwan University, Japanese—English IR using Japanese and English documents and topics, and text summarisation of Japanese text [93].
- **AMARYLLIS:** An evaluation program for text retrieval systems centred on French and co-funded by the French Ministry of Research and the Agency for the Universities of France. The second campaign, 1998–99 also included a cross-language track [13].

6.2 Advantages of an Evaluation Activity

Existing evaluation campaigns have reported on the benefits that can accrue. For example, after 3 years activity, the CLIR track at TREC reported the following results:

- areas where more R&D is needed have been identified;
- system improvement and refinement has been noted over the years;
- move from focus on pairwise retrieval (year 1) to a full multilingual task (years 2 and 3) has stimulated development of systems to handle several languages [8];
- reusable test-suites have been developed and made available for the research community.

In particular, evaluation favours experimenting of different and innovative strategies. Among other things, groups participating in the CLEF 2000 campaign tested: the use of various NLP techniques such as morphosyntactic analysis, compound processing and phrase identification in the indexing stage; the effectiveness of a translation lexicon derived from parallel corpora against an MT system; interactive query term disambiguation; the lexical triangulation proposed by Ballestreros [3] Reports can be found in the papers presented at the CLEF 2000 Workshop and posted on the Web site [92].

6.3 Difficulties

At present, it could not be claimed that the evaluation of any aspect of cross-language information retrieval is a closed issue. One of the major problems is that there is still a lack of clear vision within most of the technologies for the average level of current performance, the commonly recognised best practises, and the most promising new approaches (see [58]). Insufficient attention is still paid to the human component aspect of system use. As techniques in the different areas involved become more similar, and as the various areas start linking together, the need for coordinated and reusable evaluation techniques and measures grows. Unfortunately, large-scale evaluation activities are costly in terms of effort. Limiting factors are resources and multilingual tools for resource development. The expansion of multilingual systems will not be possible without the creation and use for evaluation purposes of common standards and resources of sufficient quality and quantity across the different languages.

7 Working Systems

The evaluation exercises outlined in the previous section have in many respects raised the standard for implementation of systems for multilingual access, given the significant undertakings of text processing and retrieval experiments across multiple languages which are necessary for successful participation in the evaluation. This has been an enormous aid to the cross-language retrieval research community, providing a common framework where different approaches and implementations can be compared in a standard benchmarking environment. No less important, these evaluation activities have provided forums for the exchange of ideas so that 'best-of-breed' solutions are picked up by research groups and integrated with different techniques in order to evolve toward better systems overall.

For a detailed overview of current systems which have participated in the various evaluation exercises, it is best to refer to the overview reports of each individual campaign [9,31,44]. Following the overview report of each evaluation, it is then possible to read further through the individual site or system reports submitted by the individual participants. These reports are available online from the respective evaluation web sites [92–94]. Over the series of TREC, NACSIS and CLEF evaluation exercises, systems dealing with English, French, German, Italian, Chinese, and Japanese have been constructed following all of the possible approaches to cross-language retrieval outlined in Sect. 3 above.

A further source of information on current systems is Doug Oard's web site [61] on resources for cross-language information retrieval under the 'working systems' link, although a recent visit to this site turned up several 'dead links' to supposedly working systems. Some of the systems listed here which are running online include:

- **APORT:** An online search engine for access to Russian and English information. A single search query is enough to search across both Russian and English content and a facility is provided for translating Russian results into English and vice versa [96].

- **ARCTOS/MUNDIAL:** A pair of systems developed at New Mexico State University's Computing Research Laboratory (CRL). The ARCTOS system [97] illustrates a presentation technique where thumbnail images of retrieved documents are displayed with terms matching the input query highlighted in colour. German, French, and Italian are the language supported, in addition to English. The MUNDIAL system [98] is intended as a multilingual access engine on top of standard Internet search engines such as AltaVista or Infoseek. A wide range of languages are supported, based on the approach of using freely available Internet dictionaries as translation resources.
- **STRATEGIS:** A Canadian government supported portal providing bilingual English-French access to information of interest to the business community [99]. An English query submitted to the bilingual search form produces an extensive list of potential French translations in dictionary format for selection by the user. The user must select the set of French terms from the translation list to create a French query.

Commercial systems which are not included in the above list also include:

- **Eurospider Information Technology:** A Swiss company that offers a 'RotondoSpider' product capable of providing multilingual access in some European languages [100].
- **AltaVista** and other online search engines allow searching in and across different languages, typically using a straightforward machine translation of queries to match foreign language documents. Altavista's BabelFish [95] for example uses Systran.
- **Document Management Partners:** A Belgian company that offers 'Scout' for cross-language retrieval based on technologies from Lernout & Hauspie and Documentum [101].
- **CINDOR:** A multilingual search system offered through Manning & Napier Information Services (MNIS) from New York [102]. This system uses a 'conceptual interlingua' framework to allow matching of many language combinations and a level of conceptual analysis designed to improve retrieval performance.

8   Conclusion

The large number of research systems that have been implemented and evaluated in standard evaluation environments is testament to the challenges involved in providing multilingual access to information, which have attracted such a large number of scientists from different backgrounds in Information Retrieval and Computational Linguistics. The growing number of commercial information systems which claim to offer multilingual information management capabilities is also evidence of the importance of this functionality for users of the global information infrastructure which is the World Wide Web.

Market research and analysis firms who specialise in forecasting trends and directions are continually pointing to the explosion of both non-English content and non-English speaking users on the Internet [103]. These forecasts reinforce the importance of ongoing research efforts toward solutions of the problems which make up the overall goal of cross-language retrieval. Much progress has been made by the research community over in the past years and substantial momentum has been built. Current efforts are focused in such areas as combining multiple sources of translational evidence to improve cross-language matching of queries and documents, multilingual access to so-called 'low-density' languages— those for which linguistic resources are not readily available in electronic form, multilingual access to multimedia content—particularly spoken documents, and presentation of results from multilingual searches—including summarisation of content across multiple documents in different languages.

The necessity of drawing together research groups from the diverse fields of Information Retrieval, Speech Processing and Natural Language Processing in order to solve these problems is part of the challenge of providing multilingual access to information. On the other hand, there is much to be said for participating in a field of multi-disciplinary research targeted at solving difficult problems related to the very real needs of a broad range of information users. There are many challenges, but also much to be learnt and many future successes to be shared.

References

1. Adriani, M., van Rijsbergen, C.J.: Term Similarity-Based Query Expansion for Cross-Language Information Retrieval. In Lecture Notes in Computer Science, Volume 1696, 1999.
2. Ballerini, J.P., Buchel, M., Domenig, R., Knaus, D., Mateev, B., Mittendorf, E., Schäuble, P., Sheridan, P., Wechsler, M.: SPIDER Retrieval System at TREC-5. In *Proceedings of the Fifth Text Retrieval Conference TREC-5*, National Institute of Standards and Technology (NIST), Gaithersburg, MD, 1996.
3. Ballesteros, L.: Cross-Language Retrieval via Transitive Translation. In Croft, W.B. (ed.): *Advances in Information Retrieval: Recent Research from the Center for Intelligent Information Retrieval*, Kluwer Academic Publishers, Boston, 2000.
4. Ballestreros, L., Croft, W.B.: Resolving Ambiguity for Cross-language Retrieval. In *Proceedings of the 20th International ACM SIGIR Conference on Research and Development in Information Retrieval*, Philadelphia, PA, 84–91, 1997.
5. Ballesteros, L., Croft, W.B.: Dictionary-based methods for cross-lingual information retrieval. In *Proceedings of the 7th International DEXA Conference on Database and Expert Systems Applications*, 791–801, 1996.
6. Ballesteros, L., Croft, W.B.: Phrasal Translation and Query Expansion Techniques for Cross-Language Information Retrieval. In *Working Notes of AAAI Spring Symposium on Cross-Language Text and Speech Retrieval*, CA, 1–8, 1997.
7. Blasband, M., Paroubek, P. (eds.): *A Blueprint for a General Infrastructure for Natural Language Processing Systems Evaluation*. Deliverable 1.1 of the ELSE project: http://www.limsi.fr/TLP/ELSE/ELSED11EN.HTM

8. Braschler, M., Kluck, M., Harman, D., Peters, C., Schäuble, P.: The Evaluation of Systems for Cross-Language Information Retrieval. In Gavrilidou, M., Carayannis, G., Markantonatou, S., Piperidis, S., Stainhaouer, G. (eds.) *Proceedings of First International Conference on Language Resources and Evaluation*, Athens, Greece, 31 May-2 June 2000, 1469–1474. See also: http://www.iei.pi.cnr.it/DELOS/CLEF/

9. Braschler, M., Krause, J., Peters, P., Schäuble, P.: Cross-Language Information Retrieval (CLIR) Track Overview, In *Proceedings of the Seventh Text Retrieval Conference (TREC-7)*. NIST, Gaithersburg, MD, 1999.

10. Brown, M., Foote, J.T., Jones, G.J.F., Sparck-Jones, K., Young, S.J.: Video Mail Retrieval by Voice: An Overview of the Cambridge/Olivetti Retrieval System. In *Multimedia Data Base Management Systems Workshop*, 2nd ACM International Conference on Multimedia, 1994.

11. Brown, M., Foote, J., Jones, G., Jones, K.S., Young, S.: Open-vocabulary Speech Indexing for Voice and Video Mail Retrieval. In *Proceedings of the ACM Multimedia Conference*, Boston, MA, 1996.

12. Cavnar, W., Trenkle, J.: N-gram Based Text Categorization, In *Proceedings of the 17th International ACM SIGIR Conference on Research and Development in Information Retrieval*, Dublin, Ireland, 161–169, 1994.

13. Chaudiron, S., Schmitt, L.:   AMARYLLIS: An Evaluation-based Program for Text Retrieval in French. In Jacquemin, C., Mariani, J. Paroubek, P. (eds.) Using Evaluation within HLT Programmes: Results and Trends. Workshop Proceedings. *LREC 2000*, 30 May 2000, Athens, Greece: http://www.inist.fr/accueil/profran.htm

14. Damashek, M.: Guaging Similarity with N-grams: Language-independent Categorization of Text. *Science*, 267(10), 1995.

15. Dunning, T.: *Statistical Identification of Language*. CRL Technical Memo MCCS–94–273, Computing Research Laboratory, New Mexico State University, 1994.

16. EMIR Consortium: *Final report of the EMIR Project Number 5312*. Commission of the European Union, Brussels, 1994.

17. Frakes, W.B., Baeza-Yates, R.: *Information Retrieval: Data Structures and Algorithms*, Prentice-Hall, 1992.

18. Gachot, D.A., Lange, E., Yang, J.: *The SYSTRAN NLP Browser: An Application of Machine Translation Technology in Cross-Language Information Retrieval*. In: [21, p. 105–118], 1998.

19. Glavitsch, U., Schäuble P.: A System for Retrieving Speech Documents. In *Proceedings of the 15th International ACM SIGIR Conference on Research and Development in Information Retrieval*, Copenhagen, Denmark, 168–176, 1992.

20. Glavitsch, U., Schäuble, P., Wechsler, M.: Metadata for Integrating Speech Documents in a Text Retrieval System. *SIGMOD Record*, 23(4):57–63, 1994.

21. Grefenstette, G. (ed.): *Cross-Language Information Retrieval*, The Kluwer International Series on Information Retrieval, Kluwer Academic Publishers, Boston, 1998.

22. Harman, D.: A Failure Analysis on the Limitations of Suffixing in an Online Environment. In *Proceedings of the 10th International ACM SIGIR Conference on Research and Development in Information Retrieval*, 102–108, 1987.

23. Harman, D.: How Effective is Suffixing? *Journal of the American Society for Information Science*, 42(1):321–331, 1991.

24. Hovy, E., Ide, N., Frederking, R. (eds.): *Multilingual Information Management: Current Levels and Future Abilities*, NSF/EC/DARPA, April 1999. See: http://www.cs.cmu.edu/~ref/mlim/index.html

25. Hull, D., Grefenstette, G.: Stemming Algorithms—A Case Study for Detailed Evaluation. *Journal of the American Society for Information Science*, 47(1):70–84, 1996.

26. Hull, D.A., Grefenstette, G.: Querying Across Languages. A Dictionary-based Approach to Multilingual Information Retrieval. In *Proceedings of the 19th International ACM SIGIR Conference on Research and Development in Information Retrieval*, Zurich, Switzerland, 49–57, 1996.

27. ISO/IEC International Standard 10646-1:1993(E): *Information technology— Universal Multiple-Octet Coded Character Set (UCS)—Part 1: Architecture and Basic Multilingual Plane*. International Organization for Standardization, Geneva 1993.

28. ISO Standard 5964–1985: *Guidelines for the establishment and development of multilingual thesauri*. First edition 1985–02–15. International Organisation for Standardisation, Technical Committee ISO/TC 46.

29. James, D.: A System for Unrestricted Topic Retrieval from Radio Broadcasts. *In Proceedings of ICASSP*, Atlanta, GA, 279–282, 1996.

30. Jones, G., Foote, J., Jones, K.S., Young, S.: Retrieving Spoken Documents by Combining Multiple Index Sources. In *Proceedings of the 19th International ACM SIGIR Conference on Research and Development in Information Retrieval*, Zurich, Switzerland, 30–38, 1996.

31. Kando, N., Kuriyama, K., Nozue, T., Eguchi, K., Kato, H., Hidaka, S., Adachi, J.: *The NTCIR Workshop: the First Evaluation Workshop on Japanese Text Retrieval and Cross-Lingual Information Retrieval*. International Workshop on Information Retrieval with Asian Languages, Nov. 11–12, 1999, Taipei, Taiwan 1999.

32. Kikui, G.: Identifying the Coding System and Language of On-line Documents on the Internet. In *Proceedings of the Sixteenth International Conference on Computational Linguistics: COLING'96*, Copenhagen, Denmark, 1996.

33. Krovetz, R.: Viewing Morphology as an Inference Process. In Proceedings of the 16th International ACM SIGIR Conference on Research and Development in Information Retrieval, Pittsburgh, PA, 191–202, 1993.

34. Lennon, M., Pierce, D., Tarry, B., Willet, P.: An Evaluation of some Conflation Algorithms for Information Retrieval. *Journal of Information Science*, 3:177–183, 1981.

35. Littman, M.L., Dumais, S.T., Landauer, T.K.: Automatic Cross-Language Information Retrieval using Latent Semantic Indexing. In Grefenstette, G. (ed.): Cross-Language Information Retrieval, The Kluwer International Series on Information Retrieval, Kluwer Academic Publishers, Boston, pp 51–62, 1998.

36. Lovins, J.: Development of a Stemming Algorithm. Mechanical Translation and *Computational Linguistics*, 11:22–31, 1968.

37. Miller, G.: WordNet: An On-line Lexical Database, International Journal of Lexicography, Special Issue, 3(4), 1990.

38. Mittendorf, E., Schäuble, P., Sheridan, P.: Applying Probabilistic Term Weighting to OCR Text in the case of a Large Alphabetic Library Catalogue. In *Proceedings of the 18th International ACM SIGIR Conference on Research and Development in Information Retrieval*, Seattle, WA, 328–335, 1995.

39. Oard, D.W.: Web Language Distribution. Web site for Research Resources on Cross-Language Text Retrieval. See:
    http://www.clis.umd.edu/dlrg/filter/papers/

40. Pevzner, B.: Comparative Evaluation of the Operation of the Russian and English variants of the Pusto-Nepusto-2 System. *Automatic Documentation and Mathematical Linguistics*, 6:71–74, 1972.

41. Picchi, E., Peters, C.: Cross-Language Information Retrieval: A System for Comparable Corpus Querying. In Grefenstette, G. (ed.): *Cross-Language Information Retrieval*, The Kluwer International Series on Information Retrieval, Kluwer Academic Publishers, Boston, 81–92, 1998.

42. Porter, M.F.: An Algorithm for Suffix Stripping. *Program*, 14(3):130–137, 1980.

43. Salton, G.: *Automatic Processing of Foreign Language Documents*. Prentice-Hill, Englewood Cliffs, NJ 1971.

44. Schäuble, P., Sheridan, P.: Cross-Language Information Retrieval (CLIR) Track Overview. In *Proceedings of the Sixth Text Retrieval Conference (TREC-6)*. NIST, Gaithersburg, MD, 1998.

45. Schäuble, P., Smeaton, A.: *An International Research Agenda for Digital Libraries: Summary Report of the Series of Joint NSF-EU Working Groups on Future Directions for Digital Libraries Research*, 1998. See: http://www.iei.pi.cnr.it/DELOS/NSF/nsf.htm

46. Schäuble, P.: *Multimedia Information Retrieval: Content-Based Information Retrieval from Large Text and Audio Databases*. Kluwer Academic Publishers, 1997.

47. Sheridan, P., Wechsler, M., Schäuble, P.: Cross-Language Speech Retrieval: Establishing a Baseline Performance. In *Proceedings of the 20th International ACM SIGIR Conference on Research and Development in Information Retrieval*, Philadelphia, PA, 1997.

48. Sheridan, P., Ballerini, J.P.: Experiments in Multilingual Information Retrieval using the SPIDER System, In *Proceedings of the 19th International ACM SIGIR Conference on Research and Development in Information Retrieval*, Zurich, Switzerland, pp 58–65, 1996.

49. Sheridan, P., Braschler, M., Schäuble, P.: Cross-Language Information Retrieval in a Multilingual Legal Domain. In *Proceedings of the 1st European Conference on Digital Libraries*, ECDL'97, Pisa, Italy, pp 253–268, 1997.

50. Sibun, P., Reynar, J.: Language Identification: Examining the Issues. In *Proceedings of the Symposium on Document Analysis and Information Retrieval*, Las Vegas, 125–135, 1996.

51. Soergel, D.: Multilingual Thesauri in Cross-Language Text and Speech Retrieval. In *Working Notes of AAAI Spring Symposium on Cross-Language Text and Speech Retrieval*, Stanford, CA, 164–170, 1997.

52. Souter, C., Churcher, G., Hayes, J., Johnson, S.: Natural Language Identification using Corpus-based Models. *Hermes Journal of Linguistics*, 13:183–203, Faculty of Modern Languages, Aarhus School of Business, Denmark, 1994.

53. Unicode Consortium: *The Unicode Standard Worldwide Character Encoding*. Version 1.0. Vols. 1 and 2, Addison-Wesley 1991.

54. van Rijsbergen, C.J.: *Information Retrieval*. Butterworths, London, second edition, 1979.

55. Wechsler, M., Schäuble, P.: Speech Retrieval Based on Automatic Indexing. In Ruthven I. (ed.), *Proceedings of the Final Workshop on Multimedia Information Retrieval (MIRO'95)*, Electronic Workshop in Computing, Glasgow, Springer, 1995.

56. Wechsler, M., Sheridan, P., Schäuble, P.: Multi-Language Text Indexing for Internet Retrieval. In *Proceedings of the 5th RIAO Conference, Computer-Assisted Information Searching on the Internet*, Montreal, Canada, June 1997.

57. Wactlar, H., Kanade, T., Smith, M., Stevens, S.: Intelligent Access to Digital Video: The Informedia Project. *IEEE Computer*, 29(5), 1996.

58. White, John (ed.): Evaluation and Assessment Techniques. In Hovy, E., Ide, N., Frederking, R. (eds.): *Multilingual Information Management: Current Levels and Future Abilities*: http://www.cs.cmu.edu/~ref/mlim/chapter8.html

59. Ziegler, D.: *The Automatic Identification of Languages Using Linguistic Recognition Signals*. PhD Thesis, State University of New York, Buffalo, 1991.

60. ACL Natural Language Software Registry. http://registry.dfki.de/

61. Oard, D.W.: Web site for Cross-Language Information Retrieval Resources, http://www.ee.umd.edu/medlab/mlir/

62. Multilingual Information Society Programme (MLIS). List of Multilingual Applications. http://193.91.44.33/mlis/en/present/applicationlist.html

63. Lernout & Hauspie Intelliscope.
http://www.lhsl.com/tech/icm/retrieval/toolkit/lr.asp

64. InXight LinguistX web site at
http://www.inxight.com/products_sp/linguistx/linguistx_tech.html

65. Alis Technologies Qué system. Web site
http://www.alis.com/castil/silc/index.html

66. Alis Technologies Flores toolkit.
http://www.alis.com/castil/flores/conversions.en.html

67. Multilingual Unicode Toolkit (MUTT) is available at:
ftp://crl.nmsu.edu/pub/misc/ A description is given at:
http://crl.nmsu.edu/Research/Projects/oleada/mutt.html

68. Rosette library from BasisTechnology. http://unicode.basistech.com

69. Ch_seg available from NMSU: ftp://crl.nmsu.edu/pub/misc/

70. Segmenter by Erik Peterson: http://www.mandarintools.com/segmenter.html

71. CHASEN for Japanese morphology:
http://cactus.aist-nara.ac.jp/lab/nlt/chasen.html

72. JUMAN: http://www-nagao.kuee.kyoto-u.ac.jp/nl-resource/juman-e.html

73. Lingsoft morphological analysis: http://www.lingsoft.fi/en/indexing/

74. Morphy for German analysis: http://psycho1.uni-paderborn.de/lezius/

75. RMA for Russian analysis: ftp://crl.nmsu.edu/pub/misc/

76. Lernout & Hauspie iTranslator: http://www.lhs.com/itranslator/

77. Systran: http://www.systran.fr/

78. Alis Technologies, Gist-In-Time: http://www.alis.com/LangSol/whatGIT.html

79. European Language Resources Association.
http://www.icp.grenet.fr/ELRA/catalog.html

80. The Linguistic Data Consortium: http://www.ldc.upenn.edu/

81. English Language Corpora and Corpus Resources
http://info.ox.ac.uk/bnc/corpora.html

82. Parallel Corpora around the World:
http://stp.ling.uu.se/~corpora/#worldcorpora

83. The Hansard Corpus of Parallel English and French:
http://morph.ldc.upenn.edu/ldc/news/release/hansard.html

84. The LINGUIST List: http://www.emich.edu/~linguist/dictionaries.html

85. The Internet Dictionary Project: http://www.june29.com/IDP/

86. THAMUS set of Italian/English bilingual terminologies: http://www.thamus.it/

87. NetGlos—The Multilingual Glossary of Internet Terminology:
http://wwli.com/translation/netglos/netglos.html

88. Universal Decimal Classification Scheme: http://www.udcc.org/about.htm

89. The Text Encoding Initiative: `http://www.tei-c.org/`
90. EAGLES: Expert Advisory Group on Language Engineering Standards: `http://www.ilc.pi.cnr.it/EAGLES/home.html`
91. DARPA program for Translingual Information Detection, Extraction and Summarization (TIDES): `http://www.darpa.mil/ito/research/tides/index.html`
92. CLEF—Cross-Language Evaluation Forum: `http://www.iei.pi.cnr.it/DELOS/CLEF`
93. NTCIR (NII-NACSIS Test Collection for IR Systems) Project: `http://www.rd.nacsis.ac.jp/~ntcadm/index-en.html`
94. The Text Retrieval Conference, TREC: `http://trec.nist.gov/`
95. AltaVista's BabelFish: `http://babel.altavista.com/`
96. APORT: `http://www.aport-ru.com/`
97. ARCTOS: `http://messene.nmsu.edu/ursa/arctos/`
98. MUNDIAL: `http://crl.nmsu.edu/users/madavis/mundial.html`
99. STRATEGIS: `http://strategis.ic.gc.ca/`
100. Eurospider Information Technology: `http://www.eurospider.com/`
101. Document Management Partners, SCOUT: `http://www.dmpartners.be/DMPartnersMain.htm`
102. CINDOR: `http://www.cindorsearch.com/`
103. Global Internet Statistics (by Language): `http://www.glreach.com/globstats/index.php3`
104. Unicode Web site: `http://www.unicode.org/`

Evaluation in Information Retrieval

Stephen Robertson

Microsoft Research Ltd, Guildhall Street
Cambridge CB2 3NH, UK
ser@microsoft.com

Abstract In this talk I summarize the components of a traditional laboratory-style evaluation experiment in information retrieval (as exemplified by TREC), and discusses some of the issues around this form of experiment. Some kinds of research questions fit very well into this framework; others much less easily. The major area of difficulty for the framework is the area concerned with the user interface and user information-seeking behaviour. I go on to discuss a series of experiments conducted at City University with the Okapi system, both of the traditional form and of a more user-oriented type. I then discuss the current TREC filtering track, which does not present quite such severe problems, but is nevertheless based on a simple model of how users might interact with the system; this has some effect on the experimental methodology.

1 Why Evaluate?

All systems designed to help humans perform tasks should be evaluated; but IR systems exhibit in extreme form some of the characteristics that make this process necessary. In particular, the task(s) to be performed by an IR system are not in general very well defined—certainly not to the point where it is obvious whether or not the computer has succeeded. On top of that, there are many design decisions (at every level of abstraction, from high principle to low-level detail) where there are many plausible possibilities, and many plausible arguments in favour of one or other possibility, but absolutely no guarantee that any such argument is watertight.

There are aspects of retrieval efficiency (e.g. speed of processing) that warrant evaluation, but this talk will concentrate on retrieval effectiveness, i.e. the ability of the system to help the user satisfy his or her information need. I will start from the idea of testing a system in a laboratory, and then consider some wider issues.

The methods and techniques associated with the evaluation of IR systems have developed over many years, and tend to be described in the methodology sections of research reports and papers. It is relatively unusual to see papers or monographs devoted to methodology *per se*. One exception to this rule is the collection of papers edited by Karen Sparck Jones and published in 1981 [1]. Although this is now old, it must be regarded as the classic source in the field. The initial part of this talk is based on a paper in that book [2].

M. Agosti, F. Crestani, and G. Pasi (Eds.): ESSIR 2000, LNCS 1980, pp. 81–92, 2000.

2   Approaches to IR Evaluation

The main components of the traditional IR laboratory experiment are: a system; a collection of documents; a collection of requests; a basic evaluation criterion; measures of performance; and an experimental design.

2.1   A System

What Is a System? A set of methods and procedures (whether human or machine based) for indexing and searching.

Traditionally the assumption is that the system is an input-output device (feed in a request and get out a result or answer) allowing for no interaction.

The system may also be interpreted simply as a computer system (software & hardware) including the user interface. In that case the inputs are all the user actions and the outputs become the system's responses. However this raises questions regarding the system's boundaries. It appears that the user is still outside the system; there are strong arguments for including the user (or some aspects of the user's behaviour) in the system, at least for some evaluation purposes.

Why Do We Need to Evaluate a Complete System? Retrieval tests have largely been concerned with system components rather than complete systems. But the main difficulty of evaluating components in isolation relates to the evaluation criteria: we need criteria which relate to overall retrieval effectiveness.

2.2   A Collection of Documents

What Is a document? A package of information structure by an author.

Traditionally retrieval systems handle document surrogates, e.g. bibliographic records of print on paper documents. Such surrogates may include human-added information, e.g. human-assigned indexing or categories, intended to help retrieval. Documents are no longer restricted to printed text formats but now may include full text, segments of texts, images and other multimedia. Many systems use whole documents in electronic form, with no human intervention. But they still retrieve on the basis of hidden surrogates—some form of automatically-extracted indexing.

2.3   A Collection of Requests

What Is a Request or a Query? Traditionally a request is a description of a topic of interest.

Now we perceive a request as a partial representation of an underlying information need or anomalous state of knowledge or a perceived problem. An initial request may also change as a result of interacting with a system.

2.4   A Basic Evaluation Criterion

What Constitutes a Good (Relevant) Document? Traditionally, one which an expert judge considers to be on the topic of interest, i.e. *topical relevance.*

Relevance is now more commonly interpreted in other ways, which may for example take account of the user's judgements as to whether or not a document is useful in the context of a particular information need or problem. (See below)

Retrieval effectiveness is usually defined in terms of retrieving relevant documents and not retrieving non-relevant documents. Here we are making some assumptions about relevance: first, that it is a simple binary property (items are relevant or not); and second, that the relevance of one item is independent of other items in the collection. There is also a substantial problem relating to the discovery of relevant items in the collection that the searching system fails to find.

2.5   Measures of Performance

What Measures?

$$\text{Recall} = \frac{\text{No. of relevant docs retrieved}}{\text{Total no. of relevant docs in collection}}$$

$$\text{Precision} = \frac{\text{No. of relevant docs retrieved}}{\text{Total no. of docs retrieved}}$$

These remain the two traditional measures of performance, although methods of analysis for averaging over queries have become more sophisticated. A number of other measures are derived from them. Although as defined here the measures seem to be appropriate to a system which produces a set of documents in response to a request ("set retrieval"), in fact they are most commonly used for evaluating systems which produce a ranked list ("ranked-output" systems). In this context it is usual to plot recall against precision, e.g. to locate positions in the ranked output which achieve certain levels of recall, and then measure precision at those points. The usual recall points for this analysis are $10\%, 20\%, \ldots, 100\%$. It is also common to measure precision at different document cut-off points (e.g. precision at 5, 10, 20, 100 ... documents retrieved), and also to calculate an "average precision" which is precision averaged over different recall levels.

The exact analysis required to evaluate these measures, given basic relevance data, is actually a little complex and has been the subject of a lot of argument. For example, if a query has 7 known relevant documents, what is the precision corresponding to a recall of 10%? Furthermore, how do we average such a measure over a number of requests? (This last is clearly necessary from an experimental design point of view; we will be able to conclude nothing at all from experiments with a single query.) There are now certain reasonably widely accepted methods; although one can argue with their validity, there is a strong compatibility argument for researchers to use the same methods as each other unless there is very good reason to depart from the norm. The norm is currently well represented by an evaluation program written for TREC by Chris Buckley [4] (more about TREC below).

On the other hand, such measures do have some limitations, and are rather crude as diagnostic tools. Other measures should also be considered when designing specific experiments.

2.6   Experimental Design

How to Design an IR Experiment? Traditionally, the same requests and documents are used repeatedly, with different systems or variants of systems. This ensures comparability. In the extreme, a large number of experiments may be conducted, to evaluate all combinations of a range of system parameters—*combinatorial* experiments.

Such methods are not necessarily compatible with all research questions or IR environments. In particular, strongly user-oriented experiments often cannot be designed in this way.

2.7   Portable Test Collections

Collections of 'portable' test materials, i.e. documents, requests, relevance judgements, can be made available to researchers to conduct retrieval tests in laboratories without having to find real users. Such collections allow for (to some extent) comparable results across systems. A number of portable collections exist, several of them small ones put together in the 70s and 80s, but the major current example is the TREC material. It is large, with a variety of documents and requests, and has a good range of relevant items. Relevance judgements come from a pooled output of many searches from many different systems.

2.8   TREC

The Text REtrieval Conference (TREC) is now the major forum for laboratory experiments and setter of standards. NIST, the National Institute of Standards and Technology in the U.S., coordinates [3]. Each year, NIST prepares some new materials, and distributes them to participants, who conduct experiments on various set tasks. Typically the retrieved documents are returned to NIST, who perform comparative evaluations. The materials are also made available for other researchers to use and evaluate locally. There are also some more recent imitations of TREC (notably in Europe and Japan). Some more details of TREC, together with some specific TREC experiments, are described below.

2.9   Some Evaluation Issues

The tradition of laboratory experiments in IR is a powerful and useful one. However, there are many issues in IR system design that seem to fall outside the scope of lab tests, or are very difficult to accommodate in the lab test framework. In general, there are inevitably substantial differences between the conditions obtaining in a laboratory and those real-life operational conditions under which systems are actually used. Perhaps the most glaring example relates to the study of highly interactive systems and of the process of interaction, or even more broadly in the study of users and the task contexts in which information seeking takes place. Designing an experiment to answer useful research questions involves balancing the need for laboratory-style control against the need for operational realism; the balance will be very different for different research questions. Some of these issues are discussed in [5]

3   More About Users

3.1   Some User Issues

We begin by making some observations about users of information retrieval systems. These observations, taken together, lead to fundamental questions about what we mean by a 'system' and about how we might interpret the term in the context of an evaluation experiment.

- Interaction
  - Users interact with systems (within sessions and between sessions).
- Relevance
  - Stated requests are not the same as information needs;
  - Relevance should be judged in relation to needs not requests.
- The cognitive view
  - An information need arises from an anomalous state of knowledge (ASK);
  - The process of resolving an ASK is essentially a cognitive process on the part of the user;
  - Information seeking is part of that process;
  - Users' models of information seeking are strongly influenced by systems.

3.2   Boundaries

Where Are the System Boundaries? Accepting the above points about users raises questions about where we might place the boundary of the system. The laboratory view seems quite happy with the notion of a core or basic system whose function is matching queries against documents. At the other extreme, from the point of view of the user trying to resolve a problem, many other components (including many the user's own perceptions) are part of the 'system' which s/he may bring to bear on the problem. The following diagram indicates some different views of the location of the boundary.

It is clear that there is no simple 'true' answer to the question: we have to choose the boundary that relates to the research question(s) we wish to answer. But also, even having made a choice, we must keep an awareness of the problem.

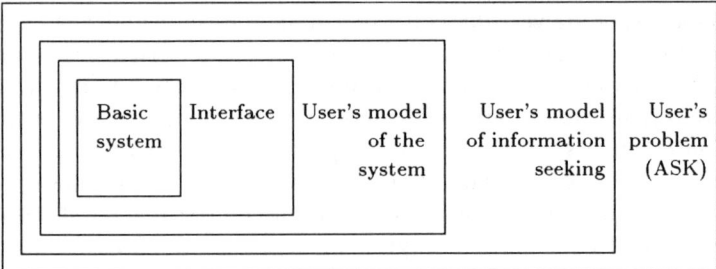

We may well be able to demonstrate, using laboratory techniques, that such-and- such a method improves the performance of the basic system. However, that will not prove the effectiveness of the method in the wider system context. This will depend on other factors in addition to those we may have investigated in the laboratory. In particular, for example, any method which changes the functionality of the system from the user's viewpoint must be tested in a realistic user environment as well as in the laboratory. A classic example is relevance feedback, on which more below.

Is it possible to adapt the traditional methods of IR system evaluation to a more user-inclusive perspective? A major problem is that the ASK is not directly visible to use; it exists only for a short time; and it is likely to be changed by interaction with the system.

4   Experiments with Okapi at City University 1989–1998

In a series of experiments at City University, we set out to investigate a number of aspects of retrieval, through experiment and observation covering the full range from TREC-style laboratory experiments to observations of real users on real information-seeking tasks. Some of this work is reported in [6]. One of the main vehicles for this work was the Okapi experimental system, together with an experimental environment; the scope of the work is indicated by the following diagram.

The environment included making the system available for use by registered users on the campus network. Having registered users (i.e. there was a logon process with individual userids) was important experimentally—it allowed us to identify individuals, examine logs of their searches, and in some cases invite them to take part in somewhat more formalized, lab-style experiments. The databases we mounted included library catalogues and scientific abstracts databases.

4.1   Okapi: A Family of Experimental IR Systems

The construction of the system (in a relatively narrow sense—the machine part of the system) may be summarized as follows. In fact it is better described as a family of systems

The Okapi System and Experimental Environment

Mechanisms	Interface	Information seeker
Functionality:	*Interaction issues:*	*Information seeking behaviour:*
functions required to support user information-seeking behaviour	user perception of system functions in relation to information-seeking task	perception of information-seeking task and approach to task
Evaluation		

Design Principles.

- Natural language queries
- Stemming
- Weighting and ranking based on probabilistic model
- Relevance feedback with query expansion

Versions.

- Character-based interactive system (VT100 system)
- Basic Search System: the retrieval engine, supporting:
  - weighting functions
  - Boolean and proximity searches
  - passage retrieval
- Query layer (supports development and maintenance of query, including relevance assessments)
- Various interfaces
  - a casual user GUI
  - an expert user interface
- Scripts for running test collection queries

4.2   Some Results

This system-and-environment was used for a series of experiments over a number of years. Many of these experiments were concerned with relevance feedback. It is one thing to demonstrate in a laboratory that suitable relevance information can be used to improve a search; quite another to provide the user with a natural way to use such a mechanism (in the context of whatever other controls they have) and expect them to use it both appropriately and effectively.

A very brief summary of some results from these studies may be made as follows:

- Careful specification of the weighting and ranking algorithms is critical ...
- ... the Okapi BM25 algorithm, devised for TRECs 2 and 3, has been very successful.
- Relevance feedback can be a very powerful device.
- In a live-use context, relevance feedback is used moderately frequently ...
- ... and to reasonable effect.
- Users commonly repeat searches, either with minor variations or identically.
- They would like to use relevance judgements experimentally/constructively.
- But giving the user more control is not always effective.

In particular, relevance feedback in the old VT100 interface, which took a very constrained form, was used to good effect by users. But they frequently complained about the constraints and asked for more control over the process. However, when we moved to a GUI (and inevitably a much richer interface), we found that use of relevance feedback dropped off substantially. A redesigned GUI increased use again somewhat, but not up to the levels seen before.

4.3   Some Conflicts in Laboratory Testing

The experience of trying to conduct relatively formalized experiments which nevertheless incorporate some aspects of the user's interactive experience made it very clear to us that the objective is fundamentally a hard one. Some of the conflicts between the laboratory approach and any attempt to cover the user experience may be summarized as follows:

- In a lab test, we try to control variables, i.e. separate the different factors ...
  - ... but in interactive searching, the user has access to a range of interactive mechanisms.
- In a lab test, we try to keep user outside the system ...
  - ... but in interactive searching, the user/searcher is inside (part of) the system
- In a lab test, we can repeat an experiment, with variations, any number of times ...
  - ... but in interactive searching, repetition is difficult and expensive and unlikely to produce identical results.

5   Routing/Filtering Experiments at TREC

This section discusses a set of experiments to evaluate methods appropriate to routing or filtering systems. First, we summarize some aspects of TREC.

5.1   TREC—The Text REtrieval Conference

A collaboration/competition with annual rounds. Basic TREC methods include:

- Accumulating collections of documents: e.g. a million documents, amounting to 2 Gb of text, consisting of an assortment of news items, news wires, scientific abstracts, US government reports, emails
- Accumulating collections of requests or 'topics': e.g. 50 each test, set by a panel of 'users'
- Old topics/documents may have relevance judgements from previous rounds
- Early TRECs:
   • 'Adhoc' test of new topics against old documents
   • 'Routing' test of old topics against new documents
- Later TRECs:
   • A wide variety of tasks
- Relevance judgements on pooled output from participants, made by the 'users'
- Various standard performance recall/precision measures based on ranked output, plus additional measures for different tasks

A number of papers on TREC (up to TREC-6) are brought together in [7]. The full proceedings from all the TREC conferences (currently at the time of writing up to TREC-8 in 1999) may be obtained from the TREC website [3].

5.2   The Routing/Filtering Task

The task as it was for TREC-8 is described in [8]. The TREC-9 task has been modified somewhat.

Assume there is an incoming stream of documents, and each user has a persistent profile representing their continuing interest. The task is to send appropriate incoming documents to the user. The form of this task suggests that it may be feasible to invite the user to provide relevance judgements on those documents s/he has been notified of; therefore the main focus has been on learning from such user feedback. Generally in the experiments the relevance judgements used for feedback have been those made previously; we simulate (to a greater or lesser degree of realism) the situation where judgements are being made in real time. Although the problem is much less than in interactive adhoc retrieval, it illustrates very well the conflict between lab and operational tests. In particular, we might expect some degree of interest drift on the part of the user in real filtering; we have not succeeded in simulating this in the TREC environment.

5.3   Batch Routing

Here the assumption is that the document stream and profile have been running for some time, and that we have accumulated a substantial set of relevance judgements. Typically we make use of all available relevance judgements for the initial time period (the training set); this is unrealistic in many ways. The object is taken to be devising an optimal profile for the next time period (test set). Evaluation has been by standard recall-precision analysis of the test set results.

The conclusions of these experiments (using Okapi and other systems) have generally been that very good performance is possible. The learning/training process typically involves some iterative exploration of combinations of terms and weights (or other search features) to find out what works best on the training set, and then applying the result to the test set. There is some danger, which needs guarding against, of overfitting the training set (i.e. learning the peculiarities of the training set which will not transfer to the test set), but provided care is taken here, learning can be very effective indeed.

5.4   Adaptive Filtering

In the adaptive filtering task, we try to make the simulation much more realistic. We assume that we start with some specification of the user's interest, and that the system has to take a yes/no decision about each incoming document (send it to the user or not). We assume that the user may provide relevance judgements about each document that we do decide to send, but not in general about any others.

The exact specification of the TREC routing/filtering task has been modified in successive TRECs. The current track has an adaptive filtering task in which it is assumed that the initial specification of the user's interest consists of a text query of the usual type, together with a couple of examples of relevant documents. It is also assumed that the incoming stream of documents was started some time ago, so that at the time of starting the simulation, there is already an accumulated collection; new documents may of course have some different characteristics, e.g. a sudden spate of interest in some topical subject, but in broad terms the stream will produce similar kinds of documents to those already seen. There is a related question about changes in the user's interest; one might assume that a user's interests will drift over time. This is not well covered by the current TREC simulation, although one of the two sets of requests used may have some such characteristics.

5.5   Evaluation Measures for Adaptive Filtering

The simulated user situation introduces some problems in terms of the standard approach to evaluation measures described above. We cannot evaluate ranked output, because the user experience is not of ranked output, and besides the decision as to whether or not to send a document to a user is the critical decision which needs evaluating. The current round of TREC is using two approaches:

1. A precision-oriented task: Maximise precision, but retrieve at least 50 documents over the time period of the simulation. Then the measure is precision, except that if less than 50 documents are returned, the denominator is 50.

2. A utility-based task: Maximise utility, measured in terms of a fixed credit per relevant document retrieved together with a fixed debit per non- relevant retrieved. (There is actually a small additional rule to do with the calculation of utility, but it does not matter for the present discussion.)

It may be seen that the specification of the task from the user point of view, the system's decision rule for whether or not to send a document to the user, and the measure of performance to be used are all intimately related. This has the disadvantage that the evaluation is specific to the task—it is not at all clear that, if we change the task slightly, our evaluation results will remain valid. On the other hand, it is also an advantage—it is much easier to see how the evaluation might relate to the user experience.

5.6   Evaluation Measures in General

If we return to the traditional measures such as average precision, it may be regarded as a serious disadvantage that some such measures would seem to be opaque from a user point of view. A measure such as average precision will mean nothing at all to a user; precision at 5 documents retrieved (P@5) would seem much more meaningful.

As against this argument, it appears that some measures are much more stable than others, and much more usable to predict performance of systems. Thus for example in the old TREC routing experiments described above, optimising a search on a training set in order to get good results on a test set, it seems to be much more reliable to optimise on average precision than on P@5. This is the case, somewhat surprisingly, *even if P@5 represents the desired outcome*. In other words, we get better P@5 in the test set by optimising on average precision in the training set, than by optimising on P@5 in the training set. An interesting paper in the last SIGIR gives some insight into this observation [9].

References

1. Sparck Jones, K. (ed.): *Information retrieval experiment*. Butterworths, London, 1981. Also available at http://www.itl.nist.gov/iad/894.02/projects/irlib/pubs/ire/ire_toc.html
2. Robertson, S.E.: The methodology of information retrieval experiment. In: Sparck Jones, K. [1] 2–31.
3. Information on the TREC programme and publications may be found at: http://trec.nist.gov/
4. This program is available for TREC participants from the TREC website [3]. It also comes as a module of the SMART system. Contact Chris Buckley (:chrisb@sabir.com) for further details.
5. Robertson, S.E. and Hancock-Beaulieu, M.: *On the evaluation of IR systems*, Information Processing & Management, 28:457–466, 1992.
6. A special issue devoted to work with the Okapi system at City University: Journal of Documentation, 53:1, 1997. Overview article: Robertson, S.E.: *Overview of the Okapi projects*, 3–7. User interface evaluation: Beaulieu, M.: *Experiments on interfaces to support query expansion*, 8–19.

7. Special issue of Information Processing & Management, 36(1), 2000.
8. Hull, D. and Robertson, S.E.: The TREC-8 Filtering Track Final Report. Available from http://trec.nist.gov/pubs/trec8/t8_proceedings.html
9. Buckley, C. and Voorhees, E.: Evaluating evaluation measure stability. In: Belkin, N.J.,Ingwersen, P. and Leong, M.-K. (eds): *SIGIR 2000*. ACM Press, New York (2000) 33–40

Indexing, Browsing, and Searching of Digital Video and Digital Audio Information

Alan F. Smeaton

School of Computer Applications, Dublin City University
Glasnevin, Dublin 9, Ireland
Alan.Smeaton@dcu.ie

Abstract In this chapter we examine various techniques for providing
content access to information stored in a continuous medium, namely
digital audio and digital video. Our coverage of audio is centered around
post-processing the output of automatic recognition of speech or phones
and we describe the various approaches than have been taken in this area.
In order to give reasonable coverage of the possibilities and limitations
of content-based access to digital video information we sketch out at a
high level, the approaches taken in various video compression algorithms,
principally the MPEG family. We then address approaches to shot and
scene boundary detection, choosing representative frames for browsing
and for search, and various browsing interfaces that have been developed.
We finish with an overview of the likely developments in this area in the
future.

1 Introduction

Having information available in digital format has many clear advantages including fast and cheap transfer of information, free and unlimited readership,
easy versioning and the capacity for easy and cheap storage of large amounts of
information. Effective and fast content based access to information is something
that has not been easy with analogue information but since practically all of
the information we use in our daily lives is in digital format, or soon will be,
content-based operations are an important goal. This will open up the prospects
of content based operations such as search, filtering, alerting, summarisation and
so on, which could not have been achieved heretofore. In this chapter we concentrate on content based operations on information stored in continuous media
such as audio and video. Although the techniques we outline can be applied to
other content-based operations besides retrieval we restrict our discussion to the
searching task which we refer to as information retrieval, though we mention
other applications in the conclusion.

Ideally, content based retrieval of any kind of information would be retrieval
based on an understanding of the semantics of the objects in a collection. For
any object, there are two approaches to the representation of content:

1. A human intermediary can interpret an object and generate keywords, captions, or some other kind of content description but the disadvantages of this
   approach are many and include at least:

M. Agosti, F. Crestani, and G. Pasi (Eds.): ESSIR 2000, LNCS 1980, pp. 93–110, 2000.

- No consistency of interpretation by a single person over time;
- No consistency of interpretation among a population of interpreters;
- No universally agreed format of the representation, whether keywords, captions or some knowledge-based formalism;
- cost!

We can see evidence of the first three of these reasons in the difficulties we have in the human classification of books, for example in the ACM Computing categories, or in the difficulties we have in classifying web pages in Yahoo! or the Open Directory Project [20].

2. The second approach to representing content is to have an automatic interpretation or transcription of objects by computer. The advantage of this is that it leads to a consistent interpretation of meaning, even if it is low-level and often wrong!

These general principles apply to information retrieval on all kinds of objects including text and other media and elsewhere in this volume other chapter authors discuss various aspects of this. Here, and specifically in the context of audio and video information, we can identify the same two general approaches where user-assigned descriptions of audio or video has more or less the same difficulties and approaches as user-assigned descriptions of text, so that isn't of much interest to us here. What is of interest to us here is the ways in which we can do automatic indexing and then information retrieval, on audio and video.

The current trend in content-based retrieval systems for non-text is based on three key ideas:

1. Successful content-based retrieval systems are domain-specific and only work in those domains though they may be ported elsewhere;
2. Automatic understanding tools have been (to date) impossible to develop and so must be replaced by interactive ones which involve users;
3. Humans should be given primitive tasks that can be performed consistently rather than complex ones which yield variable outputs;

These principles in general point to a somewhat bleak picture vis-'a-vis how we can do fully automatic indexing and retrieval of audio and of video but in fact quite a lot of progress has been made in these areas in recent years. Before examining what that progress is, and where we currently stand there are some further characteristics of multimedia objects, and of video in particular, which we will state here in order to give a full picture of the difficulties and challenges of information retrieval on these media. These are:

- Multimedia objects such as video clips have multiple dimensions and how we view an object, what our task is, what we are looking for, and so on, will all elicit different properties. Ideally, to cater for the many different interpretations of, say, a video, from many potential searchers, we would like to be able to capture all these possible features, but we cannot.

- We may eventually require retrieval based on a set of properties or types not initially captured by the system at indexing time, so our system should ideally be extensible in its index representation of multimedia objects to allow it to go back and "re-index" or perhaps index at query time.
- We should develop suites of retrieval techniques that can be used for sub-groups of features rather than developing a single retrieval technique which operates over the entire set of properties of a multimedia object. Ideally each technique should operate on the principle of an inexact match between an information need and an object, and should be based on an overall object ranking. Furthermore, we should be able to integrate these sets of ranked lists into a single overall ranked list combining individual evidences for each object into an overall Retrieval Status Value (RSV) given that each object could will involve more than one group of features.
- We must understand and allow for the fact that the automatic interpretation of objects that we handle will be both incomplete (with some parts of the description missing), inexact (some part(s) of the description may have certainty values associated) and possibly even erroneous (the interpretation probably involves automatic processes, and even human-assisted will have errors).
- We must also understand that query specifications will also be incomplete and may be refined as with document retrieval **but** in document retrieval, a document has many but a still definable number of interpretations, i.e. answers to questions. A video is even more content-rich compared to a text document and thus answers many and very diverse queries.

All these factors contribute to information retrieval on video and on audio being very difficult with almost everything stacked up against us. In fact what has happened in the area is that to date we don't have effective retrieval in the way we have come to know for text-based retrieval with the cycle of formulate and submit query, system generates ranking, browse ranked list, locate relevant document, click and read. Instead we have more of a browse-query-browse interaction with the requirement for browsing coming from the fact than one cannot easily get a *gist* of a video or audio clip compared to assessing the contents of a text document. This means that the whole concept of information retrieval on audio and on video becomes very different compared to information retrieval on text documents. We shall return to this point later on.

Before moving on to describe how current techniques for information retrieval on audio and video operate there is one other important element of the context in which we can do content operations on such media of which the reader should be aware. The huge strides that the computing industry has made over the last decade or so, to put digital multimedia information on our desktops and in our homes have been achieved by a concentrated effort into developing technologies to capture or create, store, transmit, render and display this media. Chief among this has been the development of encoding and compression formats for media which have the over-riding constraint of achieving maximum compression for minimum quality loss in order to make storing and transmitting the media possible. We thus have a situation where video and audio information is stored in a digital format which has been developed without any consideration given to how that information might be manipulated by content. The "engineering" aspect of delivering digital multimedia has been virtually the only concern in developing these encoding standards and formats, and that has started to change only very recently. When we try to do information retrieval on encoded audio and video we find that we are almost fighting against the format in which it is encoded and at the very least, unless we have huge computation resources to decode everything back to raw bits, we are constrained to leveraging whatever we can from the encoding, which as we know was driven by considerations of compression. This makes our task even more difficult with compression formats having a huge impact and limitation on the possibility for content based operations.

The organisation of this chapter proceeds as follows. In the next section we examine information retrieval on digital audio, concentrating on retrieval from spoken audio. Following that, and the main part of the chapter, we look at retrieval and browsing of digital video. Part of this section gives a thumbnail sketch of the approaches taken to video compression before we move on to cover indexing, browsing and content-based operations. In the final section we examine more general questions about retrieval aspects of audio and video.

2   Information Retrieval on Digital Audio

When we refer to digital audio information we refer to audio recordings of speech, music or other sounds. The "other sounds" category is generally restricted to specialist applications (bird sounds, whale whistles, etc.) and to sound effects (games, movies) so we are left with speech and with music.

There are several good textbooks which address issues such as psychoacoustics, the human hearing range, loudness, and the perception of sound [7, 17]. For our purposes here all we need to know is that sound is a continuous vibration which is sampled at a given rate which leads to a quantization of the analog waveform into digital format. A higher sampling rate means less quantization noise which means better quality. Audio CD recordings are sampled at a rate of 44 kHz and each of the samples is stored at 16 bits, for each (of 2) channels giving stereo reproduction. Lower sampling rates such as telephone quality audio use up less space in digital form, and require less bandwith to store and transmit files, but sound poorer, so there is a clear tradeoff.

Once audio has been digitised in this way there are literally scores of formats in which it can be represented. The WAV form is common and the samples can be 8− or 16−bit, and there are many sampling rates that can be used, but there is no compression so it is raw, and uncompressed format. Other formats achieve large compression ratios and include AU, VOX, RealAudio, TSP, VMF, AIFF and so on. MP3 is a format that has become hugely popular on the internet for encoding music and it does this by using higher compression at the parts of the audio spectrum where human hearing is at its least discerning, an approach referred to as perceptual compression.

Another audio encoding format worth noting is MIDI, an international standard for digital music which has high acceptance in the music community. In MIDI, "sounds" are encoded as one or many streams with each stream recording a specification for each of the notes, duration, volume, etc, and also the type of the sound being played, so a MIDI file is actually an ASCII text file. For example, the code 20 refers to a church organ while 117 is a taiko drum and 124 is a bird tweet! [7, pp93].

Once audio information has been digitised we can explore the possibilities for content-based access. For non-speech information the limits are a combination of our imagination and our technology. If information is stored in MIDI format then there are several approaches to finding tunes from a MIDI song database using information retrieval techniques derived from text-based IR [2]. With the explosive growth in the use of MP3 as an encoding format there are huge possibilities for content-based indexing and retrieval systems but at the present time MP3 files are accessed almost exclusively through their metadata (title, artist, etc.) rather than directly on their content, though this is an active area of research.

For audio encoding of speech, the situation is more advanced. Speech processing has always been an target of artificial intelligence and [12] is a good, short, snappy, complete and thorough survey of the problems and solutions to speech processing. Although that article is perhaps a bit dated and there has been some progress since then, speech processing is still short of human capabilities but by limiting the domain it allows it to be productive and there are commercial developments. There is an acceptance that speech will not replace the mature, established and efficient alternative for data input (keyboard/mouse) but can be combined with it. When it comes to automatic processing of spoken audio collections then the applications which are attracting most attention are in radio/TV news retrieval, searching archival radio/news broadcasts, video and audio email, searching audio archives of meetings, lectures, etc.

Two utterances of the same words by the same person under the same conditions generate very different waveforms because of the variability of human speech generation, air temperature, acoustics, etc. Given that digital audio is a waveform sampled at a given frequency and into a given bit-size (8— or 16—bits), possibly with lossy compression added, it follows that direct wave-to-wave matching of audio will not yield any kind of reasonable performance. Variations due to loudness, pitch, brightness, bandwidth, harmonisity, and others are all continuous variables and are equivalent to colour and texture in images. Thus all speech document retrieval systems are thus based on some kind of recognition of spoken words or of phones.

A spoken word is exactly the same as a written word, albeit with the difficulties of determining the boundaries between words since we tend to speak continuously and without word breaks. A phone is a sub-word unit, equivalent to a unit of pronunciation, larger than a letter, but smaller than a word. For example, the phrase "more details" consists of the 9 phones:

m oo r d ii t ei l z

with double letters used in the alphabet to represent some single phones. These phones are taken from one of several phone alphabets used commonly, with no real agreement on a standard or on which alphabet is best.

Once phones have been identified then a speech recognition system will try to group these together into words. This is a non-trivial task since there are no word bounds and since phone recognition usually outputs a lattice of phones rather than a single stream. This means that for many possible phones, a phone recogniser will output more than one candidate phone, with associated probabilities of likelihood. Phone recognition and word identification work best when they are collaborative processes, re-enforcing each other with certain phone combinations giving words which are not in a dictionary or unlikely combinations, and commonly occurring words strengthening the chances of certain phone combinations actually occurring.

Some approaches to information retrieval on speech have been based on full word recognition techniques while others have been based on indexing spoken text by the phones. These approaches can be roughly grouped as follows.

Approach 1: Word Spotting.

Instead of trying to do recognition of full speech, the Cambridge/Olivetti VMR (video mail retrieval) project [5] did word-spotting, i.e. given a pre-defined vocabulary of the order of some tens of words, process the spoken audio component of video mail looking for these words and these words only, and use them as indexing terms. By this restriction to a reduced set of key words the problem of speech recognition is reduced in complexity and becomes manageable. A user's query in this system is to search for these keywords and the keywords chosen are good discriminators between messages in a VMR application.

The reason why this works is because the speech recognition can perform effectively and this is because it has a limited vocabulary for recognition. If a word in the stream cannot be recognised then it moves on assuming it is not one of the keywords.

Approach 2: Speaker Recognition.

The Jabber project at the University of Waterloo [6] applied speaker-independent continuous speech recognition to the audio recording of a meeting but like all such attempts at such recognition has had problems because it tried to recognise all of the words spoken by everyone. However, one of the spin-off benefits of this approach is that it can recognise **who** has done the speaking at any time and a visual summary of the dialogue turn-taking can provide a kind of navigational support through meeting archives if speaker recognition can be done accurately enough.

This shows that it is possible to leverage reasonably effective retrieval from even moderate processing of the audio signal. Both the VMR and Jabber projects used off-the-shelf or tailored recognisers but even these speech recognition systems need quite an amount of training before they can be effective.

Approach 3: Phone-Based Retrieval.

Instead of recognising word-level tokens in speech recognition, an alternative is to recognise sub-word units, namely *phones*. A project at ETH-Zürich [13] indexed (German) radio news broadcasts by phones, accurately, into a lattice, so for each phone it had a set of possible candidates with probabilities. For these sets of candidates phones there are paths through the phone choices which correspond to words. At Dublin City University our own Taiscéalaí system [11, 16] took the same approach and was engineered into a real operational system. The Taiscéalaí system captured RTÉ Radio 1 news broadcasts twice daily, recognised phones, broke the stream of phones into overlapping windows, and generated a document for each window which was indexed as a retrievable unit of information. User queries (text) were turned into phones via a dictionary lookup and the matching and retrieval operation was based on a bag of tri-phones from the query matched against bags of triphones for indexed windows of audio broadcasts. Each window was 30 seconds in length with a 10 seconds overlap.

The Taiscéalaí system gives us our first glimpse of the difficulty of information retrieval where the objects being searched are continuous streams of information, rather than discrete objects such as text documents. If we assume that we are seeking a ranked list from an information retrieval operation then such an operation on a collection or library of such objects has two dimensions; the first is related to finding which how the objects are ranked and the second is related to the position or offset within each object, where the user is pointed to. A system which retrieves 30 minute video or audio clips and presents a ranked list of them to a user without any browsing or navigation within the objects is not of much assistance. In Taiscéalaí we computed a measure of similarity for each 30 seconds window and we then aggregated these into scores for regions of each broadcast and we presented, visually, the summary for each broadcast as shown in Figure 1. This screendump shows the 6th, 7th and 8th ranked broadcasts returned from the query *"head of European bank France Germany Kohl."* In the broadcast of 03 May 1998 there is a region between about 1:30 and 2:30 which the timeline shows seems to have several query term occurrences and the user has selected a short fragment of this broadcast around the 2:20 mark to be played. The vertical peaks on these timelines represent short pauses and the different shadings on the x-axis correspond to different broadcast sources, i.e. in-studio, telephone interview, outside broadcast, music, etc.

The problem of retrieval of (multimedia) objects and retrieval or navigation within these objects is analagous to passage retrieval in classical text-based information but is more complicated because it is more difficult to get an overview of an audio or video clip than a text document. This is a problem that will arise again when we look at information retrieval from digital video in the next section.

Approach 4: Word-Based Audio Retrieval.

Despite the fact that speaker independent continuous speech recognition is not 100% accurate and is computationally demanding there are several examples of work reported where speech recognition is applied to spoken audio to support subsequent information retrieval. The biggest catalyst for this has been the effect of the TREC spoken document track. TREC is an annual benchmarking exercise carried out since 1990 in the area of information retrieval. Coordinated

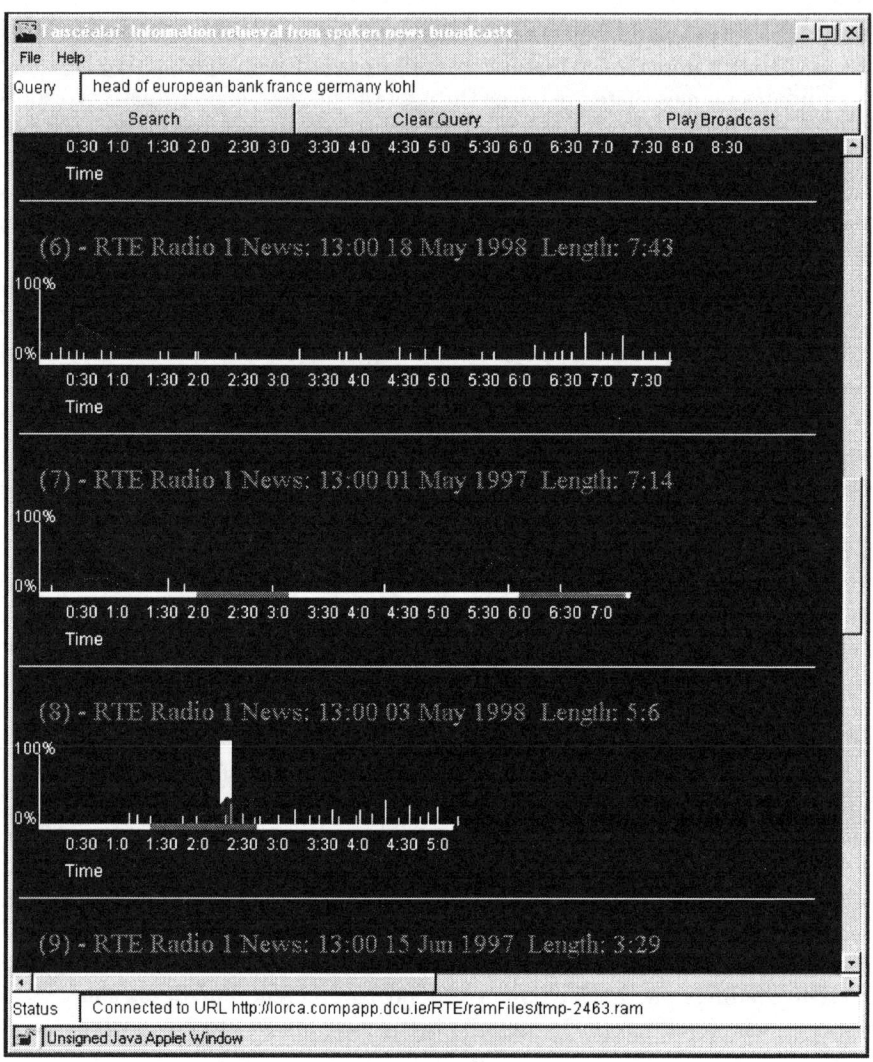

Figure 1. Sceendump from the Taiscéalaí System.

by the National Institute for Standards and Technology (NIST) in the US, NIST is a world-wide operation which has involved most of the major information retrieval research groups in industry and academia. TREC started as an initiative addressing text-based information retrieval only but then merged into almost a dozen "tracks" or variations including retrieval in different languages, cross-lingual IR, retrieval from documents corrupted from an OCR process, interactive retrieval, information filtering and information retrieval from spoken documents. In this latter track, the audio from some hundreds of hours of news broadcasts was the collection and the task was to find broadcasts which were relevant to a given query. The logistics of the operation of TREC are best described in [18].

In the spoken document track which has been ongoing for three years, many of the participating groups take the approach of training a speech recogniser to recognise spoken words and they follow this with some variation of conventional text-based information retrieval on the recognised output. Much of this work is based on taking account of and making allowances for the occurrence of the kind of speech recognition errors typically encountered in speech. Examples of systems which take this approach can be found in [4].

3   Information Retrieval from Digital Video

Video is basically a sequence of images relayed at a constant speed, normally 25 to 30 frames per second, with a synchronised audio track. Chapter 5 of [7], has details of analog video fundamentals such as aspect ratio, sync, horizontal and vertical resolutions, frame rates for motion (25 to 30), colour fundamentals (RGB), colour video and TV, video formats and worldwide TV standards such as NTSC in the US, PAL in most of Europe, and SECAM in France. It also covers video performance measurements, colour test cards and video recording equipment. Here we are concerned only with the digital encoding of video.

To display a single image of TV quality video requires 720 Kbytes and frames must be displayed at at least 25 frames per second to get the effect of smooth motion. This means that 18 Mbytes of storage is required for each second of a video without compression and for a 90 minute film this would be almost 100 Gbytes of storage. It also has the alarming implication that a CD-ROM with a storage capacity of 648 Mb and a data transfer rate of 150 Kb/second (the data transfer rate for original CD-Roms) would only be able to store 36 seconds of video, and it would take almost five seconds to download and display each frame.

Clearly the display and manipulation of TV quality video on computer screens has two technical barriers namely storage capacity and data transfer rate and these can be solved by data compression techniques and improved hardware and software. When it comes to video compression the formats that matter are the various MPEGs, H.261/p∗64 and DVI, but really the most important is the MPEG family.

A fundamental part of all video compression approaches is motion compensation, identifying motion in adjacent video frames and spotting and transmitting only the differences between adjacent frames. Of course this does not apply to adjacent frames which straddle shot or scene changes. Determining differences between frames on the basis of pixel-to-pixel comparisons is too simplistic because much video content will have some kind of camera motion as cameras are never stationary and can pan, zoom, tilt, boom, and so on or be noisy, or have slight movements. Thus in video compression algorithms, frames are divided into blocks which are larger aggregates than pixels and motion compensation is tested between the blocks. In this way, slight noisy movements of the camera can be incorporated without incurring loss of effective compression, as well as facilitating efficient encoding with the larger deliberate camera moves like panning and zooming.

Of the contemporary video encoding standards in use today it is the MPEG family which are the most important. What makes the MPEG standards attractive is that these are standards agreed upon by a large community with a broad representation, ahead of the chaos that exists with, say, image formats. What is especially notable is that during the development of the MPEG standards nobody on the development group had existing proprietary video standards that they wanted to push, so the various actual MPEG standards put forward have been more computationally and conceptually complex than anything in place at the time of their development. The implementation of the MPEG standards followed on after their specification.

At present there are four MPEG standards whose specification is complete or nearly so. MPEG-1 has been around longest and encoding and decoding is achievable on desktop computers. MPEG-2 has the same general approach as MPEG-2 but delivers higher quality and is used in digital TV broadcasting. MPEG-2 encoding requires specialist hardware and even MPEG-2 decoding and playback is not yet commonplace on desktop computing requiring, as it does, special hardware. MPEG-4 encoding and playback is a technology which has not yet been developed to the extent that it can be used in anything but laboratory test environments while MPEG-7 is still at the draft specification stage.

MPEG-1 encoding turns a 3D video sequence (x-axis, y-axis and time) into a one-dimensional bit stream for transmission [14]. MPEG-1 uses a frame size of 352×288 pixels at 25 frames/second (FPS) giving VHS quality at a fixed rate of 1.5 Mb/second or just under (which is the data rate from a CD-Rom), though larger frame sizes and different FPS rates can be encoded. MPEG decoders and players are common and available and on workstation or PC can decode in real-time for 25 FPS, but few encoders are available without hardware add-ons. Each frame is compressed breaking it into 8×8 pixel blocks for inter-frame and 16×16 pixel macroblocks for intra-frame motion compensation. Macroblocks are strung together to form slices which are combined into a picture. A number of pictures are grouped together into a group of pictures (GOP) to form a random access unit to allow forward/rewind with no dependencies between GOPs and hence handling of breaks in transmission.

In MPEG-1 there are three types of frames namely:

1. I-frames are intracoded frames, meaning they are encoded block-by-block independently of adjacent frames as if they were still images, and they are encoded with lossy compression using JPEG compression.
2. P-frames are forward-predicted frames, encoded with reference to the most recent previous I- or P-frame with motion-estimation and macroblocks vector-matched.
3. B-frames are bidirectional predicted frames coded with reference to previous and following I- or P-frames with motion-estimation and encoding similar to P-frames.

The pattern for I-, B- and P-frames will vary from encoder to another but could be something like the following

I-B-B-B-B-P-B-B-B-B-P-B-B-B-B-I- ...

A GOP is a frame pattern of I-, B- and P-frames generating a bit stream which is further compressed using Huffman coding, which yields great compression and reduces the whole video stream, including audio, to about 1.5 Mbits/second.

MPEG-1 was initially targeted at multimedia applications reading from CD-Rom but also supports frame based random access through the video, FF/Rew and reverse playback.

Beyond MPEG-1 there is MPEG-2 which has data rates of between 2 and 9.8 Mbits/sec, enough for high definition TV. MPEG-2 is 720×576 pixels and is used for the transmission of digital TV and video on DVD. It is a superset of MPEG-1 and takes the same approaches to encoding as MPEG-1.

There was an MPEG-3 slated to cater for HDTV but MPEG-2 proved adequate for these requirements so the MPEG-3 standard was dropped as work on the specification for MPEG-4 had already been started. MPEG-4 has been recently finalised and is targeted at very low bit rate encoding of audio-visual interactions requiring a completely new approach to encoding based on human-computer interactions. Part of this involves identifying objects in a frame as coloured shapes and tracking these objects from frame-to-frame and applying shape compression which is very effective, all without knowing what the shapes actually represent. Instead of being block-based as MPEG-1 and -2 are, MPEG-4 is based on object compression and represents video as a series of planes, superimposed upon each other to give the final rendered picture. This will allow future multimedia applications with extended interactive functionalities and access to actual content, i.e. the objects in the video, where the rendering of the frames can even be personalised in some way. This encoding of objects allows deconstruction and reconstruction in an object layer but the identification of objects is the biggest challenge here; tracking and compression of objects is currently achievable for synthetic or artificial video such as animated cartoons but not for video of natural scenes of objects. While the specification of MPEG-4 is complete and available, the implementation of this has not yet been achieved fully.

The final MPEG standard is MPEG-7 which is unusual in the MPEG family as it has visual and audio elements but also it has a content descriptor stream where the semantic content of the video is encoded and represented. Clearly this is targeted at content based operations such as search but as this specification is still under debate we have only speculation as to how it might end up. It is believed though that the descriptor stream will be some markup language similar to, if not part of, XML.

We now concentrate on indexing and retrieval from the digital video stream, but we note that as video is a continuous media, usually combined with an audio track and for most effective access an application should use both synchronised media for retrieval.

It is relatively straightforward to treat digital video as a binary blob and for each video to store aspects like date, title, director plus a textual description of video contents and to do little more than search the metadata associated with a video, or the video transcript. This isn't video retrieval though and we won't discuss this further.

To see how video retrieval can work we need to examine what exactly a video is and how it has been encoded. Video is a sequence of individual shots of variable lengths butted together in some way, and played as a continuous stream into a 2D window. Thus it has three dimensions: x, y and t.

The way to make progress in manipulating video content is to structure the video in some way and identify the shots and then segment the video into a list of shots using automatic shot boundary detection (SBD). This task of automatic video segmentation is quite difficult as production level video incorporates such tricks as fade-in and fade-out, dissolving, morphing, wipes and many other chromatic effects and these are surprisingly commonplace in TV and in movies. Programmes such as gardening programmes, cookery programs, TV adverts, etc. all incorporate such effects, even live coverage of sports with action replays as on-the-fly post-production effects.

Initial attempts at video segmentation were based on processing the primitives in a video which are similar to the primitives in a single-frame image, but with time added, namely colour and associated histograms and their within-frame distribution, texture, intensity/brightness, etc. These can be used to detect scene changes by measuring shifts in the overall histogram or in the distribution of colours within a frame. Essentially they are based on measuring inter-frame distances and are really an application of still image retrieval [3], but they can be confounded by commonplace camera techniques such as zooming and panning, booming, tilting and tracking, or a combination of all of these. They are even more thrown by fade-in and gradual scene changing.

In our work at Dublin City University we evaluated the effectiveness of several approaches to SBD as follows:

- Measuring inter-frame difference based on differences between colour histograms for the entire frame;
- Calculating the edges around the objects in adjacent frames using Sobel filtering and measuring the differences between these;
- Measuring colour moments between adjacent frames and using this to determine shot bounds;
- Extracting motion vectors from MPEG-1 encoding and using these to indicate shot bounds;

To evaluate these we took 8 hours of broadcast TV including many different program types like gardening programmes, news, soap operas, detective series, a comedy programme with TV commercials interspersed, and we manually marked up all shot bounds. From these 720, 000 frames of video we identified 5380 hard shot cuts and another 779 fades or dissolves and we used this as a ground truth against which to compare the different techniques. We found that all techniques perform at about the same level with both recall and precision at around 85% to

90%. As a refinement of this, instead of setting a fixed threshold we developed a method of dynamically adjusting the threshold depending on the programme genre, as determined by measuring the visual "noise" in a programme [15]. We also experimented with running all four SBD methods and combining the outputs into one decision [1]. Our conclusion from this work is that the more sophisticated approaches do give some improvement over the basic colour histogram method but not enough to merit the computational cost required. On our hardware configuration, SBD using colour histograms takes about the same time as the length of the video being analysed but using edge detection or colour moments takes twice as long. On balance, colour histogram based detection gives adequate performance.

Once a video stream has been segmented into shots we are then faced with the problem of determining how can it be indexed or browsed or viewed. It is essential to present video visually because it is a visual artifact in the first place. By segmenting a video into shots we reduce the problem to one of indexing a series of single scenes or shots. The common approach to this is to find a representative frame from each shot, above a certain length, and to present a video as a series of images, a kind of visual storyboard. A variety of approaches have been taken to choosing the representative frame for a shot. The simplest was to choose the frame in the middle of a shot but this may not be a good choice to essentially randomly pick a frame. Another approach is to choose the first frame, but in the case of a shot bound which is not a hard cut this can yield a frame which is half one shot, half the previous one. In our work on the *Fischlár* system [8] our approach is based on treating the clip as a set of individual images and the "image" or frame with the most average colour histogram or the one which is most similar to the others (using image matching techniques) is chosen. Thus the video stream is now a list of images where each image has an associated "length" of the clip from which it was taken. This approach, though not the details of our technique, is common in video indexing systems.

Once video is structured in some way we can support a visual search on keyframes from shots, but the most natural way to navigate through video is not to use search but to use browsing. The difficulty with this though is that browsing keyframes is still browsing through a very large information entity for long video streams perhaps of the order of hours, so simply structuring video into shots does not achieve much on its own. If we take an archive of many days of video content, as we have in our *Fischlár* system [8], then browsing through keyframes is adequate only for browsing within a single programme. This must be complimented by using programme metadata such as title, actors, programme genre, date, time, TV station or whatever, to select the programmes to be browsed. This returns us to the point made earlier about information retrieval through video requiring more of a search-browse interaction than for text-based information retrieval.

Once we have narrowed the "library" or collection of video to a unit of the order of size of a programme, the task then becomes browsing within this programme in order to find segments of interest. In [9] we present a framework

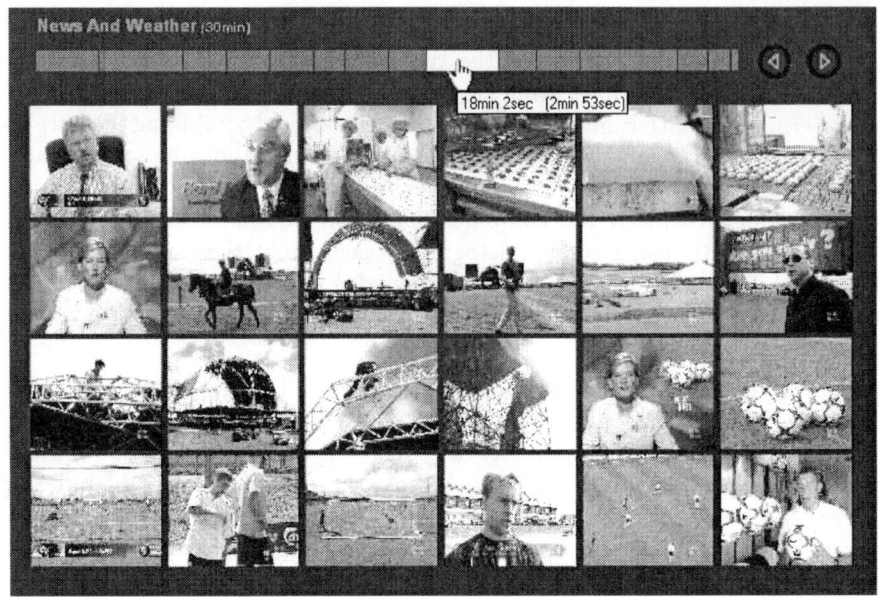

Figure 2. Screendump from Físchlár Showing Keyframes Taken from the Middle of a 30 Minute News and Weather Broadcast.

for the development of browsing interfaces to video. Two of the most interesting ones which illustrate different approaches are shown in Figures 2 and 3

In Figure 2 we see 24 keyframes, each representing a shot of length greater than 1 second, with the whole programme represented as a timeline in the top part of the frame, and the region of the programme that the 24 keyframes represents at around 18 minutes 2 seconds, clearly highlighted and visible. In Figure 3 we see a hierarchical video browser with the top line of keyframes spanning the whole 30 minute broadcast and one of these (the 4th frame from the left on the top level) selected and drilled down to the second level which covers a smaller region of the broadcast and one of these keyframes in turn is also selected and expanded to show a sub-sub region of the video.

Pages of keyframes or hierarchically organised keyframes are just two of many possible ways in which a user can be assisted in navigating a video clip. Others exist as shown in many of the research projects in this area. Many of these projects are summarised in a single web page at [21] including the AT&T DART system, DiVAN, EuroMedia, ImageMiner for Video, Informedia, NeTra-V, Pop-Eye, and about a dozen others. Most of these systems operate on video from any domain though the most successful ones concentrate on a single domain and application and the most common application is capturing, analysing and providing navigation through news broadcasts. Seminal work by Zhang and Smoliar [10] showed how a TV news programme could be parsed into its constituent storylines and classified into anchorperson, weather forecast, commercial, news/action clip,

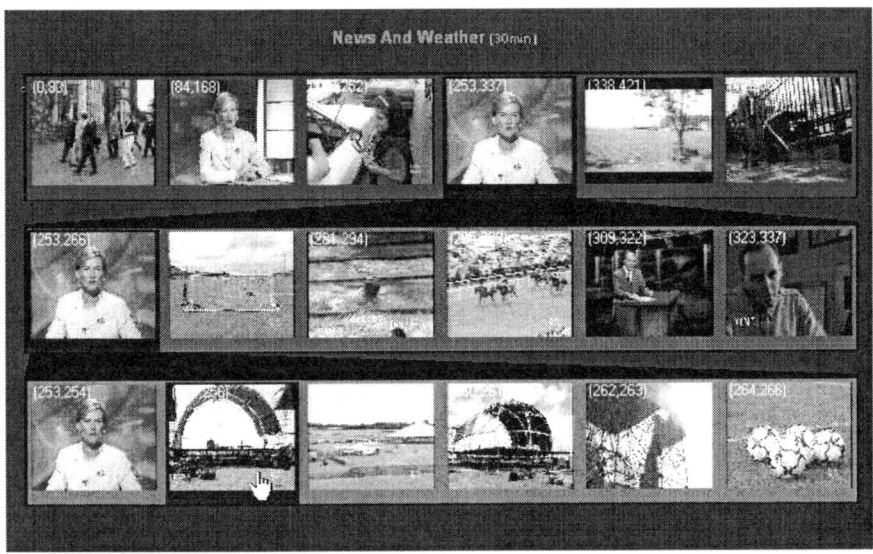

Figure 3. Screendump from News Programme Showing Hierarchically Organised Keyframe Browsing.

whatever. This is in fact parsing the entire news broadcast and this is possible because TV news has a "grammar" with opening headlines, credits, anchor, story 1, etc. Once a broadcast has been parsed in this way, then this opens the possibility for a more directed browsing of the video, though this grammar can change as a news program periodically gets a facelift.

This TV news application is one of the few where the video stream is well-structured and parsable and it is in this application that the most ambitions and successful research project in this area initially addressed its effort. The Informedia project at Carnegie Mellon University [10] was part of the US Digital Libraries initiative. The navigation/retrieval approach in Informedia was to incorporate several techniques for content retrieval and have each operate in parallel, including the following:

- speech recognition on the audio of the video using the Sphinx recogniser from CMU, at the time the best-performing speech recogniser;
- segmenting the video stream based on colour histogram changes, shape and texture measurements between frames and allowing for the kind of scene transformations mentioned earlier; there is also camera motion detection for pan, zoom, tilt, etc.;
- object detection looking specifically for faces and for text captions in the image and matching these against a database of known VIP faces in order to try to detect the presence of these VIPs;
- caption and text extraction from still frames in the videos which was then input into an OCR program;

All these tools operated on the video content and allowed the generation of video skims or summaries with transcripts, the presence of known VIPs, and so on, all presented. The retrieval tool in Informeda allows a user's text input query to be matched against the transcript (allowing for speech recognition errors) and against recognised captions to select segments of video which can be skimmed by viewing a series of representative frames with associated keywords (from the dialogue) and a user can choose a frame and run it as a query to find video clips like that one. Informedia is successful and has attracted attention because it was the first to integrate so many complimentary techniques for information management into the one system for managing video material.

4   Conclusions on Managing Digital Video and Digital Audio

In reading this chapter it should be clear that the element of browsing is an essential part of navigation through video and audio content, more so than with text or image information. This means that we cannot simply take text-based information retrieval and apply it to video but we must re-think the whole user-system interaction and integrate browsing and searching as seamlessly as possible. In practice we are only starting to do this as technology has up to now prevented us from doing so. Soon, with digital TV broadcast into our homes, the demand for control on this content will grow dramatically and as we presently stand we are not ready for these demands.

Most of the research systems developed to day have concentrated on desktop-based tools for managing video content. People managing digital TV, which will be the largest userbase and application for this work, do not sit at desktops or have mouse/keyboards for control as they lie on couches and use small remote control devices. The interfaces we develop for video content manipulation will have to reflect this and they do not to date.

Another area where there are big changes happening which will affect video content management is the unpredicted and enormous growth in mobile communications, especially in Europe. We soon will have GPRS telephony and early in 2002 we expect to have third generation mobile phones with enough bandwidth to stream MPEG-1 quality video to mobile handheld devices. This has the potential to completely change the way in which we watch TV and manage our TV viewing. Little work has been done to date, however, on video streaming and video content management on a PDA or mobile phone.

Finally, some pointers as to what the likely applications for video content management will be. Surprisingly, we would not expect to much need for classical information retrieval searching though people will want to do keyword or key phrase searching of archives of broadcast material. Applications which are based around push technology such as filtering, alerting and summarisation of video content will grow in importance, especially as the mobile communications market grows in size and importance. Users will want to have SMS or WAP alerts as to the status of the programmes they asked to be recorded and analysed.

Users will want to be able to stream video, even of preview quality, to their mobile PDAs. Users will want to be able to access trailers or summaries of video material and users will want lots of personalisation in order to make the volume of accessible material, manageable. Some demand will exist for access to broadcast and archived audio material but this will be specialist and niche. The real market and the real scientific challenges remain in the area of video content indexing and navigation and there are still lots of problems to be solved.

References

1. Browne, P., Smeaton, A.F., Murphy, N., O'Connor N., Marlow, S., Berrut, C. Evaluating and Combining Digital Video Shot Boundary Detection Algorithms. In *Proceedings of the Fourth Irish Machine Vision and Information Processing Conference*, Queens University Belfast, September 1999.
2. Downie, J.S. and Nelson, M. Evaluation of a simple and effective music IR system. In: *Proceedings of the 22nd ACM-SIGIR Conference*, Athens, Greece, July 2000.
3. Eakins, J.P. Retrieval of Still Images by Content. This volume 2000.
4. Garofolo, J., Voorhees, E., Auzanne, C., Stanford, C. and Lund, B.   TREC-7 Spoken Document Retrieval Track Overview and Results. In *NIST Special Publication 500-242: The Seventh Text REtrieval Conference (TREC 7)* 79–90, 1999. (also available at http://trec.nist.gov/pubs/trec7/t7_proceedings.html last visited 10 August 2000.)
5. Jones, G.J.F., Foote, J.T., Sparck Jones, K. and Young, S.J. Retrieving spoken documents by combining multiple index sources. In *Proceedings of SIGIR 96, Research and Development in Information Retrieval*, 30–38, Zürich, ACM Press, 1996.
6. Kazman, R. and Kominek, J. Supporting the Retrieval Process in Multimedia Information Systems. In: *Proceedings of HICSS '97*, Vol. VI, 229–238, 1997.
7. Koegel Buford, J.F. *Multimedia Systems*. ACM Press, Addison-Wesley Publishers, New York 1994.
8. Lee, H,. Smeaton AF,. O'Toole, C,. Murphy, N,. Marlow S and O'Connor, N.E. The Físchlár Digital Video Recording, Analysis, and Browsing System. In *Proceedings of RIAO '2000: Content-Based Multimedia Information Access*, Paris, France, April 12–14, 2000
9. Lee, H., Smeaton, AF, Berrut, C., Murphy, N, Marlow, S. and O'Connor, N. Implementation and Analysis of Several Keyframe-based Browsing Interfaces to Digital Video. To appear in *Proceedings of the Fourth European Conference on Digital Libraries*, Lisbon, Portugal, September 2000.
10. Perry, B., Chang, S-K, Dinsmore, J, Doermann, D, Rosenfeld, A and Stevens, S. Content-Based Access to Multimedia Information. *From Technology Trends to State of the Art*. Kluwer Academic Publishers, 69–77, 2000.
11. Quinn, G. and Smeaton, A.F. Optimal Parameters for Segmenting a Stream of Audio into Speech Documents, G. Quinn.: In *Proceedings of the ESCA ETRW Workshop on Accessing Information in Spoken Audio*: 19–20 April 1999, Cambridge, UK.
12. Rudnicky, A.I., Hauptmann,A.G. and Lee, K-F. Survey of current speech technology. *Communications of the ACM*. 37(3):52–57, 1994
13. Schäuble, P. *Multimedia Information Retrieval*. Kluwer Academic Publishers 1997.

14. Sikora, T. MPEG Digital Video-Coding Standards. *IEEE Signal Processing Magazine*, 82–99, 1997.
15. Smeaton, A.F., Gilvarry, J., Gormley, G., Tobin, B., Marlow S. and Murphy, N. An Evaluation of Alternative Techniques for Automatic Detection of Shot Boundaries in Digital Video. In: *Proceedings of the Third Irish Machine Vision and Information Processing Conference*, Dublin, September 1999.
16. Smeaton, A.F., Morony, M., Quinn G., and Scaife, R. Taiscéalaí: Information Retrieval from an Archive of Spoken Radio News. In *Proceedings of the Second European Conference on Research and Advanced Technology for Digital Libraries (ECDL)*, Crete, C. Nikolaou and C. Stephanidis (Eds.) Springer LNCS 1513, 429–442, 1998.
17. Tannenbaum, R. S. *Theoretical Foundations of Multimedia*. W. H. Freeman and Company, The Computer Science Press, New York, 1998.
18. Voorhees, E.M. and Harman, D.H. The Sixth Text REtrieval Conference (TREC-6). *Information Processing & Management* 36(1):3–35 1999.
19. Zhang, H., Low, C. and Smoliar, S. Video Parsing and Browsing Using Compressed Data. *Multimedia Tools and Applications*. 1:89–111, 1995.
20. http://www.dmoz.org visited 16 August 2000.
21. http://lorca.compapp.dcu.ie/Video/SLinksF.html Link visited 13 August 2000.

Retrieval of Still Images by Content

John P. Eakins

Institute for Image Data Research, University of Northumbria at Newcastle
Newcastle upon Tyne NE1 8ST, U.K.
john.eakins@unn.ac.uk

Abstract This chapter summarises the current state of the art in content based image retrieval (CBIR). It discusses the need for image retrieval by content, and the types of query which might be encountered. It describes the main techniques currently used to retrieve images by content at both primitive and semantic levels, describes the features of some commercial and experimental CBIR systems, assesses the capabilities of current technology, and outlines possible future developments the field.

1 Introduction

The use of images in human communication is hardly new. Our cave-dwelling ancestors painted pictures on the walls of their caves, and the use of maps and building plans to convey information almost certainly dates back to pre-Roman times. But the twentieth century has witnessed unparalleled growth in the number, availability and importance of images in all walks of life. Images now play a crucial role in fields as diverse as medicine, journalism, advertising, design, education and entertainment. Users are increasingly discovering that the process of locating a desired image in a large and varied collection can be a source of considerable frustration. Traditional methods of image indexing based on classification schemes or keywords have severe limitations [18]. This has led to the development of automatic techniques for retrieving images on the basis of features extracted from those images themselves – a technology now generally referred to as *Content-Based Image Retrieval* (CBIR). CBIR is an exciting field for research, but as yet has delivered few operational systems capable of meeting real user needs.

1.1 User Needs

Many different groups of users make use of images in a professional capacity. The police use visual information such as photographs to identify individuals and to record scenes of crimes. The use of fingerprints and shoeprints to identify criminals is widespread. In medicine, visual information in the form of X-rays, ultrasound or other types of imaging is routinely used in diagnosis and in monitoring patients' progress. Fashion and graphic designers gain inspiration from images of previous designs, and use sketches and 3-D models to present ideas to clients and colleagues. Photographs and pictures are used extensively in

M. Agosti, F. Crestani, and G. Pasi (Eds.): ESSIR 2000, LNCS 1980, pp. 111–138, 2000.
© Springer-Verlag Berlin Heidelberg 2000

the publishing world, to illustrate books and magazine articles. Most newspaper publishers maintain their own libraries of photographs, supplementing these where necessary with those from outside sources such as stock photo agencies. Computer-generated images are extensively used in architectural and engineering design, both to specify requirements to those building or manufacturing the design, and to illustrate the end-product to potential customers. Many manufacturing firms maintain design archives of standard components for reuse. And historians from a variety of disciplines use images extensively in their research. Nearly all these professions require access to images from archives at some point, often (though not always) by content rather than just by identifier.

Before discussing techniques for image retrieval, it is first necessary to understand the types of query such users might to put to an image database. Several researchers have addressed this question, though no clear consensus on user needs has yet emerged. For example, Markkula and Sormumen [57] found that journalist requests fell into four categories: concrete objects (i.e. named persons, buildings or places), themes or abstractions interpretable from the photographs, background information on the image (such as documentary information, specific news events and films and television programmes), and known photographs. Enser and McGregor [19] categorised queries put to a large picture archive into those which could be satisfied by a picture of a unique person, object or event (e.g. Kenilworth Castle) and those which could not (e.g. classroom scenes). Both categories were subject to refinement in terms of time, location, or action. Hastings [31], investigating how art historians searched photographic and digital art images, found the major classes of queries to be identification, subject, text, style, artist, category, and colour. Keister [41], reviewing queries put to an automated still picture retrieval system at the National Library of Medicine (NLM), found wide variations in the way users asked for pictures. Users who were picture professionals thought visually and used art and/or graphics jargon. Health professionals asked for images relating to specific diseases or treatments. The museum or academic community often had precise citations to the images it desired. Words describing concrete image elements appeared to make up a significant proportion of requests.

Most of the above writers attempt to categorise the uses being made of particular collections by analysing the queries put to the collections, either in the form of written statements by the end users or interpretations put on verbal enquiries by search intermediaries. This seeming emphasis on the expressed need tells us little about what the actual need is for the images, or what use will be made of retrieved images. Users' expressed needs are likely to be heavily biased by their expectations of the kinds of query the system can actually handle. Despite attempts to develop a more general framework for understanding image searching and use (e.g. [41]), we still know too little about the information needs of different types of image user to draw any firm conclusions for retrieval system design.

1.2 Characteristics of Image Queries

As indicated above, insufficient evidence is yet available to categorize in any depth the types of query users might to put to an image database. In the meantime, it has been found useful to classify image queries into three levels of increasing complexity [14]:

Level 1 comprises retrieval by *primitive* features such as colour, texture, shape or the spatial location of image elements. Examples of such queries might include "find pictures with long thin dark objects in the top left-hand corner," "find images containing yellow stars arranged in a ring" – or most commonly "find me more pictures that look like this." This level of retrieval uses features (such as a given shade of yellow) which are both objective, and directly derivable from the images themselves, without the need to refer to any external knowledge base. Its use is largely limited to specialist applications such as trademark registration, identification of drawings in a design archive, or colour matching of fashion accessories.

Level 2 comprises retrieval by *derived* (sometimes known as *logical*) features, involving some degree of logical inference about the identity of the objects depicted in the image. It can usefully be divided further into:

(a) retrieval of objects of a given type (e.g. "find pictures of a double-decker bus");

(b) retrieval of individual objects or persons ("find a picture of the Eiffel tower").

To answer queries at this level, reference to some outside store of knowledge is normally required – particularly for the more specific queries at level 2(b). In the first example above, some prior understanding is necessary to identify an object as a bus rather than a lorry; in the second example, one needs the knowledge that a given individual structure has been given the name "the Eiffel tower." Search criteria at this level, particularly at level 2(b), are usually still reasonably objective. This level of query is more generally encountered than level 1 – for example, most queries received by newspaper picture libraries appear to fall into this overall category [18].

Level 3 comprises retrieval by *abstract* attributes, involving a significant amount of high-level reasoning about the meaning and purpose of the objects or scenes depicted. Again, this level of retrieval can usefully be subdivided into:

(1) retrieval of named events or types of activity (e.g. "find pictures of Scottish folk dancing");

(2) retrieval of pictures with emotional or religious significance ("find a picture depicting suffering").

Success in answering queries at this level can require some sophistication on the part of the searcher. Complex reasoning, and often subjective judgement, can be required to make the link between image content and the abstract concepts it is required to illustrate. Queries at this level, though perhaps less common than level 2, are often encountered in both newspaper and art libraries.

As we shall see later, this classification of query types can be useful in illustrating the strengths and limitations of different image retrieval techniques. The most significant gap at present lies between levels 1 and 2. Many authors (e.g. [27]) refer to levels 2 and 3 together as *semantic* image retrieval, and hence the gap between levels 1 and 2 as the *semantic gap*.

2   Traditional Methods of Image Data Management

2.1   Classification and Indexing Techniques

The need for efficient storage and retrieval of images has been recognised by managers of large image collections such as picture libraries and design archives for many years. While it is perfectly feasible to identify a desired image from a small collection simply by browsing, more effective techniques are needed with collections containing thousands of items. The normal technique used is to assign descriptive metadata in the form of keywords, subject headings or classification codes to each image when it is first added to the collection, and to use these descriptors as retrieval keys at search time.

Many picture libraries use keywords as their main form of retrieval–often using indexing schemes developed in-house, which reflect the special nature of their collections. A good example of this is the system developed by Getty Images to index their collection of contemporary stock photographs [4]. Their thesaurus comprises just over 10,000 keywords, divided into nine semantic groups, including *geography*, *people*, *activities* and *concepts*.

Probably the best-known indexing scheme in the public domain is the Art and Architecture Thesaurus (AAT), originating at Rensselaer Polytechnic Institute in the early 1980s, and now used in art libraries across the world. AAT consists of nearly 120,000 terms for describing objects, textural materials, images, architecture and other cultural heritage material. The terms are arranged into hierarchies covering concepts such as physical attributes, styles and periods, and materials. Another popular source for providing subject access to visual material is the Library of Congress Thesaurus for Graphic Materials (LCTGM). See Greenberg [26] for a comparison between AAT and LCTGM.

A number of indexing schemes use classification codes rather than keywords or subject descriptors to describe image content, as these can give a greater degree of language independence and show concept hierarchies more clearly. Examples of this genre include ICONCLASS from the University of Leiden [25], and TELCLASS from the BBC [20]. Like AAT, ICONCLASS was designed for the classification of works of art, and to some extent duplicates its function; TELCLASS was designed with TV and video programmes in mind, and is hence rather more general in its outlook.

A number of less widely-known schemes have been devised to classify images and drawings for specialist purposes. Examples include the Vienna classification for trademark images [91], used by registries worldwide to identify potentially conflicting trademark applications, and the Opitz coding system for machined parts [64], used to identify families of similar parts which can be manufactured together.

2.2 Effectiveness of Manual Techniques

Current image indexing techniques have many strengths. Keyword indexing has high expressive power – it can be used to describe almost any aspect of image content. It is in principle easily extensible to accommodate new concepts, and can be used to describe image content at varying degrees of complexity. There is a wide range of available text retrieval software to automate the actual process of searching. But the process of manual indexing, whether by keywords or classification codes, suffers from two significant drawbacks.

Firstly, it is inherently very labour-intensive. Indexing times quoted in the literature for still images range from about 7 to 40 minutes per image [17]. Secondly, it does not appear to be particularly reliable as a means of subject retrieval of images. Markey [56] found that, in a review of inter-indexer consistency, there were wide disparities in the keywords that different individuals assigned to the same picture. Enser and McGregor [19] found a poor match between the wording of user queries and one of the indexing languages in place in the Hulton Deutsch Collection, even though it had been specially designed for the collection. There is little or no firm evidence at present that text-based techniques for image retrieval are adequate for the task in hand.

3 Content-Based Image Retrieval (CBIR)

3.1 Introduction

The limitations of the text-based approach described above have led to an upsurge of interest in CBIR, now an extremely active area for research and development. Most CBIR techniques are based on principles which are markedly different from those used in text retrieval. Features considered to capture essential aspects of image content are extracted automatically from all images in the collection. All subsequent retrieval is based on these features. More formally, feature matching involves calculating and storing a *feature vector* characterising selected aspects of the appearance of each image in the database, and then calculating the similarity between the feature vector computed from the query with that of each image in the database, using some measure such as Euclidean distance $L2 = ||\mathbf{v_i} - \mathbf{v_j}||$, where $\mathbf{v_i}$ and $\mathbf{v_j}$ represent the feature vectors of images i and j.

The commonest features used are mathematical measures of image appearance, such as colour, texture or shape; hence virtually all current CBIR systems, whether commercial or experimental, operate at level 1. A typical CBIR system allows users to formulate queries by submitting an example of the type of image being sought, though some offer alternatives such as selection of a desired colour from a palette, or input of a rough sketch of a desired shape. The system then identifies those stored images whose feature values match those of the query most closely, and displays thumbnails of these images on the screen. Some of the more commonly used techniques used for image retrieval are described below.

3.2   Retrieval by Colour

The ability to retrieve images on the basis of colour similarity is intuitively quite appealing, so it is no surprise that considerable effort has been devoted to research in this area. Colour queries can be formulated either by choosing from a palette of possible colour combinations, or by submitting an example image which is then colour matched with those in the database. Most techniques for colour retrieval are variations on the same basic idea. Each image added to the collection is analysed to compute a *colour histogram* which shows the proportion of pixels of each colour within the image. The colour histogram for each image is then stored in the database. At search time, the user can either specify the desired proportion of each colour (75% olive green and 25% red, for example), or submit an example image from which a colour histogram is calculated. Either way, the matching process then retrieves those images whose colour histograms match those of the query most closely.

The matching technique most commonly used, histogram intersection, was first developed by Swain and Ballard [83]. Variants of this technique are now used in a high proportion of current CBIR systems (see Section 5 below). Formally, a colour histogram $H(I)$ of an image I is a vector $(h_1, h_2, \ldots, h_j, \ldots, h_n)$, where each element represents the count of pixels falling within partition j of some suitable colour space, such as RGB or HSV. The similarity of two histograms A and B is then given by their intersection, defined as:

$$\sum_{j=1}^{n} \min(A_j, B_j)$$

Swain and Ballard used relatively fine histograms, partitioning the three axes rg, by and wb of opponent colour space into 16, 8 and 8 bins respectively – a total of 2048. Later workers have tended to use somewhat coarser histograms, with apparently satisfactory results. Methods of improving on Swain and Ballard's original technique include the use of cumulative colour histograms $(g_1, g_2, \ldots, g_j, \ldots, g_n)$, where

$$g_j = \sum_{i=1}^{j} h_i$$

and colour moments

$$E_n = \frac{1}{M} \sum_{m=1}^{M} p_{mn},$$

$$\sigma_n = \sqrt{\frac{1}{M} \sum_{m=1}^{M} (p_{mn} - E_n)^2} \quad \text{and}$$

$$s_n = \sqrt[3]{\frac{1}{M} \sum_{m=1}^{M} (p_{mn} - E_n)^3}$$

and representing the distribution of image pixels within each colour channel n [82]. Experiments suggested that colour moments based on HSV colour space could give particularly good results.

Colour matching of images can be applied either at the whole image or region level. A good example of the latter approach is that of Stricker and Dimai [81], who divide each image into five fuzzy regions and then compare colour moments from each of these regions. Other researchers base colour matching on automatically-segmented image regions, including Smith and Chang [77], who use *colour sets* (essentially colour histograms containing binary values) to provide rapid colour indexing of individual image regions. Corridoni et al [10] go further, using theories of human colour perception to formulate a query language which allows users to search on subjective attributes such as colour warmth or contrast as well as objective colour combinations.

3.3 Retrieval by Texture

The ability to retrieve images on the basis of texture similarity may not seem very useful. But the ability to match on texture similarity can often be useful in distinguishing between areas of images with similar colour (such as sky and sea, or leaves and grass). Techniques developed for texture retrieval have often proved useful in matching more general aspects of an image's appearance. Texture queries can be formulated in a similar manner to colour queries, either by selecting examples of desired textures from a palette, or by supplying an example query image. A variety of techniques has been used for measuring texture similarity; the best-established rely on comparing values of second-order statistics calculated from query and stored images. Essentially, these calculate the relative brightness of selected *pairs* of pixels from each image. From these it is possible to calculate measures of image texture which can be used to compare image similarity. Well-established measures include the set defined by Tamura et al [85], which includes:

$$\text{coarseness} \quad \frac{1}{mn} \sum_{i=1}^{m} \sum_{j=1}^{n} S_{\max}(i, j)$$

where m and n define image size, and S_{max} the neighbourhood size giving greatest separation of average intensity either side of any given pixel,

$$\text{directionality} \quad 1 - rn_p \sum_{p=1}^{n_p} \sum_{\phi \in w_p} (\phi - \phi_p)^2 H_D(\phi)$$

where n_p is the number of peaks and ϕ_p the direction of the pth peak in the density gradient histogram H_D, and

$$\text{contrast} \quad \sum_n n^2 \left(\sum_i \sum_j p(i,j) : |i-j| = n \right)$$

where $p(i,j)$ is the (i,j)th entry of the $n \times n$ spatial dependence matrix defined by HA number of measures are derived from pixel intensity transformations. One of the most effective methods of texture analysis for retrieval is the use coefficients derived from image transformations using Gabor filters [54].

$$G(x,y) = \left(\frac{1}{2\pi\sigma_x\sigma_y} \right) e^{\left(2\pi i W x - \frac{1}{2}\left(\frac{x^2}{\sigma_x^2} + \frac{y^2}{\sigma_y^2} \right) \right)}$$

A bank of Gabor filters can be generated by scaling and rotating this function to different degrees, effectively yielding a set of orientation and scale-dependent edge and line detectors. The mean and standard deviations of filter outputs have been shown to give good discrimination between different kinds of texture in an image. A recent extension of this technique is the texture thesaurus developed by Ma and Manjunath [53], which retrieves textured regions in images on the basis of similarity to automatically-derived codewords representing important classes of texture within the collection.

Another popular approach to texture analysis and classification is the use of the wavelet transformation (see Section 3.5 below), which has been used successfully to characterize image texture (e.g. [76]). Yet another approach is the use of the Wold decomposition [51], which has been applied to identify features characterized as *periodicity*, *directionality* and *randomness*, for use in matching images by texture similarity.

3.4   Retrieval by Shape

The ability to retrieve by shape is perhaps the most obvious requirement at the primitive level. Unlike texture, shape is a fairly well-defined concept – and there is considerable evidence that natural objects are primarily recognized by their shape [3]. As well as the ability to match human similarity judgements, the ideal shape matching technique needs to fulfil several other criteria, such as robustness to noise or small deformations in an image, and (for most applications) invariance to translation, rotation and scaling.

A wide variety of techniques meeting at least some of these criteria has been described in the literature. One important class of methods is based on direct matching of complete (information-preserving) representations of object shape, such as chain-codes or splines. Such methods can have high discriminating power, at least when matching highly similar shapes, but are often computationally very expensive. A second class of methods is based on the extraction and comparison of features such as edge direction histograms or moment invariants, which may capture important aspects of an object's appearance, but which cannot be used to reconstitute its entire shape. These methods often have lower discriminating power, but tend to scale up better to large image collections. Techniques which involve direct matching of information-preserving representations of shape boundaries include:

- **String-matching of chains of boundary pixels.** Cortelazzo et al [11] suggest a number of ways of measuring the distance between two shape boundaries represented as pixel chains, based on summation of substring differences or string rewriting rules. All can be rendered invariant to translation, rotation, scaling, and choice of starting point for string matching – though this is not a trivial problem.
- **Measurement of turning angle.** For any given shape, it is possible to represent its boundary by the turning function $\Theta(s)$, measuring the angle of the tangent to the boundary as a function of s, the normalized distance along the boundary from a given reference point. The difference in shape between two objects a and b can thus be computed [1] as

$$\int_0^1 |\Theta_a(s) - \Theta_b(s)| \mathrm{d}s$$

  Such measures are inherently invariant to translation or scaling, and can be rendered invariant to rotation given an appropriate choice of starting point.
- **Elastic deformation of templates.** A potentially powerful, though computationally expensive technique for matching unknown and query shapes is to deform the boundary of the query shape until it matches a given stored shape, and then to measure some function Φ which gives an indication of the cost of the deformation process. A good example of this technique is that of Jain et al [38], who apply displacement functions to the query template in order to compute its goodness of fit with a given image region.

Matching using non-information-preserving features involves calculating and matching a shape feature vector as outlined in Section 3.1 above. Commonly used types of feature include:

- **Simple global features.** Several computationally simple measures of a region's overall shape have been proposed over the years [47]. These include aspect ratio (L/W), circularity $(4\pi A/P^2)$, and transparency (A/H), used in the ARTISAN trademark image retrieval system [16].
- **Local features.** Features representing shape characteristics of small regions of an image can often act as a useful complement to global measures. Examples include the line-angle line triplet features devised by Eakins [13], and the longer segment sequences used by Mehrotra and Gary [58].

- **Edge direction histograms.** Another indirect measure of shape within an image is to compute a histogram of edge directions. This can give an indication of directionality within the image, though not necessarily the shape of any object it depicts. Jain and Vailaya's [39] technique identifies edge pixels, computes edge directions, and then accumulates these into bins at $5°$ intervals.
- **Fourier descriptors.** A very popular way of representing a region's overall shape is to represent the cumulative curvature around the boundary as a function of curve length, and expand this function as a Fourier series [92]:

$$\theta(t) = \mu_0 + A_k \cos(kt - a_k)$$

The coefficients A_k and a_k, the kth harmonic amplitude and phase angle respectively, known as the *Fourier descriptors* of the curve, provide a description of the curve which appears to reflect its overall shape fairly consistently.
- **Moment invariants.** For any digital image $I(x, y)$, it is possible to compute a series of central moments μ_{pq}, defined as:

$$\mu_{pq} = \sum_x \sum_y (x - \bar{x})^p (y - \bar{y})^q I(x, y)$$

from which a series of *moment invariants* ϕ_n can be derived which characterize shape in a manner which is invariant to scaling, rotation and translation [33]. Moment invariants have been widely used in image analysis for many years.
- **Zernike moments.** The Zernike moment of order n with repetition m for image $I(r, \theta)$ is defined as:

$$A_{nm} = \frac{n+1}{\pi} \sum_\rho \sum_\theta (R_{nm}(r)e^{im\theta})^* I(r, \theta)|r < 1$$

where $R_{nm}(r)$ are the set of radial polynomials originally defined by Zernike [86]. Zernike moments have the useful property of orthogonality; their use in trademark image retrieval has been investigated by Kim and Kim [42].

Shape matching of three-dimensional objects is a more challenging task – particularly where only a single 2-D view of the object in question is available. While no general solution to this problem is possible, some useful inroads have been made into the problem of identifying at least some instances of a given object from different viewpoints. One approach has been to build up a set of plausible 3-D models from the available 2-D image, and match them with other models in the database [9]. Another is to generate a series of alternative 2-D views of each database object, each of which is matched with the query image [12]. Direct matching of 3-D shapes defined as VRML (virtual reality markup language) primitives has also been attempted [65].

3.5   Retrieval by Other Types of Primitive Features

One of the oldest-established means of accessing pictorial data is retrieval by its position within an image. Accessing data by spatial location is an essential aspect of geographical information systems, and efficient methods to achieve this have been around for many years. Similar techniques have been applied to image collections, allowing users to search for images containing objects in defined spatial relationships with each other. Spatial indexing appears particularly effective in combination with other cues such as colour [77] or shape [32].

One well-established technique for rapid matching of images on the basis of similarity of spatial layout is 2-D iconic indexing, introduced by Chang et al [8] This generates a string representation of the partial ordering of objects within an image along both $x-$ and $y-$ axes, which can readily be used as the basis for similarity matching. Its lack of rotational invariance can be a problem in some contexts. An alternative method described by Gudivada and Raghavan [28] relies on computing edge graphs between the centroids of every significant object in the image. Query and stored images can then be matched by comparing the relative orientation of corresponding edges. Unlike Chang's method, the technique is insensitive to rotation – though it does require all image objects to be labelled before matching can begin.

Several other types of image feature have been proposed as a basis for CBIR. Most of these rely on complex transformations of pixel intensities which have no obvious counterpart in any human description of an image. Most such techniques aim to extract features which reflect some aspect of image similarity which a human subject can perceive, even if he or she finds it difficult to describe. The most well-researched technique of this kind uses the wavelet transform, which can be used to express any function as the sum of a set of orthonormal basis functions:

$$f(c) = c_{00}\phi(x) + \sum_{m}\sum_{n} d_{mn}\phi_{mn}(x)$$

where ϕ_{mn}, the wavelet function, is defined as:

$$\phi_{mn}(x) = 2^{-m/2}\phi(2^{-m}x - n)$$

and ϕ is a scaling function. Statistics such as the mean and variance of the wavelet coefficients d_{mn} can model a number of aspects of image appearance, including shape and texture, at different resolutions. Promising retrieval results have been reported by matching wavelet features computed from query and stored images (e.g. [36, 80]). Another method giving interesting results is *retrieval by appearance*. Two versions of this method have been developed, one for whole-image matching and one for matching selected parts of an image. The part-image technique involves filtering the image with Gaussian derivatives at multiple scales [67], and then computing differential invariants; the whole-image technique uses distributions of local curvature and phase [68].

The advantage of all these techniques is that they can describe an image at varying levels of detail (useful in natural scenes where the objects of interest may appear in a variety of guises), and avoid the need to segment the image into regions of interest before shape descriptors can be computed. Despite recent advances in techniques for image segmentation (e.g. [75]) this remains a troublesome problem.

4   Retrieval by Semantic Feature

Retrieval of images containing a specified object, scene or event is a much more formidable task than retrieval by similarity of appearance. Despite views expressed in some quarters that by image retrieval by semantic content is simply not feasible (see, for example, [72]), research in this area is beginning to gather momentum. Several different lines of investigation can be distinguished:

4.1   Automatic Whole-Image Scene Classification

Automatic classification of scenes (into general types such as *indoors*, *city street* or *beach*) can be useful, both because this is an important filter which can be used when searching, and because this can help in identifying specific objects present. Techniques of this kind permit automatic assignment of keywords such as *beach*, *mountain* or *city scene* to appropriate images. The most popular approach has been to use some combination of primitive features to train a classifier to distinguish between different kinds of scene – such as city *vs* landscape or mountain *vs* beach. For example, Szummer and Picard [84] used a combination of colour histograms and texture measures to train a nearest-neighbour classifier to distinguish between indoor and outdoor scenes with 90% accuracy. Oliva et al [63] used shape characteristics of whole-image power spectra sampled with Gabor filters to classify scenes by placing them on appropriate points on two semantic axes: artificial *vs* natural, and open *vs* closed. Vailaya et al [87] have developed a Bayesian classifier to group images into a number of semantically meaningful categories, including city *vs* landscape and forest *vs* mountain, using codebook vectors generated by vector quantization from feature vectors based on colour moments and Gabor coefficients. Reported accuracy was better than 90% for most classification tasks.

4.2   Automatic Object Classification Based on Detailed Object Models

The ability to identify a given type of object in a scene is clearly important for semantic image retrieval, both as an end in itself, and as an intermediate step in the interpretation of more complex scenes. One potentially powerful technique for object recognition in an image is to specify a model for each type of object of interest, and then examine the image for regions conforming to that model. An early system embodying these principles was ACRONYM [5], which used generalized shape modelling to identify and locate instances of desired objects in aerial photographs. After an initial edge detection step, a set of production rules was used to infer the presence of specified types of aircraft from the patterns of lines derived from the image. The more-recently developed PICTION system [79] identifies human faces in natural scenes by matching candidate face shapes generated by multi-resolution edge detection techniques with a simple three-contour model of hairline and left and right face contours.

Forsyth et al [24] have described a highly sophisticated approach based on developing a model of each class of object to be recognized, and then building up evidence for or against the presence of objects conforming to the model. Evidence includes low-level features of the candidate region itself, and contextual information such as its position and the type of background in the image. Object classification is a three-stage process: (a) segmenting images into coherent regions using a combination of edge, colour and texture information, (b) fusing colour, texture and shape information to identify possible descriptions of each region (for example, as a human arm), and (c) classifying objects from their constituents in terms of component descriptions. The method has been applied with some success to the identification of a range of object types, including unclothed human bodies, horses and trees, though retrieval effectiveness scores are fairly modest at present (15% recall at 66% precision with the horse finder, for example).

4.3   Automatic Object Classification Using Statistical Approaches

A conceptually simpler approach to image interpretation, which does not require the construction of any high-level object model, is the use of statistical techniques (often very similar to those used in scene classification) to assign appropriate semantic labels to individual regions within an image. An example of this is the method of Campbell et al [7], who use a combination of colour and texture features to train an radial basis function network to distinguish between 11 different types of region in a scene, including sky, vegetation, road, and building. They report over 80% classification accuracy for the method. Leung and Malik [46] have developed a method for identifying material within textured regions of an image (such as leather, cork, plaster, etc) using microstructures known as *3-D textons* derived from primitive texture measures.

Schiele and Crowley [74] propose a method using statistically-generated *visual classes* for object recognition. This aims to get round the problem of variability in appearance of objects such as chairs by defining more specific *visual classes*, each of which is sufficiently homogeneous to be identified purely by visual appearance. Buijs and Lew [6] have developed a method for recognising objects (such as oranges) or types of material (such as sand) in an image by inducing 'simple semantics' from primitive image features. They do this by identifying both positive and negative example images, identifying a subset of primitive features with high discriminating power, and using these to train a minimum distance classifier.

4.4   Methods for Learning and Propagating Labels Assigned by Human Users

The problems of achieving effective semantic image retrieval by purely automatic means have led many researchers to investigate methods which are capable of continuous learning through run-time interaction with end-users. Most of these are based on extensions of the principle of *relevance feedback* (see Section 6.1 below). One of the earliest systems to provide this kind of interaction was FourEyes [59], permitting a user to assign semantic labels such as *grass* or *sky* to selected image regions. Once a sufficient number of regions has been labelled, the system attempts to induce grouping rules from the positive and negative examples at its disposal. These rules can then be used to assign labels to new examples sharing the same range of feature values. Effectively, then the system can learn what areas of grass and sky look like, and can then search for images containing such areas.

Lee et al [45] also use relevance feedback to capture semantic information about an image collection. This incorporates a second feedback loop so that users' input is remembered permanently, and used to store semantic links between images as well as similarity of appearance. Initially, images are clustered purely on the basis of primitive feature similarity. Users who search the system are asked to indicate which retrieved images are relevant and which irrelevant. This information is then used to split and merge clusters of similar images, gradually introducing an element of semantic similarity in the process.

Jaimes and Chang's [37] Visual Apprentice aims to provide users with a general framework for building up visual classes which can represent specified types of object or scene. Users can define a visual class by specifying labels for objects and their key constituent parts, together with a set of training examples in which image regions are labelled according to the class definition. The system then uses a combination of lazy learning, decision trees and genetic algorithms to build up a hierarchical object definition in which image regions generated by primitive-level segmentation routines are grouped progressively into *perceptual areas* (groups of regions likely to be perceived as a whole), object parts, whole objects and scenes.

5   Current CBIR Applications and Systems

5.1   Commercial Systems

Despite the shortcomings of current CBIR technology, several image retrieval systems are now available as commercial packages, with demonstration versions of many others available on the Web. The most well-known commercial systems are:

QBIC. IBM's Query By Image Content system [23] is probably the best-known of all image content retrieval systems. It is available commercially either in standalone form, or as part of other IBM products such as the DB2 Digital

Library. It offers retrieval by any combination of colour, texture or shape – as well as by text keyword. Image queries can be formulated by selection from a palette, specifying an example query image, or sketching a desired shape on the screen. The system extracts and stores colour, shape and texture features from each image added to the database, and uses R*-tree indexes to improve search efficiency [21]. At search time, the system matches appropriate features from query and stored images, calculates a similarity score between the query and each stored image examined, and displays the most similar images on the screen as thumbnails. The latest version of the system incorporates more efficient indexing techniques, an improved user interface, and the ability to search grey-level images [61]. An online demonstration, together with information on how to download an evaluation copy of the software, is available on the World-Wide Web at `http://wwwqbic.almaden.ibm.com/`.

Virage. Another well-known commercial system is the VIR Image Engine from Virage, Inc [29]. This is available as a series of independent modules, which systems developers can build in to their own programs. This makes it easy to extend the system by building in new types of query interface, or additional customized modules to process specialized collections of images such as trademarks. Alternatively, the system is available as an add-on to existing database management systems such as Oracle or Informix. An on-line demonstration of the VIR Image Engine can be found at `http://www.virage.com/online/`. A high-profile application of Virage technology is AltaVista's AV Photo Finder (`http://image.altavista.com/cgi-bin/avncgi`), allowing Web surfers to search for images by content similarity.

Excalibur. A similar philosophy has been adopted by Excalibur Technologies, a company with a long history of successful database applications, for their Visual RetrievalWare product [22]. This product offers a variety of image indexing and matching techniques based on the company's own proprietary pattern recognition technology. It is marketed principally as an applications development tool rather then as a standalone retrieval package. Its best-known application is probably the Yahoo! Image Surfer, allowing content-based retrieval of images from the World-wide Web. Further information on Visual RetrievalWare can be found at `http://www.excalib.com/`, and a demonstration of the Yahoo! Image Surfer at `http://isurf.yahoo.com/`.

5.2   Experimental Systems

Prominent experimental CBIR systems, most of which are available as demonstration versions on the Web, include:

Photobook. The Photobook system [66] from Massachusetts Institute of Technology (MIT) has proved to be one of the most influential of the early CBIR systems. Like the commercial systems above, aims to characterize images for retrieval by computing shape, texture and other appropriate features. Unlike these systems, however, it aims to calculate *information-preserving* features, from which all essential aspects of the original image can in theory be reconstructed. This allows features relevant to a particular type of search to be computed at search time, giving greater flexibility at the expense of speed. The system has been successfully used in a number of different application areas, involving retrieval of image textures, shapes, and human faces, each using features based on a different model of the image. Further information on the Photobook system, together with an online demonstration, can be found at `http://www-white.media.mit.edu/vismod/demos/photobook/`.

Chabot. Another early system which has received wide publicity is Chabot [62], which provided a combination of text-based and colour-based access to a collection of digitized photographs held by California's Department of Water Resources. The system has now been renamed Cypress, and incorporated within the Berkeley Digital Library project at the University of California at Berkeley (UCB). A demonstration of the current version of Cypress (which no longer appears to have CBIR capabilities) can be found at `http://elib.cs.berkeley.edu/cypress.html`. Rather more impressive is UCB's recently-developed Blobworld software, incorporating sophisticated colour region searching facilities
(`http://elib.cs.berkeley.edu/photos/blobworld/`).

VisualSEEk. The VisualSEEk system [77] is the first of a whole family of experimental systems developed at Columbia University, New York. It offers searching by image region colour, shape and spatial location, as well as by keyword. Users can build up image queries by specifying areas of defined shape and colour at absolute or relative locations within the image. The WebSEEk system [78] aims to facilitate image searching on the Web. Web images are identified and indexed by an autonomous agent, which assigns them to an appropriate subject category according to associated text. Colour histograms are also computed from each image. At search time, users select categories of interest; the system then displays images from this category, which users can then search by colour similarity. Relevance feedback facilities are also provided for search refinement. For a demonstration of WebSEEk in action, see `http://disney.ctr.columbia.edu/WebSEEk/`

MARS. The Multimedia Analysis and Retrieval Ssystem project at the University of Illinois [34] is aimed at developing image retrieval systems which put the user firmly in the driving seat. Relevance feedback is thus an integral part of the system, as this is felt to be the only way at present of capturing individual human similarity judgements. The system characterizes each object within an image by a variety of features, and uses a range of different similarity measures to compare query and stored objects. User feedback is then used to adjust feature weights, and if necessary to invoke different similarity measures [71]. A demonstration of the MARS system can be viewed at `http://jadzia.ifp.uiuc.edu:8001/`

Surfimage. An example of European CBIR technology is the Surfimage system from INRIA, France [60]. This has a similar philosophy to the MARS system, using multiple types of image feature which can be combined in different ways, and offering sophisticated relevance feedback facilities. See

http://www-syntim.inria.fr/htbin/syntim/surfimage/surfimage.cgi
for a demonstration of Surfimage in action.

Netra. The Netra system uses colour texture, shape and spatial location information to provide region-based searching based on local image properties [52].
An interesting feature is its use of sophisticated image segmentation techniques. A Web demonstration of Netra is available at
http://vivaldi.ece.ucsb.edu/Netra.

Synapse. This system is an implementation of *retrieval by appearance* (see
above) using whole image matching [68]. A demonstration of Synapse in
action with a variety of different image types can be found at
http://cowarie.cs.umass.edu/~demo/.

6   General Issues

6.1   Interfacing and Search Efficiency

The ability for users to express their search needs accurately and easily is crucial
in any retrieval system. Image retrieval is no exception to this, though it is by
no means obvious how this can be achieved in practice. The use of SQL-like
query languages was advocated in some early systems, though keyboard input
hardly seems an obvious choice for formulating visual queries. The most appealing paradigm in many ways is query-by-example: providing a sample of the kind
of output desired and asking the system to retrieve further examples of the same
kind. Virtually all current CBIR systems now offer query-by-example searching, where users submit a query image and the system retrieves and displays
thumbnails of (say) the 20 closest-matching images in the database.

However, users will not always have an example image to hand. Several alternative query formulation methods have been proposed here, most based on
ideas originally developed for IBM's QBIC system [23]. The original QBIC interface allowed users to specify colour queries either by sliders varying the relative
amounts of red, green and blue in the query, or by selecting a desired colour from
a palette. Texture queries could also be specified by choosing from a palette, and
shape queries by sketching the desired object on the screen [44]. These methods
proved adequate but often cumbersome, and later versions of the QBIC system
have adopted a set of rather more intuitive *pickers* for query specification [61].
Some systems provide users with the ability to build up query shapes on the
screen from primitives such as rectangles and circles (e.g. [78]).

The ability to refine searches online in response to user indications of relevance, known as *relevance feedback*, is particularly useful in image retrieval. This
is firstly because users can normally judge the relevance of a set of images displayed on the screen within seconds, and secondly because so few current systems
are capable of matching users' needs accurately first time round. The usefulness
of relevance feedback for image retrieval has been demonstrated in several CBIR
systems (e.g. Smith and Chang [78], Rui et al [70]). However, there is still considerable scope for more research into improved interfaces for image retrieval

systems, in particular the development of better methods for users to convey individual notions of image similarity [72].

A continuing challenge facing current CBIR technology is that of efficiently retrieving the set of stored images most similar to a given query. Finding index structures which allow efficient searching of an image database is still an unsolved problem [21]. None of the index structures proposed for text retrieval has proved applicable to the problem, since CBIR techniques are based on a fundamentally different model of data. The most promising approach so far has been multidimensional indexing, using structures such as the R*-tree [2], the TV-tree [50] and the SS+-tree [43], though the overheads of using these complex index structures are considerable. Alternative approaches, which appear to avoid these problems include similarity clustering of images [40], and the use of *vantage objects* [89].

6.2   CBIR Effectiveness

Hard information on the effectiveness of automatic CBIR techniques is difficult to come by. Few of the early systems developers made serious attempts to evaluate their retrieval effectiveness, simply providing examples of retrieval output to demonstrate system capabilities. The QBIC team were among the first to take the question of retrieval effectiveness seriously [21], though even they glossed over some of the problems of determining whether a given image did in fact answer a given query. System developers do now generally report effectiveness measures such as precision and recall with a test database, though few discuss subjective measures of user satisfaction. In the absence of comparative retrieval effectiveness scores measuring the effectiveness of two different systems on the same set of data and queries, it is difficult to draw many firm conclusions. All that can be said is that retrieval effectiveness scores reported on image retrieval systems (e.g. Manmatha and Ravela [55], Eakins et al [15]) are in the same ball park as those commonly reported for text retrieval.

However, the main drawback of current CBIR systems is more fundamental. It is that the only retrieval cues they can exploit are primitive features such as colour, texture and shape. Hence current CBIR systems are likely to be of significant use only for applications at level 1. This restricts their prime usefulness to specialist application areas such as fingerprint matching, trademark retrieval or fabric selection. IBM's QBIC system has been applied to a variety of tasks, but seems to have been most successful in specialist areas such as colour matching of items in electronic mail-order catalogues, and classification of geological samples on the basis of texture. Similarly, the main commercial application of MIT's Photobook technology has been in the specialist area of face recognition.

Within specialist level 1 applications, CBIR technology does appear to be capable of delivering useful results, though it should be borne in mind that some types of feature have proved much more effective than others. It is generally accepted that colour and texture retrieval yield better results (in that machine judgements of similarity tally well with those of human observers) than shape matching [21]. Part of the problem with shape matching lies in the difficulty of automatically distinguishing between foreground shapes and background detail in a natural image [23]. Even when faced with stylized images, or scenes where human intervention has been used to distinguish foreground from background, though, shape retrieval systems often perform poorly. A major contributing factor here is almost certainly the fact that few, if any, of the shape feature measures in current use are accurate predictors of human judgements of shape similarity [73].

Although current CBIR systems use only primitive features for image matching, this does not limit their scope exclusively to level 1 queries. With a little ingenuity on the part of the searcher, they can be used to retrieve images of desired objects or scenes in many cases. A query for beach scenes, for example, can be formulated by specifying images with blue at the top and yellow underneath; a query for images of fish by sketching a typical fish on the screen. Images of specific objects such as the Eiffel Tower can be retrieved by submitting an accurate scale drawing, provided the angle of view is not too different. A skilled search intermediary could thus handle some level 2 queries with current technology, though it is not yet clear how large a range of queries can be successfully handled in this way.

Overall, current CBIR techniques may well have a part to play in specialist colour or shape-matching applications. It is also possible that they could be of use in enhancing the effectiveness of general-purpose text-based image retrieval systems. But major advances in technology will be needed before systems capable of automatic semantic feature recognition and indexing become available. Hence the chances of CBIR *superseding* manual indexing in the near future for general applications handling semantic (level 2 or 3) queries look remote. As discussed above, research into semantic image retrieval techniques gathering momentum. But it will take a considerable time before such research finds its way into commercially-available products.

6.3   CBIR and Manual Indexing

At the present stage of CBIR development, it is meaningless to ask whether CBIR techniques perform better or worse than manual indexing. Potentially, CBIR techniques have a number of advantages over manual indexing. They are inherently quicker, cheaper, and completely objective in their operation. However, these are secondary issues. The prime issue has to be retrieval effectiveness – how well does each type of system work? Unfortunately, the two types of technique cannot be sensibly compared, as they are designed to answer different types of query. Given a specialist application at level 1, such as trademark retrieval, CBIR often performs better than keyword indexing, because many of the images cannot adequately be described by linguistic cues. But for a level 2 application like finding a photograph of a given type of object to illustrate a newspaper article, keyword indexing is more effective, because CBIR simply cannot cope. It should be remembered, though, that manual classification and indexing techniques for images also have their limitations, particularly the difficulty of anticipating the retrieval cues future searchers will actually use [18]. As observed above, there is remarkably little hard evidence on the effectiveness of text keywords in image retrieval.

Attempts to retrieve images by the exclusive use of keywords or primitive image features have not met with unqualified success. Is the use of keywords and image features *in combination* likely to prove any more effective? There are in fact several reasons for believing this to be the case. Firstly, keyword indexing can be used to capture an image's semantic content, describing objects which are clearly identifiable by linguistic cues, such as trees or cars. Primitive feature matching can usefully complement this by identifying aspects of an image which are hard to name, such as a particular shape of roof on a building. Secondly, evaluation studies of the Chabot system [62] showed that higher precision and recall scores could be achieved when text and colour similarity were used in combination than when either was used separately. Finally, theoretical support for this idea comes from Ingwersen's [35] cognitive model of IR, which predicts that retrieval by a combination of methods using different cognitive structures is likely to be more effective than by any single method. However, little systematic evaluation of the effectiveness of such techniques has yet been undertaken. Hence key questions such as "can CBIR techniques bring about worthwhile improvements in performance with real-life image retrieval systems?" and "how can any such synergies most effectively be exploited?" thus remain unanswered.

6.4   CBIR in Context

Although university researchers may experiment with standalone image retrieval systems to test the effectiveness of search algorithms, this is not at all typical of the way they are likely to be used in practice. The experience of all commercial vendors of CBIR software is that system acceptability is heavily influenced by the extent to which image retrieval capabilities can be embedded within users' overall work tasks. Trademark examiners need to be able to integrate image searching with other keys such as trade class or status, and embed retrieved images in official documentation. Engineers will need to modify retrieved components to meet new design requirements. It is important to stress that CBIR is never more than the means to an end.

One implication of this is that a prime future use of CBIR is likely to be the retrieval of images by content in a multimedia system. We have already discussed possible synergies between text and image searching. Opportunities for synergy in true multimedia systems will be far greater, as demonstrated by the Informedia project [90], which combines still and moving image data, sound and text in generating retrieval cues. One example of such synergy revealed by their retrieval experiments was that in the presence of visual cues, almost 100% recall could be achieved even with a 30% error rate in automatic word recognition.

Another aspect of multimedia systems that could be much more widely exploited than at present is their use of hyperlinks to point readers to related items of data, whether elsewhere in the same document or at a remote location. This concept has been exploited in the development of MAVIS, a multimedia architecture which allows generic navigation by image content (shape, colour or texture) as well as text [48]. The authors term this process *content-based navigation* (CBN). A further development of this principle is the *multimedia thesaurus* [49], which allows a system administrator to specify semantic relationships between source items in the link database (such as a given item's set of synonyms, broader and narrower terms), whether text, image or sound.

7 Current Status of CBIR Technology

CBIR at present is still very much a research topic. The technology is exciting but immature, and few operational image archives have yet shown any serious interest in adoption. The application areas most likely to benefit from the adoption of CBIR are those where level 1 techniques can be directly applied. Trademark image searching is an obvious example – while the technology of shape retrieval may not be perfect, it is already good enough to be useful in a commercial environment. Other areas where retrieval by primitive image feature is likely to be beneficial are crime prevention (including identification of shoe prints and tyre tracks as well as faces and fingerprints), architectural design (retrieval of similar previous designs and standard components) and medical diagnosis (retrieval of cases with similar features). It is unlikely, however, that general-purpose image retrieval software will meet the needs of these user communities without a significant degree of customization.

Whether more general image database users such as stock shot agencies, art galleries and museums can benefit from CBIR is still an open question. Clearly, there is no prospect of CBIR technology *replacing* more traditional methods of indexing and searching at this level in the near future. However, there are strong indications that the combined use of text and image features might well yield better performance than either type of retrieval cue on its own. Similarly, the combined use of content-based retrieval and content-based navigation promises to be a very powerful technique for identifying desired items of any type in multimedia systems. The problem at present with both approaches is that there is as yet no body of knowledge about how these different types of access method can best be combined.

Similar considerations apply to the use of intermediaries. It has been traditional in image libraries for the custodian to perform much of the searching on behalf of users. This made excellent sense when such collections were small, and the librarian could recall the contents of most, if not all images in the collection from memory. The trend away from isolated collections and towards networked resources which can be accessed directly from users' own terminals inevitably throws the responsibility for devising an effective search strategy back on to the user. But it is questionable whether this is in fact the most effective approach. CBIR systems are not particularly easy for inexperienced end-users to understand. It is certainly not obvious to the casual user how to formulate and refine queries couched in terms of colour, texture or shape features. The use of relevance feedback can obviously help, but it is no panacea. Unless the set of retrieved images converges fairly quickly on what the user wants, disillusionment will set in quite quickly. There is thus an argument for the involvement of an experienced search intermediary who can translate a user's query into appropriate image primitives, and refine the search in consultation with the user in the light of output received.

For image database users such as graphic designers, the ability to retrieve specific images is of marginal usefulness. The role of images in stimulating creativity is little understood – images located by chance may be just as useful in providing the designer with inspiration as those retrieved in response to specific queries. In these circumstances search intermediaries are likely to be of little use, and the often capricious performance of CBIR becomes an advantage. The ability of systems like QBIC to display sets of images with underlying features in common, even if superficially dissimilar, may be just what the designer needs, particularly if any retrieved image may be used to start a further search. Such *content-assisted browsing* might turn out to be a valuable, if unforeseen, application of CBIR. There is of course a risk that future improvements in CBIR technology, enabling more accurate searching, will erode its usefulness here!

Searching the Web for images is such a chaotic process that almost any advance on current technology is likely to be beneficial. Improved search engines, capable of using both text and image features for retrieval, will become commonplace within the next few years. Users may still need considerable stamina to find the images they want, particularly if relevance feedback techniques remain too computationally expensive to operate over the Web. A variety of specialized search engines are likely to appear on the Web, such as duplicate image detectors to seek out and report on unauthorized copies of copyright material, and possibly filters to detect and block pornographic images. Pornography filters based on current CBIR technology are not likely to be very effective, as this verges on a level 3 application.

The volume of research into improved techniques for CBIR is increasing every year. How much of it is likely to make a real difference to the capabilities of CBIR technology? This is a difficult question to answer. Much current research into improved methods of primitive-level retrieval appears to be concerned with minor modifications to existing techniques. While it would be nice to have better methods for colour, texture and (particularly) shape matching, further research in this area is unlikely to lead to significantly more useful operational systems. One possible exception is research into modelling human perception of image features such as colour [10] or shape [69]. This could lead to systems capable of matching images the way people actually perceive them – what one might call *retrieval by subjective appearance*. Another is research into interface design: despite over ten years' development of CBIR systems, no really satisfactory way has yet been found to formulate a visual query. Overshadowing all these in potential importance is the fast-growing area of semantic image retrieval. While the problems involved are formidable, the potential reward – the development of CBIR systems which meet genuine user needs – is great. There are grounds for cautious optimism that advances in this area will be significant enough to feed into commercially-available CBIR technology within the next ten years. If this does happen, CBIR will indeed have come of age.

Acknowledgements

Much of the material appearing in this chapter was originally published as JISC Technology Applications Programme Report 39 (see [17] in list of references). It is reproduced here by kind permission of JISC.

8   Further Reading

- del Bimbo A. (1999) Visual Information Retrieval. Morgan Kaufmann, New York.
- Eakins J. P. (2000) Towards intelligent image retrieval. *Pattern Recognition*, in press.
- Eakins, J. P. and Graham, M. E. (1999) Content-Based Image Retrieval. *JISC Technology Applications Programme Report 39.* Available at http://www.unn.ac.uk/iidr/CBIR/report.html.
- Lew M. S. ed (2000) Principles of Visual Information Retrieval. Springer-Verlag, Berlin.
- Rui Y. et al (1999) Image retrieval: current techniques, promising directions, and open issues. *Journal of Visual Communication and Image Representation*, 10(1):39–62.

References

1. Arkin, E. M. et al (1991) An efficiently computable metric for comparing polygonal shapes. *IEEE Transactions on Pattern Analysis and Machine Intelligence*, 13(3):209–216.
2. Beckmann, N., Kriegel, H.-P., Schneider, R., and Seeger, B. (1990). R*-tree: An efficient and robust access method for points and rectangles. *SIGMOD Record (ACM Special Interest Group on Management of Data)*, 19(2):322–331.
3. Biederman, I. (1987) Recognition-by-components: a theory of human image understanding. *Psychological Review*, 94(2):115–147.
4. Bjarnestam, A. (1998) Description of an image retrieval system. presented at *The Challenge of Image Retrieval research workshop*, Newcastle upon Tyne, 5 February 1998.
5. Brooks, R. A. (1983) Model-based three-dimensional interpretations of two-dimensional images. *IEEE Transactions on Pattern Analysis and Machine Intelligence*, 5(2):140–150.
6. Buijs J. M. and Lew M. S. (1999) Visual learning of simple semantics in ImageScape. in *VISUAL99: 3rd International Conference on Visual Information and Information Systems*. Lecture Notes in Computer Science, 1614:131–138.
7. Campbell, N. W. et al (1997) Interpreting Image Databases by Region Classification. *Pattern Recognition*, 30(4):555–563.

8. Chang, S. K. et al (1987) Iconic indexing by 2-D strings. *IEEE Transactions on Pattern Analysis and Machine Intelligence*, 9(3):413–427.

9. Chen, J. L. and Stockman, C. C. (1996) Indexing to 3D model aspects using 2D contour features. in *Proceedings of IEEE Conference on Computer Vision and Pattern Recognition*, San Francisco, 913–920.

10. Corridoni, J. M. et al (1998) Image retrieval by color semantics with incomplete knowledge. *Journal of the American Society for Information Science*, 49(3):267–2.

11. Cortelazzo, G. et al (1994) Trademark shape description by string-matching techniques. *Pattern Recognition*, 27(8):1005–1018.

12. Dickinson S. et al (1998) Viewpoint-invariant indexing for content-based image retrieval. in *IEEE International Workshop on Content-based Access of Image and Video Databases (CAIVD'98)*, Bombay, India, 20–30.

13. Eakins, J. P. (1993) Design criteria for a shape retrieval system. *Computers in Industry*, 21:167–184.

14. Eakins J. P. (1998) Techniques for image retrieval. *Library and Information Briefings*, in press.

15. Eakins J. P., Graham M. E., and Boardman, J. M. (1997) Evaluation of a trademark retrieval system. in *19th BCS IRSG Research Colloquium on Information Retrieval*, Robert Gordon University, Aberdeen.

16. Eakins, J. P., Boardman, J. M., and Graham, M. E. (1998). Similarity retrieval of trademark images. *IEEE Multimedia*, 5(2):53–63.

17. Eakins, J. P., and Graham, M. E. (1999)   Content-Based Image Retrieval.   *JISC Technology Applications Programme Report*, 39. Available at http://www.unn.ac.uk/iidr/CBIR/report.html.

18. Enser P. G. B. (1995) Pictorial information retrieval. *Journal of Documentation*, 51(2):126–170.

19. Enser, P. G. B. and McGregor, C. G. (1992) Analysis of visual information retrieval queries. *British Library Research and Development Report*, 6104.

20. Evans, A. (1987) TELCLASS: a structural approach to TV classification. *Audiovisual Librarian*, 13(4):215–216.

21. Faloutsos, C. et al (1994) Efficient and effective querying by image content. *Journal of Intelligent Information Systems*, 3, 231–262.

22. Feder, J. (1996) Towards image content-based retrieval for the World-Wide Web. *Advanced Imaging*, 11(1), 26–29.

23. Flickner, M. et al (1995). Query by image and video content: The QBIC system. *Computer*, 28(9):23–32.

24. Forsyth, D. A. et al (1997). Finding pictures of objects in large collections of images. in *Digital Image Access and Retrieval: 1996 Clinic on Library Applications of Data Processing* (Heidorn, P. B. and Sandore, B, eds), 118–139. Graduate School of Library and Information Science, University of Illinois at Urbana-Champaign.

25. Gordon, C. (1990) An introduction to ICONCLASS. in *Terminology for Museums Proceedings of an International Conference, Cambridge*, 1988 (Roberts, D. A., ed), 233–244. Museum Documentation Association.

26. Greenberg, J. (1993). Intellectual control of visual archives: a comparison between the Art and Architecture Thesaurus and the Library of Congress Thesaurus for Graphic Materials. *Cataloging & Classification Quarterly*, 16(1):85–101.

27. Gudivada, V. N. and Raghavan, V. V. (1995). Guest editors' introduction: Content-based image retrieval systems. *Computer*, 28(9):18–22.

28. Gudivada, V. N. and Raghavan, V. V. (1995). Design and evaluation of algorithms for image retrieval by spatial similarity. *ACM Trans. on Information Systems*, 13(2):115–144.

29. Gupta, A. et al (1996). The Virage image search engine: an open framework for image management. in *Storage and Retrieval for Image and Video Databases IV*, Proc SPIE 2670:76–87.

30. Haralick, R. M. et al (1973). Textrual features for image classification. *IEEE Transactions on Systems Man and Cybernetics*, 3(6):610–621.

31. Hastings, S. K. (1995). Query categories in a study of intellectual access to digitized art images. *ASIS '95: proceedings of the 58th ASIS Annual Meeting*, 32:3–8.

32. Hou, Y. T. et al (1992). A content-based indexing technique using relative geometry features. in *Image Storage and Retrieval Systems*, Proc SPIE 1662:59–68.

33. Hu, M. K. (1962). Visual pattern recognition by moment invariants. *IRE Transactions on Information Theory*, IT-8: 179–187.

34. Huang, T. et al (1997). Multimedia Analysis and Retrieval System (MARS) project in Digital Image Access and Retrieval. 1996 *Clinic on Library Applications of Data Processing* (Heidorn, P. B. and Sandore, B, eds), 101–117. Graduate School of Library and Information Science, University of Illinois at Urbana-Champaign.

35. Ingwersen, P. (1996). Cognitive perspectives of information retrieval interaction: elements of a cognitive IR theory. *Journal of Documentation*, 52(1):3–50.

36. Jacobs, C. E. et al (1995). Fast Multiresolution Image Querying. Proceedings of *SIGGRAPH 95*, Los Angeles, CA (ACM SIGGRAPH Annual Conference Series, 1995), 277–286.

37. Jaimes, A. and Chang S. F. (1999). Model-based classification of visual information for content-based retrieval. in *Storage and Retrieval for Image and Video Databases VII*, Proc SPIE 3656:402–414.

38. Jain, A. K. et al (1996). Object matching using deformable templates. *IEEE Transactions on Pattern Analysis and Machine Intelligence*, 18(3):267–277.

39. Jain, A. K. and Vailaya (1996). A Image retrieval using color and shape. *Pattern Recognition*, 29(8):1233–1244.

40. Jin, J. S. et al (1998). Using browsing to improve content-based image retrieval. in *Multimedia Storage and Archiving Systems III*, Proc SPIE 3527:101–109.

41. Keister, L. H. (1994). User types and queries: impact on image access systems. in *Challenges in indexing electronic text and images* (Fidel, R. et al., eds). ASIS, 7–22.

42. Kim, Y. S. and Kim, W. Y. (1998). Content-based trademark retrieval system using a visually salient feature. *Image and Vision Computing*, 16:931–939.

43. Kurniawati, R. et al (1997). The SS+ tree: an improved index structure for similarity searches in high-dimensional feature space. in *Storage and Retrieval for Image and Video Databases V* (Sethi, I. K. and Jain, R. C., eds), Proc SPIE 3022:110–120.

44. Lee, D. et al (1994). Query by image content using multiple objects and multiple features: user interface issues. in *Proceedings of ICIP-94, International Conference on Image Processing*, Austin, Texas, 76–80.

45. Lee, C. S. et al (1999). Information embedding based on users' relevance feedback for image retrieval. in *Multimedia Storage and Archiving Systems IV* (S Panchanathan et al, eds), Proc SPIE 3846:294–304.

46. Leung, T. and Malik J. (1999). Recognizing surfaces using three-dimensional textons. presented at *Seventh IEEE International Conference on Computer Vision (ICCV-99)*, Corfu, Greece, 2:1010–1017.

47. Levine, M. D. (1985). *Vision in man and machine*, ch 10. McGraw-Hill, NY

48. Lewis, P. H. et al (1996). Media-based navigation with generic links. in Proceedings of the Seventh ACM Conference on Hypertext, New York, 215–223.

49. Lewis, P. H. et al (1997). Towards multimedia thesaurus support for media-based navigation. in *Image Databases and Multimedia Search*, (Smeulders, A. W. M. and Jain, R. C., eds), 111–118. World Scientific, Amsterdam

50. Lin, K.I., Jagadish, H. V., and Faloutsos, C. (1994). The TV-tree—an index structure for high-dimensional data. *VLDB Journal: Special Issue on Spatial Database Systems*, 3(4):517–542.

51. Liu, F. and Picard, R. W. (1996). Periodicity, directionality and randomness: Wold features for image modeling and retrieval. *IEEE Trans. Pattern Analysis and Machine Intelligence*, 18(7):722–733.

52. Ma, W.Y. and Manjunath, B. S. (1997). NeTra: A toolbox for navigating large image databases. In *Proc. of the IEEE Int. Conf. on Image Processing*, 562–571.

53. Ma, W. Y. and Manjunath, B. S. (1998). A texture thesaurus for browsing large aerial photographs. *Journal of the American Society for Information Science* 49(7):633–648.

54. Manjunath, B. S. and Ma, W.-Y. (1996). Texture features for browsing and retrieval of image data. *IEEE Trans. Pattern Analysis and Machine Intelligence*, 18(8):837–842.

55. Manmatha, R. and Ravela, S. (1997). A syntactic characterization of appearance and its application to image retrieval. in *Human Vision and Electronic Imaging II* (Rogowitz BE and Pappas TN, eds), SPIE 3016, 484–495.

56. Markey, K. (1984). Interindexer consistency tests: a literature review and report of a test of consistency in indexing visual materials. *Library and Information Science Research*, 6:155–177.

57. Markkula, M. and Sormunen, E. (1998). Searching for photos–journalists' practices in pictorial IR. presented at *The Challenge of Image Retrieval research workshop*, Newcastle upon Tyne, February 1998.

58. Mehrotra, R. and Gary J. E. (1995). Similar-shape retrieval in shape data management. *IEEE Computer*, 28(9):57–62.

59. Minka, T. (1996). An image database browser that learns from user interaction. *MIT Media Laboratory Technical Report*, #365.

60. Nastar, C. et al (1998). Surfimage: a flexible content-based image retrieval system. presented at *ACM Multimedia '98*, Bristol, UK.

61. Niblack, W. et al (1998). Updates to the QBIC system. in *Storage and Retrieval for Image and Video Databases VI* (Sethi, I. K. and Jain, R. C., eds), Proc SPIE 3312, 150–161.

62. Ogle, V. E. and Stonebraker, M. (1995). CHABOT: Retrieval from a relational database of images. *IEEE Computer*, 28(9):40–48.

63. Oliva, A. et al (1999). Global semantic classification of scenes using power spectrum templates. presented at CIR-99: *The Challenge of Image Retrieval*, Newcastle upon Tyne, UK, February 1999.

64. Opitz, H. et al (1969). Workpiece classification and its industrial application. *International Journal of Machine Tool Design Research*, 9:39–50.

65. Paquet, E. and Rioux, M. (1998). *Content-based access of VRML libraries* Lecture Notes in Computer Science 1464:20–32.

66. Pentland, A. et al (1996). Photobook: tools for content-based manipulation of image databases. *International Journal of Computer Vision*, 18(3)233–254.

67. Ravela, S. and Manmatha, R. (1998a). Retrieving images by appearance. in *Proceedings of IEEE International Conference on Computer Vision (IICV98)*, Bombay, India, 608–613.

68. Ravela, S. and Manmatha, R. (1998). On computing global similarity in images. in *Proceedings of IEEE Workshop on Applications of Computer Vision (WACV98)*, Princeton, NJ, 82–87.

69. Ren, M. et al (2000). Human perception of trademark images: implications for retrieval system design. *Journal of Electronic Imaging*, in press.

70. Rui, Y. et al (1997). Relevance feedback techniques in interactive content-based image retrieval. in *Storage and Retrieval for Image and Video Databases VI* (Sethi, I. K. and Jain, R. C., eds), Proc SPIE 3312: 25–36.

71. Rui, Y., Huang, T. S., Ortega, M., and Mehrotra, S. (1998). Relevance feedback: A power tool in interactive content-based image retrieval. *IEEE Tran on Circuits and Systems for Video Technology*, 8(5):644–655.

72. Santini, S. and Jain, R. (1997). Do images mean anything? In *Proc. of the Int. Conf. on Image Analysis and Processing, ICIP-97*, 564–567.

73. Scassellati, B. et al (1994). Retrieving images by 2-D shape: a comparison of computation methods with human perceptual judgements. in *Storage and Retrieval for Image and Video Databases II* (Niblack, W. R. and Jain, R. C., eds), Proc SPIE 2185:2–14.

74. Schiele, B. and Crowley J. L. (1997). The concept of visual classes for object classification. in *Proceedings of SCIA '97, Tenth Scandinavian Conference on Image Analysis*, Lappeenranta, Finland, 43–50.

75. Shi, J. and Malik, J. (2000). Normalized cuts and image segmentation. *IEEE Transactions on Pattern Analysis and Machine Intelligence*, in press.

76. Smith, J. R. and Chang S. F. (1994). Transform features for texture classification and discrimination in large image databases. in *Proceedings ICIP-94*, Austin, Texas, 407–411.

77. Smith, J. R. and Chang S. F. (1997a). Querying by color regions using the VisualSEEk content-based visual query system. *Intelligent Multimedia Information Retrieval* (Maybury, M. T., ed). AAAI Press, Menlo Park, CA, 23–41.

78. Smith, J. R. and Chang S. F. (1997b). An image and video search engine for the World-Wide Web. in *Storage and Retrieval for Image and Video Databases V* (Sethi, I. K. and Jain, R. C., eds), Proc SPIE 3022:84–95.

79. Srihari, R. K. (1995). Automatic indexing and content-based retrieval of captioned images. *IEEE Computer*, 28(9):49–56.

80. Stark, H-G (1996). On image retrieval with wavelets. *International Journal of Imaging Systems and Technology*, 7:200–210.

81. Stricker, M. and Dimai, A. (1996). Color indexing with weak spatial constraints. in *Storage and Retrieval for Image and Video Databases IV* (Sethi, I. K. and Jain, R. C., eds), Proc SPIE 2670:29–4.

82. Stricker, M. and Orengo, M. (1995). Similarity of color images. in *Storage and Retrieval for Image and Video Databases III* (Niblack, W. R. and Jain, R. C., eds), Proc SPIE 2420:381–392.

83. Swain, M. J. and Ballard, D. H. (1991). Color indexing. *International Journal of Computer Vision*, 7(1):11–32.

84. Szummer, M. and Picard, R. (1998). Indoor-outdoor image classification. in *IEEE International Workshop on Content-based Access of Image and Video Databases (CAIVD98)*, Bombay, India, 42–51.

85. Tamura, H., Mori, S., and Yamawaki, T. (1978). Texture features corresponding to visual perception. *IEEE Trans. on Systems, Man, and Cybernetics*, 8(6):460–473.

86. Teh, C. H. and Chin, R. T. (1988). Image analysis by methods of moments. *IEEE Transactions on Pattern Analysis and Machine Intelligence*, 10(4):496–513.

87. Vailaya, A. et al (1998). On image classification: city images vs landscapes. *Pattern Recognition*, 31(12):921–1936.
88. Vailaya, A. and Jain, A. K. (1999). Incremental learning for Bayesian classification of images. presented at *IEEE International Conference on Image Processing (ICIP'99)*, Kobe, Japan, October 1999.
89. Vleugels, J. and Veltkamp, R. (1999). Efficient image retrieval through vantage objects. presented at *VISUAL99: 3rd International Conference on Visual Information and Information Systems*. Lecture Notes in Computer Science 1614:769–776.
90. Wactlar, H. D. et al (1996). Intelligent access to digital video: the Informedia project. *IEEE Computer*, 29(5):46–52.
91. World Intellectual Property Organization (1998). *International Classification of the Figurative Elements of Marks (Vienna Classification)*, Fourth Edition. ISBN 92–805–0728–1. World Intellectual Property Organization, Geneva.
92. Zahn, C. T. and Roskies, C. Z. (1972). Fourier descriptor for plane closed curves. *IEEE Transactions on Computers*, C-21:269–281.

Digital Libraries and Information Retrieval

Ingeborg Torvik Sølvberg

Dept. of Computer and Information Science
Norwegian University of Science and Technology
N-7491 Trondheim, Norway
ingeborg.solvberg@idi.ntnu.no

Abstract The main objective of any Digital Library (DL) is to fulfil the needs of its users. A primary necessity is to make digital objects accessible using a computer network. A crucial part for Digital Libraries is that its information is managed, persistent and reliable. A Digital Library consists of digital collections, a working environment, and technology and services.

A general problem is Information Discovery; how to find information in the Internet world. Digital Libraries comprise diverse collections of digital objects representing text, sound, maps, videos, photos etceteras. The use of metadata to describe digital objects will be discussed. Metadata is often divided into three categories: descriptive, structural and administrative, and hence supports additional work tasks than the classical IR. Different metadata formats (MARC, Dublin Core, and others), the IFLA model and the Resource Description Framework (RDF) are presented.

1   Digital Libraries

The first priority for any library is to meet the information needs of its constituencies. This is also true for a digital library. A digital library is *similar* to a traditional library as it contains collections, and the information is organised, maintained, valid and persistent.

But a digital library is *different* from a traditional library as its collections are accessible using the internet; the collections—as well as the digital objects—may be distributed; a user of a digital library can be both an information consumer and an information producer. The information objects can be downloaded and used in a person's working environment. The collections are usually owned and maintained by different bodies than those responsible for the networks and for other services like storage, information retrieval software, and the information production.

Levy and Marshall [8] describes a digital library from three viewpoints: Work, Documents and Technology. These perspectives are closely linked, and one perspective cannot be fully understood without knowledge of the other perspectives.

We will in this paper broaden these perspectives and talk about *Collections, Working environment,* and *Technology and Services*.

M. Agosti, F. Crestani, and G. Pasi (Eds.): ESSIR 2000, LNCS 1980, pp. 139–156, 2000.

1.1   Collections

A collection contains information objects put together according to some rules or ideas, on the basis of one or several attributes to be described collectively. It may be a thematic collection with objects about (and by) William Shakespeare; a CD collection; a collection with objects related to a specific geographical area; or simply a collection of objects "owned by NN."

The collections in a digital library contain digital objects. Typically, a digital object consists of data, associated metadata, and an identifier. The content can be the digitised version of physical items, or it can be objects that have no physical equivalent. The digital objects can be representations of text, audio, videos, music, photos, maps, computer programs, video games, etceteras. A digital object can be an "information surrogate", i.e. it contains information (metadata) about objects which do not exist in a digital form. Examples are rare books, original manuscripts, museum artefacts, paintings. Even if digital representations of this objects are represented in a digital collection, 'the real thing' is needed in certain circumstances such as in the research on hand-written letters where the paper quality and the ink used are just as important as the text itself.

The digital objects can be static or dynamic. The Bible is an example of a static object, while Software specifications are dynamic in the specification process. The information can be valid just in a specific timeframe, like train tables, or it may be valid and should be kept for centuries, like Henrik Ibsen's "Peer Gynt."

1.2   Working Environment

A digital library is normally user-centred and shall give support to people and organisations doing intellectual work. A user may be an information producer or creator, or an information consumer or 'reader'. The same person can have both roles. Examples of information producers are authors, researchers, composers, software designers, information professionals, librarians. It is important to stress that the users can work individually or co-operate in teams towards a common goal.

The *users* are therefore persons with a great variety of needs for support and services. Later in this article we propose that a digital library shall support more than the information retrieval task, and it should include services that will allow collaboration and the exchange of ideas.

1.3   Technology and Services

William Arms [2] claims that "They (... digital libraries...) have three main functions: to help users interact with the library, to store collections of materials, and to provide services." Two typical services are *search services*, providing catalogues, indexes and services to help users in the information seeking process; and *location services*: to identify and locate information.

A digital library shall support the storage, representation and dissemination and all kinds of digital objects. It shall serve users with all kinds of computers and software. The users' computers access the collections by a communication network, where the Internet is the dominant network.

1.4   Objectives of Information Retrieval

Traditionally Information Retrieval is to search a body of information for objects that match a search query [2]. The query consists usually of descriptive terms, like subject keywords and names of persons or corporate bodies. Information retrieval is a key component of any Digital Library, and the needs and requirements from the Digital Library communities will be a challenge also to the research directions in the traditional Information Retrieval-communities.

1.5   A Digital Library Must Support More Tasks than Information Retrieval

A traditional library supports the generic tasks that are performed by a user when searching: to find, to identify, to select, and to obtain.

- using the data *to find* materials that correspond to the user's stated search criteria.
- using the data retrieved *to identify* an entity.
- using the data *to select* an entity that is appropriate to the user's needs.
- using the data in order to acquire or *obtain* access to the entity described.

A digital library shall support persons and organisations throughout several phases in the work process [11,12]. Paepke's paper "Digital Libraries: Searching is not enough" [12] describes the information needs and the work habits of workers in technical work settings. In addition to search, the paper suggests four other aspects of user tasks that should be supported by digital libraries. The five tasks are:

- locating and selecting among relevant sources,
- retrieving information from them,
- interpret what was retrieved,
- managing the filtered-out information locally,
- sharing results with others.

The same piece of information sometimes needs to be presented differently for different people and for different tasks.

This are similar requirements as the requirements to complex information systems in industry. The repositories shall contain information and give access to relevant material about the business' domain, i.e. relevant articles, journals, handbooks, documentation; the business' strategy, business-rules and regulations, project management, historic data, information about customers, etceteras. In the business environment this information systems often is called Corporate Memories.

"Corporate memory is a collection of distributed and heterogeneous knowledge-bases about individual and project experiences and tools to manage these knowledge-bases for or in (new) project simulations." [16]

A Corporate memory can include software to support co-operation and collaboration (CSCW—Computer Supported Co-operated Work), with the additional databases.

2 Metadata

Metadata in its simplest form is "data about data." A more informative description is given by Dempsey and Heery [3]:

"Metadata is data associated with objects which relieves their potential users of having to have full advance knowledge of their existence or characteristics."

2.1 Some Interactive Processes Needing Metadata

Weibel and Miller [19] gives a slightly different list than Paepcke of tasks where a digital library should give support. This list is restricted to the *interactive processes* a person will go through in order to get the correct and necessary information to do some work:

Discovery: The identification of relevant resources,
Retrieval: The transfer of resources to a local site,
Collation: The aggregation and organisation of selected sources,
Analysis: The intellectual and/or computational analysis of resources,
Re-representation: The formulation of derivative intellectual artefacts based on the resources and previous processes in sequence

2.2 Different Kinds of Metadata Are Needed

In order to give support to the whole working process, a diversity of metadata are needed, and they should assist to give good answers to queries in areas such as: [7]

Discovery: What exists? Where can I access it?
Terms and Conditions: Describes the conditions for use; access rights for groups or persons, costs, restrictions of use.
Administrative Data: Metadata related to the management of an object; modifications, date of creation, identification of the administrator.
Provenance: Data defining the source of origin of some content object.
Context: Who created it?—and why? Is it a part of a business or an intellectual process?
Structure: File format? Representation issues? Table of content?
Content: What or who is the object? What is it about?

History of Use: How has it been used in the past? Who is responsible for it?

Linkage, Relationship: Links to other works? (translations, editions etceteras). Is it part of a multimedia work?

Lagoze et. al. give the following description of the use of the different kinds of metadata needed in order to solve a composite task [7]:

> "... These processes involve events and resources distributed among institutions, machines, networks, and the minds of individuals. Metadata, then, become any one set of elements drawn from the many kinds of information necessary for decision-making within this matrix of minds, machines, and networks. For example, access to *discovery* metadata may lead to the return of terms and conditions elements, necessary for *retrieval*. *Retrieval* metadata might include the network address of a resolver from which the resource may be accessed or the publisher of an item with whom a usage agreement must be transacted. *Collation* metadata might include data about an image collection schema or the provenance of an item. *Analysis* might require a colour map for the item. *Representation* could involve information validating credit to rights holders, and might well require a link to update use history of the source object."

A variety of metadata will be needed to satisfy the requirements for each stage. As we have seen, most Metadata formats contain descriptive metadata to be used in the Information Discovery Process, with some elements that can assist in the Retrieval process. None of the standard formats support all of the processes in Papecke's model. There is still a long way to go before we have defined and developed metadata formats that will support the functionality in a Corporate Memory or an advanced Digital Library.

2.3   Various Types of Metadata

Existing metadata formats varies greatly in their complexity and granularity. Dempsey and Heery [3] give the classification of Fig. 1.

Band One includes relatively unstructured data. They are currently automatically extracted by web crawlers. A web crawler is an indexing program that follows hyperlinks and assembles lists of web pages (URIs). They extract data from resources and produce indexes automatically. The indexes may be of low quality, as the sources for indexing may give few meaningful words, sometimes even misleading. Many global services are based on these techniques, and in spite of the weaknesses the services turn out to be of great help and are useful in simple information discovery. Several of the services on the Internet work to improve the quality of their indexes. The methods and techniques are usually confidential, and they are proprietary for each service.

	Band One	**Band Two**	**Band Three**
Record characteristics	Simple formats Proprietary	Structured formats Emerging standards	Rich formats International standards
	Full text indexing	Field structure	Elaborate tagging
Record formats	Lycos Altavista Yahoo! etc	Dublin Core IAFA templates RFC 1807 SOIF LDIF	ICPSR CIMI EAD TEI MARC

Figure 1. Typology of Metadata Formats

Band Two includes structured records, and the indexes are usually produced by a mix of automatic and manual indexing. The records are simple enough to be created by non-specialists. The descriptions tend to be of discrete objects, with none or very simple relationships to other objects. The object descriptions are mainly useful for information discovery.

Band Three includes fuller descriptive formats and require specialist knowledge to create and maintain. The formats are international standards, and are costly and time-consuming to maintain or change. The formats may be used for information discovery and location, and can capture a variety of relationships at different levels.

The categorisation of the formats in these three bands can be discussed. The borders between the bands are not fixed, but the division into three categories gives a good indication of the variety of metadata formats. Some services using web-crawlers (Band one) may go into Band two, and the same may be said about CIMI-objects. This may be implementation dependent.

Metadata is often divided into three categories: descriptive metadata, structural metadata and administrative metadata. Descriptive metadata is used for bibliographic purposes and for bibliographic search and retrieval. Structural metadata relates different objects and parts of objects to each other (relationships). Administrative metadata is used to manage collections and to control access to them. Most of the metadata formats in classified in the three Bands just described, cover mainly the descriptive metadata. However, a format like RFC-1807 includes fields for administrative purposes, and the MARC format has fields of all three categories of metadata.

In the following we describe a typical format representing Band two; the Dublin Core format, and a format from Band three; the MARC format. We will not go further into formats in Band one. They are based on full text automatic indexing.

3   Dublin Core

The Dublin Core Metadata element set is defined by groups of people since the first metadata workshop in Dublin, Ohio, in 1995 [4, 18]. The major task has been to identify and define a simple set of elements for describing networked resources. The format aims at being simple and to be used by authors and information providers. The format is not an all-purpose-format, but it is meant for the information discovery process. The description was from the beginning restricted to the metadata elements required for the discovery of what was called *document-like objects*, or *DLOs*. A DLO is not rigorously defined.

The Dublin Core format, Fig. 2, is a format with few rules attached. No element is obligatory, and any element can be repeated. "It is better to give some information than none."

Title: A name given to the resource. A Title will be a name by which the resource is formally known.

Creator: An entity primarily responsible for making the content of the resource. Examples of a Creator include a person, an organisation, or a service.

Subject: The topic of the content of the resource. A Subject will be expressed as keywords, key phrases or classification codes that describe a topic of the resource

Description: An account of the content of the resource. Examples are an abstract, a table of contents, a reference to a graphical representation of content.

Publisher: An entity responsible for making the resource available. Examples include a person, an organisation, or a service.

Contributor: An entity responsible for making contributions to the content of the resource. Examples include a person, an organisation, or a service.

Date: A date associated with an event in the life cycle of the resource. A Date will be associated with the creation or availability of the resource.

Resource Type: The nature or genre of the content of the resource.

Format: The physical or digital manifestation of the resource, and may include the media-type or dimensions of the resource.

Resource Identifier: An unambiguous reference to the resource within a given context. Example formal identification systems are Uniform Resource Identifier (URI), the Digital Object Identifier (DOI) and the International Standard Book Number (ISBN).

Source: A Reference to a resource from which the present resource is derived.

Language: A language of the intellectual content of the resource.

Relation: A reference to a related resource.

Coverage: The extent or scope of the content of the resource. Coverage will typically include a spatial location or a temporal period.

Rights Management: Information about rights held in and over the resource.

Figure 2. Dublin Core's 15 Elements

The Dublin Core Format can be used in a very simple way; a person can input information about the resource in a free form, or the data can follow recommendations from organisations or bodies.

Over the years the format has been refined. The Dublin Core Metadata Initiative (DCMI) has currently recognised two classes of qualifiers: the Element Refinement Qualifiers and the Encoding Scheme Qualifiers [5]. The Element Refinement Qualifiers make the meaning of a DC element narrower or more specific. The Encoding Scheme Qualifiers identify schemes, including controlled vocabularies and formal notations. This will aid in the interpretation of an element value. Some of the recommended Encoding Schemes for the DC *Subject element* are for example Library of Congress Subject Headings (LCSH), Medical Subject Headings (MESH) and Universal Decimal Classification (UDC).

The DC *Date element* can be given dates associated with an event in the life cycle of the resource, and recommended Element Refinement Qualifiers are *created, valid, available, issued,* and *modified*. Recommended best practice for encoding the date is to use the Encoding Scheme defined in ISO 8601and follows the YYYY-MM-DD format.

The DC element *Coverage* has been much discussed. Two Refinements Qualifers are proposed. One shall give the spatial characteristics, the other the temporal characteristics, of the intellectual content of the resource (a place name, geographic coordinates, a date range a.o.)

Recommendations for use of qualifiers are given for every element in the Dublin Core format [5].

It is interesting to see how the DC *Relation element* is detailed in the proposal Refinement Qualifiers include qualifiers like i*s-version-of, has-version, has-part, is-referenced-by, requires*. The IFLA model gives similar proposals with the Relationships attributes.

4   MARC Formats

MARC (Machine Readable Catalogue Format) was developed in the 1960s as a means to exchange and share library catalogue records using magnetic tapes. The format is widely used in the library community world wide, and most library automation systems support MARC cataloguing. National libraries, as well as major library automation systems, have tended to develop their own MARC formats in order to adapt to local needs, traditions, users etceteras: USMARC in the US, UKMARC in the UK, NORMARC in Norway.

The MARC format was designed and developed a long time before the Internet introduced new needs and challenges. The large MARC-based catalogues will live and expand for years and years to come. The national libraries and the owners of other large catalogues will include descriptions of Internet resources into their existing systems.

The MARC formats are defined for three data types: Bibliographic, holdings and authority records. The Bibliographic descriptions are usually designed for the description of different forms of bibliographic material: monographs, serials, archives and manuscripts, maps, music, visual material, computer files. Data in the records is contained in fields identified by a three-digit tag.

All the MARC formats are designed according to certain rules. According to ISO-2709 a MARC record should have a record label, a directory, data field separators and record separators. The record must consist of variable length fields with content designators.

USMARC	UNIMARC
0XX Control numbers, provenance	0XX Identification block
1XX Main entry	1XX Coded information block
2XX Titles and related information	2XX Descriptive information block
3XX Physical description	3XX Notes block
4XX Series statements	4XX Linking entry block
5XX Notes	5XX Related title block
6XX Subject access	6XX Subject analysis block
7XX Added entries; linking fields	7XX Intellectual responsibility block
8XX Series added entries	8XX International use block
9XX Reserved for local fields	9XX National use block

Figure 3. Main Field Types in USMARC and UNIMARC

The Z39.50 protocol, which enables search and retrieval of bibliographic information over the Internet, is particularly designed to accommodate the search and retrieval of MARC records. The protocol can be used to pass searches of MARC fields from a Z39.50 client to a Z39.50 server fronting databases of MARC records; and retrieved records can be returned in MARC format.

There has been a tendency during the last years to standardise or converge the MARC formats, either into the USMARC format (mainly English speaking countries), or into the UNIMARC format (some European countries).

5   The IFLA Model of Digital Objects

In the information seeking process the first phase may be to find some information 'contents', and not particularly a specific item. It is important to be able to distinguish between the intellectual work itself and the possible different expressions and items in a digital library.

IFLA, the International Federation of Library Associations, presented in 1998 a study, including a conceptual model for bibliographic records. Four different levels for describing the content are proposed: *work, expression, manifestation*, and *item*; The Functional Requirements for Bibliographic Records; "the FRBR framework" or "the IFLA model" [6].

The IFLA study has two primary objectives:

- The first objective is to provide a clearly defined, structured framework for relating the data that are recorded in bibliographic records to the needs of users of those records.
- The second objective is to recommend a basic level of functionality for records created by national bibliographic agencies.

Bibliographic Description (as shown in the Norwegian BIBSYS system)	*Tittel:* **Digital libraries / William Y. Arms.** *Forfatter:* Arms, William Y *I serie:* (Digital libraries and electronic publishing) *Trykt:* Cambridge, Mass. : MIT Press, c2000. *Sidetall:* x, 287 p. : ill. *Noter:* Includes bibliographical references and index. *ISBN:* 0–262–01180–8 *Eiere:* UBB
MARC (BIBSYS MARC)	*001001011774 *008 eng *015 $alc99014773 *020 $a0–262–01180–8 *082 $c025/.00285 *100 $aArms, William Y *245 $aDigital libraries$cWilliam Y. Arms *260 $aCambridge, Mass.$bMIT Press$cc2000 *300 $ax, 287 p.$bill. *440 $aDigital libraries and electronic publishing *500 $aIncludes bibliographical references and index. *650 $aLibraries$zUnited States$xSpecialcollections Electronic information resources *650 $aDigital libraries$zUnited States *096d $aUBBRB$n00d042953
Dublin Core (in its simplest form)	*Title.* Digital libraries *Creator.* Arms, William Y. *Publisher.* MIT Press. *Subject.* Digital libraries. *Subject.* Electronic publishing. *Subject.* Electronic information resources. *Date.* 2000 *Identifier.* ISBN 0–262–01180–8 *Language.* English

Figure 4. Example of an Information Resource Described in MARC and Dublin Core

The study takes into account that the users of bibliographic records belongs to different professions as information specialists, distributors, publishers, and also outside of the traditional library community. The study does also clarify that bibliographic records are to be used in a wide range of applications. However, they do all belong to the traditional library world: purchasing and acquisitions, cataloguing, inventory, circulation and inter-library-loan, preservation, and reference and information retrieval.

The material to be included in the model are textual, music, cartographic, audio-visual, graphic and three-dimensional. The functional requirements for bibliographic records are defined in relation to the generic tasks that are performed by user when searching: *to find, to identify, to select,* and *to obtain.*

- Using the data *to find* materials that correspond to the user's stated search criteria
- Using the data retrieved *to identify* an entity
- Using the data *to select* an entity that is appropriate to the user's needs
- Using the data in order to acquire or *obtain* access to the entity described.

The IFLA study divides the entities into three groups:

Group 1 comprises the products of intellectual or artistic endeavour; the *Product Model* (the four level content model).

Group 2 comprises the those entities responsible for the intellectual or artistic content physical production a.o., the *Responsibility Relationship Model*.

Group 3 gives an additional set of entities , the *Subject Relationship Model*.

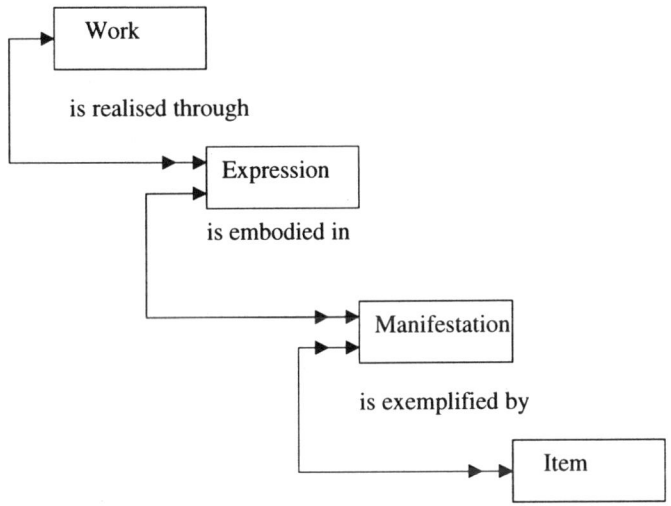

Figure 5. The Product Model. IFLA Group 1.

5.1   Product Model. (Group 1 Entities)

The IFLA model proposes four levels for describing content. They are *Work, Expression, Manifestation,* and *Item*.

Work. A work is the underlying abstraction: a distinct intellectual or artistic creation, i.e. a work such as William Shakespeare's "Romeo and Juliet" or Edvard Grieg's "Solveig's Song".

Expression. A work is realised through an expression. The expression may be in the form of alpha-numeric, musical, or choreographic notation, sound, image, object, movement etc., or any combination of such forms. For example will an Italian translation of "Romeo and Juliet" be an expression, and a translation into Norwegian will be another expression.

"Solveig's Song" arranged for a violin is one expression of the Grieg's work, and "Solveig's Song" made for a symphony orchestra and a soprano are others.

Computer software has separate expressions as source code and as machine code.

Defining expression as an entity enables us to draw relationships between specific expressions of a work.

Manifestation. An expression is given form in one or more manifestations. The text of "Romeo and Juliet" has been manifest in several books. "Solveig's Song" is manifest on CDs, videos, films. Software is manifest as files, and can be stored or transmitted in any digital medium.

Item. A single exemplar (copy) of a manifestation is called an item. This is a concrete entity.

The entities of the first group, the Product Model, represent the different aspects of user interests in the products of intellectual or artistic endeavour. The entities *work* and *expression* reflects intellectual or artistic content, while *manifestation* and *item* reflect physical form.

There are many ambiguities in the models, and strict rules can not be applied. The notion of a work is abstract, and the boundaries may not be distinct. However, when the modification of a *work* involves a significantly degree of independently intellectual or artistic effort, this may be viewed as a new *work*.

Examples of separate works:

- William Shakespeare's "Romeo and Juliet"
- Franco Zeffirelli's motion picture "Romeo and Juliet"
- Baz Lurhmann's motion picture "William Shakespeare's Romeo and Juliet"

5.2   Responsibility Relationship Model. (Group 2 Entities and "Responsibility" Relationships)

The group is divided into two entities: Person and Corporate Body; i.e. the persons or corporate bodies responsible for the intellectual or artistic content of the work, for the physical production and the dissemination of the products.

5.3   Subject Relationship Model. (Group 3 Entities and "Subject" Relationships)

The entities in this group represent an additional set of entities that serve as the subject of works. The four entities are *concept* (an abstract notion or idea), *object* (a material thing), *event* (an action or occurrence), and a *place* (a location).

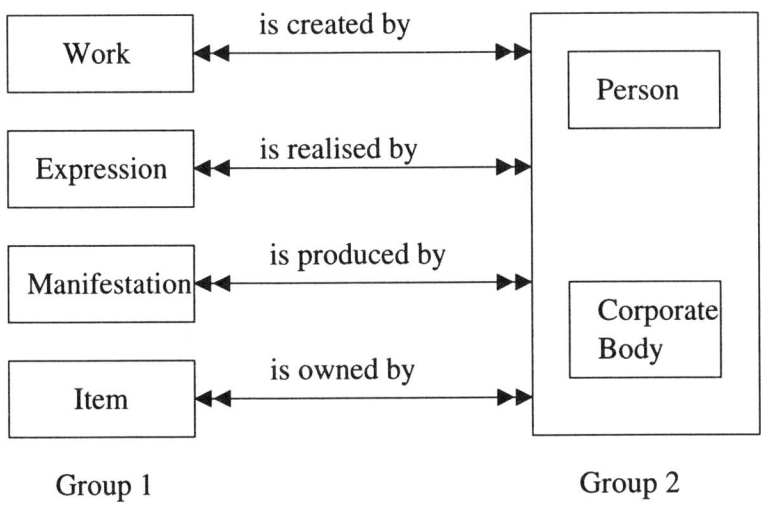

Figure 6. Responsibility Relationships Model. (IFLA Group 2).

Examples:

A Concept: Information Retrieval
An Object: Lake Como (treated as an object only to the extent that it is subject of a work).
An Event: ESSIR 2000.
A Place: Villa Monastero.

Figure 7 describes that a *work* may have as its subject one or more entities from each of the first, second or third groups.

The entities in each of the three groups has associated with it a set of attributes. The attributes are selected in order to be used in the query process and to improve the quality of the information seeking process, with emphasis on the generic tasks *find, identify, select* and *obtain*. The entities can be linked using specific relationships. In the IFLA-study the main relationships described are the relationships that operate between the entities in the Product Model (*work, expression, manifestation, item*). Some relations are shown in the Figs. 5, 6 and 7, and in Table 2.

The users have different objectives when searching. One user wants to find all of the manifestations for works on a specific subject; works in a given series; or the various expressions for a given work. Another user wants to obtain a specific manifestation; an item, of a work; or to identify a work or an expression.

Which attributes are the most important to assist in the information seeking process?

The IFLA-study makes suggestions. In Table 1 some of these are given. Table 2 gives relations between works and between a work and an expression, proposed by IFLA to be of 'high value.' There are no relations of 'high value' proposed between manifestations or items to other entities.

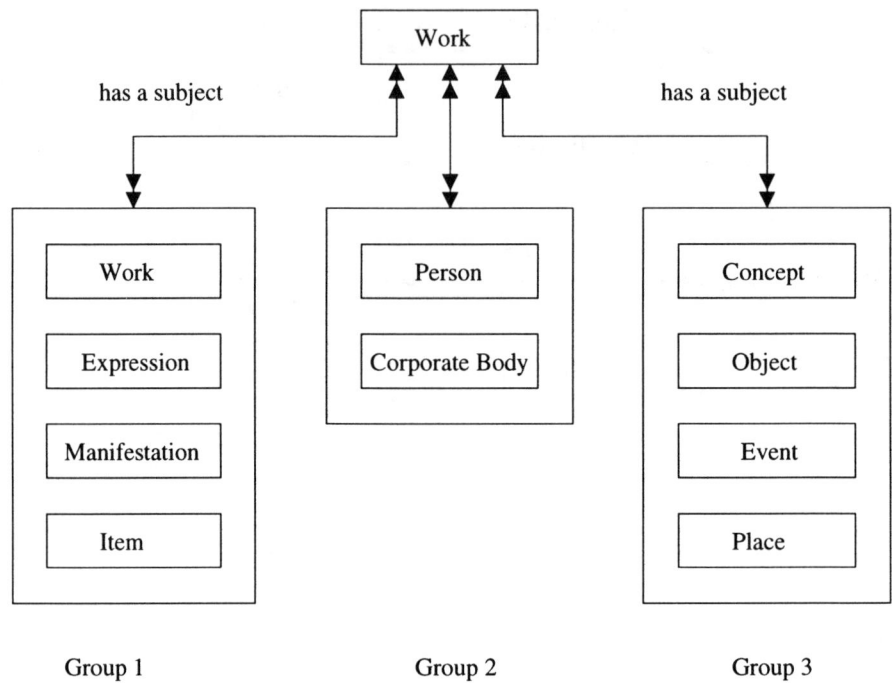

Figure 7. Subject Relationships Model. (IFLA Group 3)

Table 2 gives a few relations of 'moderate value'. The IFLA model has had a great impact on the library community [10,15]. The discussions will continue.

It is interesting to see how the DC *Relation element* is detailed in the proposal [5]. Refinement Qualifiers includes qualifiers like *is-version-of, has-version, has-part, is-referenced-by, requires*. The IFLA model gives similar proposals with its Relationships attributes.

6   Naming of Digital Objects

The paper [1] identifies four main modules in a digital library: *user interface, repository, handle system,* and *search system.* The User Interface is the interface to the user. Digital objects are stored and maintained in the Repository. The Search system is used by the user. A digital object consists of an identifier for the object, data types (the 'content') and structural metadata. The content description of the digital object (the descriptive metadata) can be stored in a the digital object or in a separate digital object (a 'document surrogate'). Traditional library catalogues for example consists of this kind of information objects. Many are accessible on the Internet. The Handle System is a locator system for identificators to digital objects on the Internet. Handles is a naming system, compatible with the URNs (Uniform Resource Name); a naming system which is location independent.

Table 1. Attributes, and 'high value'.

	Find				Identify				Select				Obtain			
	Work	Expression	Manifestation	Item	Work	Expression	Manifestation	Item	Work	Expression	Manifestation	Item	Work	Expression	Manifestation	Item
Attributes of a Work																
Title	X				X				X							
Form									X							
Co-ordinates (maps)					X				X							
Intended termination					X											
Attributes of a Expression																
Form						X				X						
Language						X				X						
Use restrictions										X						
Other disting. Characteristics						X				X						
Attributes of a Manifestation																
Title	X	X	X		X	X	X								X	
Responsible						X	X		X	X					X	
Edition/issue						X	X		X	X					X	
Publisher/distributor						X									X	
Date of publ./distribution						X						X			X	
Form of carrier						X						X			X	
Identifier				X		X									X	
Access restrictions																
Attributes of an Item																
Identifier				X				X								X
Access restrictions																X

7   The Resource Description Framework RDF

The Resource Description Framework (RDF) [13, 14] is an infrastructure that enables the encoding, exchange, and reuse of structured metadata. RDF uses XML (eXtensible Markup Language) as a common syntax. The XML syntax is, however, only one possible syntax for RDF. The basic RDF data model consists of three object types: *resources, properties, and statements.*

All the things being described by RDF expressions are called *resources.* This may be an entire Web page, or a part if one. It may be a whole collection of

Table 2. Relationships, and 'high value', 'X', and of 'moderate value', '(x)', for Manifestation and Item

	Find				Identify				Select				Obtain			
	Work	Expression	Manifestation	Item	Work	Expression	Manifestation	Item	Work	Expression	Manifestation	Item	Work	Expression	Manifestation	Item
Between a Work *And* other works:																
Title	X				X				X							
Form									X							
Co-ordinates (maps)					X				X							
Intended termination					X											
Between an Expression *And* other expressions/works:																
Form						X				X						
Language						X				X						
Use restrictions										X						
Other disting. Characteristics						X				X						
Between a Manifestation *And* a:																
Title	X	X	X		X	X	X								X	
Responsible						X	X			X	X				X	
Edition/issue						X	X			X	X				X	
Publisher/distributor							X								X	
Date of publ./distribution							X				X				X	
Form of carrier							X				X				X	
Identifier				X			X								X	
Access restrictions							X								X	
Between an Item *And* other items:																
Identifier				X				X								X
Access restrictions																X

digital objects, or a physical object like a printed book. A Uniform Resource Identifier, URI, always names a resource. A *property* is a specific aspect, attribute, characteristic, or relation used to describe a resource. A RDF *statement* is a specific resource together with a named property plus the value of that property. These three parts of a statement are called, respectively, the subject, the predicate, and the object. A resource is identified by a resource identifier, a URI.

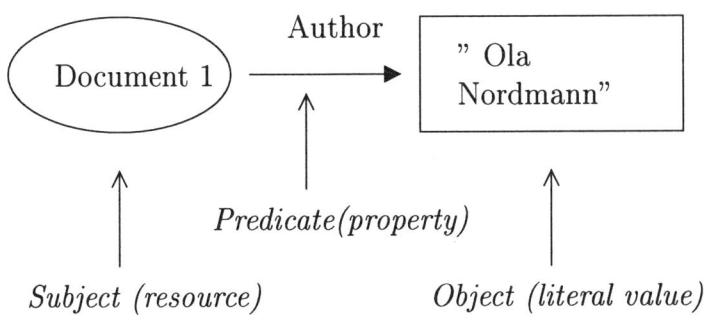

Figure 8. The RDF Data Model: "Ola Nordmann" Is the Author of Document 1.

RDF provides a framework where independent communities can develop application-specific vocabularies, or formats. RDF is a recommendation from the World Wide Web Consortium, W3C [17]. W3C co-operates with the Dublin Core Initiative, bringing the digital library perspective actively into the Web infrastructure.

Figure 9 gives an example of the RDF used in a XML document describing a HTML-document using the Dublin Core metadata elements. DC is specified using XML Name Space (xmlns).

```
<?xml version="1.0"?>
<rdf:RDF
    xmlns:rdf="http://www.w3.org/TR/REC-rdf-syntax/"
    xmlns:dc="http://purl-org/metadata/dublin_core">
    <rdf:Description about="http:///www.ifi.ntnu.no">
        <dc:Title>IDI NTNU Home Page</dc:Title>
        <dc:Creator>IDI Webmaster</dc:Creator>
    </rdf:Description>
</rdf:RDF>
```

Figure 9. Example of RDF Used in a XML Document.

8 Conclusions

There are many actors working world wide to improve the quality of information on the Internet. The development of infrastructures, standards and formats that enables the encoding, exchange and reuse of structured metadata will improve the access to the digital objects. The development and maintenance of a successful Digital Library need interdisciplinary co-operation. In the area of metadata and document modelling promising co-operation between disciplines has started.

References

1. William Arms, C. Blanchi, and E.A. Overly: An architecture for Information in Digital Libraries. *D-Lib Magazine*, February 1997. http://www.dlib.org/dlib/february/cnri/02arms1.html
2. William Arms: Digital Libraries. MIT Press, 2000. ISBN 0-262-01880-8
3. Loran Dempsey, Rachel Heery: DESIRE-RE1004. A review of metadata: A survey of current resource description formats. http://www.ukoln.ac.uk/metadata/desire/overview/rev_toc.htm
4. The Dublin Core Home Page: http://purl.oclc.org/dc/documents/rec-dces-19990702.htm
5. http://purl.org/DC/documents/rec/dcmes-qualifiers-20000711.htm
6. IFLA. The Functional Requirements for Bibliographic Records. http://www.ifla.org.sg/VII/s13/frbr/frbr.pdf
7. Carl Lagoze, Clifford A. Lynch and Ron Daniel Jr. The Warwick Framework: A Container Architecture for Aggregating Sets of Metadata. *D-Lib Magazine*, July 1996 http://www.dlib.org/dlib/july96/lagoze/07lagoze.html
8. David M. Levy, Catherine C. Marshall: Going Digital: A Look at Assumptions Underlying Digital Libraries. CACM, April 1995, pp 77–84.
9. Eric Miller: An Introduction to the Resource Description Framework. *D-Lib Magazine*, May 1998 http://www.dlib.org/dlib/may98/miller/05miller.html
10. Murtomaa, Eeva: The Impact of the Functional Requirements for Bibliographic Records Recommendations on the ISBD(ER). 64th IFLA General Conference 16–21 August, 1998 http://www.ifla.org/IV/ifla64/065-74e.htm
11. David M. Nichols and Michael B. Twidale: Computer supported co-operative work and libraries. http://www.comp.lancs.ac.uk/computing/research/cseg/projects/ariadne/docs/vine.html Also in Vine, 109, 10-15, (special issue on Virtual communities and information services).
12. Andreas Paepcke: Digital Libraries: Searching is not enough. *D-lib Magazine*, May 1996. http://www.dlib.org/dlib/may96/stanford/05paepcke.html
13. W3C Resource Description Framework (RDF) Schema Specification. http://www.w3.org/TR/PR-rdf-schema/
14. W3C Resource Description Framework (RDF) Model and Syntax Specification. http://www.w3.org/TR/REC-rdf-syntax/
15. Strunck, Kirsten: About the use of "Functional Requirements for Bibliographic Records" in teaching cataloguing. 65th IFLA Council and General Conference Bangkok, Thailand, 20–28 August, 1999 http://www.ifla.org/IV/ifla65/papers/108-131e.htm
16. Vanwelkenhuysen, J.: What is a Corporate Memory?, 1996 http://www.inria.fr/acacia/personnel/jvanwelk/projects/section3_1.html
17. The World Wide Web Consortium Home Page: http://www.w3.org/
18. Stuart Weibel Metadata: The Foundations of Resource Description. *D-Lib Magazine*, July 1995, http://www.dlib.org/dlib/July95/07weibel.html
19. Stuart Weibel, Eric Miller: Image Description on the Internet. A Summary of the CNI/OCLC Image Metadata Workshop. *D-Lib Magazine*, January 1997. http://www.dlib.org/dlib/january97/oclc/01weibel.html

Users in Context

Peter Ingwersen

Royal School of Librarianship and Information Science
Birketinget 6, DK 2300 Copenhagen S, Denmark
pi@db.dk

Abstract Users as actors in interactive information retrieval (IIR) are seen in the contexts of their perceived work tasks and information seeking behaviour. The paper models IIR processes by demonstrating a variety of approaches, ranging from Ingwersen's cognitive communication model for IR interaction, over Saraceveic' stratified model which includes a typology of relevance conceptions, to Borlund's model of work task perception, information need development and relevance assessments. Other associated models and perspectives of IIR are discussed when appropriate to the major focus points of the contribution: information need development and typology; understanding of relevance in IIR; and experimental problems in IIR.

1 Introduction

Mainstream IR research, e.g. the Cranfield and TREC traditions [11,17], assumes users as an experimental constant, commonly represented in models by sets of queries. Only in interactive IR (IIR), e.g. in the interactive TREC track as well as in all cognitive and user-driven IR research, users are seen as (more) dynamic actors, that is, as variables in the research settings [23].

In a typical TREC-like experiment one operates with a set of approximately 60 queries. Each query is regarded as a *true* representative of a *stable* information need. In non-interactive IR one expects that user requests always are identical to the information need or gap of knowledge expressed by the request. If a request for information is consisting of few terms, like often on the Web, that is what the user asks for—not that the knowledge gap might be vague. Since the non-interactive experiment assumes the query as a constant, the information need or gap *must* be seen as a stable phenomenon throughout a retrieval session. Aside from the problem of keeping the non-interactive experiment under control there exist at least two reasons for keeping requests and information needs constant. First, the goal of non-interactive experiments is to observe the *retrieval performance* of competing systems or algorithms—not really to find out why algorithms function as they do in real-life settings. Secondly, it is paramount that an assessor judges the retrieval outcome for relevance. In the non-interactive TREC experiments the role of the assessor is to generate the query and later to make assessments after one run of the systems. Thus, he acts like a user in batch mode. Obviously, if other users (or assessors) participated in experiments with

M. Agosti, F. Crestani, and G. Pasi (Eds.): ESSIR 2000, LNCS 1980, pp. 157–178, 2000.

several consecutive iterations or runs, human learning processes might occur and vary, and the one-run assessments would turn out to be inadequate or wrong.

Belkin et al. as well as Iivonen looked into this phenomenon in the early interactive track of TREC [4,19] during which one assessor per query indeed was used like in common TREC. They found that searcher inconsistency was paramount but that one of the applied search strategies led to the "best" performance. That "best" strategy is of course unpredictable. In one-run non-interactive experiments, where several assessors are used per query, there are required more than 30 different queries in order to make the variation between assessors statistically insignificant. Below this number the ranking of the involved systems may alter in terms of performance measures [45].

The investigative problem in IIR is consequently to allow for the inclusion of the disturbing variable during experimentation, i.e. the user framed by his or her world, and, at the same time, to keep control of the experiment or investigation. Otherwise it becomes difficult to compare what one wants to compare, for instance, two best-match algorithms, two different human query modification methods, two ways of visualisations in interfaces, etc. Below, we discuss central concepts that should be taken into account in IIR research with users in action.

First, the paper discusses the basic IIR models, including the simplistic mainstream model. The models in focus are those by Ingwersen [23] and Saracevic [33], and their precursors and derivatives. The models are viewed in context of information seeking. This is followed by a discussion of information need development and dynamics over time in relation to perceived work tasks or interests, and a section on relevance conceptions and models. Some examples of experimental design conclude the paper.

2   Interaction Information Retrieval Models

Figure 1 outlines the interactive IR model as depicted by Ingwersen within the framework of the cognitive viewpoint [22,23]. The model has gone through several modifications due to new empirical research results in international cooperation.

Basically the model operates with five central components. From the left the information objects and their representations, including thesaural nets, are in interaction with the IR system setting during retrieval. The interface component would commonly be seen as part of the entire system and functions as query generator, based on some input from the user component, for instance, in the form of a request or by selection of some visual object on the interface. The individual user—or team of individuals—displays a cognitive space that is assumed to consist of a world model developed over time from cultural and social experiences. The world model is represented by different and dynamic cognitive structures. These are assumed responsible for the actual *perception* of a work task or interest framed by the current cognitive state of the individual. According to this state, which deals with both conceptual domain-related knowledge *and* retrieval and seeking knowledge, the individual user may be in a problematic situation and state of uncertainty in the attempt to solve the problem derived from the perceived work task. If not solvable intrinsically by the cognitive state, including tacit knowledge, the individual may recognise a knowledge gap [14] or need for information. This is the intentionality behind engaging into information seeking behaviour and IIR. This view of the cognitive processes involved in IIR on the user side derives from the well-known ASK hypothesis put forward by Belkin et al. in 1982 [5]. The hypothesis operates with the similar concepts of problematic situation, cognitive uncertainty, and information need. In Fig. 1 the concept of work task or interest, e.g. also of cultural nature, is introduced to explain why people get into problematic situations. There is hence a strong emphasis on the social interaction between the individual user and the situated context surrounding that individual, also over time. The actual work task may thus originate from the social-organisational environment or be produced by the user himself. The environment may take the form of scientific, professional, or social domains with recognised strategies, goals and preferences as well as tasks to be fulfilled.

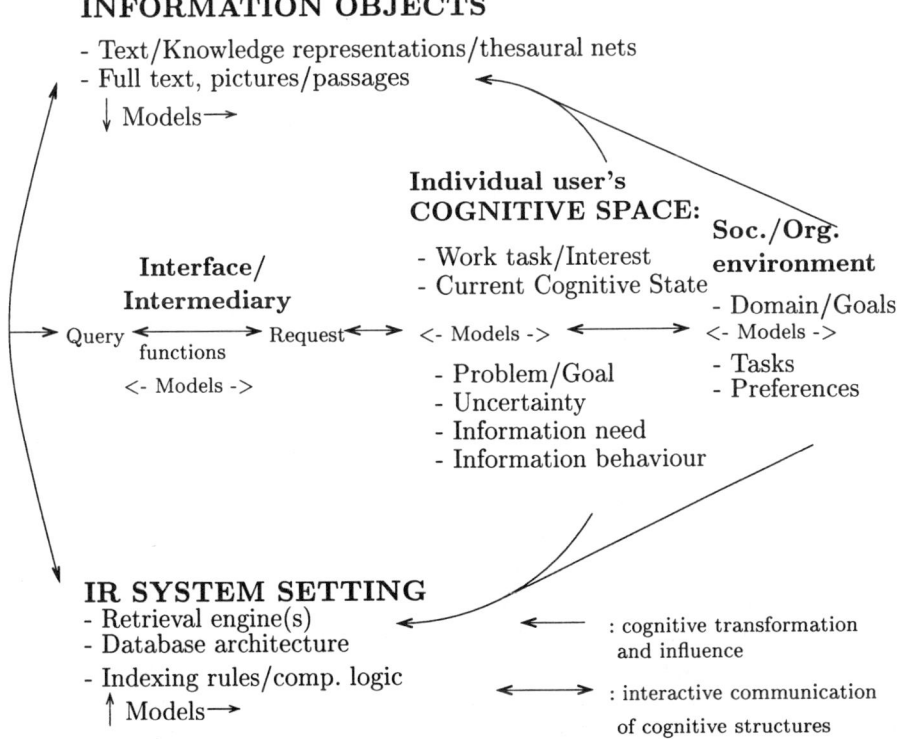

Figure 1. Cognitive Model of IR Interaction. Extension of Ingwersen [22, p. 16]

In IIR *situated context* plays a central role [49]. For each of the five components there exists context. Context is signified by the notion of "models" associated with each component. The notation signifies that models of activities and solutions, behaviour and possible future situations external but crucial to the function of the component are embedded in that component, e.g. by the designer or generator or by learning. With respect to information objects the system setting, interface, user, and the social environment act as context, situated in a given retrieval or seeking activity. Authors do commonly attempt to envisage that context, for instance by generating their texts or images in such a way that they are acceptable by the prevailing domain paradigm and by (at least some) future readers or viewers. On the Internet authors also think about the system settings to which they load their objects.

The individual user is in an interesting position by being dynamic and self-contained. He or she is *influenced* by the social-organisational environment, domain, and work tasks as kinds of situated context. In fact, he or she may seek the required information to lessen the uncertainty and fill the knowledge gap by social interaction with that environment. For instance, the individual user may inquire a colleague about information. On the other hand, the same individual may look to available retrieval systems and engage in IIR—indeed also preceding or proceeding social interaction activities. One might ague that the IR systems, information objects and interfaces form part of the social-organisational environment. This would typically be the case in enterprises or organisations, but also in scientific communities. The problem for the person is now twofold. He or she must engage the information objects in order to obtain data concerning the *perceived work task* and problem. This engagement requires adequate domain knowledge to form part of the current cognitive state. However, in order to engage a system, that is, to perform *search tasks*, the cognitive state in addition must possess adequate retrieval knowledge.

We may consequently observe that the IIR consists of different types of engagements during acts of interaction. Seen from the user point of view the interaction with the social environment certainly requires conceptual (domain) knowledge but also behavioural and personal communicative skills. In order to assess the relevance of the incoming information adequate cognitive structures (conceptual presuppositions or pre-understanding) are required [51]. When interacting with IR systems the personal communicative skills are replaced by levels of retrieval knowledge, including system knowledge. Simultaneously, the user must possess sufficient conceptual domain knowledge to reach into information space to find some objects. When the system feeds back some data from retrieved information objects, the semantics or original contextual properties of that data are not supported by any behavioural signs or attitudes, as is the case in personal communication. The conceptual demand on the user as the recipient of data to carry out interpretations, assess relevance, to learn something and to fulfil his work task is hence of higher magnitude during IIR. This phenomenon also concerns the search task data fed back from the system through the interface: does the user understand the retrieval and system structures, the logic, commands, icons, etc.?

Figure 1 incorporates the simplistic retrieval model applied to mainstream system-driven retrieval research. If we make a vertical cut on the left-hand side of the model between the notion of "query" and the interface component, we observe a triangular interactive model consisting of the information objects, the system setting, and a set of queries. We then take the set of queries and one of the other two components as constants in an experimental setting typical of the mainstream approach. The remaining component is the only variable to be studied across systems.

From the rather complex scenario, Fig. 1, that involves users and their social contexts, cognitive as well as probabilistic uncertainties in objects, we may understand that experimental settings in IIR fundamentally are forced to apply social science methodologies—rather than methods and settings adhering to an early age of Physics [31].

2.1   Complementary IIR Models

Quite recently Belkin et al. [3] generated a four-dimensional model of IIR strategies seen as episodes of information seeking. Based on this model and that of Ingwersen, Fig. 1 [23], Saracevic made a comprehensive alternative model of IIR incorporating a relevance typology [33].

Belkin et al.'s episodic model of information seeking strategies (ISS) considers the types of search a system must support. It might hence be regarded a model of IR interaction behaviour rather than an information seeking model. The underlying idea is that people commonly engage in multiple searching behaviour, both during single IR sessions and across sessions in a longitudinal sense. The goal of the model is to support retrieval (or seeking) by making design and implementation of IR systems adapt to the changing requirements of the systems. The model consists of 16 types of episodes by means of a four-dimensional classification of IR modes. Each mode contains a binary number of values and each type of behaviour is hence defined by the four-dimensional values. The four modes are *method of searching* (scanning or browsing); *mode of retrieval* (recognition or specification of relevant objects); *the goal of retrieval* (learning about the system and information space or finding relevant information); and the *resource considered* (information objects or meta-information).

The model has been applied to Web searching and navigation studies, for instance by Pharo. Pharo's test seems to show that the model is not exhaustive enough and that there is a potential for interdependency between the method of searching and mode of retrieval [30, p. 211].

Saracevic' alternative model of *stratified interaction* displays a three level structure consisting of surface, cognitive, and situational strata [33]. The surface level deals primarily with the computational data processing based on a query. In relation to Fig. 1 this level concerns the interaction between information objects and system setting instigated by a query. The cognitive level embraces the process of perceiving information during man-machine interaction in relation to the perceived need for information. Here, the interaction involves the user through an intermediary mechanism. The situational level refers to the *information use* with respect to a perceived work task in context of an environment. As a central point we observe the longitudinal dimension of use or utility stressed in the models. Saracevic stresses that ideally the system components ought to adopt to users and vice versa. The model is clearly associated to that of Ingwersen from 1992 [22, p. 148] and its extended version [23, p. 9] depicted on Fig. 1. Its strength is its comprehensiveness. The model incorporates a typology of relevance consisting of five different types of relevance. 1) Algorithmic relevance, which is the relation between the system output matched with the query features; 2) Topical relevance, i.e. the relation between the aboutness of information objects and the query; 3) Pertinence or cognitive relevance, i.e. the association between the perceived information need of the user and system output; 4) Situational relevance, which is seen as the usefulness of the objects to the current interest or work task of the user; 5) Affective / motivational relevance, associated with the goal of the user.

Situational relevance and information utility are not new concepts in information science and IR [48]. However, with the re-incorporation of situational relevance and situated context into contemporary IR research and information seeking models the issues of *informativeness* and *information use* become central research objects. This issue extends the *timeline* commonly observed during IR investigations.

Traditionally IIR research stops the experiment with users assessing the retrieval output after a number of iterations during one session. The assessments can be of situational nature where the user judges the *perceived usefulness* of the retrieved objects by means of interpretation on site of titles, summaries, or full objects. Obviously, the real usefulness or degree of informativeness and the ensuing *actual use* of (parts of) the information objects in relation to a work task is a quite different measure. It can only be taken when the user has digested their contents and associated information with the task in question, often after social interaction. Informativeness and actual use makes it obvious increasingly to view information seeking and retrieval as a whole, as proposed analytically by Vakkari [40, 41]. Longitudinal studies of information behaviour and search processes should hence play a more central role as an empirical foundation for future Information Seeking and Retrieval (ISR) models and research.

Long-term investigations of cognitive behaviour and interactive retrieval over time by Wang come here to mind [46]. Wang studied empirically from a cognitive approach the alterations of the perceived information needs over a research project, represented by the distribution of articulated unique and novel versus overlapping search terms. Wang and White goes further by investigating the actual application of documents at the *reading stage*, in particular in relation to the decisions of giving citations to the works used.

Hence, we observe how bibliometric citation studies and mapping of scientific communication patterns, using citations as representations of use, may walk hand in hand with IIR, for instance in terms of presentation of information spaces [15, 23]. The original idea of applying citation indexing as an alternative form of representation in IR derives from Garfield in 1968 [16]. Figure 1 illustrates the spiral of user inquiry, IIR, and use in context by the arrows re-connecting the user / environment to the information objects. In scientific communication the latter contains the results of author interpretations and selections of earlier contributions in the form of citations provided on the reference lists in their journal articles.

The close association between information seeking and IIR has very recently been addressed in a number of general models of information behaviour. Wilson [50] outlines 1999 the central earlier models of information seeking and other aspects of information behaviour. In the form of a nested model he places retrieval in IR systems within the sphere of information seeking processes that again are under the general umbrella of information behaviour. The discussion concerns, for instance, the sense-making framework by Dervin and Nilan [14], Kuhlthau's phenomenological stage process model [26], Belkin et al.'s episodic model [3], Ingwersen's cognitive communication model for interactive IR [23], and Saracevic' stratified IR model [33]. Wilson suggests that the discussed models are *complementary* rather than conflicting, and that his proposed problem-solving model [50, p. 266], provides a basis for relating the models in relevant research strategies.

3   The Work Task—Information Need Relationship

In a pioneering effort Vakkari [40] provides a detailed analysis of theory growth in information seeking, in particular the growth of a theoretical research program on the relation between work task complexity and information seeking. This analytical work refers back to the empirical studies made by Byströ and Järvelin [9] on work task complexity and information needs from 1995. The general trend observed is that the more complex the work task the less the user know about or can define his or her information need, i.e. what is unknown at present. In a cognitive sense that implies that one may assume that basically only something is known about the task or problem at hand, and perhaps nothing about what is required of information to fulfil it. In less complex situations, e.g. in the case of routine tasks or problems to be solved, the information need seems more articulated. To IIR this means that one should not always ask what the user wants, but rather about *why* he or she wants it. This goes very well together with the holistic cognitive IR theory proposed 1996 by Ingwersen [23] in which poly-representation (or multi-evidence) of the information space *as well as* of the user's cognitive space is suggested as a way to avoid dead end retrieval situations. The theory is associated with the aforementioned ASK hypothesis on the user side [5], and the plausible inference technique by Turtle and Croft [39] as well as the Dempster-Shafer uncertainty logic and multiple-evidence principles proposed by van Rijsbergen and Lalmas [44].

Ingwersen [23] proposes to view the *perceived work task* as a rather stable cognitive state during retrieval session time, but not in a longitudinal sense. The

Table 1. Matrix of four distinct cases of human intrinsic information needs, given a perceived work task situation, and the corresponding seeking and interactive information retrieval behaviour—simplified version of Ingwersen [23, p. 15].

Intrinsic information need variables—given a perceived work task	**Well-defined**	**Ill-defined**
Stable	**Verificative** **Conscious topical** *Querying* Filtering behaviour	**Muddled task and info. need** Search loops
Variable	**Conscious topical** *Query-Navigation* Dynamic interaction	**Defined work task Muddled info. need** *Browsing* Try-and-error behaviour

corresponding information need, however, may be dynamic and develop simultaneously due to interpretation and learning processes during IIR. According to Ingwersen one may view the basic cases of information needs in the form of a matrix, defined by two dimensions. One is the degree of perception of the need, i.e. how well is the information need defined in the mind of the user at a given point in time. The other dimension corresponds to the degree of variability of the need over time, i.e. the motivation and ability for change. In line with the holistic cognitive view each individual user will act differently to the same given work task due to differences in the perception influenced by the socio-cultural history of the person and his or her perception of the current context. Notwithstanding, each user should have a degree of understanding of the work task. Otherwise there would not exist any *reason* or cause for engaging in information seeking or IIR. Depending on the current cognitive state, the user may belong to one of the four cases of human information needs at the initiation of the IIR session, Table 1. During retrieval he or she may move to other cases and hence require different kinds of retrieval support.

On Table 1 the transition between the four cases is continuous. The matrix operates with three kinds of intrinsic information needs [21]. *Verificative* needs signify that the user wishes to verify information objects with known non-topical (structured) data, such as author names, client address, cited authors, journal name, etc. This type is assumed to be stable during a session period until objects have (not) been retrieved. *Conscious topical* needs for information imply that the user wants to clarify, review or pursue information in known subject matter and domain. Known subject matter signifies topical (unstructured) data on contents, such as terms, concepts, image representation, etc. This type is assumed to be either of intrinsically stable nature, like the verificative one, or variable over session time. The third kind of information need is called *muddled* or ill-defined. The user is engaged in the exploration of new concepts and relations outside known subject matter or domain, or the known data are incomplete and cognitively vague. In reality one may observe needs that are mixed of verificative and conscious topical ones. We will functionally regard such blends as belonging to the conscious topical kind of information need. We can see that OPACs commonly deal with verificative needs, having some difficulty with the topical ones. Bibliographic and full-object databases are traditionally suited to both verificative and topical information needs.

If users constantly acted rationally, that is, if they expressed *everything they know* about their perceived need and work task, IIR could possibly handle the well-defined information needs quite properly. Besides, the system-driven approach to IR, that information needs are stable and queries (requests) exactly mirror the underlying needs, would be much more in line with reality. However, the problems in IIR are not confined to muddled need situations alone, whether stable or variable. People tend to act at random, to be *uncertain*, and *not to express everything* they know. Instead they express what they assume is enough and/or suitable to the intermediary and/or IR system. They compromise their statements under influence of the current *context and situation*. This context involves the perceived work task or domain *as well as* the perception of the search task, i.e. the understanding of the system and knowledge sources to engage with. This phenomenon is called the *Label Effect*. The effect was predicted by Taylor in 1968 [38] and empirically verified and discussed by Ingwersen 1982 [20, 22].

The Label Effect means that users, even with well-defined knowledge of their information gap, tend to label their initial request for information verbally by means of very few terms or single concepts. It implies two obstacles to successful IR: First, intermediary mechanisms have difficulty in reaching out into the proper directions in information space where data are located relevant to that particular user. Due to the lack of *context* in the request a multitude of directions are indeed possible. This is what we observed in the scientific online age 10–20 years ago, and the same phenomenon is dominant today in web searching. Secondly, intermediary mechanisms may not be capable of distinguishing between users with detailed, some or no knowledge about their information requirements, that is, whether the user is intrinsically well or ill-defined concerning the ASK. It becomes hence difficult for the system to support adequately the user in his or her retrieval endeavour.

A closer observation of the matrix, Table 1, suggests the following issues of concern to IIR research. Mainstream IR research is fundamentally concerned with the investigation of the well-defined and stable case of the matrix. Indeed, we have such kinds of needs, for instance, in connection with patent retrieval and filtering, i.e. selective dissemination of information (SDI) as it is called in information science. In this case IR may support users by means of querying and/or confined navigation. Users will be expected to be less uncertain and be capable of query modification as well as assessing topical relevance as well as pertinence due to the rich cognitive state and situational relevance due to work task perception.

In the case concerned with well-defined but variable information needs people are assumed to be willing (or forced) to learn and shift focus after initial engagement. We may expect exploratory navigation and *stages of uncertainty* throughout the IR session, in line with the "berry-picking" exploratory behaviour suggested and modelled by Bates [1]. The cognitive uncertainty is empirically found to increase during the initial stages of IR (and seeking) processes due to interpretative problems of the retrieved data [27] and the quality of the cognitive state. Situational relevance assessments are possible due to known work task, but query modification as well as topicality and pertinence assessments may be unreliable at initial stages of engagement with the system.

The muddled and variable kind of information needs seem to require means of browsing rather than querying due to the inherent Label Effect. Cognitive uncertainty will be expected to be high and we may observe try and error behaviour during searching, since new adequate search features may be hard to recall from memory or non-existent. However, the motivation and curiosity of the user may make the session progress. With the exception of situational relevance assessments judgements of topicality or pertinence are assumed very cumbersome during many stages of the IIR process, as is query modification. In fact, the only cognitive structures assumed to be present are those associated with the perceived work task or interest.

The final case of ill-defined but stable information needs also assumes uncertainty as to the work task definition. It might be highly complex [9] but the work task may also be vaguely represented in a cognitive sense for another reason. In the case of human mediators (librarians), Ingwersen found [20] that they rarely possess a complete picture of the work task or problem of the end-user. What they often only know is "something"—a few terms or concepts—extracted from the user during personal communication. The Label Effect clearly appears in such cases and the mediator runs into search loops. In order to break the dead end the mediator's cognitive state must rapidly absorb knowledge about the user situation. In generalist circumstances, for instance, in public libraries, this "getting to know" the underlying situation is often hampered by lack of domain knowledge on the mediator side. On the other hand, in specialised information services in organisations the mediators often know of the current tasks of their end-users, due to collaboration, and the muddled case can be solved or moved to another case in the matrix. However, when being in the fourth case the searcher have severe difficulty with respect to all kinds of relevance assessments as well as query modification activity. The reason that public librarians after all often succeed is grounded in their extensive retrieval knowledge that may guide them to probably proper locations in information space.

The matrix, Table 1, demonstrates that only in one-two cases can we expect users to act according to plans in rational ways, i.e. in the well-defined cases. This difference also lies in the notions of navigation versus browsing. Navigation is seen as purposeful moves by links or similar activity in networks of information objects. The user seeks to fulfil a goal, either by navigating in a confined space or by a more exploratory behaviour—but constantly with the work task or end goal in mind. Browsing signifies an activity of randomness in searching. The searcher is open to novel paths and serendipity effects may occur. Recently, Hong [52] has published a model of intentions and shifts that take place during IIR, also applying the episodic IIR model by Belkin et al. [3]. Hong's model primarily concerns the well-defined cases discussed above.

Due to the randomness, vagueness, and Label Effects of users, at least during the initial stages of IIR, retrieval research might profit from also concentrating on the perceived work tasks and their function in IIR. Essentially, the concern is to make possible for the system to obtain several *simultaneous evidences* or representations of the user work task and underlying situation. Such representations do not exclude non-topical data types, such as meta-data. The system is hence better equipped to support the user in his or her information retrieval activities.

4 Relevance Issues in IIR

Relevance has become a major area of study in information science. A wide variety of subject fields have tried to deal with this concept. Theoretical frameworks abound, and yet, relevance is also a concept that is intuitively understood, but very difficult to define. Nevertheless, since information science was first seen as a distinct discipline in the 1940s, relevance has been identified as one of its fundamental and central concept [35].

In the past, studies have concentrated on either a systems-centred or user-centred or cognitive approaches to information retrieval. In systems approaches to IR, relevance is considered to be a property of the system, whereas in user-oriented and cognitive traditional, relevance is *directly associated* to the cognitive processes of the users and their changing knowledge and needs regarding information, stimulated by the context. Furthermore, there are many kinds of relevance, not one only, as discussed by Mizzaro [28]. It is clear that the concept of relevance covers a very wide area of knowledge, and it is perhaps owing to this diversity that the latest studies concentrate on the *interaction* between the user and the system in trying to establish what relevance really is. It is during this interaction that an important dimension must be added, namely that of *time*. As the cognitive state may change over session time or across sessions both the information need and relevance may change for the same user. This time dimension can be measured and plotted in terms of *information-seeking* stages and successive searches, as empirically shown by Wang [46] and Spink et al. [36].

Saracevic' stratified model of IIR also offers an integrated framework to incorporate a system of relevance, and states that "The effectiveness of IR depends on the effectiveness of the interplay and adaptation of various relevance manifestations, organised in a system of relevances. Thus the major direction of R&D in information science should be toward increasing the effectiveness of relevance inter-plays and interactions. This should be the whole point of relevance research in information science" [33, p.216]. Following the framework, discussed above, relevance manifests itself on different levels or strata. Relevance inferences may differ at various levels, but the inferences are always interdependent, and IR evaluation is all about comparing relevance inferences from different levels. Relevance can be typified at different levels of manifestation, and we can study its behaviour and effects within and between strata. As briefly defined above, Saracevic' relevance system contains the following relevance manifestations: algorithmic; topical; cognitive relevance or pertinence; situational; and motivational and affective relevance.

Saracevic' underlying assumption is that relevance is rooted in human cognition. This is summarised by the following words: "As a cognitive notion relevance involves an interactive, dynamic establishment of a relation by inference, with intentions toward a context" [33, p.206]. On the surface it would mean that relevance is a subjective phenomenon. However, also an objective manifestation can be found, namely that made available by the IR system itself directly through its algorithms. Since the algorithms are cognitive representations the assumption holds. In the early days of IR experimentation [11], and during the following two decades, relevance was seen as either objective, i.e. system relevance that could be measured, e.g., by recall and precision, or a subjective relevance in the form of utility. With the article by Schamber et al. in 1990 [35] this dual notion of relevance was scattered by the introduction of situational relevance manifestations, and more recent analytical as well as empirical contributions on the matter all treat relevance as a multi-dimensional phenomenon. Simultaneously, relevance is not anymore consisting of a binary scale used during assessment activities in all IR experiments. The empirical studies by Borlund and Ingwersen [7] as well as Greisdorf and Spink [13,36] are examples of a non-binary approach to relevance *and* scaling.

4.1   Dimensions of Relevance

Saracevic operates with the following attributes that makes it possible to distinguish between the above mentioned five manifestations of relevance, Table 2.

Table 2. Attributes of Relevance According to Saracevic [33].

Attributes of Relevance	
Relation	Relevance always implies a relation, often in communication or exchange.
Intention	The relation in expression of relevance involves intentions such as objectives, roles, expectations (motivation).
Context	Intention always comes from a context, and is always directed toward that context.
Inference	Assessment (often graduated) of the effectiveness of a given relation.
Interaction	Inference is accomplished as a dynamic process of interaction, and interpretations of the other attributes change as cognition changes.

Looking at the attributes of relevance as listed above, Table 2, it is clear that relevance always indicates a relation. Different manifestations of relevance indicate different relations. It would therefore seem that the trend moves toward viewing relevance in IR not as a single definition of relevance, but as a system of relevances (note the plural). Consequently no single relevance in the system can be viewed in isolation. Relevance exists as an interacting system of manifestations on different levels.

According to Cosijn and Ingwersen [13] who analysed Saracevic' framework [33] and plotted his manifestations against the attributes, it is interesting to note that the relevance manifestations are moving from a systems approach to a user- and socially oriented approach. Thus the whole spectrum is included in relation to the IIR components, Fig. 1. More importantly their analysis demonstrates that the attributes function in *different dimensions* for the different manifestations of relevance, Table 3.

This raises two issues associated with the original framework: First, should the defined manifestation of *affective or motivational relevance* be regarded as part of a linear scale of moving from objective to subjective relevance? One may argue that motivational relevance is the same as the *intent attribute*. Cosijn and Ingwersen suggest to replace it by a *socio-cognitive relevance* as the ultimate manifestation of relevance on a linear scale, as proposed by Ørom under the label of contextual relevance [29], and corresponding to domain-related relevance proposed by Hjørland [18]. Secondly, one may regard affective relevance as a dimension of relevance influencing *all* the preceding subjective relevance types. Cosijn and Ingwersen argue [13] that affective relevance is *not* a discrete category or part of a linear scale. It should rather be viewed as part of, and influencing the subjective types of relevance (topical, pertinence, situational and socio-cognitive relevance).

Table 3 displays in tabular form the final analysis result with the socio-cognitive relevance manifestation replacing affective or motivational relevance. The table illustrates the difference between topicality observed by a person external to the user-system interaction process, for instance, an assessor, and topicality assessed by a user having a real information need. The relation and intention attributes work differently depending on whether the judge is internal or external to an investigation. External observers can only assess the aboutness of the *expressed need*, in the form of a query or request, in relation to retrieved information objects. Due to the Label Effect such an assessment may be rather different from that made by the user, in particular if he or she possesses an intrinsically well-defined information need. The Borlund and Ingwersen model, Fig. 2, originating in a simplified form from [7], takes this distinction into account, naming the user's topical assessment as intellectual topicality.

External assessors may judge algorithmic relevance by means of (intellectual) topicality, as done in non-interactive TREC after a one-run session. However, the *time* issue plays a distinctive role, as discussed earlier on. The more IIR iterations by users the more likely the inconsistency in between users and between users and assessors. *Pertinence* as well as situational relevance belongs clearly to the sphere of the individual user. Pertinence is a result of pragmatic interpretations of objects, for instance, their novelty, also over session time, their way

Table 3. Attributes and Manifestations of Relevance. Revision of Saracevic' Framework [33] by Cosijn and Ingwersen [13]. Socio-cognitive relevance has replaced affective-motivational relevance in right-most column.

At-tributes of Rele-vance	Manifestations of Relevance				
		⇔ Affective	Relevance	⇔	
	Algorithmic	**Topical**	**Cognitive / Pertinence**	**Situational / Utility**	**Socio-Cognitive**
Relation	Query ⇒ Information objects (feature-based)	Subject / topic expressed in query ⇒ information objects	State of knowledge / cognitive information need ⇒ Information objects	Situation, work task or problem at hand as perceived ⇒ Information objects	Situation, task or problem at hand as perceived in socio-cultural context ⇒ Information objects
Intention	(a) System dependent (b) Intent / motivation behind algorithm	(a) User / assessor expectations (b) Intent / motivation behind query	Highly personal and subjective, related to information need, intentions and motivations	Highly personal and subjective or even emotional. Related to goals, intentions and motivations	Personal, subjective / org. strategy. Related to user's experience, traditions, scientific paradigms
Context	Tuning search engine performance (e.g. TREC)	All types of subjective relevance are, by context definition, dependent (user's / assessor's context)			
Infer-ence	Weighting and ranking functions	Interpretation of aboutness and subject matter at semantic level	Subjective and individualised process of cognitive / pragmatic interpretation, selection and filtering	User's ability to utilise information objects in a way meaningful to user	Users' (or group's) ability to utilise information objects, meaningful to environment
Interac-tion	Automatic relevance feedback or query modification	Relevance judgements are content dependent	Relevance judgements are content, feature, form and presentation dependent	Including interaction *with* environment	Including interaction *within* environment
		Increasing Time Dependence		⇒	

of being presented, their credibility, and/or in relation to features different from subject matter, such as a publishing journal. Affective issues come into play, like in connection to the situational and socio-cognitive relevance manifestations. *Situational relevance* is influenced by the context, e.g. the domain, the perceived work task, organisational preferences, etc., Fig. 1, but the individual user is the deciding factor in relation to usefulness of objects on site. At a later stage in the process of fulfilling the work task the user may be further influenced by social interaction. Hence, we move into the region of *socio-cognitive* relevance. Examples of this manifestation are, for instance, reviewer meetings in editorial boards or conference programme committees assessing contributed papers, co-author negotiations of which articles to use and cite, or workshop and research seminar discussions of papers and ideas. Schamber provides a comprehensive review of the historical and contemporary issues of relevance up towards 1994 [34].

4.2   Experimental Issues on Relevance and Work Tasks in IIR

Saracevic' typological relevance framework as well as the work task-information retrieval issue have inspired several empirical research efforts and further modelling of relevance phenomena recently. For instance, Borlund and Ingwersen [7] explored the possibility of applying situational relevance and topicality assessments in interactive IR experiments using non-binary relevance assessments and by modelling Saracevic' framework [33] in relation to real as well as simulated work tasks. That model can be modified to emphasise the relation between a *perceived* work task, the dynamic information need developing over time, and relevance categories for test persons as well as assessors in IR experiments—Fig. 2. The same approach also evaluates performance measures that relate types of relevance and suggests novel relevance ranking measures, also suitable for non-interactive IR [8]. Järvelin and Kekäläinen [25] are also concerned with relevance ranking in non-binary mode by proposing and testing the cumulative gain the user obtains by examining the retrieval results up to a given ranked position. Spink et al. [36, 37] empirically investigate what they call regions of relevance, including the application of non-binary assessments in large-scale interactive studies. They develop the relevance framework further. In an empirical research environment Vakkari [42] and Vakkari and Hakala [43] investigate the development of relevance, relevance criteria and contributing information types of searched documents in task performance over an academic term period. Similarly, Wang and White investigate and provide a cognitive model of the actual application of documents at the reading stage in particular in relation to the decisions of giving citations to the works used [47].

In Fig. 2 cognitive agents are symbolised by ellipses. A cognitive agent may in this setting be a user or an assessor. The traditional and most commonly used type of relevance is the algorithmic relevance (a) which expresses the degree of match between the request/query version (r^{1-n}) and the retrieved information objects (O^{1-n}) resulting in a ranked output. The topical founded, though intellectually influenced type of relevance, intellectual topicality (Int. t), is signified by the topical nearness (aboutness) between the retrieved objects (O^{1-n}) and

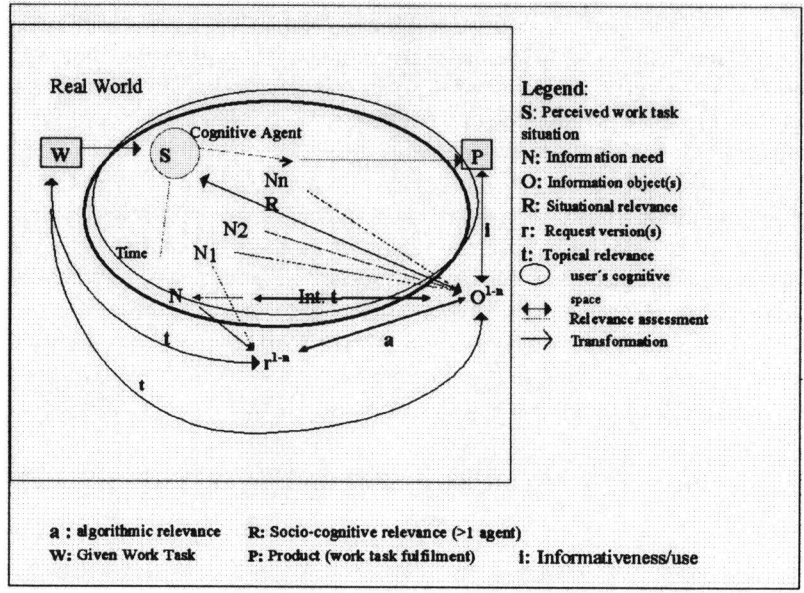

Figure 2. Manifestations of relevance in interactive information retrieval with a given work task, cognitive spaces of (two) cognitive agents (ellipses), information objects retrieved from a system (not shown), and the final information product.

the topic of the information need version (N^{1-n}). Situational relevance (R) signifies the relationship between the retrieved objects (O^{1-n}) and the perceived cognitive work task situation (S) originated from (W), for instance in the form of usefulness. Because intellectual topicality may continue into pertinence assessments, i.e. the relation between objects and current information need, e.g. in the form of novelty or applicable features of objects, a dotted line continues the intellectual topicality line of assessment towards the need (N). In short, the two relevance manifestations might be difficult to distinguish during experiments. If two users interact as a team, socio-cognitive relevance assessments may be observed as negotiated decisions on the usefulness of objects, under influence of the understanding by the agents of the work task. The fulfilment of (part of) a work task commonly results in a product which can be observed in the real world. The relationship between previously observed relevance assessments, e.g. situational, intellectual topical, or algorithmic, and the actual use of objects in the product provides an observable measure of informativeness (i), as done by Wang and White [47].

It is important to note that the *time dimension* is incorporated into the model, Fig. 2, signified by the sequential versions of the information need (N1-n) and the corresponding request versions (r1-n). The perceived work task (S) is regarded rather stable during session time, but not across sessions. Since the request versions/queries form part of the real world they are observable. One may hence assess the relationship between requests and the given work task in order to observe manifestations of *interpretations* of the original work task (t), also across test persons.

This sort of assessment is *ideally* of topical nature. Similarly, an observer might focus on the nearness of the given work task and the retrieved objects, also those that have been judged highly relevant by the body of users (or systems). Indeed, this is what TREC assessors commonly do. They create the task and observe the (topical) relevance of the output, pooled from the algorithmic results of the involved IR systems. In this respect one may refer back to Saracevic' notion that relevance inference are interdependent and IR evaluation is all about comparing relevance inferences from different levels or strata [33]. However, it is easy to see that such ideally objective observations and measurements in fact are *subjective. The observer turns into a cognitive agent,* as depicted in the model, Fig. 2, in line with a user. Consequently, the observer/assessor suffers from the *same problems* of perception and interpretation of the work task, as do users. The objective "topical" assessments by the assessor turn out to be of intellectual nature or perhaps in the form of pertinence or even situational relevance. In particular, if the assessor has generated the task, he or she should have an idea about in which situated context the task is supposed to function. The assessor is then like a user with a real information need. How do we then know which relevance manifestation the assessor actually applies when assessing? How much influence has the context on him? Some of these facets of relevance assessments were already discussed in 1973 by Cooper [12].

If the assessor has not generated the work task he or she becomes similar to a user during either a brief one-run session (in non-interactive TREC) or a real IIR experiment with multiple runs with given simulated topics or information needs to fulfil. In the latter case the *presentation and form* of the given work task becomes crucial for the outcome. Common TREC "topics" are rarely situated or expressing a context of use. This is the reason for explicitly to apply cover stories or *simulated work task situations* during IIR experiments [6–8], preferably in a classic social science setting (placebo experiments) if comparing two systems or features of interfaces [31].

The model, Fig. 2, demonstrates the influence of a real or a given simulated work task. Simulated work tasks or cover stories provide a context or *reason* for that people should look for information. Each test person is then free to make his or her own perception and interpretation of that context, forming his own perceived information need. The more limited the context the more open semantically the possibilities for interpretation. Borlund currently evaluates this research methodology, by comparing real needs for information with simulated ones, and by investigating characteristics of well-functioning simulated work tasks [6], including their domain-dependency. Other proposals for applying search and work tasks as instrumental in IIR investigations are currently under development [32]. The advantage of applying such simulations is that users are free to interpret the situations which, when given to a number of test persons, makes the experimental setting controllable and manageable.

5   Concluding Remarks

In contrast to non-interactive IR experiments IIR investigations rely on a relatively high number of test persons and work tasks/information need situations (search jobs) that make the results statistically reliable, whether the goal is measuring performance, functionality or behavioural aspects of retrieval interaction. The rule of thumb is that behavioural or cognitively related investigations of quantitative nature require, as a minimum, 40–50 participants and 2–3 work tasks of simulated and/or real nature per person in order to be reliable. In the case of qualitative empirical studies the number of persons may be less. Since we clearly are talking about sampling the numbers will depend on the target population. The sample population as well as the chosen test situations and systems under study should always belong to a defined knowledge or work domain. Naturally, if the entire population, say in an organisation, is analysed smaller studies are still valid since no sampling takes place. But one may not be able to generalise beyond the organisation or domain. In performance comparisons between systems or interface features one may decrease the number of test persons to minimum 25–30 but should apply an increased number of test situations or search jobs per person. In particular care should be taken of the cross tabulation of test situations applied between two groups of test persons where one acts as the control group of the other. Similarly, the test situations can be made to function as sets of control. The search jobs should be permuted in order to normalise learning effects using the systems under testing and to avoid that particular job sequences define the searching behaviour [7].

Another dimension of IIR and information seeking studies and investigations is the question of who to use as test persons. We observe often in information research that information or computer science students are used as participants, since they are easy to approach. This is not a good idea if the purpose of the study is to observe how a chemical information system and interface function. Another facet of this dimension is the problem that face interface investigations. Novel interfaces or interface functionality are always new to everybody. Many consecutive sessions are thus required in order for the participants to accustom to the interface prior to the serious investigation of the interaction is carried out. Too many interface solutions have prematurely been disregarded due to studies made over a few sessions by users new to the system/interface.

Users in IIR evaluations cannot be asked to perform an unlimited number of work tasks. On average, a test search may take 20–30 minutes per person. Four work tasks per test session are consequently seen as the maximum, in particular if the researcher also applies post search interviewing. Since the investigation often requires more than four tasks to be performed by each participant, several test sessions are necessary and (unwanted) learning processes may take place between sessions. Careful planning, the application of several data collection methods (triangulation) and normalisation of the test situations can solve some of these problems [31].

By applying several simulated work task situations it becomes possible to induce controlled parameters in the search jobs, such as features unfamiliar to the user population, in order to investigate IR system functionality and performance during interaction with knowledge weak populations. In general, IIR experiments should make more use of *differentiated* work task situations in order to observe, for instance, which kind of situations or information needs are best fulfilled by which kinds of interface functions or retrieval algorithms. As we have seen there exists a variety of work task situations, of corresponding information need types as well as of relevance types. We also know about several algorithmic means to retrieve information objects at the theoretical level or as black box experiments. Such means include methods of visualisation, query modification and relevance feedback. From of these features studies involving users we experience often that their theoretical attractiveness in practical interaction raises new issues and problems. For instance, Beaulieu has found that users have severe problems in understanding what relevance feedback and human query modification entail [2]. Further, the common probabilistic weighting methods often produce the same information objects again and again via relevance feedback algorithms on the top of the ranked output, only changing the ranking order of relevance from iteration to iteration. This is because all relevant objects chosen over the session have equal weights. Campbell [10] has thus investigated to alter the algorithms so that the present visualised objects that are chosen to be of interest have highest weights. One should note that not only the direct interactions between man and system are researchable in IIR. In fact, the entire system of interactions and transformations, demonstrated on the model, Fig. 1, are contributing to our understanding of IIR. However, our comprehension of how the information and system spaces interact with the cognitive and social ones is far from complete [24]. The grey areas on the IIR research map are *legio*.

References

1. Bates, M.J. The Design of Browsing and Berry-Picking Techniques for the Online Search Interface. *Online and CD-ROM Review*, 13(5):407–424, 1989.
2. Beaulieu, M. Experiments with Interfaces to Support Query Expansion. *Journal of Documentation*, 53:8–19, 1997.
3. Belkin, N.J., Cool, C., Stein, A., Thiel, U. Case, Scripts, and Information Seeking Strategies: On the Design of Interactive Information Retrieval Systems. *Expert Systems with Applications*, 9:379–395, 1995.
4. Belkin, N.J., Kantor, P., Fox, E.A., Shaw, J.A. Combining the Evidence of Multiple Query Representation for Information Retrieval. *Information Processing & Management*, 31:431–448, 1995.
5. Belkin, N.J., Oddy, R., Brooks, H. ASK for Information Retrieval. *Journal of Documentation*, 38(3):61–71, 1982.
6. Borlund, P. Experimental Components for the Evaluation of Interactive Information Retrieval Systems. *Journal of Documentation*, 56(1):71–90 (2000).
7. Borlund, P., Ingwersen, P. The Development of a Method for the Evaluation of Interactive Information Retrieval Systems. *Journal of Documentation*, 53(3):225–250, 1997.

8. Borlund, P., Ingwersen, P. Measures of Relative Relevance and Ranked Half-Life: Performance Indicators for Interactive IR. In: Wilkinson, R., Croft, B.W., van Rijsbergen, C.J. (eds.): *Proceedings of the 21st ACM-Sigir Conference on Research and Development of Information Retrieval*. York Press, Melbourne, Australia (1998) 324–331.

9. Byström, K., Järvelin, K. Task Complexity Affects Information Seeking and Use. *Information Processing & Management*, 31(2):191–214, 1995.

10. Campbell, I. Interactive Evaluation of the Ostensive Model Using a New Yest Collection of Images with Multiple Relevance Assessments. *Information Retrieval*, 2:87–114, 2000.

11. Cleverdon, C.W., Keen, E.M. Factors Determining the Performance of Indexing Systems. Vol. 1: Design. Vol. 2: Results. *Aslib Cranfield Research Project*, Cranfield, UK, 1966.

12. Cooper, W.S. A Definition of Relevance for Information Retrieval. *Information Storage and Retrieval*, 7(1):19–37, 1971.

13. Cosijn, E., Ingwersen, P. Dimensions of Relevance. *Information Processing & Management*, 36:533–550, 2000.

14. Dervin, Brenda, Nilan, M. Information Needs and Uses. In: Williams, M.E. (ed.): *Annual Review of Information Science and Technology*, Vol. Learned Information for the Am. Soc. for Information Science, Medford, NJ (1986) 3–33.

15. Ding, Y., Chowdhury, G.. Foo, F. Mapping the Intellectual Structure of Information Retrieval Studies: An Author Co-Citation Analysis, 1987–1997. *Journal of Information Science: Principles and Practice*, 25(1):67–78, 1999.

16. Garfield, E. From Citation Indexes to Informetrics: Is the Tail Wagging the Dog? *Libri: International Library Review*, 48:67–80, 1998.

17. Harman, D.K. The TREC Conferences. In: Sparck Jones, K. and Willett, P. (eds.): *Readings in Information Retrieval*. Morgan Kaufmann, San Francisco (1997) 247–256.

18. Hjørland, B. *Information Seeking and Subject Representation: An Activity-Theoretical Approach to Information Science*. Greenwood Press, London, 1997.

19. Iivonen, M. Consistency in the Selection of Search Concepts and Search Terms. *Information Processing & Management*, 31(2):173–190, 1995.

20. Ingwersen, P. Search Procedures in the Library Analysed from the Cognitive Point of View. *Journal of Documentation*, 38(3):165–191, 1982.

21. Ingwersen, P. Cognitive Analysis and the Role of the Intermediary in Information Retrieval. In: Davies, R., (ed.): *Intelligent Information Systems*. Horwood, Chichester, West Sussex, England, 1986. 206–237.

22. Ingwersen, P. *Information Retrieval Interaction*. Taylor Graham, London, 1992.

23. Ingwersen, P. Cognitive Perspectives of Information Retrieval Interaction: Elements of a Cognitive IR Theory. *Journal of Documentation*, 52(1):3–50, 1996.

24. Ingwersen, P. Cognitive Information Retrieval. In: Williams, M. (ed.): *Annual Review of Information Science and Technology*, 34, (2000), In press.

25. Järvelin, K., Kekälainen, J. IR Evaluation Methods for Retrieving highly Relevant Documents. In: Belkin, N.J., Ingwersen, P., Mun-Kew Leong (eds.): *Proceedings of the 23rd ACM-Sigir Conference on Research and Development of Information Retrieval*. SIGIR Forum, 34:41–48, 2000.

26. Kuhlthau, C.C. Inside the Search Process: Information Seeking from the User's Perspective. *Journal of the American Society for Information Science*, 42:361–371, 1991.

27. Kuhlthau, C.C. The Role of Experience in the Information Search Process of an early Career Information Worker: Perceptions of Uncertainty, Complexity, Construction, and Sources. *Journal of the American Society for Information Science*, 50(5):399–412, 1999.
28. Mizzaro, S. Relevance: The Whole History. *Journal of the American Society for Information Science*, 48(9):810–832, 1997.
29. Ørom, A. 2000. Information Science, Historical Changes and Social Aspects: A Nordic Look. *Journal of Documentation*, 56:12–26, 2000.
30. Pharo, N. Web Information Search Strategies: A Model for Classifying Web Interaction. In: Aparac, T., Saracevic, T., Ingwersen, P., Vakkari, P. (eds.): *Proceedings from the 3rd International Conference on Conceptions of Library and Information Science, CoLIS 3: Digital Libraries: Interdisciplinary Concepts, Challenges and Opportunities*. University Of Zagreb, Zagreb, Croatia (1999) 207–218.
31. Pors, N.O. Information Retrieval, Experimental Models and Statistical Analysis. *Journal of Documentation*, 56(1)(2000) 55–70.
32. Reid, J. A New, Task-Orientated Paradigm for Information Retrieval: Implications for Evaluation of Information Retrieval Systems. In: Aparac, T., Saracevic, T., Ingwersen, P., Vakkari, P. (eds.): *Proceedings from the Third International Conference on Conceptions of Library and Information Science, CoLIS 3: Digital Libraries: Interdisciplinary Concepts, Challenges and Opportunities*. University of Zagreb, Croatia (1999) 97–108.
33. Saracevic, T. Relevance Reconsidered '96. In: Ingwersen, P., Pors, N.O. (eds): *Information Science: Integration in Perspective. Royal School of Library and Information Science*, Copenhagen, Denmark (1996) 201–218.
34. Schamber, L. Relevance and Information Behavior. In: Williams, M. (ed.): *Annual Review of Information Science and Technology*, 29:3–48, 1994.
35. Schamber, L., Eisenberg, M., Nilan, M. A Re-Examination of Relevance: Toward a Dynamic, Situational Definition. *Information Processing & Management*, 26(6):755–776, 1990.
36. Spink, A., Greisdorf, H., Bateman, J. From Highly Relevant to not Relevant: Examining Different Regions of Relevance. *Information Processing & Management*, 34(5):599–621, 1998.
37. Spink, A., Greisdorf, H. Regions of Relevance Study, Part 1: Measuring and Mapping Users' Relevance Judgements. *Journal of the American Society for Information Science*, 51, (2000). In press.
38. Taylor, R.S. Question Negotiation and Information Seeking in Libraries. *College and Research Libraries*, 29:178–194, 1968.
39. Turtle, H., Croft, W.B. Inference Methods For Document Retrieval. *ACM-SIGIR Forum*. June, 1–24, 1990.
40. Vakkari, P. Growth of Theories on Information Seeking: An Analysis of Growth of a Theoretical Research Program on the Relation between Task Complexity and Information Seeking. *Information Processing & Management*, 34:361–382, 1998.
41. Vakkari, P. Task Complexity, Problem Structure and Information Actions: Integrating Studies on Information Seeking and Retrieval. *Information Processing & Management*, 35(6):819–837, 1999.
42. Vakkari, P. Relevance and Contributing Information Types of Searched Documents in Task Performance. In: Belkin, N.J., Ingwersen, P., Mun-Kew Leong (eds.): *Proceedings of the 23rd ACM-Sigir Conference on Research and Development of Information Retrieval. SIGIR Forum*, 34:2–9, 2000.
43. Vakkari, P., Hakkala, N. Changes in Relevance Criteria and Problem Stages in Task Performance. *Journal of Documentation*, 56(5):540–562, 2000.

44. van Rijsbergen, C.J., Lalmas, M. An Information Calculus for Information Retrieval. *Journal of the American Society for Information Science*, 47:385–398, 1996.

45. Voorhees, E.M. Variations in Relevance Judgements and the Measurement of Retrieval Effectiveness. In: Croft, B.W., Moffat, A., van Rijsbergen, C.J., Wilkinson, R. and Zobel, H. (eds): *Proceedings of the 21st ACM SIGIR Conference on research and development of Information retrieval.* ACM Press/ York Press, Melbourne, Australia 315–323, 1998.

46. Wang, P. Users' Information Needs at Different Stages of a Research Project: A Cognitive View. In: Vakkari, P. (eds): *Information Seeking in Context.* Taylor Graham, London (1997) 307–318.

47. Wang, P., White, M.D. A Cognitive Model of Document Use during a Research Project. Study II. Decisions at the Reading and Citing Stages. *Journal of the American Society for Information Science*, 50(2):98–114, 1999.

48. Wilson, P. Situational Relevance. *Information Storage and Retrieval*, 9:457–471, 1973.

49. Wilson, T.D. On User Studies and Information Needs. *Journal of Documentation*, 37(1):3–15, 1981.

50. Wilson, T.D. Models in Information Behaviour Research. *Journal of Documentation*, 55(3):249–270, 1999.

51. Winograd, T., Flores, C.F. *Understanding Computers and Cognition: A New Foundation for Design.* Addison-Wesley, Norwood, NJ, 1986.

52. Xie, H. Shifts of Interactive Intentions and Information-Seeking Strategies in Interactive Information Retrieval. *Journal of the American Society for Information Science*, 51:841–857, 2000.

Logic and Uncertainty in Information Retrieval

Fabio Crestani[1] and Mounia Lalmas[2]

[1] Department of Computer Science
University of Strathclyde, Glasgow G1 1XH, Scotland
fabioc@cs.strath.ac.uk
[2] Department of Computer Science
Queen Mary, University of London, London E1 4NS, England
mounia@dcs.qmw.ac.uk

Abstract The use of logic in Information Retrieval (IR) enables one to formulate models that are more general than other well known IR models. Indeed, some logical models are able to represent, within a uniform framework, various features of IR systems, such as hypermedia links, multimedia content, and users knowledge. Logic also provides a common approach to the integration of IR systems with logical database systems. Finally, logic makes it possible to reason about an IR model and its properties. This latter possibility is becoming increasingly important since conventional evaluation methods, although good indicators of the effectiveness of IR systems, often give results which cannot be predicted, or for that matter satisfactorily explained. However, logic by itself cannot fully model IR. In determining the relevance of a document to a query the truth value or the validity of a logical formula relating the two is not enough. It is necessary to take into account the uncertainty inherent in such a formulation. This paper gives an overview of how past and current research have combined the use of logical and uncertainty theories for the formulation of more advanced models for the representation and retrieval of information.

1 Introduction

Information retrieval (IR) is the science and technology concerned with the effective and efficient retrieval of information for the subsequent use by interested parties. The central problem in IR is the quest to find the set of relevant documents, amongst a large collection, containing the information sought thereby satisfying an information need usually expressed by a user with a query. The documents may be objects (items) in any medium, text, image, audio, or, indeed a mixture of all three. An important area of research concentrates on the modelling of objects and processes involved in the retrieval of information.

Well known models of IR are the Boolean, vector space, probabilistic, and fuzzy models; these have been studied in detail and implemented for experimentation, as well as, commercial purposes. Nevertheless, the known limitations of these models have caused researchers to propose new models. One such model is the logical model for IR [15, 23, 24, 54, 57, 90].

M. Agosti, F. Crestani, and G. Pasi (Eds.): ESSIR 2000, LNCS 1980, pp. 179–206, 2000.
© Springer-Verlag Berlin Heidelberg 2000

In recent years there have been several attempts to define *a logic for IR* along the so-called *logical approach*, initiated by Cooper [21] and given decisive impulse by van Rijsbergen [103, 104]. Logical IR models were studied to provide a rich and uniform representation of information and its semantics, with the aim to improve retrieval effectiveness. The earliest approaches were directed to the use of classical logic, like Boolean logic. The basis of a logical model for IR is the assumption that queries and documents can be represented effectively by logical formulas. In order to retrieve a document, an IR system has to infer the formula representing the query from formulas representing the document. This logical interpretation of query and documents emphasises that *information retrieval is an inference process* that computes whether a document d is relevant to a query q using both information present in the document itself and external information, like for example, user knowledge. An example is given in classical logic where inference is often associated with *logical implication*: a document is relevant to a query if it implies the query, or in other words, if the query can be inferred from the document. Such an evaluation formally embodies the semantics of the information represented in the query and in the document.

This way of viewing IR is especially fascinating once we consider, instead of the proof-theoretic "symbol-crunching" level of logic, its model-theoretic, semantic level. In terms of the latter, the logical approach to IR amounts to sanctioning that relevance coincides with (set-)inclusion of information content, or semantics: only documents whose information content includes that of the information need are to be retrieved.

In addition, the use of logic to build IR models enables one to obtain models that are more general than earlier well known IR models. Indeed, some logical models are able to represent within a uniform framework various features of IR systems, such as hypermedia links [13, 97], multimedia content [19, 67], users knowledge [75], cross-lingual [73], and structured documents [58]. It also provides a common approach to the integration of IR systems with logical database systems [37]. Finally, logic makes it possible to reason about an IR model and its properties [47, 69, 89]. This latter possibility is becoming increasingly important since conventional evaluation methods, although good indicators of the effectiveness of IR systems, often give results which cannot be predicted, or satisfactorily explained.

However, logic by itself cannot fully model IR. In determining the relevance of a document to a query, the success or failure of an implication relating the two is not enough. It is necessary to take into account the *uncertainty* inherent in such an implication. The introduction of uncertainty can also be motivated from the consideration that a collection of documents cannot be considered as a consistent and a complete set of statements. In fact, documents in the collection could and often do contradict each other in any particular logic, and not all the necessary knowledge is available.

It has been shown [18, 56, 103] that classical logic, the most commonly used logic, is not adequate to represent query and documents because of the intrinsic uncertainty present in IR. To cope with uncertainty a logic for *uncertain infer-*

ence needed to be introduced. In fact, if $d \to q$ is uncertain, then we can measure its degree of uncertainty by $P(d \to q)^1$.

In 1986 Van Rijsbergen proposed the use of a non-classical conditional logic for IR [103]. This would enable the evaluation of $P(d \to q)$ using the following *logical uncertainty principle*:

> "Given any two sentences x and y; a measure of the uncertainty of $y \to x$ related to a given data set is determined by the minimal extent to which we have to add information to the data set, to establish the truth of $y \to x$."

This principle was the first attempt to make an explicit connection between non-classical logics and IR uncertainty modelling. However, when proposing the above principle, Van Rijsbergen was not specific about which logic and which uncertainty theory to use. As a consequence, various logics and uncertainty theories have been proposed and investigated. The choice of the appropriate logic and uncertainty mechanisms has been a main research theme in logical IR modelling leading to a number of different approaches over the years.

In this paper we present a number of approaches to the use of logical and uncertainty models in IR. We will not address models based on classical logic, since their limitations (but also strengths) have long been recognised [56, 95]. Here we will only present models attempting to capture the uncertainty of the IR inference process, either through non-classical logics or some uncertainty theory defined on logical basis. We will call these two classes of models "logical models" and "logical-uncertainty models," respectively.

Another completely different class of models that will be presented in this paper is that of so called "meta-models." Meta-models attempts to formally study the properties and the characteristics of IR systems within a uniform logical framework. They aim at making it possible to compare IR models through formal properties of these models, instead of through their effectiveness, that can only be evaluated by means of expensive experimentation.

Thus, this paper is structured as follows. In Section 2 we introduce the concept of logical relevance, that is at the basis of the use of logic in IR. In Section 3 we present a selection of logical models of IR, while in Section 4 we present a number of logical-uncertainty models. Finally, in Section 5 we present work carried out towards developing meta-models of IR.

This paper is not intended to provide a complete survey of all attempts to using logics and uncertainty theories in IR. Such a task is outside the purpose of this paper. Also, it is not our intention to state that logical or logical-uncertainty IR models are better than other IR models, or to decide which of these models is the most appropriate. Instead, we are trying to highlight the approaches that we believe to be most interesting to future generations of IR researchers. We hope that the lessons learned will be carried forward and new interesting development will arise in this exciting area of research.

---

[1] In most of the models presented here uncertainty is measured using probability. In this case $P(\alpha)$ stands for "the probability that α."

2   A Logical Definition of Relevance

Relevance is one of the most important, if not "the fundamental," concept in the theory of IR. The concept arises from the consideration that if a user of an IR system has an information need, then some information stored in some documents in a document collection may be "relevant" to this need. In other words, the information to be considered relevant to a user's information need is the information that might help the user satisfy his or her information need. Any information that is not considered relevant to a user's information need, is to be considered "irrelevant" to that same information need. This is a consequence of accepting a dichotomous concept of relevance [2].

A logical definition of relevance was considered for the first time in the context of IR by Cooper in a paper written almost 30 years ago [21]. For Cooper *logical relevance* was another name for topic-appropriateness, and he addressed the problem of giving a definition of logical relevance for IR by analogy with the same problem in question-answering systems. The analogy goes only as far as having questions with a yes-no (true-false) type of answer, and while Cooper's work started by analysing question-answering systems, later he abandoned the analogy. Relevance is defined by Cooper as "logical consequence." To make this possible both queries and documents need to be represented by sets of declarative sentences. In the case of a yes-no query, the query is represented by two formal statements of the form p and $\neg p$. The two statements representing the query are called "component statements." A subset of the set of stored sentences is called "premiss set" if and only if the component statement is a logical consequence of that subset. A "minimal premiss set" for a component statement is one that is as small as possible in the sense that if any of its members were deleted, the component statement would no longer be a logical consequence of the set. Logical relevance is defined as a two-place relation between stored sentences and the query represented as component statements (the representation of the information need). A first definition of logical relevance says:

> "A stored sentence is logically relevant to (a representation of) an information need if and only if it is a member of some minimal premiss set of stored sentences for some component statement of that need."

This definition of relevance is essentially just a proof-theoretic notion that has been generalised to be applicable to information needs involving more than one component statement.

Although logical relevance was initially defined only for sentences, it can be easily extended to apply to stored documents: a document is relevant to an information need if and only if it contains at least one sentence which is relevant to that need.

In the same paper Cooper attempted to tackle a generalisation of such a definition to natural language queries and documents. However, without a formalised language, no precise definition of the logical consequence relation is at

---

[2] We will not address here the work challenging this binary view of relevance. The interested reader can look at the chapter in this book dealing with fuzzy approaches to IR or refer to other work using probabilistic approaches, like for example [2, 7].

hand, and thus we lose a precise definition of relevance. The problems of ambiguity and vagueness of natural language deny the possibility of extending the previous logical notion of relevance, despite the fact that the general idea of implication in natural language is a reasonably clear one. The definition of relevance, so far as natural language in concerned, is only a definition-in-principle — a conceptual definition — but not yet defined on a mathematical level.

Cooper also tried to tackle the problem of having "degrees of relevance," or as he wrote: "shades of grey instead of black and white" [21, pp.30]. The idea was to extend the system of deductive reasoning used to access logical relevance to a system of plausible reasoning. Cooper argued that plausible or probabilistic inference was not as well defined as deductive inference, even for formalised languages. However, he added that when such tools are formalised enough then this development would become a "sensible and indeed inescapable idea," because it would enable the ranking of documents according to an estimated probability of relevance. What he proposed was to assign a higher probability of relevance to a sentence or a document that has greater probability of belonging to a residual minimal premiss set.

Cooper went on extending the previous definition of relevance to the case of non-inferential systems and to the case of topical queries, but the extensions are not of interest in the context of this chapter. What should be retained from this discussion is that Cooper was the first to associate the topic-appropriateness sense of relevance [91] with logical implication and that he recognised the importance of evaluating the uncertainty of such implication to rank documents in relation to their estimated measure of relevance. Many other researchers followed this idea proposing the use of different logics to capture relevance.

An early common belief was that the logical implication needed to capture relevance was not the classical material implication. The reasons why the use of the classical material implication $d \supset q$ is not appropriate for IR is in the definition of material implication itself, and there are many ways of explaining why material implication is not suitable for IR (see for example [18]). For reasons of brevity, we repeat only the most important argument, that is the one most often used to dismiss the suitability of classical material implication for IR. The argument relates to the fact that the truth of the material implication $d \supset q$ is to be determined relative to a particular evaluation situation. To determine the truth of $d \supset q$ we have to compare the truth of d with that of q. Using a truth table for $d \supset q$ one can see that when d is false, no matter what the query q is, $d \supset q$ will always be true. Herein lies the problem. In fact, d is true only when d is retrieved, but, given a retrieval situation in which q is submitted, a document d is always false since it has not been retrieved yet. Therefore the real retrieval situation corresponds to the case of d false and such a document is relevant to any query q. This obviously does not provide a suitable definition of relevance.

The idea that a non-classical form of logical implication was needed for defining relevance was first proposed by Van Rijsbergen in [103]. That initial idea was supported with stronger arguments in [102], where the logical uncertainty principle was formulated. It is now clear that it is not possible to apply the logical uncertainty principle without a combination of a (non-classical) logic formalism and uncertainty theory. Both logic and uncertainty theory alone cannot fully capture this view of relevance. Depending on where the focus lays, one can use a non-classical logic combined with a theory of uncertainty or a theory of uncertainty defined in terms on a non-classical logic. In the following we will present some examples of these two classes of approaches to the use of non-classical logics and uncertainty theories in IR.

3   Logical Models of Information Retrieval

Some logical models are able to capture the uncertainty inherent in the IR process. These models capture the uncertainty mainly in two ways: qualitatively by the logic itself (for example, via default rules, non-monotonicity, or background conditions), or quantitatively by adding an uncertainty theory to the logic (for example, fuzzy logic). In the following we will present some of these models, just those that we think are most representative of the work done in this area.

3.1   Models Based on Modal Logic and Conceptual Graphs

Modal Logic [43] adopts the notion of possible worlds [52] that correspond to the interpretations in classical logic, but which are connected to each other via an accessibility relation. The evaluation of the truth of a proposition is with respect to a possible world, and may involve the evaluation of the truth of the proposition in connected worlds (see more about possible worlds semantics in Section 4.3).

Modal Logic was first used to develop a logical model for IR by Nie [71, 72]. Documents are worlds, and queries are formulae. A document represented by a world d is relevant to a query represented by a formula q if q is "true" in d, or if it is true in a world d' accessible from d.

The accessibility relation captures the transformation of documents; the fact that the world d is connected to the world d' is interpreted as d being transformed into d'. For example, d' could contain terms that are synonymous to those contained in d. The accessibility relationship can have different properties. For example, transitivity, meaning that if a world d is related to a world d', which is itself related to a world d'', then the world d is also related to the world d''. Consider the example of a hypertext system. Using Modal Logic, worlds can represent texts (nodes) and the accessibility relation can represent the links between the texts. Let d be a text-world, linked to a second text-world d', itself linked to a third text-world d''. If d does not contain information relevant to a query, but d' does, we may still want to retrieve d. It could be that only d'' contains information relevant to the query. Do we still want to retrieve d? This decision can be formally represented by allowing the accessibility relation to be transitive or not. This example gives an indication on how it is possible to reason about the type of system needed.

The model also allows the transformation of both the query and the data set. One query can be transformed into another one using, for example, thesaural information. Query transformation is not a new approach in IR (e.g., query expansion). The novelty is that the transformation process can be formally represented, and hence reasoned upon. Transforming a data set can capture the modelling of a user's state in the retrieval process. The data set can be transformed until it reaches one that reflects the user's state.

The above approach has been implemented in a medical context [20, 69]. The results showed that such an approach was promising, but the experiment was carried out on only 36 documents, so these results are only an indication of the effectiveness of the model. Another implementation of the model uses the WordNet thesaurus to transform queries, and is applied to the CACM test collection [66]. The results showed a positive increase in effectiveness.

A variant of this model was proposed in [17]. The logic was instantiated by the formalism of conceptual graphs [96], which are graphs built out of concepts and their associated semantics. Documents and queries are represented by conceptual graphs, and the transformation process is instantiated by operations performed on the graphs. For example a graph could be transformed to another one, where one concept in the initial graph is replaced by a more general one. This formalism has been used for instance to represent medical documents and software components. The problem, however, is the automatic construction of graphs from documents or queries (see [76] for further work, and its application to image retrieval).

3.2   Models Based on Situation Theory

Situation Theory is a theory of information that provides an analysis of the concept of information and the manner in which intelligent organisms (referred to as cognitive agents) handle and respond to the information picked up from their environment [35]. The theory defines the nature of information flow and the mechanisms that give rise to such a flow. Information items are represented by types. For example, $\phi = [\dot{s} | \dot{s} \models << Swimming; Mounia; 1 >>]$ represents the information item that Mounia is swimming. Nothing is said about the truth of this type; a type is just the representation of an item of information. What makes a type true is the situation (a partially defined world) from which the information represented by that type is extracted. Situation Theory models the notion of "make true" by the support relation, denoted $\models$. If s is a situation that makes the information "Mounia is swimming" true, then one can write $s \models \phi$, which should be read as "s supports ϕ."

Some IR logical model were developed based on Situation Theory [59]. A document is a situation s and the query is a type ϕ. The document is relevant to the query if there exists a flow of information from a situation s to a situation s' such that $s' \models \phi$. The nature of the flow depends on the so-called "constraints" which capture semantic relationships (e.g., the relationships that many people attach to white wine and Australian wine, the relationships based on synonymy, etc.). More formally, constraints are defined between types. Let ϕ and ψ be two types that constitute the constraint $\phi \rightarrow \psi$. The application of this constraint to a situation s is possible if first $s \models \phi$ and then informs of the existence of a situation s' such that $s' \models \psi$: the fact $s \models \phi$ carries the information that $s' \models \psi$.

A flow of information circulates between the situations s and s', and the nature of the flow is defined by the constraint $\phi \to \psi$.

Flows of information do not always materialise because of the unpredictable nature of situations, thus flows are often uncertain. In Situation Theory, an uncertain flow is modelled by a conditional constraint of the form $\phi \to \psi | B$, which highlights the fact that $\phi \to \psi$ holds if some background conditions captured within B are met. If the background conditions are satisfied, the corresponding flow arises. The use of background conditions in an IR model acknowledges the important fact that information is seen to be dependent on a context. For example, background conditions can represent context with respect to polysemic words.

Situation theory also allows the representation of uncertainty via background conditions, although only qualitatively [53]. It can be argued that the quantitative representation of the relevance of documents to queries is there only to rank documents, the numerical values have no real significance. Therefore, a qualitative representation of uncertainty may be enough to rank documents according to their estimated relevance to a query. Based on the background conditions, the fact that a document modelled by a situation $s1$ "supports more" the information item T than the document represented by the situation $s2$ would mean that the first document is more relevant to the query than is the second document. There is however much work to be done before such expressions become possible, but an elegant formalism that may be used for this purpose has already been advanced in [5].

The problem, however, with a Situation Theory based IR model is the difficult implementation of the model. The power of the theory is too complex to capture in an implementation [9]. For example, in [55], the WordNet thesaurus [66] was used to build the constraints. The implemented constraints were inappropriate (too general) for the test collection used in the experiments, hence, poor experimental results were obtained. There is however interesting work where ontologies are being developed to provide a "semantic for the Web" [3], in order to formally represent and qualitatively reason about the content of Web information objects. Situation Theory would provide an excellent framework for that purpose.

Situation Theory has also been used to develop a framework for searching on a thesaurus [8], and a meta-theory of IR [45], where the notion of aboutness was defined in terms of the flow of information. An extension of Situation Theory, called Channel Theory, was also used to develop logic-based IR models. This is discussed in the next section.

3.3 Models Based on Channel Theory

It is often the case that two situations are systematically related to each other, by way of a flow of information. For example: a situation where smoke is perceived is related to a situation where a fire has occurred; a situation where a person hears the door bell ringing is related to a situation where a second person is at the door pressing the bell; a situation representing a HTML document is related to a

---

[3] See http://www.semanticweb.org/

situation representing one it links to; a situation where a user views non-relevant retrieved document is related to a situation where the user adjusts his or her information need. Therefore, in addition to constraints, there are relationships that link situations. The concept of a channel is introduced in [6] to express the relationships, by way of an information flow, between two situations.

Channel theory defines formally channels, together with the mathematical properties that support the flow of information. For example, two operations are defined on channels: the sequential combination of channels and the parallel combination of channels. Their definitions satisfy fundamental properties of information and its flow.

One major asset of the use of channels is that the physical link between situations is conceptually defined. This allows formal representation at two levels: the link and its nature. For example, a document contains information about another document, either implicitly (e.g., the two documents are on the same topic) or explicitly, by way of citations, or links (e.g., hypermedia systems). Both of these cases can be captured with channel theory. In the first case, the nature of the flow can be defined in terms of thesaural relationships, but the link between one document and another that contains information relevant to the query is unknown. In the second case, the nature of the link is often unknown. However, the relevance of a document to a query can be calculated, since it is known that a flow of information circulates between that document and one that contains the information being sought after.

Similarly to the case for situation theory, the main problem with an IR model based on channel theory is its difficult implementation. Here in addition to the implementation of constraints, we must also provide an implementation of channels.

The use of channel theory to model IR has been investigated in [106], where the connection between IR, logic, probability and information containment was made. It was indicated that the use of channels present many potentials for theoretical IR modelling because they can apply to various IR processes present in advanced IR systems.

3.4   Models Based on Terminological Logic

Terminological logics come from the area of artificial intelligence, in particular, knowledge representation. Terminological logics derive from a large group of knowledge representation language (such as, for example, KL-ONE) based on semantic networks and inspired by the notion of frames. They provide object-oriented flavoured representations. The primary syntax starts with terms, which are either individuals or relations. Concepts are defined on top of those. For example, the concept:

$$(and\ paper\ (forall\ author\ european))$$

denotes the class of papers written by European authors only. Concepts come with a partial order $\leq$ which stands for conceptual containment. The fact that two concepts are ordered constitutes an axiom that describes thesaural knowledge. For example:

$$dog \leq (and\ animal(exactly\ 4\ leg))$$

states that dogs are four-legged animals (but not all four-legs animals are dogs).

The fact that a particular individual is an instance of a concept, is written as an assertion. For example, the following:

$$(and\ paper(forall\ author\ european))[paper1]$$

means that the individual document, named $paper1$, belongs to the concept that denotes the class of papers where all authors are European.

Given a concept C, defining whether an individual i is an instance of this concept, that is, evaluating whether $C[i]$ holds, uses the set of given assertions describing various facts, axioms that describe thesaural knowledge, and the notion of subsumption (hierarchical domination) defined by $\leq$. The evaluation of $C[i]$ is defined similarly to classical logic. However, the semantics of the terms go beyond truth and falsity; for example, the semantics of the concept "author" will be the set of individuals that are authors.

The use of terminological logic for IR was proposed in [64]. There, documents are represented by individual constants, whereas a class of documents is represented as a concept. Queries are described as concepts. Given a query represented by a concept Q, the retrieval task is to find all those documents d such that $Q[d]$ holds. The evaluation of $Q[d]$ uses the set of assertions describing documents, that is, we are not evaluating whether $d \rightarrow q$, but rather whether individual d is an instance of the class concept Q.

The model has been extended to include probabilities with respect to possible-world semantics [94]. That is, all interpretations (worlds) are considered, each of them with a given probability. For example, the proposition $w(\gamma) > 0.8$ means that the summation of the probability of those worlds (a probability distribution is defined on worlds) where γ is true is greater than 0.8. It was shown that this approach allows the representation of subjective beliefs (e.g., the belief that a document is about a given concept is of 0.8) as well as statistical information (e.g., 80% of worlds contain some given information).

In [65], a different class of terminological logic is used, based on a variation of relevance logics and four-valued semantics proposed in [77]. The terminological logic used in [64, 94] was discovered to have poor computational properties [16]. By contrast, relevance logics have language ALC as their base, which is the standard description logic on which people conduct experiments (i.e., integrations or deviations, such as probabilistic extensions, fuzzy extensions, etc.).

3.5   Models Based on Abductive Logic

Abduction is a way of explaining observations, expressed as formulae, by minimally extending a theory with some added hypotheses. More formally, given a theory T, and a formula p that needs to be explained in terms of T, abduction leads to a set of hypotheses H such that $T \cup H \models p$. The hypotheses are also referred to as abductive sentences.

A logical model based on *abductive reasoning* has been developed in [97] to build a hybrid system, where IR and hypertext facilities are combined. In this case, p is a query, and T is a knowledge base which captures semantic relationships (e.g., synonymy). The abductive sentences correspond to information related to documents (e.g., author, topic, etc.). The abduction process yields a structured proof, which is used to compute a solution space (a formula can be explained in different ways, so several sets of hypotheses, or solutions, can be found). Each solution generates a model that constitutes a starting point for a user to browse, either to access relevant documents, or related documents (e.g., same authors). This work is particularly attractive because it defines a logical framework that integrates IR and hypertext.

This approach was also used in an image retrieval system [67] where images were described by qualitative rules about contour, colour, texture, etc., and hence expressed as formulae.

In [87], relevance feedback is viewed as a process of explanation. In this case, a relevance feedback theory should provide an explanation of why a document is relevant to an information need. Such an explanation can be based on how information is used within documents. Abductive logic is used to provide a framework for an explanation-based account of relevance feedback.

3.6   Models Based on Default Logic

Default reasoning is concerned with the modelling of assumption of the form "birds usually fly" which are assumptions that do not always hold (e.g. penguin, ostrich). One instance of default reasoning is default theory [81], which is composed of two parts: a set of axioms, referred to as the basic theory, and a set of default rules. The inference rules are those of classical logic plus an additional mechanism for default rules. In default logic, the following rule

$$\frac{a : b}{c}$$

indicates that if a is true, and b cannot be inferred, then infer c. The application of default rules to the basic theory consists of an extension. Several extensions can be obtained since default rules can lead to different conclusions, thus capturing the non-monotonicity nature of the reasoning.

The use of default logic in IR was proposed in [48, 49] as a means to obtain a uniform and comprehensive framework for reasoning with keywords, for example for implementing sound query expansion. The proposed framework allows the representation of context in IR (e.g. polysemy) and the handling of exception.

3.7   Model Based on Belief Revision

Belief revision is an approach from non-monotonic reasoning that has been used in many domains [41]. The approach provides a means to formalise changes done to a knowledge base after the arrival of new information. The most interesting case arises when contradiction occurs between the old knowledge base and new knowledge (new information); the change (revision) must always lead to a consistent knowledge base. In addition, the revised knowledge base must contain the new information. Therefore, old knowledge maybe be deleted from the knowledge base, but this deletion should be minimal.

The use of belief revision in IR was attempted in [61] as a way to compute the similarity of a document to a query for retrieval purpose. The Dalal's revision operator was chosen for implementing the belief revision process, since it provides an order among proposition interpretations, where propositions model index terms. The ordering is used to formulate a similarity measure between a document and a query (expressed as formulae) based on the number of revisions necessary for the document to "reach" the query. It should be noted that both documents and queries can have, each, several interpretations, so normalisation becomes necessary.

The proposed belief revision framework has been extended in two ways. First, a syntactic characterisation of the logical formulae using DNF was advanced to overcome the problem arising from a direct implementation of logical interpretations which has an exponential complexity [62]. The characterisation allows the design of polynomial-time algorithms. Such work is crucial for the efficient implementations of logical IR models. On the other hand, in [63], retrieval situations were formally expressed in the belief revision model, which enable to formally capture, for example, user knowledge (e.g. of the collection), user information-seeking tasks (e.g. precision vs. recall search), and so on.

Finally, other work on the use of belief revision in IR can be found in [1, 34].

3.8   Models Based on Fuzzy Logic

Fuzzy set theory is a formal framework well suited to model vagueness and imprecision [108]. In IR it has been successfully employed at several levels [26, 27, 51], in particular for the definition of a superstructure of the Boolean model, with the appealing consequence that existing Boolean IRS systems can be improved without redesigning them completely. Through these extensions the gradual nature of relevance of documents to user queries can be modelled.

In this paper we do not address this area of research since it is presented extensively in the paper by Bordogna and Pasi in this same book.

4   Logical-Uncertainty Models of Information Retrieval

Logical-uncertainty models (sometimes referred to as uncertain inference models) are based on an uncertainty theory (for instance, probability theory, semantic theory, imaging) that is defined on a logical basis. They enable a more complex definitions of relevance than other IR models (than probabilistic relevance model, for instance, which are based mainly upon statistical estimations of the probability of relevance). With logical-uncertainty models, information not present in the query formulation may be included in the evaluation of the relevance of a document. Such information might be domain knowledge, knowledge about the user, user's relevance feedback, and so on.

Another characteristic of logical-uncertainty models is that they are not as strongly collection-dependent as most other IR models. In most IR models, parameters (e.g., normalisation and weight combination parameters) are only valid for the current collection, while logical-uncertainty models can use knowledge of the user or the application domain that can be useful with many other collections.

In this section we will present some logical-uncertainty models, with particular attention to models based on an uncertainty theory defined using a non-classical logic.

4.1 Models Based on Probability Theory

In IR, probabilistic modelling refers to the use of a model that ranks documents in decreasing order of their evaluated probability of relevance to a user's information need [83]. Past and present research has made use of formal theories of probability and of statistics in order to evaluate, or at least estimate, those probabilities of relevance. These attempts are to be distinguished from looser ones like, for example, the "vector space model" [88] in which documents are ranked according to a measure of similarity with the query. A measure of similarity cannot be directly interpretable as a probability. In addition, similarity based models generally lack the theoretical soundness of probabilistic models.

A treatment of models based on Probability Theory is beyond the scope of this section. Good surveys of probabilistic modelling in IR are [25, 36] and we refer the interested reader to them. The models presented in this section are based on the idea that IR is a process of uncertain inference. This research area is promising in that it is attempting to move away from the traditional approaches, and may provide the breakthrough that appears necessary to overcome the limitations of current IR systems.

There are two main types of probabilistic uncertain inference models. The first is based on non-classical logic, to which probabilities are mapped, and the second is based on Bayesian inferences. Models based of the first class can be found in Section 3, here we will only address models of the second class.

A probabilistic formalism for describing inference relations with uncertainty is provided by *Bayesian inference networks*, which have been described extensively in [68, 78]. Turtle and Croft [98, 99] applied such networks to IR. Figure 1 depicts an example of such a network. Nodes represent IR entities such as documents, index terms, concepts, queries, and information needs. We can choose the number and kind of nodes we wish to use according to how complex we want the representation of the document collection or the information needs to be. Arcs represent probabilistic dependencies between entities. They represent conditional probabilities, that is, the probability of an entity being true given the probabilities of its parents being true.

The inference network is usually made up of two component networks: a document network and a query network. The document network represents the document collection. It is built once for a given collection and its structure

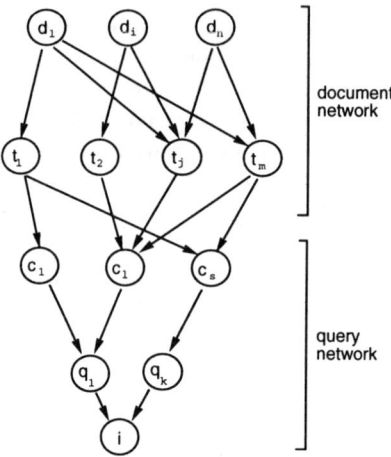

Figure 1. An Inference Network for IR.

does not change. A query network is built for each information need and can be modified and extended during each session by the user in a interactive and dynamic way. The query network is attached to the static document network in order to process a query.

In a Bayesian inference network, the truth value of a node depends only upon the truth values of its parents. To evaluate the strength of an inference chain going from one document to the query we set the document node d_i to "true" and evaluate $P(q_k = true \mid d_i = true)$. This gives us an estimate of $P(d_i \rightarrow q_k)$. It is possible to implement various traditional IR models on this network by introducing nodes representing Boolean operators or by setting appropriate conditional probability evaluation functions within nodes [100].

One particular characteristic of this model that warrants exploration is that multiple document and query representations can be used within the context of a particular document collection (e.g., a Boolean expression or a vector). Moreover, given a single information need, it is possible to combine results from multiple queries and from multiple search strategies.

The strength of this model comes from the fact that most classical retrieval models can be expressed in terms of a Bayesian inference network by estimating in different ways the weights in the inference network [100]. Nevertheless, the characteristics of the Bayesian inference process itself, given that nodes (evidence) can only be binary (the evidence is either present or not) limits its use to where "certain evidence" [68] is available. The approach proposed by van Rijsbergen in [105], which makes use of "uncertain evidence" by using Jeffrey's conditioning [50], therefore appears more attractive.

Other approaches to the use of Bayesian inference networks in IR are presented in [38,82,92].

4.2   Models Based on Probabilistic Datalog

This area of research is based on the fact that logical IR retrieval could be viewed as a generalisation of logical database retrieval; uncertainty is introduced in the former. Datalog is a predicate logic that has been developed in the database field, and makes the link between the relational model and rule-based systems. *Probabilistic Datalog* is the probabilistic extension of Datalog [37]. For example:

$$0.7 \; term(d_1, IR)$$
$$0.8 \; term(d_1, DB)$$

represent two facts $term(d_1, IR)$ and $term(d_1, DB)$ they indicate that the document $d1$ is indexed by "IR" and "DB"; the weights represent the probability that the two facts are true. Retrieving documents that deal with both of these topics can be expressed by the following inference rule:

$$q_1(D) : -term(D, IR) \wedge term(D, DB)$$

If term dependence is assumed (i.e., $P(a \wedge b) = P(a) \cdot P(b)$), then the document $d1$ is retrieved with probability 0.56. If we want to retrieve every document about "IR" or "DB," the following query can be used:

$$q_2(D) : -term(D, IR)$$
$$q_2(D) : -term(D, DB)$$

The above document d_1 is retrieved with probability 0.94. This comes from that $P(a \vee b) = P(a) + P(b) - P(a \wedge b)$ and assuming term independence.

The rule-based approach allows for easy formulation of various retrieval models and advanced IR systems. Consider the example of a hypermedia system. We may want to express that a document is about a term if that term indexes the document, or if the document is linked to one that is indexed by the term. This can be expressed by the following rule:

$$about(D, T) : -term(D, T)$$
$$about(D, T) : -link(D, D1) \wedge term(D1, T)$$

Consider the following query:

$$q_3 : -about(D, IR)$$

The query is looking for document directly or indirectly about "IR." The use of Probabilistic Datalog to model retrieval in hypermedia has been presented in [85]

Probabilistic Datalog is not itself a logical IR framework, but more a platform in which logical probabilistic IR models, as well as other IR models can be expressed (see for example [28]).

One of the major assets of Probabilistic Datalog is that, since it is a general-isation of the Datalog model, it can be used as standard query language for both database and IR. It can then deal with both structured data (as in database) and unstructured data (as in IR) within the same system. It also allows the uniform representation, retrieval and querying of content, fact and structural knowledge.

The work has been further extended via the development, implementation and evaluation of the POOL (Probabilistic Object-Oriented Logic) model, which allows the representation of inconsistency (using then a four-valued logic), the modelling of the document and query representation using the object-oriented paradigm [84, 86]. The result is a running IR platform, called HySpirit, that is currently being further developed and commercialised for large volumes of data [4].

4.3   Models Based on Logical Imaging

Several models have been developed based on the frameworks of imaging [60] and general imaging [39]. *Logical imaging* is an approach that defines the prob-ability of conditional $P(d \rightarrow q)$ based on the notion of possible-worlds. In this approach the possible worlds (e.g., retrieval situation, document representation) are spanned by an accessibility relation defined in terms of similarity. The truth value of the implication $p \rightarrow q$ in a world w depends on two cases. If p is true in w, then $p \rightarrow q$ is true (false) in that world if q is also true (false) in that world. In the other hand, if p is not true in w, then the implication is evaluated in the worlds that differ minimally from w and in which p is true. The worlds in which p is true are referred to as p-worlds.

The set of worlds comes with a probability distribution P, reflecting the probability of each world. The probability of a proposition p is the summation of the probability of those worlds in which p is true. The computation of the probability of $p \rightarrow q$ involves a shift of probability (the imaging process) from non-$p - worlds$ to their closest p-worlds. It can be proved that [60]:

$$P(p \rightarrow q) = P_p(q)$$

where P_p is a new probability distribution, a "posterior probability," derived from P by imaging on p.

Conditionalisation by imaging causes a revision of the prior probability on the possible worlds w in such a way that the posterior probability is obtained by shifting the original probabilities from non-p-worlds to p-worlds. Each non-p-world moves its probability to its closest p-world (or set of p-worlds in the case of general imaging). Probability is neither created or destroyed, but just moved according to the accessibility relation (and to the opinionated probability function, in the case of general imaging). Bayesian conditionalisation, on the other hand, is obtained by cutting off all non-p-worlds and then proportionally magnifying the probabilities of the p-worlds so that the posterior probabilities

---

[4] See http://www.hyspirit.de/

still add up to 1, as required by Probability Theory. The magnification is done in the same way for every p-world, thus keeping constant the ratios between the probabilities assigned to these worlds. It is therefore clear that imaging and Bayesian conditionalisation yield, in general, different results [40].

However,since the transfer of probabilities is directed towards the closest p-worlds, this technique is just what it is needed to implement Van Rijsbergen's logical uncertainty principle. If d represents the document and q the query, then the relevance of the document to the query can be evaluated as:

$$P(d \rightarrow q) = P_d(q) = \sum_{t \in q} P_d(t)$$

by imaging on the document. This formula is compatible with Van Rijsbergen's logical uncertainty principle since the probability revision is minimal with regard to the accessibility relation. Alternatively, it is possible to evaluate:

$$P(q \rightarrow d) = P_q(d) = \sum_{t \in d} P_q(t)$$

by imaging on the query. Nie showed in [70] that the two conditionals $d \rightarrow q$ and $q \rightarrow d$ have a very interesting interpretation in the context of IR. The conditional $d \rightarrow q$ expresses the "exhaustivity" of the document to a query, i.e. how much of a document content is specified by the query content. In fact, $d \rightarrow q$ is intuitively equivalent to $d \subseteq q$. The conditional $q \rightarrow d$, on the other hand, expresses the "specificity" of a document to a query, i.e. how much of a query content is specified in the document content. In fact, $q \rightarrow d$ is intuitively equivalent to $q \subseteq d$. The choice of either $d \rightarrow q$ or $q \rightarrow d$ depends on the particualr requirements of the application, that is, if the application requires high recall or high precision.

The application of imaging to IR requires that:

– in any given possible world, a sentence is either true or false,
– possible worlds are more or less similar to each other (imaging uses this similarity), and
– the set of possible worlds is finite.

From an IR perspective, the second and third assumptions are acceptable. The first one, however, is problematic. For example, consider that a possible world and a sentence represent a document and an index term, respectively. The uncertainties inherent in the indexing process make a true-false assignment to index terms (sentences) within documents (worlds) an error prone task.

To build an IR system based on imaging, the similarity relation between worlds must be available. If documents correspond to worlds, then a similarity measure between documents must be computed. In practice, this measure is computed using not the documents, but their representations. As a consequence, the integrity of the similarity relation is compromised as, in practice, a document representation is an incomplete reflection of the actual document content. This is due to limitations in automatic indexing algorithms. For example, in a primitive system, the representations of a document on "Gone with the Wind" and a document on "Meteorology and Wind" may be considered fairly similar because they both contain the keyword "wind," whereas in reality the two documents are different. As a consequence, there are errors inherent in the calculation of $P(d \rightarrow q)$ when using document representation as input to the similarity calculation. Nevertheless, this approach gives a conceptually neat and concise realization of the logical uncertainty principle. Moreover, it provides a direct route for calculating $P(d \rightarrow q)$, which can be used to rank documents on likelihood of their relevance to the user. Imaging sidesteps the troublesome question of the semantics of the implication via its probabilistic basis.

General imaging [39] relaxes two earlier assumptions by asserting that: (i) truth assignments of sentences in worlds need not be true or false, and (ii) the most similar world need not be unique.

Two logical-probabilistic IR models have been developed on the concept of imaging. In the first one [31, 32], worlds model terms, and propositions model documents and queries. A term t "makes a document true" if that term belongs to that document. Imaging with respect to d gives the closest term to t that is contained in d. Of course, this is t itself if t is contained in the document. Imaging consists then of shifting the probabilities from term not contained in d to the terms contained in d (i.e., the terms that make d true). The evaluation of the relevance takes into account the semantics between terms by shifting probabilities to those (semantically) closer terms contained in the document [30]. Models based on imaging and general imaging has been successfully implemented and tested on some standard test collections [32], but results with larger scale testing were inconclusive [29].

A second model based on imaging includes user's knowledge in the evaluation of the relevance of a document to a query [75]. In this model both documents and queries are propositions. Possible worlds represent different states of the data set, for example possible states of knowledge that can be held by users. A document d is true in a world w if the document is "consistent" (the term is used here in a broad sense) with the state of knowledge associated with that world. Worlds differ because they represent different states of knowledge and, given a metric on the world space, we can identify the closest world to w for which d is true. This model has the advantage that user modelling is formally included, while the model presented in [32] and detailed above only takes into account a system evaluated relevance. However, no implementation and evaluation of this model has been produced so far.

4.4   Models Based on Semantic Information Theory

Semantic Information Theory is concerned with studies in Logic and Philosophy on the use of the term information, "in the sense in which it is used of whatever it is that meaningful sentences and other comparable combinations of symbols convey to one who understands them" [42]. Notwithstanding the large scope of this description, Semantic Information Theory has primarily to do with the question of how to weigh sentences according to their informative content. The main difference with conventional information theory is that information is not conveyed by an ordered sequence of binary symbols, but by means of a formal language in which logical statements are defined and explained by a semantics. The work on Semantic Information Theory in IR concerns two research directions: the axiomatisation of the logical principles for assigning probabilities or similar weighting functions to logical sentences and the relationship between information content of a sentence and its probability. Both directions were investigate in [3,4].

In [3], it is argued that the notion of amount of information content in IR is determined by some entropy measures, especially by one axiomatised first by Hilpinen. By using different utility functions which combine entropy and probability, several old and new models of IR are derived. In addition, the principles of a "duality theory" are presented. Retrieval based on probability theory requires the definition of an event space. When one deals with probabilities, one measures a Boolean, or a sigma algebra, of events. According to the duality theory, used also in [32] to give a representation semantics to logical imaging in the context of IR, one can either consider the set of terms T of the term space as the set of the elementary events, or consider the set D of documents as the set of elementary events. In the first case one can work on a term probability space, in the second on a document probability space. Working on the term probability space leads on to the standard application of probability theory to IR. On the other hand, working on the document probability space it is possible to show how to tightly link the vector space model to the standard probabilistic model.

In [4], the concepts of simplicity, regularity, randomness, and shortest description length are studied with the purpose of formalising the informative content of documents. It is shown that the Zipf's law and the inverse document frequency weight are derived from first principles involving these concepts.

4.5   Models Based on Probabilistic Argumentation Systems

One basic assumption of probabilistic models of IR is that terms and documents are independent. Although this assumption has been reshaped in recent times [22], a number of investigations have demonstrated the potential usefulness of incorporating dependencies or relationships between terms (for example [80,101]) and between documents (for example [33,93]). When attempting to incorporate these features in the matching process, the limits of the traditional term matching approach appear more clearly, and one is often left to the use of ad-hoc schemes. For this reason and others, it has been argued by a number of researchers that the best way to model the IR process is by the use of an appropriate logic that captures these features. In fact, the expressiveness of logic makes it a very attractive framework for modelling relationships between terms and/or documents, but the complexity of its implementation makes it difficult to have large-scale applications. A possible way out of this "impasse" could be found in integrating logic in large-scale classic IR systems as a tool for solving specific problems which cannot be formalised within more conventional approaches. The different steps of the retrieval process could be done as usual, and logic could be used as a formal tool for modifying the output of certain components of the retrieval system. In this way the "logical components" could be integrated to any retrieval system working on soft term matching, e.g. the vector-space or probabilistic models, even in large-scale applications.

The work described in [79] starts from this premise and from the consideration that IR can be seen both as an inference process under uncertainty involving complex relationships between information items, and as a task of proper assessment of uncertainty. The originality of this work is in the choice of the framework used: *probabilistic argumentation systems*. Probabilistic argumentation systems provide techniques for reasoning under uncertainty which emphasise both the inference process and the assessment of uncertainty, by clearly distinguishing the qualitative and quantitative aspects of uncertainty. Probabilistic argumentation systems represent uncertainty in a clear and easily understandable way: the qualitative part is handled with propositional logic and the quantitative part is treated with probability theory. They offer a natural way to model relationships between terms and between documents, and allows complex inferences. In [79] two applications of probabilistic argumentation systems to IR are presented, aimed at:

1. taking into account existing hypertext links in order to improve an initial ranking of documents
2. considering statistical similarities between query terms to improve query weighting.

These two applications can be easily integrated in a classic IR system based on term matching, even for large-scale applications [79]. It is worth noticing that even though the symbolic part of uncertain knowledge is naturally modelled with probabilistic argumentation systems, the numerical assessment of probabilities is often a very difficult problem. It is clear that if the uncertainty is incorrectly assessed, combined or propagated, the inference carried out by the logic will very probably be unable to improve retrieval effectiveness. The transformation of easily estimated statistical similarity information into a measure of uncertainty (e.g. probabilities) is one major difficulties and is still an open problem. Nevertheless, the work presented in [79] highlights that in IR the numerical and symbolic aspects of uncertainty are profoundly interlaced, and a purely symbolic or numerical approach would not bring the same insight in these problems. The theoretical foundations of probabilistic argumentation systems, which rely on the theory of evidence, make them a reliable technique for approaching problems in which the quantitative and qualitative aspects of uncertainty are of equal importance.

5   Meta-models

Meta-models are a completely different class of models from those presented earlier. Meta-models attempts to formally study the properties and the characteristics of IR systems within a uniform logical framework [89,107]. The advantage is that it will then be possible to compare IR systems not only with respect to their effectiveness, but also with respect to formal properties of the underlying models. For example, an application may require a system that retrieves all relevant documents (recall-oriented system), or that retrieves only relevant documents (precision-oriented system).

The use of logic to formally conduct proofs for IR purposes originated in [69], where it was showed that a logical model is a general form of many other IR models. The idea was later thoroughly investigated in [10,47], where a framework was proposed in which different models of IR could be theoretically expressed, formally studied and compared. The framework was developed within a logic, thus allowing formal proofs to be conducted. Here meta-models are based on non-monotonic reasoning approaches.

The framework defines the aboutness relationship, denoted $\models$, which aims at capturing the notion of information containment primary to IR. Given two objects a and b, $a \models b$ means that object a is about object b. Axioms are defined that represent possible properties of IR systems. Examples of axioms include:

- Reflexivity: $a \models a$
- Symmetry: if $a \models b$ then $b \models a$
- Transitivity: if $a \models b$ and $b \models c$ then $a \models c$

Most IR models seem to satisfy reflexivity because if objects are documents, then if a document is submitted as a query, then this document should be retrieved. However, if only new documents should be retrieved in response to a query, then another aboutness relationship should be defined, one which is not reflexive. The IR models satisfying symmetry are the vector space model, and those based on overlap measures such as Jaccard's, or Dice's. The models based on overlap measures were shown to not satisfy transitivity.

A rule often used by meta-models and borrowed from non-monotonic reasoning is [14]:

- Right weakening: if $a \models b$ and $b \Rightarrow c$ then $a \models c$[5]

An aboutness relationship that satisfies the above rule can be precision degrading. For example, a document about "microbes" should probably not be retrieved in response to a query about "animal" although $microbe \Rightarrow animal$. This is because most preferred documents about animals would presumably deal with "birds," "dogs," and similar.

Monotonicity is another rule being investigated. Consider for example the left monotonicity rule:

- Left Monotonicity: if $a \models b$ then $a \oplus c \models a$, where $a \oplus c$ is an item yielded from the combination of a and c

Where the combination is not restricted to the logical "and". Clearly the above rule produces inferences that are not sound (e.g. take $a = surfing$, $b = wave$ and $c = internet$). It is however not a solution to drop the rule, for example for

---

[5] Here $b \Rightarrow c$ means that c follows from b or that c is informationally contained in b.

expressing the query expansion process. Cautious monotonicity rules have been investigated for that purpose.

This research has led to the theoretical comparison of IR models [10, 44, 46]. This proceeds as follows. Two IR models are mapped down into a logic-based framework. The aboutness properties that a given model supports is then filtered out. The two models can be compared by using the particular aboutness properties they each embody. For example, if retrieval system A supports a monotonic notion of aboutness and retrieval system B does not, then this may suggest that system B will offer more precise retrieval than A. Boolean retrieval and (strict) coordinate retrieval have been compared in this fashion. Boolean retrieval represents a document d and query q as propositional formulae. Document d is deemed to be about query q iff $d \models q$. Strict coordinate retrieval represents d and q as sets of index terms. Document d is deemed to be about q iff $d \subseteq q$.

The relationship between particular aboutness properties and IR effectiveness is currently an open problem. Also, which underlying logic-based framework should be used? More investigation and experience with these frameworks may lead to an integrated, underlying theory of IR. Nevertheless, through this research, IR is gaining a clearer understanding of what aboutness is, and what properties are desirable (and not desirable) for this notion [11, 12].

6   Conclusions and Future Directions

This paper describes some of the work done in developing logical and logical-uncertainty models for IR. The aim in using logic to model IR is to provide expressive and uniform IR models not only to improve effectiveness, but also to have a framework where the semantics of the retrieval process can be formally described and investigated. Uncertainty theories enable to take into account the uncertainty inherent in such a formulation.

We have presented in this paper a number of approaches that address different issues. The variation in approaches reflects different vehicles deemed suitable for the modelling of IR. So far, no consensus has been reached regarding what the best vehicle is. Investigations into various logic-based frameworks will hopefully lead to a unified information-based model theory for expressing the semantics of information retrieval. Such a theory will allow us to predict the behaviour of IR systems, compare them and prove properties about them. This, we believe, is one of the major strength of logical models.

Another major asset of logical and logical-uncertainty models is that they are able to represent within a uniform framework various features of advanced IR systems, such as hypermedia objects, structured multimedia documents, users knowledge and agents. One main advantage in having a general model in IR is that it becomes possible to reason about various IR features of the model. This possibility is becoming increasingly important because conventional evaluation methods such as experimentally measuring precision and recall are sometimes insufficient.

Finally, the use of logic and uncertainty theory in IR is still in its early stages. Substantial theoretical progress has been made, but further investigation and development are required before the effectiveness of these models can be established. For instance, the implementation of logical models can be complex, and when possible, often only small document collections can be handled. Despite some implementations have provided positive results [32, 74], more experimental work is necessary to demonstrate the effectiveness of logical and logical-uncertainty models.

Note

This paper is heavily based on some introductory and survey papers on the use of logic and uncertainty theory in IR that we already published, in particular on [27, 56,57]. In addition, large part of the work on logic and uncertainty in IR reviewed in this paper can be found in *Information Retrieval: Uncertainty and Logics* edited by Crestani, Lalmas, and van Rijsbergen [24] and in the proceedings of the "Workshop on Logical and Uncertainty Models for Information Systems" [15,23].

References

1. G. Amati and P.D. Bruza. A logical approach to query reformulation motivated from belief change. In *Proceedings of the Workshop on Logical and Uncertainty Models for Information Systems*, pages 36–45, London, UK, July 1999.
2. G. Amati and F. Crestani. Probabilistic learning by uncertain samplying with non-binary relevance. In F. Crestani and G. Pasi, editors, *Soft Computing in Information Retrieval: techniques and application*, pages 292–314. Physica-Verlag, Heidelberg, Germany, 2000.
3. G. Amati and C.J. van Rijsbergen. Semantic Information Retrieval. In F. Crestani, M. Lalmas, and C.J. van Rijsbergen, editors, *Information Retrieval: Uncertainty and Logics*, pages 189–220. Kluwer Academic Publishers, Norwell, MA, USA, 1998.
4. G. Amati and C.J. van Rijsbergen. Simplicity and Information Retrieval. In F. Crestani, M. Lalmas, and C.J. van Rijsbergen, editors, *Information Retrieval: Uncertainty and Logics*, pages 281–293. Kluwer Academic Publishers, Norwell, MA, USA, 1998.
5. Z. An, A. Bell, and J.G. Hughes. Res - a logic for relative evidential support. *International Journal of Approximate Reasoning*, 8:205–230, 1993.
6. J. Barwise. *Handbook of Mathematical Logic*. Elsevier Science Publishers B.V., Amsterdam, The Netherlands, 8th edition, 1993.
7. R.K. Belew. Rave reviews: acquiring relevance assessments from multiple users. In *Proceedings of the AAAI Spring Symposium on Machine Learning in Information Access*, Stanford, CA, USA, March 1996.
8. F. C. Berger and T. W. C Huibers. A framework based on situation theory for searching on a thesaurus. In J. Rowley, editor, *The New Review of Document and text Management*, volume 1, pages 253–276, Crewe, England, 1995.
9. A. W. Black. *A Situation Theoretic Approach to Computational Semantics*. PhD thesis, University of Edinburgh, 1992.
10. P. D. Bruza and T. W. C. Huibers. Investigating aboutness axioms using information fields. In *Proceedings of ACM SIGIR*, pages 112–121, Dublin, Ireland, 1994.
11. P. D. Bruza and T. W. C Huibers. How monotonic is aboutness? Technical report, Utrecht University, The Netherlands, 1995. Technical Report UU-CS-1995-09.

12. P. D. Bruza and T. W. C Huibers. A study of aboutness in information retrieval. *Artificial Intelligence Review*, 10:1–27, 1996.
13. P.D. Bruza. *Stratified Information Disclosure: a synthesis between Hypermedia and Information Retrieval*. PhD Thesis, Katholieke Universiteit Nijmegen, The Netherlands, 1993.
14. P.D. Bruza. Intelligent filtering using nonmonotonic inference. In *Proceedings of the Australian Document Computing Symposium*, pages 1–7, Royal Melbourne Institute of Technology, Melbourne, Australia, 1996.
15. P.D. Bruza, F. Crestani, and M. Lalmas. Second Workshop on Logical and Uncertainty Models for Information Systems (DEXA-LUMIS 2000). In *Proceedings of DEXA 2000*. IEEE Press, Greenwich, London, UK, 2000.
16. P. Buongarzoni, C. Meghini, R. Salis, F. Sebastiani, and U. Straccia. Logical and computational properties of the description logic MIRTL. In *Proceedings of DL 95*, pages 80–84, Rome, Italy, 1995.
17. J. P. Chevallet. *Un modèle logique de recherche d'information appliqué au formalisme des graphes conceptuels. Le prototype ELEN et son expérimentation sur un corpus de composants logiciels*. PhD thesis, Université Joseph Fourier, Grenoble I, 1992.
18. Y. Chiaramella and J.P. Chevallet. About retrieval models and logic. *The Computer Journal*, 35(3):233–242, 1992.
19. Y. Chiaramella, P. Mulhem, and F. Fourel. A model for multimedia information retrieval. Technical report, ESPRIT Basic Research Action, Project Number 8134 - FERMI, Department of Computing Science, Glasgow University, Glasgow, UK, 1996.
20. Y. Chiaramella and J. Nie. A retrieval model based on an extended Modal Logic and its application to the RIME experiment approach. In *Proceedings of ACM SIGIR*, pages 25–43, Brussels, Belgium, 1990.
21. W.S. Cooper. A definition of relevance for Information Retrieval. *Information Storage and Retrieval*, 7:19–37, 1971.
22. W.S. Cooper. Some inconsistencies and misnomers in probabilistic Information Retrieval. *ACM Transactions on Information Systems*, 13(1):100–111, 1995.
23. F. Crestani and M. Lalmas, editors. *Proceedings of the First Workshop on Logical and Uncertainty Models for Information Systems (LUMIS 99)*, London, UK, July 1999. Available online at: http://www.dcs.gla.ac.uk/lumis99/.
24. F. Crestani, M. Lalmas, and C.J. van Rijsbergen, editors. *Information Retrieval: Uncertainty and Logics*. Kluwer Academic Publisher, Norwell, MA, USA, 1998.
25. F. Crestani, M. Lalmas, C.J. van Rijsbergen, and I. Campbell. Is this document relevant? ... probably. A survey of probabilistic models in Information Retrieval. *ACM Computing Surveys*, 30(4):528–552, 1998.
26. F. Crestani and G. Pasi. Soft Information Retrieval: applications of fuzzy sets theory and neural networks. In N. Kasabov and R. Kozma, editors, *Neuro-fuzzy Techniques for Intelligent Information Systems*, pages 287–315. Physica Verlag, Heidelberg, Germany, 1999.
27. F. Crestani and G. Pasi, editors. *Soft Computing in Information Retrieval: techniques and applications*. Physica-Verlag, Heidelberg, Germany, 2000.
28. F. Crestani and T. Rölleke. Issues on the implementation of imaging on top of probabilistic datalog. In *Proceedings of the First Workshop in IR, Uncertainty and Logic*. Glasgow, Scotland, UK, September 1995.
29. F. Crestani, I. Ruthven, M. Sanderson, and C.J. van Rijsbergen. The troubles with using a logical model of IR on a large collection of documents. Experimenting retrieval by logical imaging on TREC. In *Proceedings of the TREC Conference*, pages 509–525, Washington D.C., USA, November 1995.

30. F. Crestani, M. Sanderson, and C.J. van Rijsbergen. Sense resolution properties of logical imaging. *The New Review of Document and Text Management*, 1:277–298, 1996.

31. F. Crestani and C.J. van Rijsbergen. Information Retrieval by Logical Imaging. *Journal of Documentation*, 51(1):1–15, 1995.

32. F. Crestani and C.J. van Rijsbergen. A study of probability kinematics in rnformation retrieval. *ACM Transactions on Information Systems*, 16(3):225–255, 1998.

33. W.B. Croft and R.H. Thompson. I^3R: a new approach to the design of Document Retrieval Systems. *Journal of the American Society for Information Science*, 38(6):389–404, 1987.

34. W.T. da Silva and R.L. Milidiú. Belief function model for Information Retrieval. *Journal of the American Society for Information Science*, 44(1):10–18, 1993.

35. K. Devlin. *Logic and Information*. Cambridge University Press, Cambridge, UK, 1991.

36. N. Fuhr. Probabilistic models in Information Retrieval. *The Computer Journal*, 35(3):243–254, 1992.

37. N. Fuhr. Probabilistic Datalog - a logic for powerful retrieval methods. In *Proceedings of ACM SIGIR*, pages 282–290, Seattle, WA, USA, 1995.

38. R. Fung and B. Del Favero. Applying bayesian networks to Information Retrieval. *Communications of the ACM*, 38(3):42–48, 1995.

39. P. Gärdenfors. Imaging and conditionalization. *Journal of Philosophy*, 79:747–760, 1982.

40. P. Gärdenfors. *Knowledge in flux: modelling the dynamics of epistemic states*. The MIT Press, Cambridge, Massachusetts, USA, 1988.

41. P. Gärdenfors, editor. *Belief Revision*. Cambridge University Press, Cambridge, UK, 1992.

42. J. Hintikka. On semantic information. In *Information and inference*. Synthese Library, Reidel, Dordrecht, The Netherlands, 1970.

43. G.E. Hughes and M.K. Cresswell. *An Introduction to Modal Logic*. Muthuen and Co. Ltd, London, UK, 1968.

44. T. Huibers, I. Ounis, and J. P. Chevallet. Axiomatization of a conceptual graph formalism for information retrieval in a situated framework. Technical Report RAP95-004, Group MRIM of the Laboratoire de Génie Informatique, Grenoble, France, 1995.

45. T. W. C. Huibers and P. D. Bruza. Situations, a general framework for studying information retrieval. In *Proceedings of the 16th British Computer Society Colloquium in Information Retrieval*, Drymen, Scotland, UK, March 1994.

46. T. W. C Huibers and N. Denos. A qualitative ranking method for logical information retrieval models. Technical Report RAP95-005, Groupe MRIM of the Laboratoire de Génie Informatique, Grenoble, France, 1995.

47. T.W.C Huibers. *An Axiomatic Theory for Information Retrieval*. PhD thesis, Utrecht University, The Netherlands, 1996.

48. A. Hunter. Intelligent text handling using default logic. In *Proceedings of IEEE Conference on Tools with Artificial Intelligence*, 1996. (to appear).

49. A. Hunter. Using default logic for lexical knowledge. In *Qualitative and Quantitative Practical Reasoning (ECSQARU'97/FAPR'97)*. Springer-Verlag, Heidelberg, Germany, 1997.

50. R.C. Jeffrey. *The logic of decision*. McGraw-Hill, New York, USA, 1965.

51. N. Kasabov and R. Kozma, editors. *Neuro-fuzzy techniques for intelligent information systems*. Physica Verlag, Heidelberg, Germany, 1998.

52. S.A. Kripke. Semantical considerations on modal logic. In L. Linsky, editor, *Reference and modality*, chapter 5, pages 63–73. Oxford University Press, Oxford, UK, 1971.

53. M. Lalmas. From a qualitative towards a quantitative representation of uncertainty on a situation theory based model of an information retrieval system. Technical report, Department of Computing Science, Technical Report TR-1995-18, University of Glasgow, Scotland, 1995.

54. M. Lalmas, editor. *Proceedings of the First International Workshop on Information Retrieval, Uncertainty and Logics*, Glasgow, Scotland, UK, July 1995.

55. M. Lalmas. Modelling Information Retrieval with Dempster-Shafer's theory of evidence: a study. In *Proceedings of the ECAI Workshop on Uncertainty in Information Systems: questions of viability*, Budapest (Hungary), September 1996.

56. M. Lalmas. Logical models in Information Retrieval: introduction and overview. *Information Processing & Management*, 34(1):19–33, 1998.

57. M. Lalmas and P.D. Bruza. The use of logic in information retrieval modelling. *Knowledge Engineering Review*, 13(2):19–33, 1998.

58. M. Lalmas and I. Ruthven. Representing and retrieving structured documents with Dempster-Shafer's theory of evidence: Modelling and evaluation. *Journal of Documentation*, 54(5):529–565, 1998.

59. M. Lalmas and C.J. van Rijsbergen. A model of an Information Retrieval system based on Situation Theory and Dempster-Shafer theory of evidence. In *Proceedings of the 1st Workshop on Incompleteness and Uncertainty in Information Systems*, pages 62–67, Montreal, Canada, 1993.

60. D. Lewis. *Conterfactuals*. Basil Blackwell, Oxford, UK, 2nd edition, 1986.

61. D.E. Losada and A. Barreiro. Using a belief revision operator for document ranking in extended boolean model. In *Proceedings of ACM SIGIR*, pages 66–73, Berkeley, CA, USA, 1999.

62. D.E. Losada and A. Barreiro. Efficient algorithms for ranking documents. In *Proceedings of SIGIR Workshop on Formal/Mathematical Methods for Information Retrieval*, pages 16–24, Athens, Greece, 2000.

63. D.E. Losada and A. Barreiro. Retrieval situations and belief changes. In *Proceedings of DEXA-LUMIS 2000*, Greenwich, London, UK, 2000.

64. C. Meghini, F. Sebastiani, U. Straccia, and C. Thanos. A model of Information Retrieval based on a Terminological Logic. In *Proceedings of ACM SIGIR*, pages 298–307, Pittsburgh, PA, USA, June 1993.

65. C. Meghini and U. Straccia. A relevance terminological logic for information retrieval. In *Proceedings of ACM SIGIR*, Zurich, CH, August 1996.

66. G. A. Miller. WordNet: An on-line lexical database. *International Journal of Lexicography*, 3(4):235–312, 1990.

67. A. Müller. A flexible framework for multimedia Information Retrieval. In F. Crestani, M. Lalmas, and C.J. van Rijsbergen, editors, *Information Retrieval: Uncertainty and Logics*, pages 97–128. Kluwer Academic Publishers, Norwell, MA, USA, 1998.

68. R.E. Neapolitan. *Probabilistic reasoning in expert systems*. John Wiley and Son Inc., New York, USA, 1990.

69. J. Y. Nie. *Un Modèle de Logique Générale pour les Systemes de Recherche d'Informations. Application au Prototype RIME*. PhD Thesis, Université Joseph Fourrier, Grenoble, France, 1990.

70. J.Y. Nie. An outline of a general model for Information Retrieval. In *Proceedings of ACM SIGIR*, pages 495–506, Grenoble, France, June 1988.

71. J.Y. Nie. An Information Retrieval model based on Modal Logic. *Information Processing & Management*, 25(5):477–491, 1989.

72. J.Y. Nie. Towards a probabilistic modal logic for semantic based Information Retrieval. In *Proceedings of ACM SIGIR*, pages 140–151, Copenhagen, Denmark, June 1992.

73. J.Y. Nie. CLIR and query expansion as logical inference. In *Proceedings of SIGIR Workshop on Formal/Mathematical Methods for Information Retrieval*, pages 8–15, Athens, Greece, 2000.

74. J.Y. Nie and M. Brisebois. An inferential approach to information retrieval and its implementation using a manual thesaurus. *Artificial Intelligence Review*, 10:409–439, 1996.

75. J.Y. Nie, F. Lepage, and M. Brisebois. Information Retrieval as counterfactuals. *The Computer Journal*, 38(8):643–657, 1995.

76. I. Ounis. *Un modele d'indexation relationnel pour les graphes conceptuels fonde sur une interpretation logique*. PhD Thesis, Université Joseph Fourrier, Grenoble I, 1998.

77. P. F. Patel-Schneider. A four-valued semantics for frame-based description languages. In *AAAI-86, 5th Conference of the American Association for Artificial Intelligence*, pages 344–348, Philadelphia, 1986.

78. J. Pearl. *Probabilistic reasoning in intelligent systems: networks of plausible inference*. Morgan Kaufmann, San Mateo, California, 1988.

79. J. Picard. Logic as a tool in a term matching information retrieval system. In *Proceedings of the Workshop on Logical and Uncertainty Models for Information Systems*, pages 77–90, London, UK, July 1999.

80. Y. Qiu and H.P. Frei. Concept based query expansion. In *Proceedings of ACM SIGIR*, pages 160–171, Pittsburgh, PA, USA, June 1993.

81. R. Reiter. A logic for default reasoning. *Artificial Intelligence*, 13(1):81–132, 1980.

82. B. Ribeiro-Neto, I. Silvia, and R. Muntz. Bayesian network models for Information Retrieval. In F. Crestani and G. Pasi, editors, *Soft Computing in Information Retrieval: techniques and application*, pages 259–291. Physica-Verlag, Heidelberg, Germany, 2000.

83. S.E. Robertson. The probability ranking principle in IR. *Journal of Documentation*, 33(4):294–304, December 1977.

84. T. Rölleke. *POOL: Probabilistic Object-Oriented Logical Representation and Retrieval of Complex Objects - A Model for Hypermedia Retrieva*. PhD Thesis, Department of Computer Science, University of Dortmund, Germany, 1999.

85. T. Rölleke and M. Blömer. Probabilistic logical Information Retrieval for content, hypertext and database querying. In *Proccedings of HIM Conference*, Dortmund, Germany, September 1997.

86. T. Rölleke and N. Fuhr. Retrieval of complex objects using a four-valued logic. In *Proceedings of ACM SIGIR*, pages 206–214, Zurich, Switzerland, 1996.

87. I. Ruthven, M. Lalmas, and C.J. van Rijsbergen. Retrieval through explanation: Inference approach to relevance feedback. In *Proceedings of 10th Annual Irish Conference on Artificial Intelligence & Cognitive Science (AICS)*, Cork, Ireland, 1999.

88. G. Salton. *Automatic information organization and retrieval*. McGraw Hill, New York, 1968.

89. S. Dominich. Formal foundation of classical information retrieval. In *Proceedings of SIGIR Workshop on Formal/Mathematical Methods for Information Retrieval*, pages 69–75, Athens, Greece, 2000.

90. S. Dominich, M. Lalmas, and C.J. van Rijsbergen. SIGIR Workshop on Formal/Mathematical Methods for Information Retrieval. *Technology Letters*, 4(1), 2000.

91. T. Saracevic. The concept of "relevance" in information science: a historical review. In T. Seracevic, editor, *Introduction to Information Science*, chapter 14. R.R. Bower Company, New York, USA, 1970.

92. J. Savoy. Bayesian inference networks and spreading activation in hypertext systems. *Information Processing & Management*, 28(3):389–406, 1992.

93. J. Savoy. A learning scheme for Information Retrieval in hypertext. *Information Processing & Management*, 30(4):515–533, 1994.

94. F. Sebastiani. A probabilistic terminological logic for modelling Information Retrieval. In *Proceedings of ACM SIGIR*, pages 122–131, Dublin, Ireland, 1994.

95. F. Sebastiani. On the role of logics in Information Retrieval. In *Proceedings of the MIRO Workshop*, Glasgow, September 1995.

96. J.F. Sowa. *Conceptual structures: information processing in mind and machine.* Addison-Wesley Publishing Company, Reading, MA, USA, 1984.

97. U. Thiel and A. Müller. Why was this item retrieved?: new ways to explore retrieval results. In M. Agosti and A.F. Smeaton, editors, *Information Retrieval and Hypertext*, chapter 8, pages 181–201. Kluwer Academic Publishers, Dordrecht, NL, 1996.

98. H.R. Turtle and W.B. Croft. Inference networks for document Retrieval. In *Proceedings of ACM SIGIR*, Brussels, Belgium, September 1990.

99. H.R. Turtle and W.B. Croft. Evaluation of an inference network-based retrieval model. *ACM Transactions on Information Systems*, 9(3):187–222, July 1991.

100. H.R. Turtle and W.B. Croft. A comparison of text retrieval models. *The Computer Journal*, 35(3):279–290, 1992.

101. C.J. van Rijsbergen. A theoretical basis for the use of co-occurence data in Information Retrieval. *Journal of Documentation*, 33(2):106–119, June 1977.

102. C.J. van Rijsbergen. A new theoretical framework for Information Retrieval. In *Proceedings of ACM SIGIR*, pages 194–200, Pisa, Italy, 1986.

103. C.J. van Rijsbergen. A non-classical logic for Information Retrieval. *The Computer Journal*, 29(6):481–485, 1986.

104. C.J. van Rijsbergen. Toward a new information logic. In *Proceedings of ACM SIGIR*, pages 77–86, Cambridge, USA, June 1989.

105. C.J. van Rijsbergen. Probabilistic retrieval revisited. *The Computer Journal*, 35(3):291–298, 1992.

106. C.J. van Rijsbergen and M. Lalmas. An information calculus for information retrieval. *Journal of the American Society of Information Science*, 47(5):385–398, 1996.

107. S.K.M. Wong and Y.Y. Yao. On modelling Information Retrieval with probabilistic inference. *ACM Transactions on Information Systems*, 13(1):38–68, 1995.

108. L. A. Zadeh. *Fuzzy sets and Applications: Selected Papers.* Wiley, New York, 1987.

Modeling Vagueness in Information Retrieval

Gloria Bordogna and Gabriella Pasi

Istituto per le Tecnologie Informatiche Multimediali
Consiglio Nazionale delle Ricerche—Milano, Italy
{gloria.bordogna,gabriella.pasi}@itim.mi.cnr.it

Abstract This paper reviews some applications of fuzzy set theory to model flexible information retrieval systems, i.e., systems that can represent and interpret the vagueness typical of human communication and reasoning. The paper focuses on the following topics: a description of fuzzy indexing procedures defined to represent structured documents, the definition of flexible query languages which allow the expression of vague selection conditions, and some fuzzy associative retrieval mechanisms based on fuzzy pseudo-thesauri of terms and fuzzy clustering techniques.

1 Introduction

The objective of this paper is to provide an overview of some applications of fuzzy set theory to design flexible Information Retrieval Systems. By flexible IRSs we mean systems that can represent and manage the vagueness which is characteristic of the process of information searching and retrieval.

Based on the considerations that index terms only offer an approximate view of the document content, that the query languages (such as the Boolean one) usually do not allow users to express vague requirements for specifying selection conditions tolerant to imprecision, and that the documents' relevance is a subjective and an imprecise notion, we will show how the imprecision and vagueness can be managed in the formal framework of fuzzy set theory [63]. In this way, retrieval mechanisms capable of both modelling the human subjectivity and estimating the partial relevance of documents to the user needs can be designed [30].

The retrieval activity will be introduced as a fuzzy multi-criteria decision making activity in the presence of vagueness. The documents constitute the set of the alternatives described on the basis of weighted index terms; the query specifies a set of soft constraints on the documents representation, and the retrieval mechanism performs a fuzzy decision to the aim of ranking the documents on the basis of their partial satisfaction of the soft constraints.

The paper is organized as follows: in the next section the basic concepts of fuzzy set theory used in the rest of the paper to model the vagueness in IR are introduced. In Sect. 3 the notions of imprecision and vagueness are analysed in the context of information retrieval. In Sect. 4 an overview of the main approaches to apply fuzzy set theory to model flexible Information Retrieval

M. Agosti, F. Crestani, and G. Pasi (Eds.): ESSIR 2000, LNCS 1980, pp. 207–241, 2000.
© Springer-Verlag Berlin Heidelberg 2000

Systems is presented. In Sect. 5 a description of the traditional fuzzy document representation is first illustrated; then both a fuzzy representation of documents structured into logical sections that can be adapted to the user having specific information requirements, and a fuzzy representation of HTML documents are presented.

Section 6 is devoted to the description of a flexible query language for Information Retrieval Systems based on soft constraints expressed by linguistic selection conditions which capture the vagueness of the user needs and simplify the query formulation. Two kinds of linguistic selection conditions are introduced to qualify term's importance, and to specify soft aggregation operators of query terms. In Sect. 7 a description of fuzzy associative retrieval models based either on fuzzy pseudothesauri of terms or fuzzy clustering techniques are introduced.

2   Modelling Vagueness within Fuzzy Set Theory

2.1   Definition of a Fuzzy Set

A fuzzy set is a class of elements with unsharp boundaries suitable to represent vague concepts [63]. A fuzzy subset A of a universe of discourse U is defined through a membership function $\mu_A : U \to [0,1]$; the value 1 indicates full membership of an element of U to A, the value 0 no membership, and a value between 0 and 1 partial membership. When a fuzzy subset A is defined on a finite set U it is denoted by $A = \sum_{u \in U} \mu_A(u)/u$. If U is an infinite set, A is denoted by: $A = \int_U \mu_A(u)/u$.

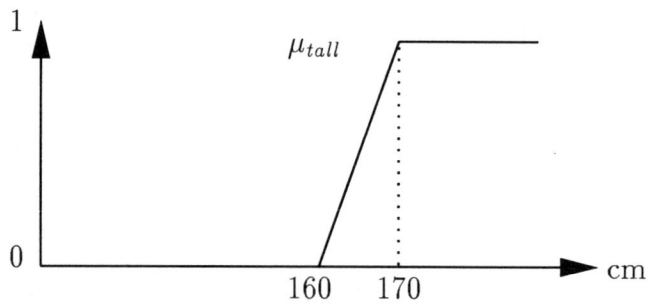

Figure 1. Membership Function of the Fuzzy Set *tall*.

For example, the vague characterisation *tall* on the set of the persons' heights can be defined as a fuzzy subset of the numeric values of the height. Each numeric value x of height belongs to the fuzzy set *tall* to a given degree: this membership degree is indicated by $\mu_{tall}(x)$ (see Fig. 1).

The most common definition of the cardinality of a fuzzy set A, indicated by Count(A) is defined as: Count(A) $= \sum_{u \in U} \mu_A(u)$ in which $\mu_A(u)$ is the membership degree of u to A.

A fuzzy binary relation R is defined on the Cartesian product $X \times Y$, and takes values in $[0, 1]$; it is then a fuzzy set $R = \sum \mu_R(x, y)/(x, y)$ in which the membership value $\mu_R(x, y)$ is a measure of the intensity or strength of the relation R existing between the elements x and y. For example, the fuzzy relation "close to" can be defined on the set R^2 with a membership function $\mu_{close\ to}$ so that: $\mu_{close\ to}(x, y) = e^{k*(x-y)^2}$, and $k < 0$. If the universes X and Y are finite, a fuzzy relation on $X \times Y$ can be represented by a matrix [25].

2.2 Basic Operations on Fuzzy Sets

Given two fuzzy subsets A and B defined on the universe U with membership functions μ_A and μ_B, they can be combined by applying different operators to obtain a new fuzzy subset of U. Here, we recall three main classes of aggregation operators: the t-norms denoted by $T(\mu_A(u), \mu_B(u))$, the t-conorms, $S(\mu_A(u), \mu_B(u))$ and the mean operators, $M(\mu_A(u), \mu_B(u))$; these classes of operators satisfy the following:

$$T(\mu_A(u), \mu_B(u)) \leq \min(\mu_A(u), \mu_B(u)) \quad \text{and}$$
$$\max(\mu_A(u), \mu_B(u)) \leq S(\mu_A(u), \mu_B(u))$$

Moreover:

$$\min(\mu_A(u), \mu_B(u)) \leq M(\mu_A(u), \mu_B(u)) \leq \max(\mu_A(u), \mu_B(u)).$$

A t-norm operator is a mapping $T : [0, 1] \times [0, 1] \to [0, 1]$ that is symmetric, associative, and has 1 as neutral element. Examples of t-norms include: $\min(a, b)$; $1 - \min(1, [1 - (1 - x)^w + (1 - y)^w]^{1/w})$ for $w \geq 1$; $\max(x + y - 1, 0)$; and $x * y$.

A t-conorm operator is a mapping $S : [0, 1] \times [0, 1] \to [0, 1]$ that is symmetric, associative, and has 0 as neutral element. Examples of t-conorms include: $\max(x, y)$; $\min(1, (x^w + y^w)^{1/w})$; $\min(1, x + y)$; and $x + y - x * y$.

Notice that the min and the max are the only t-norm and t-conorm operators which satisfy the idempotence property, and they are usually adopted for the union and intersection operations respectively [20].

The complement of a fuzzy set is a unary operation generally defined as: $1 - \mu_A(u), \forall u \in U$.

A mean operator is a continuous function $M : [0, 1] \times [0, 1] \to [0, 1]$ that is idempotent, symmetric, and monotonic. These properties imply that mean operators lie between *min* and *max*. Example of mean operators include the harmonic mean $2xy/(x + y)$, the geometric mean $\sqrt{xy}$, the arithmetic mean $(x + y)/2$ and generalized p-means $[(x^p + y^p)/2]^{1/p}$ with $p \geq 1$ [22].

2.3 Linguistic Quantifiers

In [65] two types of linguistic quantifiers have been defined as fuzzy subsets, i.e. the absolute and the relative quantifiers. Absolute quantifiers, such as *about 7, almost 6*, etc. are defined as fuzzy sets with membership function $\mu_Q : \Re \to [0, 1]$, where $\forall x \in \Re$, $\mu_Q(x)$ indicates the degree to which the amount x satisfies the concept associated with the quantifier Q. Relative quantifiers like *most*, or *about 70%*, are defined as fuzzy subsets of the unit interval: $\mu_Q : [0,1] \to [0,1]$, where $\forall x \in [0,1], \mu_Q(x)$ indicates the degree to which the proportion x satisfies the concept Q. In Fig. 2 a possible definition of the quantifier *most* is showed. For an introduction to linguistic quantifiers see [58, 60, 65].

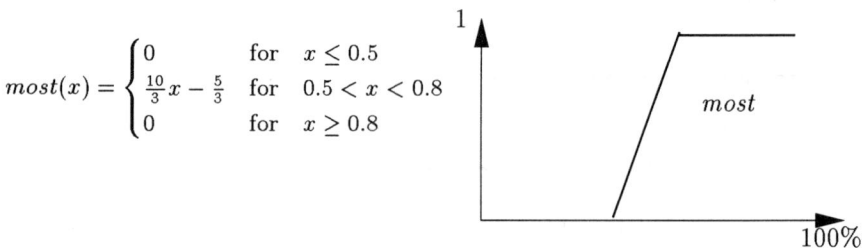

$$most(x) = \begin{cases} 0 & \text{for} \quad x \leq 0.5 \\ \frac{10}{3}x - \frac{5}{3} & \text{for} \quad 0.5 < x < 0.8 \\ 0 & \text{for} \quad x \geq 0.8 \end{cases}$$

Figure 2. Representation of the Linguistic Quantifier *most*.

For example the absolute quantifier *at least 5* depicted in Fig. 3 acts as the specification of a fuzzy or tolerant threshold of value 5 on its argument. If its argument x is equal or greater than 5, the value *at least*$5(x)$ is 1. When $2 \leq x < 5$, the value *at least*$5(x)$ is greater than zero.

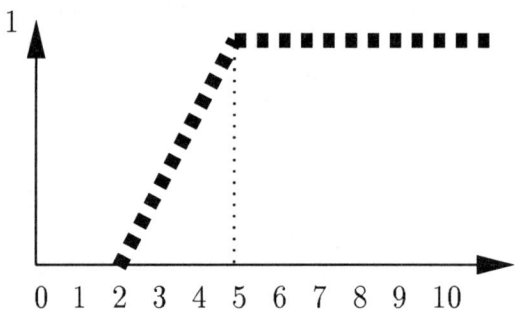

Figure 3. Representation of the Absolute Linguistic Quantifier *at least 5*.

Linguistic quantifiers can be associated with aggregation operators; to this aim in the next subsection Ordered Weighted Averaging Operators (OWA) are introduced.

2.4   Ordered Weighted Averaging Operators

An Ordered Weighted Averaging (OWA) operator of dimension n is a non linear aggregation operator OWA : $[0,1]^n \to [0,1]$ with a weighting vector

$W = [w_1, w_2, \ldots, w_n]$ such that:

$$\sum_{j=1}^{n} w_j = 1 \quad \text{with} \quad w_j \in [0,1]$$

and

$$\text{OWA}(x_1, x_2, \ldots, x_n) = \sum_{j=1}^{n} w_j * \text{Max}_j(x_1, x_2, \ldots, x_n) \tag{1}$$

in which $\text{Max}_j(x_1, x_2, \ldots, x_n)$ equals the j-th biggest element of all the x_i [58].

For example, $\text{Max}_1(x_1 = 0.8, x_2 = 0.5, x_3 = 1) = x_3 = 1$; $\text{Max}_2(x_1 = 0.8, x_2 = 0.5, x_3 = 1) = x_1 = 0.8$; $\text{Max}_3(x_1 = 0.8, x_2 = 0.5, x_3 = 1) = x_2 = 0.5$.

OWA operators are mean operators, the values produced as a result of their aggregation lie between those produced by the AND (min) and those produced by the OR (max). The degree of *orness* of an OWA aggregation operator expresses its closeness to the OR behaviour, and it is defined as:

$$\text{orness}(W) = \left(\frac{1}{n-1}\right) \sum_{j=1}^{n} ((n-j)w_j) \tag{2}$$

The OWA operator with the weighting vector W* defined as $[1, 0, \ldots, 0]$ so that $w_1 = 1$ corresponds to the OR operator, i.e., the max. In this case, $orness(W^*) = 1$. The OWA operator with the weighting vector W_* defined as $[0, \ldots, 0, 1]$ so that $w_n = 1$ corresponds to the AND operator, i.e., the min. In this case, $orness(W_*) = 0$.

An OWA operator can be defined with a weighting vector W modelling a linguistic quantifier such as for example *most of*, *at least k*, etc. This definition of linguistic quantifiers allows to interpret them as aggregation operators in multicriteria decision making. The linguistic quantifiers *all* and *at least one* correspond to the OWA operators with weighting vector W_* and W^* respectively.

OWA operators modelling the semantics of a linguistic quantifier with a soft behaviour between the two extremes *all* and *at least one* can be defined as follows: first, as it has been explained is Sect. 2.3, the membership function of the fuzzy subset representing the monotone non-decreasing relative quantifier Q is defined: $Q : [0,1] \to [0,1]$. Then the N elements $w_i \in [0,1]$ of the weighting vector W are obtained as:

$$w_i = Q(i/n) - Q((i-1)/n) \quad \forall i = 1 \ldots n \tag{3}$$

The weighting vector of the OWA associated with the quantifier *most* depicted in Fig. 2 is defined by $W_{most} = [0, 0, 0, 5/9, 4/9, 0]$.

A proposed definition of OWA operator when distinct importance degrees $I_1, \ldots, I_n \in [0,1]$ are associated with its arguments, is based on a modification of the values $x_1, x_2, \ldots, x_n$ so as to increase the contrast between the more important arguments with respect to the less important ones. The modified degrees $a_1, \ldots, a_N$ are obtained as follows:

$$a_i = \left[I_i \vee (1 - orness(W)) \right] * (x_i)^{I_i \vee orness(W)} \tag{4}$$

where W is the OWA weighting vector, and $\vee$ is defined as the max operator. Then, the OWA operator is applied to the modified values $a_1, \ldots, a_N$.

2.5   Linguistic Variables

A linguistic variable is a variable whose values are linguistic terms rather than numbers [64]. For example the linguistic variable Age can be defined, which takes as values the linguistic terms *very old, old, not very old, not very young, young, very young*. Each linguistic variable has a base variable associated with it that takes numeric values: for example the base variable of *Age* may take values in $[0, 120]$.

Formally a linguistic variable is defined by a quintuple: $\{V, T(V), D_V, G_V, M_V\}$ where V is the name of the linguistic variable;
$T(V)$ is the term set of V, i.e., the set of linguistic terms that V can assume as values;
D_V is the universe of discourse of the base variable, i.e., the set of all the numeric values that the base variable can assume and on which the membership functions of the linguistic terms are defined.
G_V is the context-free grammar that generates all values belonging to $T(V)$. The composite terms are generated from the primary terms, the hedges (such as *less, more or less, very*, etc.), the negation *not* and connectives (and, or) by applying production rules. For example, the composite term *very old* is generated from the primary term *old* and the hedge *very* by applying the production rule:

<composite term>:=<hedge><primary term>

M_V is the set of meanings of the terms in $T(V)$. The meaning of primary terms is defined by membership functions defined on the domain U_V of the base variable; these functions express the compatibility between the concept expressed by the linguistic value and the values of the base variable. For example the meanings of the primary terms *old* and *young* are defined by the functions $\mu_{old} : [0, 120] \rightarrow [0, 1]$ and $\mu_{young} : [0, 120] \rightarrow [0, 1]$. The meaning of composite terms is obtained by modifying those of the primary terms through the operators associated with the hedges, the connectives and the *not*. For example *very* can be associated with a concentrator operator such as
$op_{very}(f) = (f)^2$ so that:
$\mu_{very\ old}(u) = (\mu_{old}(u))^2$, $\forall u \in U_V$.
The *not* unary operator is generally defined as the complement to one $op_{not}(f) = 1 - f$ and the connectives *and* and *or* are generally defined as the *min* and the *max* operators respectively (more generally they are defined by t-norms and t-conorms respectively).

3   Vagueness and Imprecision in Information Retrieval

In many real situations of information searching and retrieval one has to deal with information characterized to some extent by some kind of *imperfection*. The word *imperfection* has been introduced to indicate one of the following faults of information [38]: imprecision, vagueness, uncertainty, and inconsistency, which are briefly discussed in the following.

Vagueness and imprecision are related to the information content of a proposition. For example, when an unexperienced user having some information needs is faced with a human intermediary of an information source she/he can more easily express her/his requirements by a natural language query containing linguistic terms, such as:

> "find *recent* scientific papers *mainly* dealing with the *early* stage of infectious deseases by HIV."

In this query, the terms *recent, mainly* and *early* specify vague selection conditions on the values of the publication date, significance of the terms "infectious deseases by HIV" in characterizing the document content, and temporal evolution of a desease. The automatic evaluation of this query assumes that the IRS represents documents by weighted terms (content descriptors), and also by the meta-data "publication date" and "desease temporal evolution" [1]; further it must be able to interpret the semantics of the vague terms. In the previous example the information expressing the publication date, the weights of index terms and the phase of an infectious desease is numeric; as it has been illustrated in Sect. 2, in the framework of fuzzy set theory the vagueness is expressed by means of linguistic terms with a semantics which is compatible to a gradual extent with several "numeric" values of the scale on which this numeric information is defined. Imprecision is just a case-limit of vagueness since imprecise values have a full compatibility with a subset of values of the reference scale. In Fig. 4 a representation of the compatibility function of the vague term *recent* with respect to the numeric values of the time scale (measured in years) is depicted, together with a representation of the imprecise term *between one year ago and next year*.

Uncertainty is related to the truth of a proposition, intended as the conformity of the information carried by the proposition with the considered reality. Linguistic expressions such as *"probably"*, and *"it is possible that"*, can be used to declare the partial ignorance about the truth of the stated information.

Further, there are cases in which information is affected by both uncertainty and imprecision or vagueness, like for example in the proposition *"probably* document *d* is *relevant* to query *q*." However, the same information content can be expressed by choosing a trade-off between the vagueness and the uncertainty embedded in a proposition. For example, one can express the content of the previous proposition by the new one "document *d* is *more or less relevant* to query *q*." In this last sentence the uncertain term *probably* has been eliminated, but the specificity of the vague term has been reduced; in fact, the term *more or less relevant* is less specific than the term *relevant*.

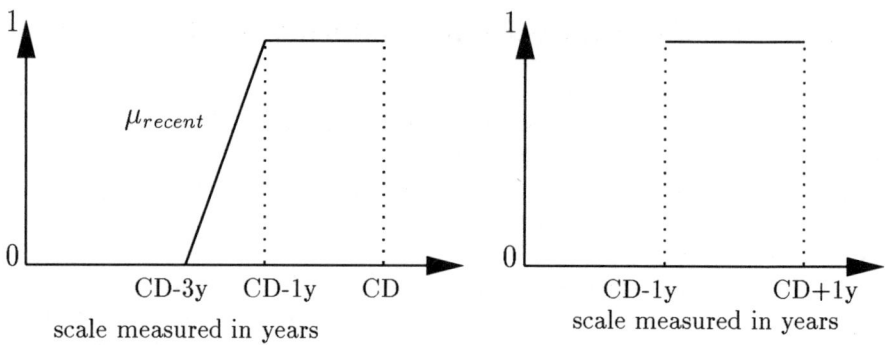

Figure 4. Compatibility functions of the vague term *recent* and of the imprecise term *between one year ago and next year* referred to the publication date of a scientific paper, where CD=Current date, y=years

In IR, when judging if a document is relevant to a query, one is invariably faced with the uncertainty implied by this decision process and deriving by the fact that, on the one side, one can only partially interpret the user's information needs, and on the other side, has only an incomplete and rough description of the document information content, generally synthesised by index terms, sometimes weighted.

On the basis of what has been said about the trade-off between uncertainty and vagueness to express the same information content, there are two alternative ways to model a flexible query evaluation mechanism.

One possibility is to model the query evaluation mechanism as an uncertain decision process: by this approach the concept of relevance is considered binary (crisp) and the query evaluation mechanism computes the probability of relevance of a document d to a query q. The approach which models the uncertainty of the retrieval process has been introduced and developed by the probabilistic IR models [19, 23, 56].

Another possibility is to interpret the query as the specification of soft "elastic" constraints that the representation of a document can satisfy to a partial extent, and to consider the term *relevant* as a gradual (vague) concept. This is the approach adopted by fuzzy IR models [6, 30]: in this case, the decision process performed by the query evaluation mechanism computes the degree of satisfaction of the query by the representation of each document. This degree, named Retrieval Status Value (RSV) is considered as an estimate of the *relevance* of the document with respect to the query: RSV = 1 maximum relevance, RSV=0 no relevance; $0 < \text{RSV} < 1$ intermediate degrees of relevance, RSV = 0.5 means average relevance.

Inconsistency comes from the simultaneous presence of contradictory information about the same reality: an example of inconsistency is obtained when submitting the same query to several IRSs that adopt different representations of documents and produce distinct results: this is a very common case that can occur when searching information over the Internet by using different search engines. To solve this kind of inconsistency some fusion strategies can be applied on the ranked lists [44, 61].

Possibility theory [21, 62] together with the concept of linguistic variable defined within fuzzy set theory [64] provides a unifying formal framework to formalize the management of imperfect information. The four aspect of imperfect information are all present in database applications; recently, some models of data base management systems able to cope with them have been defined within possibility theory [11].

In this contribution we analyse the management of vagueness as a means to improve the flexibility of IRSs. In particular, since fuzzy set theory provides a natural framework to model vagueness and imprecision, we will focus on the modelling of vagueness in fuzzy IR models.

In an IRS, the information is managed at two distinct levels:

- documents' representation;
- information request formulated through queries.

The document representation based on a selection of index terms is invariably incomplete. When synthesizing the content of a text manually by asking an expert to select a set of index terms one introduces subjectivity in the representation. On the other side, automatic full-text indexing introduces imprecision since the terms are not all fully significant to characterise the document content, but they can have a partial significance that can depend also on the context in which they appear, i.e., document subpart.

In query formulation, often users have only a vague idea of the information they are looking for and they find it difficult to translate their needs in a precise request of a formal query language such as the Boolean one. A flexible IRS should then be capable of providing more detailed and rich representations of documents and of interpreting vague queries so as to perform a retrieval activity which tolerates and accounts for this vagueness.

4   Fuzzy IR Models

Fuzzy IR models have been defined to the following aims:

1. to reduce the incompleteness and to deal with the imprecision which characterise the indexing process;
2. to manage the user's vagueness in queries
3. to deal with discriminated answers reflecting the partial relevance of the documents with respect to queries.

Extended Boolean models based on fuzzy sets have been defined which face one or more of the above aspects [5, 7, 8, 12, 14, 16, 28, 45, 57]. In [6, 29] surveys of fuzzy extensions of IRS and of fuzzy generalizations of the Boolean IR model are provided.

Fuzzy "knowledge based" models [31, 32], and fuzzy associative mechanisms based on thesauri or clustering techniques [34–36, 39] have been defined in order to cope with the incompleteness characterizing either the representation of documents or the users' queries. In [33] a wide range of methods for generating fuzzy associative mechanisms is illustrated.

4.1   Fuzzy Generalizations of the Boolean Models

Fuzzy generalizations of the Boolean model have been defined to extend existing Boolean IRSs without redesigning them. Their definition was first motivated by the need of IRSs able to produce discriminated answers in response to users' queries. Basically, Boolean IRSs apply an exact matching between a Boolean query and the representation of each document defined as a set of index terms. They partition the archive of items into two sets: the retrieved documents and the rejected ones. As a consequence of this crisp behaviour, they are liable to reject useful items as a result of too restrictive queries, and to retrieve useless material in reply to general queries [52].

Thus, the softening of the retrieval activity to rank the retrieved items in decreasing order of their relevance to a user query can greatly improve the effectiveness of such systems. This objective has been approached by extending the Boolean model at different levels hereafter listed; the basic idea is to conceive the IR activity as a MCDM activity tolerant to imprecision in query evaluation and allowing the expression of soft constraints in the users' queries.

- **Fuzzy techniques for documents' indexing**: the aim is to provide more specific and exhaustive representations of documents' information content than those generated by the existing indexing procedures. In the following section, the fuzzy interpretation of the weighted document representation is introduced, and a fuzzy representation of documents structured in logical sections that can be adapted to the user having subjective criteria for interpreting the content of documents is presented [8]. Also an indexing procedure for HTML documents is shortly described [37].
- **Definition of flexible query languages**; the objective is to define query languages more expressive and natural than the Boolean language, in order to capture the vagueness of user needs as well as to simplify the user system interaction. This aim has been pursued at two levels:
  - through the definition of soft selection criteria (soft constraints), which allow the specification of the different importances of the search terms. Query languages based on numeric query term weights with different semantics have been first proposed as an aid to define more expressive selection criteria [5, 15–17, 57]. Then, an evolution of these approaches has been defined, which introduces linguistic query weights, specified by fuzzy sets such as *important* or *very important*, in order to express the different importances of the query terms [9].
  - by introducing soft aggregation operators of the selection criteria, characterized by a parametric behaviour which can be set between the two

extremes AND and OR adopted in the Boolean language. Different approaches have been proposed. In [7] the Boolean query language has been generalized by defining aggregation operators as linguistic quantifiers such as *at least k* or *most of*.

As it will be shown, the incorporation of a weighted documents' representation in a Boolean IRS is a sufficient condition to improve the system with a document ranking ability. As a consequence of this extension the exact matching applied by a Boolean system can be softened to a partial matching mechanism, evaluating the degree of satisfaction of the user's query for each document retrieved. This value is called a Retrieval Status Value (RSV), and can be used for ranking documents.

4.2 Fuzzy Associative Mechanisms

Fuzzy associative mechanisms employ fuzzy thesauri, fuzzy pseudothesauri, and fuzzy clustering techniques to serve three distinct but compatible purposes:

1. fuzzy thesauri and pseudothesauri can be used to expand the set of index terms of documents with new terms by taking into account their varying significance in representing the topics dealt with in the documents; the degree of significance of the associated terms depends on the strength of the associations with the documents' descriptors.
2. An alternative use of fuzzy thesauri and pseudothesauri is to expand each of the search terms in the query with associated terms, by taking into account their distinct importance in representing the concepts of interest; the varying importance is dependent on the associations' strength with the search terms.
3. fuzzy clustering can be used to expand the set of the documents retrieved by a query with associated documents; their degrees of association with respect to the documents originally retrieved influence their Retrieval Status Value.

5 Fuzzy Document Indexing

The primary objective of the research in information retrieval is to define models which allow to design IRSs with a high effectiveness. The aim is to make a system able to retrieve from the considered archive the documents concerned with the topics required in a user query. The production of effective retrieval results depends on both subjective factors, such as the users' ability to express their information needs in a query, and the characteristics of the Information Retrieval System.

In order to increase the effectiveness of IRSs, the indexing process plays a crucial role: in fact, to achieve effective results it is not sufficient to provide information retrieval systems with powerful query languages or sophisticated retrieval mechanisms if the representation of documents oversimplifies their information content.

The vector space model and the probabilistic models generally adopt a weighted document representation, which has improved the Boolean document representation, by allowing the association of a numeric weight with each index term [52, 56]. The automatic computation of the index term weights is based on the occurrences count of a term in the document and in the whole archive [51, 54, 55]. In this case the indexing function computes for each document d and each term t a numeric value, by means of a function F; an example of definition of the function F is the following, in which the index term weight is proportional to the frequency of term t in the document d, and inversely proportional to the frequency of the term in the documents of the archive:

$$F(d, t) = tf_{dt} \times g(\text{IDF}_t) \qquad (5)$$

where:

- tf_{dt} is a normalized term frequency which can be defined as: $tf_{dt} = \frac{\text{OCC}_{dt}}{\text{MAXOCC}_d}$; OCC_{dt} is the number of occurrences of t in d, and MAXOCC_d is the number of occurrences of the most frequent term in d;
- IDF_t is an inverse document frequency which can be defined as: $\text{IDF}_t = \log \frac{N}{\text{NDOC}_t}$; where N is the total number of documents in the archive and NDOC_t is the number of documents indexed by t. The computation of IDF_t is particularly costly in the case of large collections which are updated online; g is a normalizing function.

The definition of such a function F is based on a quantitative analysis of the text which makes it possible to model the qualitative concept of significance of a term in describing the information carried by the text. The adoption of weighted indexes allows for an estimate of the relevance or of a probability of relevance of the documents to the considered query [52, 56].

Based on such an indexing function and by maintaining the Boolean query language, the first fuzzy interpretation of an extended Boolean model has been to adopt a weighted document representation and to interpret it as a fuzzy set of terms [13]. From a mathematical point of view this is a quite natural extension: the concept of the significance of index terms in describing the information content of a document can then be naturally described by adopting the function F (such as the one defined in (5)) as the membership function of the fuzzy set representing a document. Formally a document is represented as a fuzzy set of terms: $R_d = \sum_{t \in T} \mu_{Rd}(t)/t$ in which the membership function is defined as $\mu_{Rd} : D \times T \to [0, 1]$. In this case $\mu_{Rd}(t) = F(d, t)$, i.e. the membership value can be obtained by the indexing function F. As it will be described in Sect. 6, through this extension of the document representation, the evaluation of a Boolean query produces a numeric estimate of the relevance of each document to the query, expressed by a numeric score, called the Retrieval Status Value (RSV), which is interpreted as the degree of satisfaction of the constraints expressed in a query.

Fuzzy set theory has been applied to define new and more powerful indexing models than the one based on the function specified in (5). The definition of new indexing functions has been motivated by the following considerations: first, the F function previously defined does not take into account that a term can play a different role within a text, according to the distribution of its occurrences. Moreover the text is considered as a sort of black box, "closed" to the interpretation of the user, who, on the contrary, would naturally filter the information by emphasizing certain subparts on the basis of her/his subjective interests. This last consideration outlines the fact that relevance judgments are driven by a subjective interpretation of the document's structure, and supports the idea of *dynamic* and *adaptive* indexing [2,8]. By adaptive indexing we intend indexing procedures which take into account the users' indications to *interpret* the document contents and to "build" their synthesis on the basis of this interpretation.

In Sect. 5.1 we synthesize a fuzzy representation of structured documents which takes into account the user interpretation of the document [8]. A document is represented as an entity composed of sections (such as *title, authors, introduction, references*, in the case of a scientific paper). When generating an archive from a set of documents, first it is necessary to identify the sections in which one wants to structure each document; this choice depends on the semantics of the documents and on the accuracy of the indexing module that one wants to achieve. The formal representation of a document is constituted by a fuzzy binary relation defined on the Cartesian product $T \times S$ (where T is the set of index terms and S is the set of identifiers of the documents' sections): with each pair <section, term>, a significance degree in $[0, 1]$ is computed, expressing the significance of the term in the document section. To obtain the overall significance degree of a term in a document these values are *dynamically* aggregated, by taking into account the indications that a user explicitates in the phase of query formulation. The aggregation function is defined on the basis of a two level interaction between the system and the user. At the first level the user expresses preferences on the document sections, outlining those that the system should more heavily take into account in evaluating the relevance of a document to a user query. At the second level, the user can decide which aggregation function has to be applied for producing the overall significance degree. This is done by the specification of a linguistic quantifier such as *at least k* and *most* [65]. By adopting this document representation the same query can select documents in different relevance order depending on the user indications.

In Sect. 5.2 another representation of documents is synthesized, which produces a weighted representation of documents written in HyperText Markup Language [37]. An HTML document has a syntactic structure, in which its subparts have a given format specified by the delimiting tags. In this context tags are seen as syntactic elements carrying an indication of the importance of the associated text: when writing a document in HTML, one associates a distinct importance with distinct documents' subparts, by delimiting them by means of appropriate tags. On the basis of these considerations, an indexing function has been proposed, which computes the significance of a term in a document by taking into account the different role of term occurrences according to the importance of tags in which they appear.

5.1   An Adaptive Indexing Function for Structured Documents

In many existing applications of IR, the documents in the considered archive are structured in logical sections, such as for example *title, author, introduction,* etc., in scientific papers. In these documents, the occurrences of a given term play a distinct role depending on the subpart in which they appear: a single occurrence of the term in the *title* indicates that the paper is concerned with the concept expressed by the term, while a single occurrence in the *reference* suggests that the paper refers to other publications dealing with that concept. The information role of each term occurrence depends then on the semantics of the subpart where it is located. This means that to the aim of defining an indexing function for structured documents the single occurrences of a term may contribute differently to the significance of the term in the whole document. Moreover, the document's subparts may have a different importance determined by the users' needs. For example, when looking for papers written by a certain author, the most important subpart is the *author name*, while when looking for papers on a certain topic, the *title, abstract,* and *introduction* subparts are those preferred.

In [8] an indexing model has been proposed by which the occurrences of a term in the different documents' sections are taken into account according to specific criteria, and the user's interpretation of the text is modelled. To this aim, first the archive is generated so that the system can recognize and manage the sections in which one wants to structure the documents. The sections are defined depending on the semantics of the documents.

Then, during the retrieval phase, the user can specify the distinct importance (preference) of the sections and decide that a term must be present in *all* the sections of the document or in *at least a certain number* of them in order to consider the term fully significant. A section is a logical subpart identified by s_i, where $i \in 1, \ldots, n$ and n is the total number of the sections in the documents. We assume here that an archive contains documents sharing a common structure.

Formally a document is represented as a fuzzy binary relation:

$$R_d = \sum_{(t,s) \in T \times S} \mu_d(t, s)/(t, s) \qquad (6)$$

The value $\mu_d(t, s) = F_s(d, t)$ expresses the significance of term t in section s of document d. A function $F_s : D \times T \to [0, 1]$ is then defined for each section s. The overall significance degree $F(d, t)$ is computed by combining the single significance degrees of the sections, the $F_s(d, t)$s, through an aggregation function specified by the user. This function is identified by a fuzzy linguistic quantifier such as *all, at least k, at least 1*, and it aggregates the significance degrees of the sections according to their importance values, also specified by the user.

The criteria for the definition of F_s are based on the semantics of section s and are specified by an expert during the indexing of the documents. For example, for sections containing short texts or formatted texts, such as the *author* and the *keywords*, a single occurrence of a term makes it fully significant in that section: in this case, it could be for example assumed that $F_s(d,t) = 1$, if t is present in s, $F_s(d,t) = 0$ otherwise. On the other side, for sections containing textual descriptions of variable length such as the *abstract* and *title* sections, $F_s(d,t)$ can be computed as a function of the normalized term frequency in the section as for example:

$$\mu_s(d,t) = tf_{dst} * \text{IDF}_t \tag{7}$$

in which IDF_t is the inverse document frequency of term t (see definition (5)), tf_{dst} is the normalized term frequency defined as:

$$tf_{dst} = \frac{\text{OCC}_{dst}}{\text{MAXOCC}_{sd}}$$

in which OCC_{dst} is the number of occurrences of term t in section s of document d and MAXOCC_{sd} is a normalization parameter depending on the section's length so as not to underestimate the significance of short sections with respect to long ones. For example, it can be computed as the frequency of the term with the highest number of occurrences in the section. To simplify the computation of this value it is possible to heuristically approximate it: during the archive generation phase, the expert indicates the estimated percentage of the average length of each section with respect to the average length of documents (PERL_s). Given the number of occurrences of the most frequent term in each document d, MAXOCC_d, an approximation of the number of occurrences of the most frequent term in section s of document d is:

$$\text{MAXOCC}_{sd} = \text{PERL}_s * \text{MAXOCC}_d$$

To obtain the overall degree of significance of a term in a document, in [8] an aggregation scheme of the $F_s(d,t)s$ values has been suggested, based on a twofold specification of the user. When setting a retrieval session, the user can specify her/his preferences on the sections s by a numeric score $\alpha_s \in [0,1]$ (the most important sections have an importance weight close to 1). Moreover the user can select a linguistic quantifier to specify the aggregation criterion; the quantifier can be chosen among *all* (the most restrictive one), *at least one* (the weakest one), or *at least k* which is associated with an intermediate aggregation criterion.

In [58] the linguistic quantifiers have been defined as Ordered Weighted Averaging operators. When processing a query the first step accomplished by the system for evaluating $F(d,t)$ is the selection of the OWA operator associated with the linguistic quantifier lq, OWA_{lq}. When the user does not specify any preferences on the documents' sections, the overall significance degree $F(d,t)$ is obtained by applying directly the OWA_{lq} operator to the values $\mu_1(d,t), \ldots, \mu_n(d,t)$:

$$F(d,t) = \text{OWA}_{lq}(\mu_1(d,t), \ldots, \mu_n(d,t))$$

When distinct preference scores $\alpha_1, \ldots, \alpha_n$ are associated with the sections, it is first necessary to modify the values $\mu_1(d,t), \ldots, \mu_n(d,t)$ in order to increase the "contrast" between the contributions due to important sections with respect to those of less important ones. The modified degrees $a_1, \ldots, a_n$ of significance of the sections are obtained by applying formula (4) as explained in Sect. 3.4. The evaluation of the overall significance degree $F(d,t)$ is obtained by applying the operator OWA_{lq} to the modified degrees $a_1, \ldots, a_n : F(d,t) = \text{OWA}_{lq}(a_1, \ldots, a_n)$.

In the following we briefly sketch a compared evaluation of the effectiveness of a system adopting a simple weighted representation and the system with the structured weighted representation. In particular, the different rankings of two documents by adopting the two different representations are outlined by an example. The two documents considered in the archive of CNR research projects contain the term "genoma."

Table 1 shows the normalized frequency of "genoma" in the sections of the two documents; as it can be noticed, the term "genoma" has the same total number of occurrences in both the documents. Since the normalization factors are the same, by applying function (5) the significance of "genoma" in both documents gets the same value $F(d_1, \text{genoma}) = F(d_2, \text{genoma}) = 0.8$.

Table 2 shows the significance degrees for each section in which the term "genoma" occurs. These degrees are obtained using the fuzzy representation of structured documents; since the title and keywords sections are short texts, μ_{title} and μ_{keywords} are defined so as to take values in $\{0,1\}$. After estimating that the objective section takes up averagely 30% of the documents' length, and the description section is around 40%, $\mu_{objective}$ and $\mu_{description}$ are defined based on formula (7).

Table 1. Normalized Frequency of "genoma" in the Sections of the Two Documents

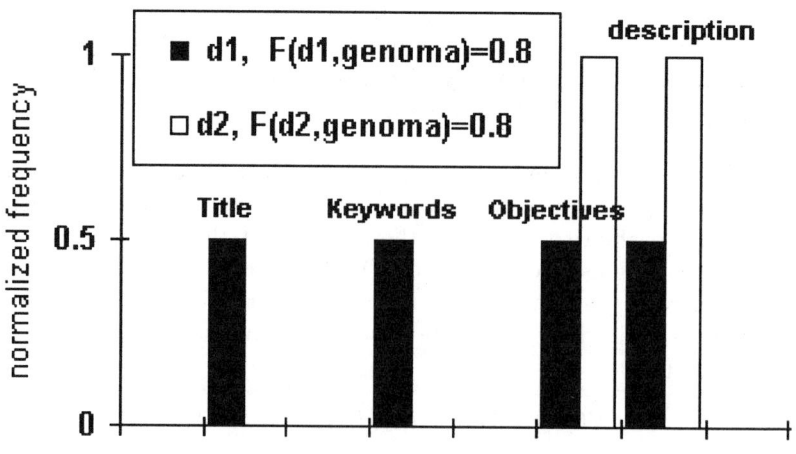

Table 2. Significance Degrees of "genoma" in Each Section of the Two Documents

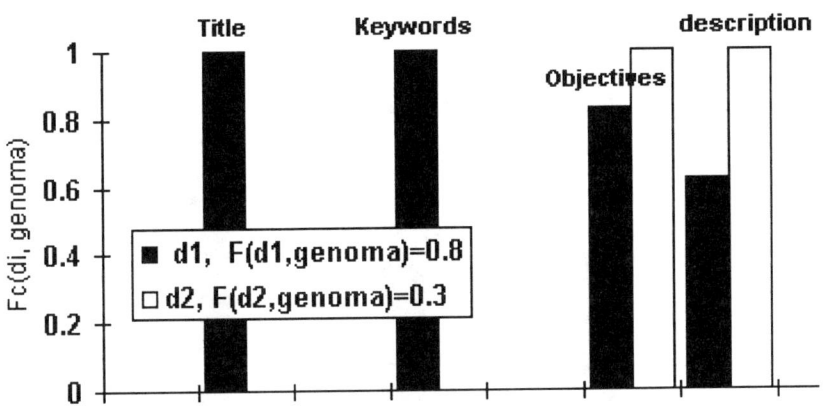

When the user does not specify any criterion to aggregate the single degrees of the sections a default aggregation operator is used [7]. Since no importance is specified to differentiate the contributions of the sections, all of them are assumed with the same importance weight 1. Notice that the document d_1 which contains "genoma" in the keywords and title is now considered more significant with respect to the document d_2 containing the term just in the objective and description. These results can be reversed, for example, when the user specifies that the presence of the term "genoma" in the objective is fundamental. Table 3 illustrates this situation: it shows the modified degrees of significances of the sections when the user sets the aggregation criterion equal to *at least 1* and $\alpha_{objective} = 1$, $\alpha_{title} = \alpha_{keywords} = \alpha_{description} = 0.5$, and $\alpha_i = 0$ otherwise.

A compared evaluation of the system results produced by using the traditional fuzzy representation of documents and the fuzzy representation of structured documents can be found in [8]. In this experiment a collection of 2500 textual documents about descriptions of CNR research projects has been considered. The indexing module of the prototypal information retrieval system named DOMINO, used for the experiment, has been extended in order to be able to recognize in the documents any structure simply by specifying it into a definition file. In this way it is not necessary to modify the system when dealing with a new collection of documents with a different structure. The definition of the documents sections has been made before starting the archive generation phase. During this phase it was also necessary to specify the criteria by which to compute the significance degrees of the terms in each section. Two kinds of sections have been identified: the "structured" sections, i.e., the research code, title, research leader, and the "narrative" sections, containing unstructured textual descriptions, i.e., the project description and the project objective. It has been observed that while the values of precision remain unchanged in the two versions of the system, the values of recall are higher by using the structured representation than those obtained by using the traditional fuzzy representation.

Table 3. Modified Significance Degrees of the Term "genoma" in the Documents Sections.

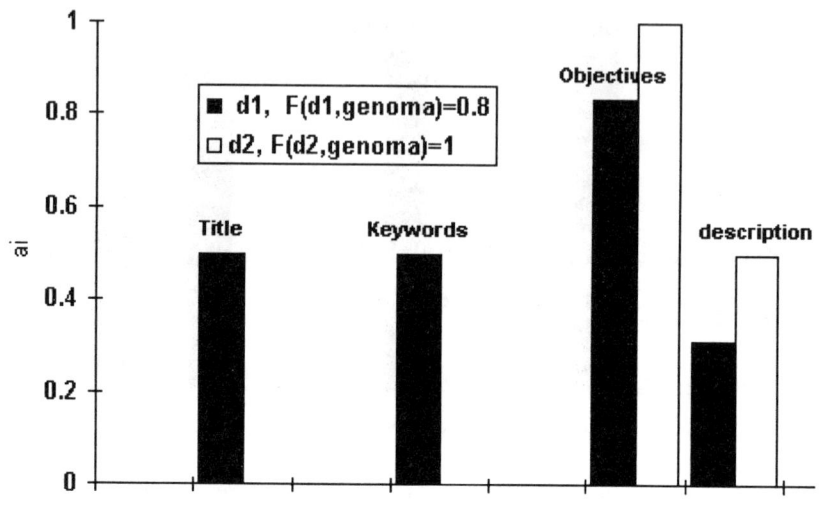

5.2   An Indexing Function for HTML Documents

An HTML document can be seen as a structured entity, in which documents' subparts are identified by tags, and each subpart is constituted by the text delimited by a distinct tag. Since a certain tag can be employed more than once, and in different positions inside the document, the concept of document subpart is not meant as a unique, adjacent piece of text. Such a structure is subjective and carries the interpretation of the document provider; it can be applied in archives which collect heterogeneous documents, i.e. documents with possibly different "logical" structures. When generating a HTML document a user exploits the importances associated with different subparts of the text: if characters of different dimensions are used, it is assumed that the bigger the dimension, the more important the information carried by the text; to bold or to italicize characters generally means to highlight a portion of the text with respect to others. Tags constitute then indicators of the importance of documents' subparts; in [37] an indexing function has been proposed which differently weights the occurrences of a given term in the document, depending on the tags by which they are delimited. The overall significance degree $F(d,t)$ of a term t in a document d is computed by first evaluating the term significance in the different document tags, and then by aggregating these contributions through a function $A : [0,1]^m \to [0,1]$, in which m is the number of the tags considered. To simplify the hierarchy of the tags, since certain tags can be employed to a similar aim, some of them are grouped into different classes. With each class of tags denoted by tag, a function $F_{tag} : D \times T \to [0,1]$ is associated together an importance weight $\alpha_{tag} \in [0,1]$; the higher the emphasis of the text associated with a tag, the higher its importance weight. It is assumed that the members of a class have the same importance weight. The text that is not delimited by any tag is included into the lowest class. A possible identification of classes of tags, together with a proposal of their ranking has been suggested in [37]. The definition of such a list is subjective, although based on objective assumptions suggested by commonsense such as: the bigger the character the higher the importance of the text; text in bold, italics or appearing in lists can be assumed as having a high importance, etc.

A simple procedure to compute numeric importance weights starting form the proposed ranking is described and here reported in the following. The definition of F_{tag} depends on the characteristics of the considered class of tags. For example, tags such as title and authors have to be used just once in a document, and they should contain short texts; for this reason it could be assumed that a single occurrence of a term makes it fully significant inside these tags. Functions F_{title} and $F_{authors}$ could then be defined as functions which take the value 1 if the term appears in the the title and authors respectively, the value 0 otherwise. For the others tags, as the length of the text they are delimiting in a document varies, a more general definition must be considered, based on the frequency of the term inside the tags. The following normalized frequency is then proposed:

$$F_{tag}(d, t) = \frac{\text{NOCC}_{tag\ dt}}{\text{MAXOCC}_{tag\ d}}$$

in which $\text{NOCC}_{tag\ dt}$ is the number of occurrences of term t inside class tag in document d, and $\text{MAXOCC}_{tag\ d}$ is the number of occurrences of the most frequent term inside the class of tags.

Once the single significance degrees of a term into the tags have been computed, these have to be aggregated in order to produce an overall significance degree of the term into the document. In the aggregation all the significance degrees should be taken into account, so as to consider the contribution of each tag, modulated by their importances. To this aim a weighted mean can be adopted:

$$A(F_{tag1}(d, t), \ldots F_{tagn}(d, t)) = \sum_{i=1\ldots n} F_{tagi}(d, t) * w_i$$

in which $\sum_{i=1\ldots n} w_i = 1$.

Starting from the list of tags in decreasing relative order of their importances, the numeric weights w_i are computed through a simple procedure: it is assumed that tag_i is more important than tag_j iff $i < j$ (being i and j the positions of tag_i and tag_j respectively in the ordered list); the numeric importance weight w_i associated with tag_i can be computed as: $w_i = (n - i + 1)/\sum_{i=1\ldots n} i$.

In the computation of the overall significance degree $F(d, t)$, the inverse document frequency of term t could be taken into account:

$$F(d, t) = \left(\sum_{i=1\ldots n} F_{tagi}(d, t) * w_i \right) * g(\text{IDF}_t)$$

in which the definition of $g(\text{IDF}_t)$ is given in formula (5).

6   Flexible Querying

By flexible query language we mean a query language that incorporates some
elements of the natural language so as to make possible a simple and powerful
expression of subjective information needs. Flexible query languages have been
defined as generalizations of the Boolean query language within fuzzy set theory;
a flexible query may consists of either one of the following two soft components
or just one: the first component is constituted by selection conditions that are
interpreted as soft constraints on the significance of the index terms in each
document representation. The second component is constituted by soft aggregation operators which can be applied to the soft constraints in order to define
compound selection conditions. The atomic selection conditions are expressed
by pairs <term, weight>, in which weight can be either a numeric value in [0,1]
(which identifies a soft constraint) or a linguistic value of the variable *Importance*,
and the compound conditions are expressed by means of linguistic quantifiers
used as aggregation operators. The concept of linguistic variable introduced in
Sect. 2.5 provides a suitable framework to represent and manage linguistic concepts and for this reasons it has been used to formalize the semantics of linguistic
terms introduced in the Boolean query language to generalize it.

In the following section we introduce a general view of the IR activity and
a formalization of the query evaluation mechanism of an IRS. According to this
view the definition of the query evaluation mechanism is strongly dependent on
the query language adopted. In the subsequent sections the various soft extensions of the Boolean language will be described together with their evaluation
functions. Specifically, in Sect. 6.2 the most common semantics of numeric query
weights and their evaluation functions are described. In Sect. 6.3 an evaluation
function of linguistic query weights is introduced. Finally, in Sect. 6.4 the evaluation function of a query language with linguistic quantifiers is presented.

6.1   Query Evaluation Mechanism

An Information Retrieval activity can be interpreted as a decision making activity; its aim is to evaluate a set of alternatives or possible solutions, on the basis
of a set of criteria or selection conditions in order to select the best ones.

In the Boolean IR context, the alternatives are the documents represented as
sets of index terms. The selection conditions are expressed by query terms: each
query term specifies a constraint requiring the presence of the term in the document representation; the selection conditions can be connected by aggregation
operators (which in the Boolean query language are the AND, and OR) and negated by the NOT operator. The decision process is performed through an exact
matching function, which evaluates the satisfaction of the query constraints by
each document representation. Relevance is here modelled has a binary property
of documents with respect to a user query.

In the fuzzy approach the IR activity is regarded as a decision activity affected
by vagueness: the query is seen as the specification of a set of soft constraints, i.e.
vague selection conditions, that the documents can satisfy to a partial extent.

The documents are represented by means of weighted index terms and constitute the alternatives to be evaluated. The query evaluation mechanism is regarded as a fuzzy decision process that evaluates the degree of satisfaction of the query constraints by each document representation by applying a partial matching function. This degree, named Retrieval Status Value, is interpreted as the degree of relevance of the document to the query and is used to rank the documents. Then, as a result of a query evaluation, a fuzzy set of documents is retrieved in which the RSV is the membership value. The definition of the partial matching function is strictly dependent on the query language definition and specifically on the semantics of the soft constraints.

In [57] and successively in [16], a so called wish list of requirements that a matching function of an IRS must satisfy has been proposed. Among these requirements, the separability property states that, in a query evaluation process, the evaluation of an atomic selection condition should be independent of the evaluation of the other query atomic components, or their Boolean connectives. The matching function should then be solely based on a function evaluating atomic conditions and on their logical Boolean connections. Also in Fuzzy IR models this property has been considered, and in the definition of flexible query languages a particular care has been paid in trying to satisfy this property.

This property is guaranteed by designing the partial matching mechanism bottom-up: first, each atomic selection condition (soft constraint) in the query is evaluated by a function, denoted by E, for a given document, and then the aggregation operators are applied to the results starting from the inmost operator in the query to the outermost operator by a function denoted by E^*.

The E function evaluates the soft constraints associated with the query atoms on the fuzzy set R_d representing each document ($E : D \times A \to [0,1]$, where A is the set of the atomic selection conditions). The soft constraints are defined as fuzzy subsets of the set $[0,1]$ of the index term weights; the membership value $\mu_{atom}(i)$ is the degree of satisfaction of the soft constraint associated with the query atom denoted by atom by the index term weight i, i.e. $E(d, <atom>) = \mu_{atom}(F(d,t))$. In other words, E evaluates how well the value $F(d,t)$ satisfies the soft constraint specified by $atom$; the result of the evaluation is a fuzzy set:

$$\sum_{d \in D} \mu_{atom}(F(d,t))/d$$

in which $\mu_{atom}(F(d,t))$ is interpreted as the RSV of document d with respect to the query atom denoted by $atom$.

The function $E^* : D \times Q \to [0,1]$ (where Q is the set of all the legitimate queries of the language) evaluates the final RSV of a document, reflecting the satisfaction of the whole query. The definition of E^* depends strictly on the query language structure and specifically on the aggregation operators used to combine the atomic components. The AND is generally defined as the min and the OR as the max. The NOT is defined as the complement operator. These definitions preserve the idempotence property. In [7] a fuzzy generalization of the Boolean query language has been defined in which the Boolean operators are replaced by linguistic quantifiers. In this context, linguistic quantifiers are used as aggregation operators of the satisfaction degrees of the soft constraints. In the Sects. 6.2 and 6.3 we present some possible definitions of soft constraints that can be specified in a flexible query; in Sect. 6.4 the aggregation operators specified by linguistic quantifiers are introduced.

6.2   Query Weights

To make the Boolean query language more user friendly and less limited in its expressiveness, the selection conditions have been extended by introducing numeric query term weights, which allow users to quantify the importance of query terms as descriptors of their information needs [5, 10, 14, 45]. An example of weighted query is the following: $<t_1, w_1>$AND$(<t_2, w_2>$ OR $<t_3, w_3>)$ in which t_1, t_2, t_3, are search terms and $w_1, w_2, w_3 \in [0, 1]$ are numeric weights. The weight w can be considered implicit and equal to 1 in the Boolean query language. A selection condition $< t, w >$ identifies a soft constraint on the weighted document representations; the semantics of the soft constraints depends on the interpretation of the query weight w. Different interpretations of the soft constraint imposed by a pair $<t, w>$ have been proposed in the literature; each interpretation determines a distinct definition of the E function (which is interpreted as the membership function of the fuzzy set associated with the soft constraint identified by w, and defined on the set $[0, 1]$ of the index term weights).

The query weight w was first interpreted as a relative importance weight, in this case the separability property does not hold and two distinct definitions of E have been proposed for conjunctive and disjunctive queries respectively [5, 59]. In other models [14, 45, 57] the query weight w was interpreted as a threshold on the index term weight, and finally as an ideal index term weight [10].

In the following subsections we introduce distinct query weight semantics; we denote by μ_w the membership function of the soft constraint identified by a weight w (where $\mu_w(F(d, t)) = E(d, <t, w>)$).

Implicit Query Weights. The simplest extension of the Boolean model consists in adopting a weighted document representation and the Boolean query language [13]. In this case the retrieval mechanism ranks the retrieved documents in decreasing order of their significance with respect to the user query. In fact, in this case an atomic query consisting of a single term t is interpreted as the specification of a pair $<t, 1>$ in which $w = 1$ is implicitly specified. The soft constraint associated with $<t, 1>$ is then interpreted as the requirement that the index term weight be *"close to 1"* and its evaluation is defined as:

$$\mu_w(F(d, t)) = \mu_{close\ to\ 1}(F(d, t)) = F(d, t) \qquad (8)$$

This means that the desired documents are those with maximum index term weight for the specified term t, i.e. index term weights closest to 1; this interpretation implies that the evaluation mechanism tolerates the undersatisfaction of the soft constraint associated with $<t, 1>$ with a degree equal to $F(d, t)$.

Relative Importance Query Weights. By this semantics query weights are interpreted as measures of the "relative importance" of each term with respect to the others in the query [5, 59]; this semantics demands for retrieval results conditioned more heavily by the most heavily weighted terms.

Since it is not possible to have a single definition for the soft constraint μ_w that preserves the relative importance semantics independently of the connectives in the query, two distinct definitions of μ_w have been proposed, depending on the aggregation operators in the query, thus giving up the separability property. Two alternative definitions have been proposed for conjunctive and disjunctive queries [5, 59]. The first proposal [5] is the following:

$$\mu_w(F(d,t)) = w * F(d,t) \quad \text{for disjunctive queries} \tag{9}$$
$$\mu_w(F(d,t)) = \max(1, F(d,t)/w) \quad \text{for conjunctive queries} \tag{10}$$

The second proposal [Yager, 1987] is the following:

$$\mu_w(F(d,t)) = \min[w, F(d,t)] \quad \text{for disjunctive queries} \tag{11}$$
$$\mu_w(F(d,t)) = \max[(1-w), F(d,t)] \quad \text{for conjunctive queries} \tag{12}$$

Notice that any weighted Boolean query can be expressed in Disjunctive Normal Form, and then any query can be evaluated just by using one of these two definitions.

Threshold Query Weights By specifying thresholds the user is asking to see all documents "sufficiently about" a topic [15, 45]. In this case the soft constraint identified by the numeric query weight can be linguistically expressed as "more or less over w." The lower the threshold, the greater the number of documents retrieved. The threshold allows to define a point of discrimination between its under and oversatisfaction.

The simplest formalization of threshold weights has been suggested by [45] who proposes a crisp threshold:

$$\mu_w(F(d,t)) = \begin{cases} 0 & \text{for} \quad F(d,t) < w \\ F(d,t) & \text{for} \quad F(d,t) \geq w \end{cases} \tag{13}$$

In this case, the threshold defines the minimally acceptable document. Due to its discontinuity this definition may cause the abrupt variation of the number of documents retrieved even for small changes in the query weights. This led [14] to define continuous thresholding functions such as:

$$\mu_w(F(d,t)) = \begin{cases} P(w) * \frac{F(d,t)}{w} & \text{for} \quad F(d,t) < w \\ P(w) + Q(w) * \frac{(F(d,t)-w)}{(1-w)} & \text{for} \quad F(d,t) \geq w \end{cases} \tag{14}$$

in which: $P(w) = \frac{1+w}{2}$ and $Q(w) = \frac{1-w^2}{4}$.

For $F(d,t) < w$, the μ_w function measures the closeness of $F(d,t)$ to w; for $F(d,t) \geq w$, $\mu_w(F(d,t))$ expresses the degree of oversatisfaction with respect to w, and undersatisfaction with respect to 1.

Ideal Query Weights. In [10] a third semantics for the query weight w has been defined: the pair $<t, w>$ identifies a set of ideal or perfect documents, so that the soft constraint μ_w measures how well $F(d, t)$ comes "close to w":

$$\mu_w\left(F(d, t)\right) = e^{\ln(k)*(F(d,t)-w)^2} \tag{15}$$

The k value, $k \in [0, 1]$ determines the steepness of the Gaussian slopes and, as a consequence, it affects the strength of the soft constraint "*close to w*"; the higher the k value, the weaker the constraint. This parametric definition makes it possible to adapt the constraint interpretation to the user concept of "*close to w*" .

The retrieval operation associated with a pair $<t, w>$ corresponds in this model to the evaluation of a similarity measure between the importance value w and the significance value of t in $R_d : w \approx F(d, t)$.

Example of Comparisons of the Three Semantics for Query Weights. Let us analyse the different results that are obtained by the different semantics associated with the query weight w.

Let us consider the archive represented by the fuzzy sets in Table 4, in which an element of row d_i and column t_j is the value $F(d_i, t_j)$, and the query: $q = <t_1, 1>\text{AND}<t_2, 0.6>\text{AND}<t_4, 0.2>$ represented in Table 5. Depending on

Table 4. Each Row is a Fuzzy Set Representing a Document.

	t_1	t_2	t_3	t_4
d_1	1	0.9	1	0.2
d_2	0.7	0.6	0.3	0.8

Table 5. Query q (ANDed Weighted Pairs).

	t_1	t_2	t_4
q	1	0.6	0.2

the semantics chosen for w, i.e. on the definition of the soft constraint μ_w and by assuming that the AND operator is evaluated as the minimum, the results of the evaluation of q are given in Table 6.

6.3   Linguistic Query Weights

The main limitation of the numeric query weights is their inadequacy in dealing with the imprecision which characterizes the concept of importance that they represent. In fact, the use of numeric query weights forces the user to quantify

Table 6. Results of Query q in Table 5 Referred to Documents in Table 4.

Query Weight Semantics	d_1	d_2
Ideal index term weight	0.3	0.6
Relative importance	0.8	0.6
Threshold on index term weight	0.2	0

a qualitative and rather vague concept and to be well aware of the weight semantics. This is why in [9] a fuzzy retrieval model with linguistic query weights
has been proposed; a linguistic extension of the Boolean language is defined,
based on the concept of linguistic variable [64]. By this language the user can
select the primary term *"important"* together with linguistic hedges (e.g., *"very"*
or *"almost"*) to qualify the desired importance of the search terms in the query.
When defining a query language based on linguistic query term weights, first the
term set, i.e., the set of all the possible linguistic values of the linguistic variable
Importance must be defined: this definition depends on the desired granularity
that one wants to achieve. The greater the number of the linguistic terms, the
finer the granularity of the concepts that are dealt with. Then the semantics
for the primary terms must be defined. A pair $<t, important>$, expresses a soft
constraint $\mu_{important}$ on the term significance values (the $F(d, t)$ values). The
evaluation of the relevance of a given document d to a query consisting solely of
the pair $<t, important>$ is based on the evaluation of the degree of satisfaction
of the associated soft constraint; this value is obtained by applying the function
$\mu_{important}$ to the value $F(d, t)$.

The problem of giving a semantics to numeric weights reappears here in
associating a semantics with the linguistic term *important*. In [9] the $\mu_{important}$
function is defined based on the ideal semantics of the numeric weight (from
definition (15)):

$$\mu_{important}(F(d,t)) = \begin{cases} e^{\ln(k)*(F(d,t)-i)^2} & \text{for} \quad F(d,t) < i \\ 1 & \text{for} \quad i \leq F(d,t) \leq j \\ e^{\ln(k)*(F(d,t)-j)^2} & \text{for} \quad F(d,t) > j \end{cases}$$

In this definition, if $F(d, t)$ is less than the i value or greater than the j value, the
constraint is under-satisfied. The strength of the soft constraint $\mu_{important}$ depends on both the width of the range $[i, j]$ and on the k value. The values i and j
delimit the full satisfaction of the concept *important*. The larger the value $|i-j|$,
the less precise is the constraint; as in the case of the ideal semantics of numeric
query term weights, k determines the sharpness of the constraint: the higher
the k value, the fuzzier the constraint.

In [30] the $\mu_{important}$ function is defined based on the threshold semantics (from definitions (14) and (15)) as follows:

$$\mu_{important}(F(d,t)) = \begin{cases} \frac{1+i}{2} * e^{\ln(k)*(F(d,t)-i)^2} & \text{for} \quad F(d,t) < i \\ \frac{1+F(d,t)}{2} & \text{for} \quad i \le F(d,t) \le j \\ \frac{1+j}{2} * \left(1 + \frac{F(d,t)-j}{2}\right) & \text{for} \quad F(d,t) > j \end{cases}$$

It can be observed that this compatibility function is continuous and non-decreasing in $F(d,t)$ over the interval $[0,1]$. For $F(d,t) < i$, $\mu_{important}$ increases as a Gaussian function. For $F(d,t)$ in the interval $[i,j]$, $\mu_{important}$ increases at a linear rate. For $F(d,t) > j$, $\mu_{important}$ still increases, but at a lesser rate.

The compatibility functions of non-primary terms, such as *very important*, *fairly important*, etc. are derived by modifying the compatibility functions of primary terms: this is achieved by defining each linguistic hedge as a modifier operator. For example, in [30] the linguistic hedges are defined as translation operators:

$\mu_{very important}(x) = \mu_{important}(x)$
with $i_{very} = i + 0.2$ and $j_{very} = j + 0.2$ and $\forall x \in [0,1]$.

$\mu_{averagely\ important}(x) = \mu_{important}(x)$
with $i_{averagely} = i - 0.3$ and $j_{averagely} = j - 0.3$ and $\forall x \in [0,1]$.

$\mu_{minimally\ important}(x) = \mu_{important}(x)$
with $i_{minimally} = i - 0.5$ and $j_{minimally} = j - 0.5$ and $\forall x \in [0,1]$.

in which i and j are values in $[0,1]$ delimiting the range of full satisfaction of the constraint $\mu_{important}$.

With these definitions any value $F(d,t)$ of the basic domain of the *Importance* variable fully satisfies at least one of the constraints defined by the linguistic query terms.

6.4   Linguistic Quantifiers to Aggregate the Selection Conditions

In the Boolean query language, the AND and OR connectives allow only for crisp aggregations which do not capture any vagueness. For example, the AND used for aggregating M selection conditions does not tolerate the unsatisfaction of a single condition; this may cause the rejection of useful items. To face this problem, other extensions of Boolean queries have been provided, which concern the replacement of the AND and OR operators with soft operators for aggregating the selection criteria [43, 52, 53].

Within the framework of fuzzy set theory a generalization of the Boolean query language has been defined in [7], based on the concept of linguistic quantifiers: they are employed to specify both crisp and vague aggregation criteria of the selection conditions. New aggregation operators can be specified by linguistic expressions, with a self-expressive meaning such as *at least k* and *most of*. They are defined with a behaviour between the two extremes corresponding to the AND and the OR connectives, which allow, respectively, requests for *all* and *at least one of* the selection conditions. The linguistic quantifiers used as aggregation operators, are defined by Ordered Weighted Averaging (OWA) operators defined in Sect. 2.4.

By adopting linguistic quantifiers, the requirements of a complex Boolean query are more easily and intuitively formulated. For example when desiring that *at least 2* out of the three selection conditions "politics", "economy", "inflation" be satisfied, one should formulate the following Boolean query:

(politics AND economy)

OR

(politics AND inflation)

OR

(economy AND inflation)

which can be replaced by the simpler one:

at least 2(politics, economy, inflation)

The expression of any Boolean query is supported by the new language via the nesting of linguistic quantifiers. For example a query such as:

AND (<processing> OR <analysis>) AND <digital>

can be translated into the following new formulation:

all(<image>, *at least 1 of* (<processing>, <analysis>), <digital>)

A quantified aggregation function can thus be applied not only to single selection conditions, but also to other quantified expressions.

Then, the E^* function evaluating a whole query q yields a value in $[0, 1]$ for each document d in the archive D; let us indicate by S the set of atomic selection conditions and by Q the set of legitimate queries. The E^* function is formalized by recursively applying the following rules:

1. if $q \in S$ then $E^*(d, s) = \mu_w(F(d, t))$ in which $\mu_w(F(d, t))$ is the satisfaction degree of a pair $< t, w >$ by document d with w being either a numeric weight or a linguistic weight.
2. if $q = quantifier(q_1, \ldots, q_n)$ and $q_1, \ldots, q_n \in Q$ then
   $E^*(d, q) = \mathrm{OWA}_{quantifier}(E^*(d, q_1), \ldots, E^*(d, q_n))$
3. $E^*(d, \mathrm{NOT}\ q) = 1 - E^*(d, q)$

in which $\mathrm{OWA}_{quantifier}$ is the OWA operator associated with *quantifier*.

The formal definition of the query language with linguistic quantifiers can be found in [7]. The following quantifiers have been proposed:

- *all*: it replaces the AND;
- *at least k*: it acts as the specification of a crisp threshold of value k on the number of selection conditions. It is defined by a weighting vector $W_{at\ least\ k}$ in which $w_k = 1$, and $w_j = 0$, for $i \leq k$. Notice that *at least 1* selects the maximum of the satisfaction degrees and it has thus the same semantics of the OR.
- *about k*: this is a soft interpretation of the quantifier *at least k* in which the k value is not interpreted as a crisp threshold, but as a fuzzy one. This means that the user is fully satisfied if k or more conditions are satisfied, but she/he gets a certain degree of satisfaction even if $k-1, k-2, \ldots, 1$ conditions are satisfied. This quantifier is defined by a weighting vector $W_{about\ k}$ in which $w_i = \frac{i}{\sum_{j=1}^{k} j}$ for $i \leq k$, and $w_i = 0$ for $i > k$.
- *most of*: it is defined as a synonym of *at least $\frac{2}{3}n$* in which n is the total number of selection conditions.

7   Fuzzy Associative Mechanisms

Associative retrieval mechanisms are defined to enhance the retrieval of traditional IRSs. They work by retrieving additional documents that are not directly indexed by the terms in a given query but are indexed by other terms, associated descriptors. The most common type of associative retrieval mechanism is based on the use of a thesaurus to associate entry terms with related terms. In traditional associative retrieval the associations are crisp.

The fuzzy associative retrieval mechanisms are based on the concept of fuzzy associations. A fuzzy association between two sets $X = \{x_1, \ldots, x_m\}$ and $Y = \{y_1, \ldots, y_n\}$ is formally defined as a fuzzy relation $f : X \times Y \rightarrow [0,1]$: the value $f(x,y)$ represents the degree of strength of the association existing between the values $x \in X$ and $y \in Y$.

In information retrieval, different kinds of fuzzy associations can be derived depending on the semantics of the sets X and Y.

Fuzzy associative mechanisms employ fuzzy thesauri, fuzzy pseudothesauri, and fuzzy clustering techniques to serve three alternative, but compatible purposes:

- to expand the set of index terms of documents with new terms,
- to expand each of the search terms in the query with associated terms,
- to expand the set of the documents retrieved by a query with associated documents.

7.1   Fuzzy Thesauri for Terms

A thesaurus is an associative mechanism that can be used to improve both indexing and querying. It is well known that the development of thesauri is very costly, as it requires a large amount of human resources. Moreover, in highly dynamic situations, where terms are added and new meanings derived for old terms quite rapidly, the thesaurus needs frequents updates. For this reason, methods for the automatic construction of thesauri have been proposed, based on statistical criteria such as the terms' co-occurrences, i.e., the simultaneous appearance of pairs (or triplets, or even larger subsets) of terms in the same documents.

In a thesaurus the relations defined between terms are of different type: if the associated descriptor has a more general meaning than the entry term, the relation is classified as broader term (BT), while a narrower term (NT) is the inverse relation; synonyms or near-synonyms are associated by a related term (RT) relation.

Some authors have proposed the definition of fuzzy thesauri, see [33,34,40,46], where the links between terms are weighted to indicate strength of association. Moreover, this notion includes generalizations such as fuzzy pseudothesauri [36], and fuzzy associations based on a citation index [41].

The first works on fuzzy thesauri introduced the notion of fuzzy relations to represent associations between terms [46,47].

Miyamoto [34,35] has proposed a formal definition of a fuzzy thesaurus. Let us consider T to be the set of index terms, and let C be a set of concepts. Each term $t \in T$ corresponds to a fuzzy set of concepts $h(t)$:

$$h(t) = \{< c, t(c) > | c \in C\}$$

in which $t(c)$ is the degree to which term t is related to concept c. A measure M is defined on all the possible fuzzy sets of concepts, and which satisfies:

$$M(\varnothing) = 0$$
$$M(C) < \infty$$
$$M(A) \leq M(B) \quad \text{if} \quad A \subseteq B$$

A typical example of M is the cardinality of a fuzzy set.

The fuzzy RT relation is represented in a fuzzy thesaurus by the s-similarity relation between two index terms, t_1 and $t_2 \in T$, defined as:

$$s(t_1, t_2) = M\big[h(t_1) \cap h(t_2)\big] \big/ M[h(t_1) \cup h(t_2)].$$

This definition satisfies the following:

- if terms t_1 and t_2 are synonymous, i.e., $h(t_1) = h(t_2)$, then $s(t_1, t_2) = 1$.
- if t_1 and t_2 are not semantically related, i.e., $h(t_1) \cap h(t_2) = \varnothing$, then $s(t_1, t_2) = 0$.
- $s(t_2, t_1) = s(t_1, t_2)$ for all $t_1, t_2 \in T$.
- if t_1 is more similar to term t_3 than to t_2, then $s(t_1, t_3) > s(t_1, t_2)$.

The fuzzy NT relation, indicated as nt, which represents grades of inclusion of a narrower term t_1 in another (broader) term t_2 is defined as:

$$nt(t_1, t_2) = M\big[h(t_1) \cap h(t_2)\big] \,/\, M[h(t_1)]$$

This definition satisfies the following:

- if term t_1's concept(s) is completely included within term t_2's concept(s), i.e. $h(t_1) \subseteq h(t_2)$, then $nt(t_1, t_2) = 1$.
- if t_1 and t_2 are not semantically related, i.e., $h(t_1) \cap h(t_2) = \varnothing$, then $nt(t_1, t_2) = 0$.
- if the inclusion of t_1's concept(s) in t_2's concept(s) is greater than the inclusion of t_1's concept(s) in t_3's concept(s), then $nt(t_1, t_2) > nt(t_1, t_3)$.

By assuming M as the cardinality of a set, s and nt are given as:

$$s(t_1, t_2) = \sum_{k=1}^{M} \min\big[t_1(c_k), t_2(c_k)\big] \,/\, \sum_{k=1}^{M} \max\big[t_1(c_k), t_2(c_k)\big]$$

$$nt(t_1, t_2) = \sum_{k=1}^{M} \min\big[t_1(c_k), t_2(c_k)\big] \,/\, \sum_{k=1}^{M} t_1(c_k)$$

A fuzzy pseudothesaurus can be defined by replacing the set C in the definition of $h(t)$ above with the set of documents D, with the assumption that $h(t)$ is the fuzzy set of documents indexed by term t. Thus, we get

$$h(t) = \{(d, t(d)) | d \in D\}$$

in which $t(d) = F(d, t)$ is the index term weight defined above. F can be either a binary value defining a crisp representation or a value in $[0, 1]$, defining a fuzzy representation of documents. The fuzzy RT and the fuzzy NT relations now are defined as:

$$s(t_1, t_2) = \sum_{k=1}^{M} \min\big[F(t_1, d_k), F(t_2, d_k)\big] \,/\, \sum_{k=1}^{M} \max\big[F(t_1, d_k), F(t_2, d_k)\big]$$

$$nt(t_1, t_2) = \sum_{k=1}^{M} \min\big[F(t_1, d_k), F(t_2, d_k)\big] \,/\, \sum_{k=1}^{M} F(t_1, d_k)$$

Note that $s(t_1, t_2)$ and $nt(t_1, t_2)$ are dependent on the co-occurrences of terms t_1 and t_2 in the set of documents, D. The set of index terms of document d, i.e., $\{t|F(d,t) \neq 0 \text{ and } t \in T\}$, can be augmented by those terms t_A which have $s(t, t_A) > \alpha$ and/or $nt(t, t_A) > \beta$ for parameters α and $\beta \in [0, 1]$.

Suppose that in the definition of F as given above, the set T is a set of citations which are used to index documents, in place of the set of terms. In this case a fuzzy association on citations can be defined through the fuzzy relations s and/or nt as defined above. By using citations, a user may retrieve documents that cite a particular author or a particular reference. In [42] a keyword connection matrix is proposed to represent similarities between keywords so as to reduce the difference between relationship values initially assigned using statistical information, and a user's evaluation. The authors also propose a new method in which keywords that are attached to a document and broader concepts are hierarchically organized, calculating the keyword relationships through the broader concepts. In [4] a thesaurus is generated based on the max-star transitive closure for linguistic completion of a thesaurus generated initially by an expert linking terms.

In [56] a probabilistic notion of term relationships is used; it is assumed that if one given term is a good discriminator between relevant and nonrelevant documents, then any term that is closely associated with that given term (i.e., statistically co-occurring) is likely to be a good discriminator, too. Note that this implies that thesauri are collection-dependent.

In [27] the Salton's use of the $F(d, t)$ values is expanded [48]. One can manipulate the $F(d, t)$ values in order to generate co-occurrence statistics to represent term linkage weights. In [49] document section similarities are also used to infer term relationships.

In [27] a synonym link is considered, defined as:

$$\mu_{synonym}(t_1, t_2) = \sum_{d \in D} \left[F(d, t_1) \leftrightarrow F(d, t_2) \right]$$

where $F(d, t_1) \leftrightarrow F(d, t_2) = \min[F(d, t_1) \to F(d, t_2), F(d, t_1) \leftarrow F(d, t_2)]$ and $F(d, t_1) \to F(d, t_2)$ can be defined in variety of ways: for instance, $F(d, t_1) \to F(d, t_2)$, i.e., the implication operator, can be defined as $[F(d, t_1)^c \vee F(d, t_2)]$, where $F(d, t_1)^c = 1 - F(d, t_1)$ is the complement of $F(d, t_1)$ and $\vee$ is the disjunctive (OR) operator defined as the max. An other alternative definition of the implication operator is $\min(1, [1 - F(d, t_1) + F(d, t_2)])$.

In [27] a narrower term link is also considered (where term t_1 is narrower than term t_2, so term t_2 is broader than term t_1), which is defined as:

$$\mu_{narrower}(t_1, t_2) = \sum_{d \in D} \left[F(d, t_1) \to F(d, t_2) \right]$$

7.2   Fuzzy Clustering for Documents

Clustering in information retrieval is a method for partitioning a given set of documents D into groups using a measure of similarity (or distance) which is defined on every pairs of documents. The similarity between documents in the same group should be large, while it should be small for documents in different groups. A common method to perform clustering of documents is based on the simultaneous occurrences of citations in pairs of documents. Documents are so clustered using a measure defined on the space of the citations. Generated clusters can then be used as an index for information retrieval; that is, documents which belong to the same clusters as the documents directly indexed by the terms in the query are retrieved.

Often, similarity measures are suggested empirically or heuristically [50,52, 54]. When adopting the fuzzy set model, clustering can be formalized as a kind of fuzzy association. In this case, the fuzzy association is defined on the domain $D \times D$, where D is the set of documents. By assuming $R(d)$ to be the fuzzy set of terms representing a document d with membership function values $d(t) = F(d,t)$ being the index term weight of term t in document d, the symmetric fuzzy relation s, as originally defined above, is taken to be the similarity measure for clustering documents:

$$
\begin{aligned}
s(d_1, d_2) &= \sum_{k=1}^{M} \min\left[d_1(t_k), d_2(t_k)\right] \bigg/ \sum_{k=1}^{M} \max\left[d_1(t_k), d_2(t_k)\right] \\
&= \sum_{k=1}^{M} \min\left[F(t_k, d_1), F(t_k, d_2)\right] \bigg/ \sum_{k=1}^{M} \max\left[F(t_k, d_1), F(t_k, d_2)\right]
\end{aligned}
$$

in which M is the cardinality of the set of index terms T.

In fuzzy clustering, documents can belong to more than one cluster with varying degree of membership [3]. Each document is assigned a membership value to each cluster. In a pure fuzzy clustering, a complete overlap of clusters is allowed. Modified fuzzy clustering, or soft clustering, approaches use thresholding mechanisms to limit the number of documents belonging to each cluster. The main advantage of using modified fuzzy clustering is the fact that the degree of fuzziness is controlled.

References

1. Agosti M., Crivellari F., Melucci M. The Effectiveness of Meta-data and other Content Descriptive Data in Web Information Retrieval. *Proc. of Third IEEE Meta-Data Conference (META-DATA '99)*, Bethesda, Maryland, USA, April 6–7, 1999.
2. Berrut C, Chiaramella Y. Indexing medical reports in a multimedia environment: the RIME experimental approach. *ACM-SIGIR 89*, Boston, USA, 187–197, 1986.
3. Bezdek, J. C., *Pattern recognition with Fuzzy Objective Function Algorithms*, Plenum Press, New York, NY, 1981.
4. Bezdek, J. C., Biswas, G., and Huang, L. Y. Transitive closures of fuzzy thesauri for information-retrieval systems. *International Journal of Man-Machine Studies*, 25(3):343–356, 1986.
5. Bookstein, A. Fuzzy requests: An approach to weighted boolean searches. *Journal of the American Society for Information Science*, 31(4):240–247, 1980.

6. Bordogna G., and Pasi G. The Application of Fuzzy Set Theory to Model Information Retrieval. In *Soft Computing in Information Retrieval: Techniques and Applications*, F. Crestani and G. Pasi eds., Physica-Verlag,Heidelberg, Germany, 2000.

7. Bordogna G., and Pasi G. Linguistic aggregation operators in fuzzy information retrieval. *International Journal of Intelligent systems*, 10(2):233–248, 1995.

8. Bordogna, G. and Pasi G. Controlling Information Retrieval through a user adaptive representation of documents. *International Journal of Approximate Reasoning*, 12:317–339, 1995.

9. Bordogna, G. and Pasi, G. A fuzzy linguistic approach generalizing Boolean information retrieval: A model and its evaluation. *Journal of the American Society for Information Science*, 44(2):70–82, 1993.

10. Bordogna, G., Carrara, P., and Pasi, G. Query term weights as constraints in fuzzy information retrieval. *Information Processing & Management*, 27(1):15–26, 1991.

11. Bosc P. Fuzzy Databases. In *Fuzzy sets in approximate reasoning and information systems*, Bezdek J., Dubois D., Prade H., eds., The Handbooks of Fuzzy Sets Series, Kluwer Academic publishers, 1999.

12. Buell, D. A. A problem in information retrieval with fuzzy sets. *Journal of the American Society for Information Science*, 36(6):398–401, 1985.

13. Buell, D. A. An analysis of some fuzzy subset applications to information retrieval systems. *Fuzzy Sets and Systems*, 7(1):35–42, 1982.

14. Buell, D. A. and Kraft, D. H. A model for a weighted retrieval system. *Journal of the American Society for Information Science*, 32(3):211–216, 1981.

15. Buell D.A., and Kraft D.H. Threshold values and Boolean retrieval systems. *Information Processing & Management*, 17:127–136, 1981.

16. Cater, S. C. and Kraft, D. H. A generalizaton and clarification of the Waller-Kraft wish-list. *Information Processing & Management*, 25:15–25, 1989.

17. Cater, S. C. and Kraft, D. H. TIRS: A topological information retrieval system satisfying the requirements of the Waller-Kraft wish list. In *Proceedings of the tenth annual ACM/SIGIR International Conference on Research and Development in Information Retrieval*, New Orleans, LA, June, 171–180, 1987.

18. Chen S.J., Hwang C.L., Hwang F. *Fuzzy Multiple Attribute Decision Making: Methods and Applications*, Lecture Notes in Economics and mathematical Systems series 375, Springer-Verlag, 1992.

19. Crestani, F., Lalmas, M., van Rijsbergen, C.J., and Campbell, I., "Is this document relevant? ... probably": A survey of probabilistic models in information retrieval. *ACM Computing Surveys*, 30(4):528–552, 1998.

20. Dubois, D., Prade, A. A review of fuzzy sets aggregation connectives. *Information Sciences*, 3:85–121, 1985.

21. Dubois D., Prade H., *Possibility Theory: An Approach to Computerized Processing of Uncertainty*, Plenum Press: New York, 1988, 1988.

22. Fodor J.C., and Rubens M., *Fuzzy Preference Modelling and Multicriteria Decision Support*, Kluwer Academic Publisher, Dordrecht, 1994.

23. Fuhr, N., Models for retrieval with probabilistic indexing. *Information Processing & Management*, 25(1):55–72, 1989.

24. Kamel, M., Hadfield, B., and Ismail, M. Fuzzy query processing using clustering techniques. *Information Processing & Management*, 26(2):279–293, 1990.

25. Klir G.J., Folger T.A. *Fuzzy Sets, Uncertainty and Information*, Prentice Hall PTR Englewood Cliffs, 1988.

26. Kohout, L. J. and Kallala, M. The use of fuzzy information retrieval in knowledge-based management of patients, clinical-profiles. In *Uncertainty in Knowledge-Based Systems,Proceedings of the International Conference on Information Processing and Management of Uncertainty in Knowledge-Based Systems*, Bouchon, B. and Yager, R. R. (eds.) 30 June-4, July, 1986, Paris, France, Berlin, Germany: Springer-Verlag, 275–282, 1987.

27. Kohout, L. J., Keravanou, E., and Bandler, W. Information retrieval system using fuzzy relational products for thesaurus construction. In *Proceedings IFAC Fuzzy Information*, Marseille, France, 7–13, 1983.

28. Kraft, D. H. Advances in Information Retrieval: Where is That /#*%@^ Record? In *Advances in Computers*, Yovits, M. (ed.), 24, New York, NY: Academic Press, 277–318, 1985.

29. Kraft D., Bordogna G., Pasi G., Fuzzy Set Techniques in Information Retrieval, in *Fuzzy Sets in Approximate Reasoning and Information Systems*, J. C. Bezdek, D. Dubois and H. Prade eds. The Handbooks of Fuzzy Sets Series, Kluwer Academic Publishers, 469–510, 1999.

30. Kraft, D. H., Bordogna, G. and Pasi, G. An extended fuzzy linguistic approach to generalize Boolean information retrieval. *Journal of Information Sciences, Applications*, 2(3):119–134, 1995.

31. Lucarella, D. and Morara, R. FIRST: fuzzy information retrieval system. *Journal of Information Science*, 17(2):81–91, 1991.

32. Lucarella, D. and Zanzi A. Information Retrieval from hypertext: An approach using plausible inference. *Information Processing & Management*, 29(1):299–312, 1993.

33. Miyamoto, S. *Fuzzy sets in Information Retrieval and Cluster Analysis*. Kluwer Academic Publishers, 1990.

34. Miyamoto, S. Information retrieval based on fuzzy associations. *Fuzzy Sets and Systems*, 38(2):191–205, 1990.

35. Miyamoto, S. Two approaches for information retrieval through fuzzy associations. *IEEE Transactions on Systems, Man and Cybernetics*, 19(1):123–130, 1989.

36. Miyamoto, S. and Nakayama, K. Fuzzy information retrieval based on a fuzzy pseudothesaurus. *IEEE Transactions on Systems, Man and Cybernetics*, SMC-16(2):278–282, 1986.

37. Molinari, A. and Pasi, G. A Fuzzy Representation of HTML Documents for Information Retrieval Systems. In *Procedings of the IEEE International Conference on Fuzzy Systems*, 8–12 September, New Orleans, U.S.A., Vol 1, 107–112, 1996.

38. Motro, A., Imprecision and Uncertainty in Database Systems, in: *Fuzziness in Database Management Systems*, P. Bosc, J. Kacprzyk (eds.), Physica-Verlag, Heidelberg, 3–22, 1995.

39. Murai, T., Miyakoshi, M., and Shimbo, M. A fuzzy document retrieval method based on two-valued indexing. *Fuzzy Sets and Systems*, 30(2):103–120, 1989.

40. Neuwirth, E. and Reisinger, L. Dissimilarity and distance coefficients in automation-supported thesauri. *Information Systems*, 7(1):47–52, 1982.

41. Nomoto, K., Wakayama, S., Kirimoto, T., and Kondo, M. A fuzzy retrieval system based on citation. *Systems and Control*, 31(10):748–755, 1987.

42. Ogawa, Y., Morita, T., and Kobayashi, K. A fuzzy document retrieval system using the keyword connection matrix and a learning method. *Fuzzy Sets and Systems*, 39(2):163–179, 1991.

43. Paice, C. D. Soft evaluation of Boolean search queries in information retrieval systems. *Information Technology: Research Development Applications*, 3(1):33–41, 1984.

44. Pasi G., Yager R.R., Document Retrieval from Multiple Sources of Information, in *Uncertainty in Intelligent and Information Systems*, B. Bouchon-Meunier, R.R. Yager and L. Zadeh eds., World Scientific, 2000.

45. Radecki, T. Fuzzy set theoretical approach to document retrieval. *Information Processing & Management*, 15(5):247–260, 1979.

46. Radecki, T. Mathematical model of information retrieval system based on the concept of fuzzy thesaurus. *Information Processing & Management*, 12(5):313–318, 1976.

47. Reisinger, L. On fuzzy thesauri. In *COMPSTAT 1974*, Bruckman, G., et al. (eds.) Vienna, Austria, Physica Verlag, 119–127, 1974.

48. Salton G. *Automatic text processing: The transformation, analysis and retrieval of information by computer*, Addison Wesley, 1989.

49. Salton, G., Allan, J. Buckley, C., and Singhal, A. Automatic analysis, theme generation, and summarization of machine-readable texts. *Science*, 264, June 3, 1421–1426, 1994.

50. Salton, G. and Bergmark, D. A citation study of computer science literature. *IEEE Transactions on Professional Communication*, 22(3):146–158, 1979.

51. Salton, G. and Buckley, C. Term weighting approaches in automatic text retrieval. *Information Processing & Management*, 24(5):513–523, 1988.

52. Salton, G. and McGill, M.J. *Introduction to modern information retrieval*. New York, NY: McGraw-Hill, 1983.

53. Sanchez, E. Importance in knowledge systems. *Information Systems*, 14(6), 455–464, 1989.

54. Sparck Jones, K. A. *Automatic keyword classification for information retrieval*. London, England: Butterworths, 1971.

55. Sparck Jones, K. A. A statistical interpretation of term specificity and its application in retrieval. *Journal of Documentation*, 28(1):11–20, 1972.

56. Van Rijsbergen, C. J. *Information Retrieval*. London, England, Butterworths & Co., Ltd, 1979.

57. Waller, W. G. and Kraft, D. H. A mathematical model of a weighted Boolean retrieval system. *Information Processing & Management*, 15:235–245, 1979.

58. Yager, R. R. On ordered weighted averaging aggregation operators in multi criteria decision making. *IEEE Transactions on Systems, Man and Cybernetics*, 18(1), 183–190, 1988.

59. Yager, R. R. A note on weighted queries in information retrieval systems. *Journal of the American Society for Information Science*, 38(1):23–24, 1987.

60. The Ordered Weighted Averaging Operators: Theory and Applications, R.R Yager and J. Kacprzyk eds., Kluwer Academic Publishers, 1997.

61. R.R.Yager, A. Rybalov, On the Fusion of Documents from Multiple Collections Information Retrieval Systems. *Journal of the American Society for Information Science*, 1999.

62. Zadeh L.A., Fuzzy Sets as a Basis for a Theory of Possibility. *Fuzzy Sets and Systems*, 1:3–28, 1978.

63. Zadeh, L.A. Fuzzy sets. *Information and control*, 8:338–353, 1965.

64. Zadeh, L. A. The concept of a linguistic variable and its application to approximate reasoning, parts I, II. *Information Science*, 8:199–249, 301–357, 1975.

65. Zadeh L.A. A computational Approach to Fuzzy Quantifiers in Natural Languages, *Computing and Mathematics with Applications*. 9:149–184, 1983.

Information Retrieval on the Web

Maristella Agosti and Massimo Melucci

Department of Electronics and Computer Science
University of Padova, Via Gradenigo 6/a, 35131 Padova, Italy
{agosti,melo}@dei.unipd.it

Abstract Information Retrieval (IR) on the Web can be considered
from many different perspectives, but one objective and relevant aspect
to consider is that on mid-1999 the estimated number of pages being
published and available for indexing in the Web was 800 millions for 6
terabytes of textual data. Those Web pages were estimated to be distributed over 3 millions Web servers. This means that anyone cannot effort
to explore all the information distributed over those pages, but anyone
necessarily needs to be supported by tools that help the end users to
choose the most relevant Web pages to answer any specific request of
information. The Web has started to operate only 10 years ago, and
just few years after the first information retrieval tools have been made
available to help Web users to find Web pages with relevant information. To deal with the complexity and heterogeneity of the Web, we need
search tools implementing algorithms for indexing and retrieval that are
more advanced than those currently employed in IR. These advanced
algorithms need to exploit the structure of, and the inter-relationships
among Web pages.

From a research point of view, we need also to re-think evaluation because of the different characteristics of Web IR, which can be expressed
in terms of data, functionalities, architecture, and tools. These characteristics affect 'how' to carry evaluation out and 'what' to evaluate.

This chapter faces the different aspects of IR on the Web that can be
considered and analysed, that is: history of IR on the Web, different
types of tools for performing IR on the Web which have been designed
and developed to answer different user requirements, architecture and
components of those IR Web tools, indexing and retrieval algorithms
that can be employed for making Web IR effective, and methods for
evaluation of Web IR.

1 Introduction and Vocabulary

This initial section addresses the main topic of the chapter explaining what
we mean by "Information Retrieval (IR) on the Web", and along with this
explanation the necessary vocabulary is introduced.

First of all, it is useful to recall that we use the term IR to identify all those
activities that we can use to choose from a given *collection* of *documents*, those
documents that are of interest in relation to a specific *information need*. Those

M. Agosti, F. Crestani, and G. Pasi (Eds.): ESSIR 2000, LNCS 1980, pp. 242–285, 2000.
© Springer-Verlag Berlin Heidelberg 2000

activities, we are concerned with, are those that permit us to reach the target of choosing the documents that are probably relevant to the initial information need in an *automatic* way, because our concern is on collections of documents that are available in a *digital form* and we are going to have an *automatic IR system* that we can use in choosing documents. Since we are going to use an automatic system, we imagine that the problem of translating the user *information need* is external to the IR system, and the IR system is going to have to answer to an information need already translated in a *query*. Where the query is the transformation of the information need in a phrase of a language that the IR system has been programmed to understand and to answer.

In traditional IR, the *collection* of *documents* is a set of documents that has been put together, because it is related to a specific context of interest for the users that are going to use it. An IR collection is a set in the mathematical sense, because all the documents of the collection have certain properties or features in common, those features are usually related to a specific subject or thematic area, and often also to a time span.

The set of all the digital copies of the articles published in the journals and magazines of the ACM (where ACM stands for "Association for Computing Machinery"), of the last 10 years can be an example of collection of documents of interest for the computer scientists of an academic department; so those scientists can ask to have them represented in and managed by an IR system; another example can be the set of all the published laws of a western country, that can be of interest for the lawyers but also for the citizens of that country. This means that the collection of documents that an IR system manages is clearly identified and the user of the system knows exactly, when he receives an answer from the system to a submitted query, that the answer is related only to that a-priori identified set.

Normally, one of the *documents* of the collection that is managed by an IR system is the digital ASCII version of the corresponding original document of the collection of interest for a group of users; as for the previous examples, it is the file containing the ASCII version of one ACM article or of one law. In fact, the IR system is going to use the complete textual version of the original document to index it and representing its semantic content for further matching with the user query in the matching process that permits of choosing of some probably relevant documents of the managed collection. This indexing process is often named *full text*, since the full text of the document is used in extracting words or terms to represent its semantic content.

In the Web, it is possible to continue to use a traditional IR system, and its specific managed documents collection. To do so, the IR system is made available to the user through a gateway program which connects the IR system to a Web page or a Web presentation that plays the role of interface between the user and the IR system. It is through this interface that the IR system is made available through a general Web access. The same IR system can also be used to manage different collections of documents. In this case the user can access an *IR service* through a Web page, that gives access to different document collections as the one depicted in Fig. 1.

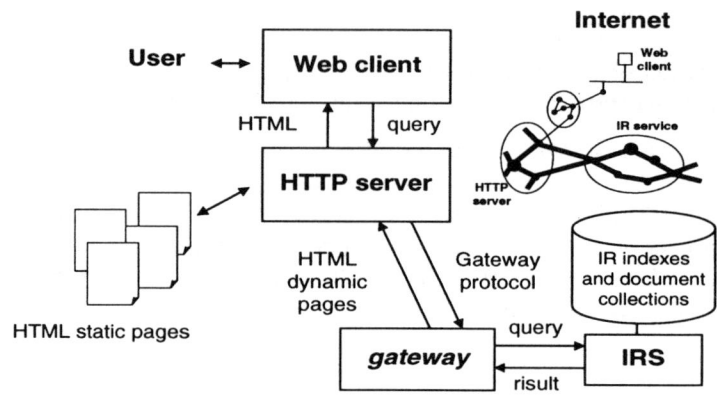

Figure 1. Use of an IR Service through a Browser Web

In this case, we continue using a traditional IR service, even though its access is made easier than before the Web availability, because it is not necessary to install on the user machine a specific client software related to that specific IR service. In this case the Web browser, that the user normally uses for navigating the Web, it is used as interface for accessing the IR service of interest and the gateway program needs to have the capability of managing a connection-oriented service, since the user of an IR service is used to have a dialogue with the IR system during the search session. We do not consider this situation as one of IR on the Web, being only a different type of access to a traditional IR service.

"IR on the Web" concerns all those activities that we can use to identify, in the Web, those documents that are of interest in relation to a specific information need. In IR we normally speak about documents, and, in the context of IR on the Web, we can consider a *Web page* as a document. It is worth to note, that Web pages can be really different in size and in the different number and types of files that can constitute them, since a single page can contain text and many other media, such as graphics, sounds or videos. A Web page is different from a common textual document also for the hypertext *links* it contains, where a link is an explicit logical association between two Web pages that are considered by the Web pages author to be in some way related. So, the Web page author has decided to relate a page to another to make explicit this relationship. Most of textual parts of Web pages contains links to other Web pages, and each link associates a Web page to a different Web page related to it. In this way Web pages are related and the reading can be done by navigation or browsing. In fact the Web can be considered as a vast hypertext, and, if the Web is considered in this way, all the studies have been conducted on Hypertext IR (HIR) are of interest; the interested reader can refer to [4] as a general reference addressing the different aspects of HIR.

IR on the Web considers as collection of documents of interest the Web itself, and more precisely the part of the Web that is publicly indexable. This part was estimated, in the assessment of Lawrence and Giles of mid-1999 [30], to contain about 800 million Web pages, encompassing about 6 terabytes of text data on about 3 million servers; when, in December 1997, the same authors were estimating that the Web publicly indexable contained at least 320 million pages, that makes the growth of the number of Web pages, in those 20 months, of a monthly average of roughly 24 millions new Web pages a month. Where the *publicly indexable Web* is constituted by the pages that can be indexed for representing their semantic content for further searching, and it excludes pages that cannot normally considered for indexing, such as pages with authorisation requirements, pages excluded for indexing using the robots exclusion standard, and pages that are dynamically generated following a submission of a search form by a user. This means, that the Web pages available for navigation were on mid-1999 many more than 800 million, where by *navigation* we intend to identify one of the methods we can use to locate information on the Web, that is:

- direct request of a Web page knowing the correct URL,
- indirect request of a Web page using the hypertext link presents in an available Web page, and
- availability of a Web page given by a "narrowcast" service that "push" to the user Web pages related to a user profile.

There is another method that a user can use for locating Web pages, and it is that of using a *Web service* that supports also the searching for specific information in the Web and the presentation of possible pertinent Web pages, as results of the search, to the users. That is a service that permits the location of Web pages implementing, at least, a two-steps process: the initial step of searching and presentation of a list of essential information of possible pertinent Web pages, is followed, on a second moment, by a step of location by navigation of possible pertinent pages. Possible Web services that support the searching for information in the Web are:

- A *Web search engine* (SE), that is the generic term in common use for identifying a collection of different types of complex software tools that implement the effective functions of "IR on the Web". That is, IR functions using as collection of documents of interest the Web that is publicly indexable.
- A *Web search service*, that is a service made available on the Web for searching of information. It usually makes use of a SE, but it could also use more

than one SE combining in a dynamic way characteristics of many of them together also with other software tools and taking into account some indications received from its user. A *Web meta-search engine* can be considered as a Web search service which answer to a query of a user using different search engines, and combining their different result together as a unique answer to present to the final user.

– A *Web portal*, that is a "port of entry" into the Internet and the Web, a sort of information gateway to the Web, which often includes a search engine plus additional organisation of services by content, because portals are often concentrated on a particular topic.

With the introduction of the concepts of SE and search service, we have completed the presentation of all introductory concepts and pertinent vocabulary, thus in the following sections we can concentrate on the specific topics of the chapter, that are: history, types of tools for performing IR on the Web, architecture and components of such tools, algorithms, and finally, evaluation of IR on the Web.

2   History

The World Wide Web is available to the general public from less than 10 years and we often speak about the "History of the Web", when the western tradition suggests to speak about the "history" of an event or happening when at least 50 years have been passed from it. In fact it is believed that it is necessary for speaking about an historical happening that the time interval between the present time and the event is long enough to permit to consider it on a sufficient distance from the day by day life and in its complex context. As regards the Web, the notion of historical event is different, probably because we are facing so many differences in just a year time in technology and methods that we have the possibility to use in relation to the Web in our working and private life, that the time span of 10 years seems to be long enough to speak about history.

Some Web Search Engines historical information can be found on Web pages and journal documents, but they are conflicting, also if the time span of availability of this sort of complex software tools is so short. As example, Susan Davis Herring reports in [14] that *Lycos*, developed at Carnegie Mellon University (USA), was the first of such tools, while Michael Maudlin in [33] reports that *WebCrawler*, developed at the University of Washington (USA), was the first tool that allowed the user to search the full text of entire Web documents, because the first release of WebCrawler was made available on April 1994, and Lycos was made available on July 1994.

Anyway, Web users started having the availability of such types of tools during 1994, before that year, it was possible to use tools that were indexing and managing only the title, the URL, and some small parts of Web pages [33]. So, we can say that from 1994 on it has been possible to have Web tools with effective IR functionalities, so we can fix 1994 as the year of starting of "IR on the Web".

From that year on, it has been a flourishing of these tools. In December 1995 *Altavista* entered the scene with a number of innovative features, and in the following years many other search tools were made available together with different types of them. The range of tools that are now available is so wide, that we believe it is worthwhile to try to identify some aspects of them, that permit us to have a sort of reference for understanding what are their features that are relevant to IR and that make them similar or different to each other. In the following section with introduce such sort of reference.

3   Types of Tools for Performing IR on the Web

It is possible to face the problem of presenting the characteristics of tools, that perform activities of IR on the Web, in many different ways. Often the choice of the characteristics that need to be analysed depends on the targets of the study of the problem, and in relation to these it is decided what characteristics to take into considerations. Because of that, many different ways of classifying these tools have been proposed over the years. Since our target is the study of the complex and different characteristics of these tools in performing information retrieval functions on the Web, we believe it can be very effective to examine them making reference to the abstract scheme of phases of the IR process, as it is depicted in Fig. 2.

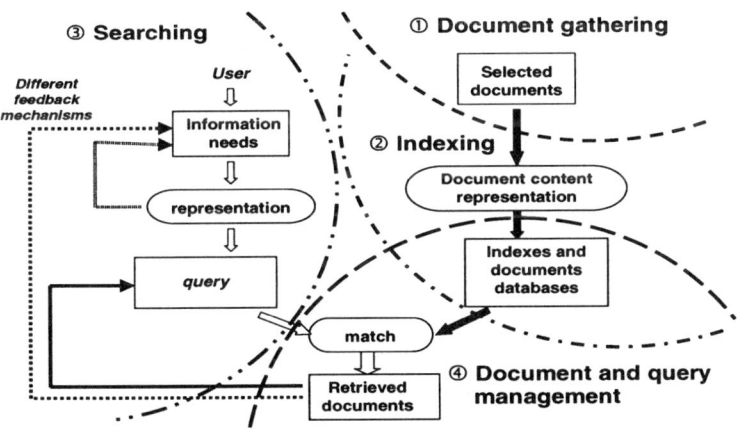

Figure 2. Phases of the IR Process

The main phases of the IR process that can be in general totally or partially automated with the support of software tools are:

1. *Document Gathering,*
2. *Indexing,*
3. *Searching,* and
4. *Document and Query Management.*

In the case of tools for performing IR on the Web, there are differences with traditional IR tools, not in the specific four phases and specific functions, that are fairly similar, but in the way specific functionalities need to be performed in the Web and on Web documents, as it has been underlined by many other authors, and in particular by Gordon and Pathak [21], and by Gudivada et al [22]:

1. *Document Gathering* is the phase of the IR process which produces as output the construction and maintenance over time of a virtual and/or physical collection of Web documents. The objective of this phase is the construction of the collection of the Web documents that form the universe of interest that the software tools have to index and manage; and this is the set of Web documents from which the user is going to search and retrieve. It can be a virtual and/or a physical collection of Web documents, because each original document can be discarded after indexing ("virtual collection") or maintained ("physical collection") together with all the data that are in any case maintained in auxiliary indexes for permitting other types of user searches. Among those auxiliary data, there are the date in which the document has been collected for indexing, and other basic information such as the URL where the document has been found, title, and author. The decision of maintaining the original indexed version of the Web document can be made, because the document can change over time and the new one can be really different from the version which has been indexed, and it can constitute a surprise for the user when he sees it as one of the documents selected by the system to answer his query.
   The software tools can gather the documents for building the collection of interest mainly in two different ways:
   (a) *Web Pages are* submitted *to the Search Engine*: Specific Web users or companies directly contact the search engine or the search service submitting new Web pages.
   (b) *Web Pages are* collected *by a tool of the Search Engine*: The search engine has a software component which navigates the Web using as starting points of the process of navigation and collection of new Web pages, some URL addresses that are known to be useful and interesting starting points for the type of service that the search engine is used for. That software component of the search engine is identified by different and typical names, that evoke their main function of traversing the Web looking for useful new or not previously visited pages, some of these typical names are: *crawler, spider, worm,* and *robot.* In effect the software characteristics of such a component are those that are typical of *autonomous agents,* and in particular the specific class of *task-specific agents* which is named *information agents,* as it can be seen in the classification of those types of software tools which is reported in Fig. 3 from [29].

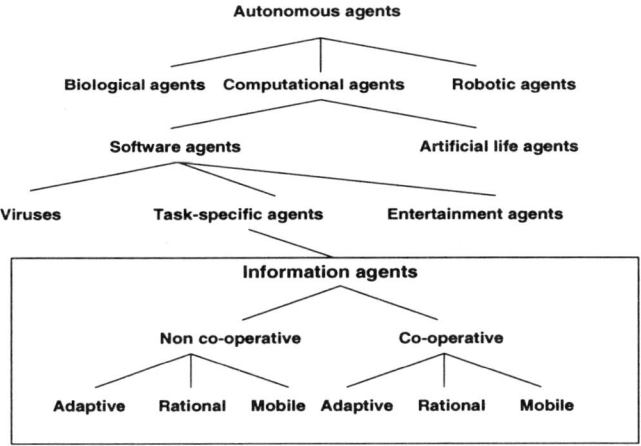

Figure 3. A Classification of Information Agents, Reported from Klusch, 1999 [29]

Another effective and general name which is used to identify such type of tools is *Web Search Agent* (WSA), which is particularly effective because it recalls the software characteristics it is based upon and its main target, which is that of searching for Web pages to consider in the construction of the documents collection of interest. A WSA is programmed to use some known Web pages as starting points, and from those pages it visits related Web pages passing from link to link.

2. *Indexing*: is the phase of the IR process which takes each single document, of the collection of interest, as input and represents its content to make this representation usable by a computer process or program. It is possible to conduct the indexing process following many different approaches, at the extremes of the range of the possible approaches there are: the complete automatic indexing approach of a full text document, and the human association of the document to a class of a knowledge hierarchy which has been built and is maintained by people. If we emphasise the importance of the way indexing is conducted, that is automatically versus manually, it is possible to consider this way as a criterion to be used in classifying search engines, distinguishing them in two types:

(a) *Query-based Engines*, where indexes are maintained and used in searching for pertinent documents to answer the user query.

(b) *Classified Lists*, where subject directory catalogues are built and maintained.

Since we have specified in Sect. 1 that the process of doing IR needs to be based on a completely automatic approach, only *Query-based Engines* can be considered tools that really implement functions of IR on the Web, and in Sect. 5, the innovative algorithms that can be used to really implement IR functions are presented and discussed.

3. *Searching*: This is the phase which manages the user's query making use of information retrieval algorithms and with the purpose of choosing from the managed collection of Web documents, the most relevant ones to the user's query. Searching functions are strongly related to the indexing algorithms which have been employed in the representation of the content of the documents, because of that these aspects are dealt in details in Sect. 5 of this chapter.

4. *Document and Query Management*: This phase partially overlaps both indexing and searching, because document management is related to indexing and query management to searching. The necessity of considering it also as a separate phase is related to the necessity of considering as a separate issue the effective storage and management of indexes, as they logically result from the indexing process, and the different documents databases that can be useful to manage for offering different services to final users, also if the logical Web document collection of documents is a single one. In relation to the way the collection of documents is stored, the search engine can offer a different service to its users. As an example, a single collection can be searchable only as a unique one, or the user can ask to query only the subset of it which is constituted of documents written in Italian language, or the one of documents written in English language; this aspect does not change the type of algorithms are used in indexing and in searching, but it changes the types of offered services.

The differences that can be implemented as part of this phase are only confined by imagination, and it is often in relation to these particularities, that search engines are offering different services also if those different search engines are not really different in the aspects which are peculiar to IR. Because of that, these differences are not taken into account here as aspects that can are useful in specifying or classifying search engines.

4   Architecture and Components of IR Web Tools

In correspondence to the main phases of the IR process, depicted in Fig. 2, there is a component of the software tool that is implementing the process itself. In traditional IR, no software component does exist for document gathering, since the document collection is built in relation to some specific criteria that are external to the IR process, as it has been exemplified in Sect. 1.

In traditional IR the indexing procedure is applied to each document of the collection of interest, and the output of this procedure is the creation of the databases of indexes of interest, together with the different document databases that are useful to answer final user queries. The indexing of a collection of textual documents together with the production of useful databases of documents and structured data are depicted in Fig. 4.

A specular phase to indexing is the phase of information search and retrieval, that makes use of indexes produced during the indexing phase, and the query is

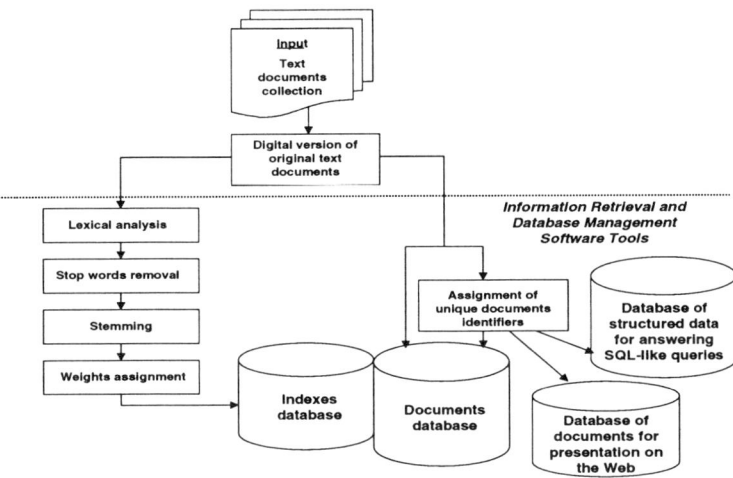

Figure 4. Indexing of Textual Documents and Production of the Databases for Information Management

managed as a document, which needs to be indexed to produce a representation that can be compared to that of documents, as depicted in Fig. 5.

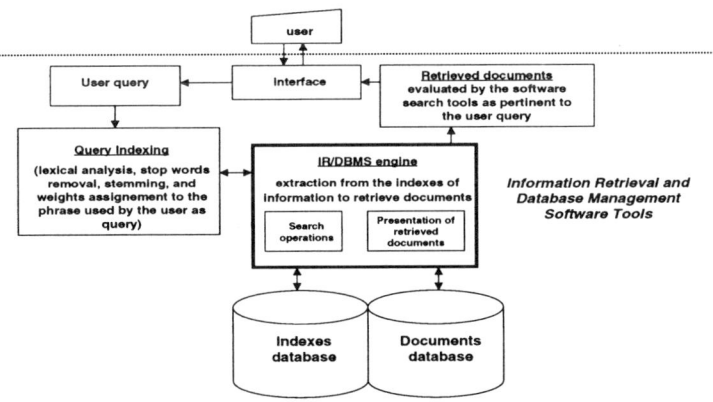

Figure 5. Phase of Information Search and Retrieval

From an architectural point of view, the two main differences from traditional IR and IR on the Web are:

- the phase of construction of the Web document collection, that needs to be done automatically traversing the Web using a WSA;
- the management of the collection, which is in most cases a virtual collection of documents, because to manage a real collection would be unmanageable, since the storing and managing of a Web collection of interest would require a storing space and a management capability that is not possible to concentrate on one search engine only site.

Figure 6 shows these main differences, that can be appreciated in comparing it with Fig. 4, where IR traditional indexing phase is depicted.

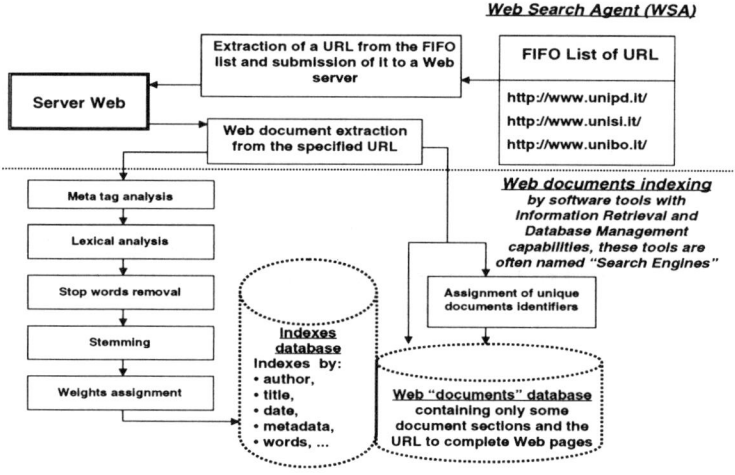

Figure 6. Functions of the Web Search Agent (WSA) and the Search Engine (SE)

5   Algorithms for Information Retrieval on the Web

The main difference between the algorithms for IR on the Web and the ones for classical IR is the massive presence of Web links, which can be used as source of evidence for indexing and retrieving pages. The basic idea, and the importance, underlying the use of Web links is that they represent a explicit logical association between two Web pages that are considered by the Web pages author to be in some way related, as it has been stated in Sect. 1. Basically, Web links can be useful for IR purposes because they can connect relevant documents.

This is not a completely new idea: The Cluster Hypothesis, for example, states that closely associated documents tend to be relevant to the same requests [44]. It is then natural to use Web links to disclosure the semantic relationships between pages, because linked documents may tend to be relevant to the same requests. For example, a Web link from a relevant page can point to another relevant page, or relevant pages can frequently be linked by pages being rich of links.

The idea of using relationship representations, such links or citations between informative objects, e.g. documents, has been exploited some decades ago in bibliographic citation analysis. Garfield described, for example, the notion of impact factor as a means to assess the importance of a scientific journal [19]. Recently, some studies focussed on Web link analysis to understand how, and the extent to which, Web pages and sites are inter-connected; for example, the notion of Web impact factor has been introduced and defined as the sum of the number of in-links or self-links pointing to a given page, site, or domain, divided by the number of pages found in that page, site, or domain [27]. A link with respect to an object p is called "in-link" if it starts from a different object and points to p; a link is called "self-link" if it starts from and points to p. The numbers of pages that link to a page, which is necessary to compute Web impact factors, are calculated using the advanced search capabilities of the search engines, e.g. AltaVista [16]. Some researchers discussed the appropriateness of Web impact factors and of the methods for calculating it; some contributions on this subject are reported in [32,40,41]. Further, and previous research work on link analysis was obviously conducted in the field of hypertext systems, and specifically in hypertext IR, as reported in [4], for instance.

5.1 Hypertext Structure Analysis

The work by Botafogo et al. is in a sense paradigmatic of the research work done in the field of hypertext systems regarding the analysis of hypertextual structure. That work consisted in discovering clusters of hypertext nodes, identifying nodes playing predefined roles, such as hierarchy roots, internal nodes, or leaves, and computing metrics that give an idea about the characteristics of a hypertext. In [18], the authors report an evaluation and comparison of hypertexts using hypertext structuring and analysis methods. Specifically, they describe an analysis of inter-linked consistency, and i.e. the degree to which humans author similar hypertexts. Their findings explained why research in automatic link generation, that increase inter-linker consistency, can be useful.

The importance of these methods within hypertext systems is due to their application to help author "good" hypertexts, which minimize the risk of encountering the "lost in hyperspace" problem, that is the end user's disorientation from long navigation paths. As regards to clustering, for instance, if the end user gets lost in the hypertext, the system can cluster nodes and provide a map of the hypertext. The elements of a such a map are clusters that identify coherent nodes, i.e. contexts, and separate nodes that are about different contexts. The detection of hierarchies, for example, help author a "good" hypertext because a hierarchical structure can communicate to the end user a more comprehensible hypertext semantics than other types of structure. Indeed, hierarchies are considered as the most adequate structure to minimize the risk of disorientation [9]. Thus, transforming a hypertext structure into hierarchy, discovering hierarchies, or supporting hypertext authors in writing hierarchies, are useful procedures to produce comprehensible hypertexts.

In case of the Web, structural analysis, cluster analysis, or hypertext topology metrics help discover regularities of portions of the Web. The discovered regularities is a knowledge that can be exploited in Web IR because the regularities are likely to implement specific types of Web pages. For example, a hierarchy can be a regularity that signal the presence of a home page and some referred pages. The metrics described in [9] implement a complementary means to analyze the hypertext structure. These metrics measure some properties of the hypertext and provide some directions to author the hypertext itself. For example, these metrics measure the connectivity, and the chance of accessing to every node from any node. These metrics can be employed to automatically restructure a Web site to make the discovery of hidden regularities easier than the discovery of poorly structured Web sites. For example, if discovering hierarchies in a Web site were possible, that knowledge could be exploited to extract hierarchical relationships, such as specialization-generalization or aggregation relationships, among the Web pages.

In [8], by "cluster analysis" is meant as the identification of clusters of hypertext nodes. In some hypertexts, nodes can tend to be associated with other nodes, and be dissociated from others. We can then speak about internal association and external dissociation, respectively. Clusters can be used to explain if and why nodes are characterized by an internal association and/or external dissociation. The advantages of clustering hypertexts is that clustered nodes provide a context, which can be represented by means of a summary, and they reduce the amount of data to be stored to represent the content of nodes, and communicated to the end user.

Nodes are clustered on the basis of the topology of manually inserted links, rather than the content of the nodes themselves [8]. The advantage of using links, rather than the semantic content of nodes, is that manually inserted links are readily available, while semantic content representations, such as index terms, and content-based links need to be constructed automatically. The rationale of using links is that, if nodes are likely to be about homogeneous semantic content, i.e. included in the same context, then some pieces of the content of a node can be linked to some pieces of the content of another node. The resulting subgraph is then strongly connected. Therefore, a strongly connected subgraph is likely to represent a cluster of nodes that are homogeneous in content and then can provide a homogeneous context.

Clusters of nodes connected by a high number of independent paths [8]. The number of independent paths can be used as measure of the degree of membership in a cluster because the presence of a link; generally speaking, a path indicates a relationship between two nodes, and the higher the number of independent paths between two nodes, the stronger the relationship between them.

Technically speaking, k-components are used to implement clusters in [8]. A k-component of a graph G is a subgraph A such that, for every partition (A_1, A_2) of A, there are at least k links of A are each incident with a node of A_1 and with a node of A_2. A k-component must be a maximal subgraph, i.e. no subgraph $B, A \subset B$ exists and is a k-component [8].

The starting point of structural analysis is a distance matrix M, such that the element M_{ij} is the shortest path length from node i to node j. If no path exists between nodes i, j, M_{ij} is set to a high arbitrary constant value K, which is for example twice the longest path length. The distance matrix can help compute index and reference nodes. Index nodes are nodes that can be used as an index or home to many other nodes, while reference nodes are the converse of index nodes [9]. Index and reference nodes can be detected using in-degree and out-degree: The out-degree of node i is the the sum of the elements placed in the same row i of M, while in-degree of node j is the the sum of the elements placed in the same column j of M.

Index and reference nodes can be detected as follows: Let μ and μ' be the average in-degree and out-degree, respectively, which have been computed over all the nodes. Let σ and σ' be the corresponding standard deviations. Then, an reference node is a node whose in-degree is greater than $\mu + 3\sigma$, and a index node is a node whose out-degree is greater than $\mu' + 3\sigma'$. Centrality is another measure that is useful in analyzing hypertexts [9]. In the latter work, the authors define distance as $D = \sum_i \sum_j M_{ij}$ and define a central node as one whose distance to all other nodes is small. Specifically, they define out- and in-distances for nodes i and j as $\sum_j M_{ij}$ and $\sum_i M_{ij}$, respectively. Therefore, the relative out-centrality O_i can be defined for node i as $D / \sum_j M_{ij}$, while the relative in-centrality I_j can be defined for node j as $D / \sum_i M_{ij}$.

The relative out-centrality can be used to detect roots of hypertext hierarchies. The root of a hierarchy should satisfy three requirements [9]: The root has to reach every node, the distance from the root to any node should be short, and the number of children nodes should be low. The latter can be controlled using a predefined threshold, which depends of the specific hypertext. The nodes with a high relative out-centrality satisfy the other two properties because they are central, and then reach almost all the nodes, and the total distance to the nodes is the lowest.

In the following, we give an example of computation of out- and in-centrality measures. Let consider the following table that represents the connections between the nodes of Fig. 7.

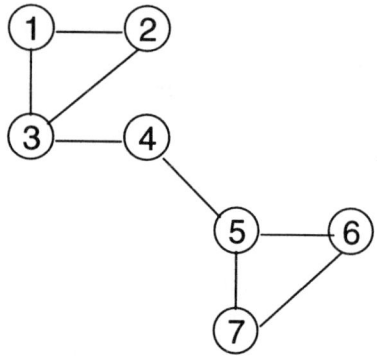

Figure 7. Án Example of Hypertext and Two Potential Node Clusters: {1,2,3,4} and {5,6,7}.

	1	2	3	4	5	6	7	O_i
1	−	1	1	∞	∞	∞	∞	5.7
2	1	−	1	∞	∞	∞	∞	5.7
3	1	1	−	1	∞	∞	∞	6.3
4	∞	∞	1	−	1	∞	∞	5.7
5	∞	∞	∞	1	−	1	1	6.3
6	∞	∞	∞	∞	1	−	1	5.7
7	∞	∞	∞	∞	1	1	−	5.7
I_j	5.7	5.7	6.3	5.7	6.3	5.7	5.7	

If the value of the table entry of index (i, j) is 1, then, there is a direct connection between nodes i and j. If there is no direct connection, the value id ∞. To allow the computation of the out- and in-centrality measures, it is necessary to replace ∞ with a constant value K which is the highest of all the entries. If we set K to 2, out- and in-centrality can be measured using the following two expressions, respectively:

$$O_i = \frac{D}{\sum_j M_{ij}} \qquad I_j = \frac{D}{\sum_i M_{ij}}$$

where, $D = \sum_i \sum_j M_{ij}$. As regards to the example, $D = 57$ and nodes 3 and 5 can be considered as index nodes, e.g. homes or roots, because their out-centrality (O_i), which is equal to the in-centrality (I_j) because of symmetry, is higher than any other centrality measures.

A modification can be applied to the table by considering, for example, indirect connection, other that direct connection, so that the symbol ∞ is used to mean that no path connects two nodes, while a finite value is the distance of the shortest path between the two nodes.

Starting from the distance matrix, two additional metrics can be computed to give a global view of the hypertext, or of a part of it. In [9], compactness and stratum are developed to capture the notions of complexity and connectedness in hypertexts. For example, a measure of compactness can be the average number of in- or out-links per node; a measure of stratum can be the average minimum number of links to be followed to go from a node to another node. An end user navigating a compact hypertext can reach almost all nodes through a dense network of links. As every node is linked to many nodes, the hypertext results rather unstructured and thus the end user may get lost in the hyperspace. In contrast, a low compactness can indicate a hypertext with few links, and then the end user is unable to reach every node from a given node; however, the end user is unlikely to be disoriented. In IR, the notions of precision and recall correspond to the notions of low compactness and high compactness, respectively. Indeed, if the end user exploit a hypertext to retrieve information that are stored in the nodes, a high compactness may make recall high, because many relevant documents can be reached, but precision may be low, because many irrelevant documents can be reached as well. In contrast, a low compactness may make recall low and precision high. Stratum gives an idea of the degree to which the end user has to reach intermediate nodes before reaching the desired node. The higher the stratum, the higher the number of intermediate node.

In the following, we report an example of computation of a compactness measure. The following three hypertexts are represented both as matrix and as graph.

	1	2	3	4
1	0	K	K	K
2	K	0	K	K
3	K	K	0	K
4	K	K	K	0

	1	2	3	4
1	0	1	1	1
2	1	0	1	1
3	1	1	0	1
4	1	1	1	0

	1	2	3	4
1	0	1	1	2
2	1	0	2	1
3	1	2	0	3
4	2	1	3	0

The leftmost hypertext is one where each node is disconnected from any other node, thus, compactness has the lowest value. The hypertext in the middle is partially connected, the, compactness is higher than the previous one. The rightmost hypertext is one where each node is connected to every node, thus, compactness has the highest value. If the table entry is K, then, no path exists between two nodes, otherwise, the value is the shortest distance between two nodes. A non-normalized compactness value is $C = \sum_i \sum_j M_{ij}$; the maximum value is $MAX = n(n-1)K$, while the minimum is $MIN = n(n-1)$. In case of the totally disconnected hypertext, $C = MAX$, then the relative compactness value is $C^* = 0$; in case of the totally connected hypertext, $C = MIN$, then the relative compactness value is $C^* = 1$.

Hypertext structural analysis, clustering and metrics can be employed within IR on the Web because they provide some useful tools to implement algorithms for IR automatically. Note that there are some fundamental differences between the Web and other information systems that make Web hypertext analysis important, so one should pay a great deal of attention in employing these methods. However, some suggestions can briefly be given, which can be the seed of further research.

- Link- and content-based clustering methods can be combined by taking advantage of their strengths and weaknesses. Link-based methods are independent of the content, so they can help overcome some keyword mismatch problems; content-based methods can discover relationships that are not coded by Web links.
- Structural analysis, e.g. hierarchy discovering, help detecting Web link types; for example, links of a hierarchy may represent specialization or aggregation relationships.
- Clusters and other structures, like hierarchies, can be indexed, retrieved and displayed as an individual object; for example, metadata of root nodes, e.g. home pages, can be used to index children nodes; clusters can be presented to be further examined.
- Metrics can help discover hidden structures, guide the generation of clusters and the selection of hierarchies; for example, select clusters with a given internal connectivity, select hierarchies with a given out-centrality.

5.2   Bibliographic Citation Analysis

The work reported, for example, in [39] investigate the effectiveness of bibliographic citations in IR. If one looks at bibliographic citations as links, one can consider those results in designing techniques dealing with IR on the Web. In [13], Croft and Turtle described a comparison between a heuristic spreading activation strategy and a probabilistic retrieval model incorporating inter-document links. The main findings are that the use of hypertext links makes retrieval more effective than strategies without links. Specifically, manually constructed links, such as bibliographic citations, are more effective than automatically constructed ones, such as the nearest neighbor links. The authors stress the importance of implementation issues, as the use of hypertext links in retrieval strategies requires additional computation resources to store and process links.

Savoy has evaluated the effectiveness of inter-document links designed and implemented on the grounds of three kinds of bibliographic citations, i.e. bibliographic references, bibliographic coupling, and co-citations, as well as links based on nearest neighbor nodes [39]. Two test collections, i.e. CACM and CISI were employed [17]. The former also included bibliographic citations between documents. The results confirmed the findings reported in [13] and demonstrated that links based on bibliographic citations are more effective than links based on nearest neighbors, as the former are carefully inserted by the document authors.

The important lesson to be learned from the work presented in [39] and [13] is that man-made links (such as bibliography-based links), if available, are more effective than, and are an "upper limit" to automatically made links. Therefore, it is necessary to dedicate more research work on the evaluation of automatically constructed links to understand whether they are effective enough whenever links made by a human expert are absent, or in what proportion the effectiveness of automatic links is less than that of manual links.

5.3   Web Page Authority Analysis

HITS (Hyperlinked Induced Topic Search) [28] and PageRank [10] are among the most recent algorithms dealing with Web links. They represent a rather large set of similar algorithms. The design of techniques for IR on the Web can consider those results because the latter allow of capturing some structural characteristics of the Web that can make indexing and retrieval methods more effective. For example, HITS or PageRank detect "important" pages in playing some roles, such as index or reference. If these pages are about the end users' topic, they can be important in IR on the Web because they may be relevant, or allow for reaching pages that are relevant to the end user's topic. HITS and PageRank resembles that reported in previous papers on impact factors, citation analysis or structural analysis of hypertext. There are some fundamental differences between the Web and other information systems that make these algorithms more important. The Web is much more complex than a local hypertext or a bibliographic database, such as those considered, for example, in [9, 39]. The high heterogeneity of Web pages and the absence of link typing are two out of the reasons why the Web is very complex. Therefore, the requirement for algorithms for link analysis is stronger than in the case of classical hypertext systems or bibliographic database. Additionally, the Web is a highly dynamic entity in terms of size and structure. So, capturing its structure as pages and links are added or removed is important to make search tools effective continuously in different time periods. Finally, while classical hypertext systems and bibliographic databases are managed and accessed locally by a limited number of users, the Web is the result of the convergence, or the divergence, of a myriad of contributions from million of end users. Therefore, capturing some regularities in the Web would allow for detecting those pages that are considered as "important" in a specific role by many end users; for example, HITS and PageRank aim to detect those pages that end users consider as authoritative as regards to a given topic.

HITS focuses on broad topic queries, i.e. queries that are likely to be answered with too many pages. The problem with broad topic queries is that the number of pages is too large to allow the end user to examine them effectively and find relevant information. As corollary, the estimation of recall for broad topic queries is almost impossible since the set of relevant pages is unknown. HITS aims to extract authority pages from large set of retrieved pages under the assumption that relevant information are still stored in these sets, and that authority pages are more likely to contain relevant information than other pages. The notion of authority is then central to HITS. Therefore, understanding what an authority page is, and how it can be detected, is crucial.

An evidence to assess a page as authoritative can be the number of links pointing to it, because a link pointing to it would mean a citation made from the pointing page author. However, universally popular pages, but not authoritative with respect the query topic have also a large number of links pointing to them. The problem is that universally popular pages are expected to have a large in-degree regardless of the underlying query; they are likely to be assessed as authoritative for every query, and then they would appear in any B_q. The question is then whether distinguishing between authoritative relevant pages and popular pages is still possible.

The heuristics used in HITS to detect authority pages is based on two types of page—hub and authority—and on the number of links citing a page and of links that cite pages—the former being called in-links, and the latter being called out-links. An authority is a page being cited frequently, i.e. with a high number of in-links, while a hub is a page citing other pages frequently, i.e. with a high number of out-links. HITS detects hubs and authorities with a given degree of uncertainty measured by the number of in-links and out-links. Authority and hub pages correspond to those defined in [9], but there is circular mechanism relating them, as explained below. Figure depicts an intuitive view of hubs and authorities.

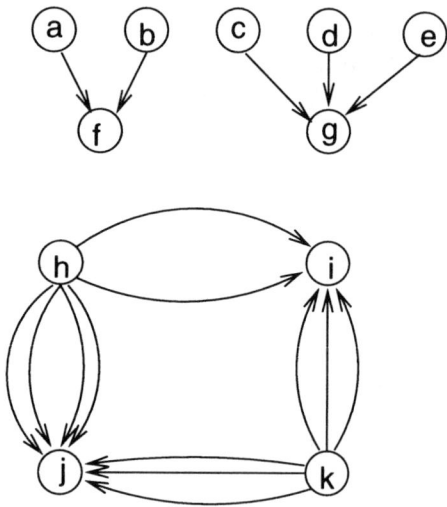

Figure 8. A Pictorial Description of Hubs and Authorities.

Nodes f, g, i, j are popular pages because they are pointed to by many pages; specifically, i, j are also authoritative pages because they are pointed to by h, k which are hub pages.

HITS ranks authorities and hubs by the number of in-links and of out-links, respectively, in two different lists; top ranked pages of a list are "good" authorities or those of the other list are "good" hubs. The techniques is hinged on a circular mechanism: The degree of goodness of a page as authority depends on the degree of goodness of the hub pages citing it. Viceversa, the degree of goodness of a page as hub depends on the degree of goodness of the authority pages being cited. Therefore, a "good" authority is cited by "good" hubs and a "good" hub cites "good" authorities.

The iterative algorithm that computes hubs and authorities makes use of the circular mechanism relating good hubs and good authorities. At the first level of decomposition, the algorithm can be defined as follows:

q: a query
R_q: the root set, i.e. the set of pages retrieved
                  to answer q
B_q: the base set, i.e. R_q expanded using links
A_q: the authorities
H_q: the hubs
S_q: the result set
k: a natural number
σ: a threshold
for each q
                  $R_q = \text{answer}(q)$
                  $B_q = \text{expand}(R_q)$
                  $(A_q, H_q) = \text{iterate}(B_q, k)$
                  $S_q = \text{filter}(A_q, H_q, \sigma)$
end for

For each query q, the routine takes the root set R_q as seed set to start the algorithm; the root set is the usual retrieval result produced by a search system. The subroutine "expand" returns the base set B_q by adding to R_q the pages that are not in R_q and are pointed to by, or point to a page in R_q. The subroutine computes the weight vectors that measure a value representing the importance of each page in B_q as authority (A_q) or as hub (H_q), as regards to the query topic q. Finally, the subroutine "filter" selects the most important authorities and hubs given a threshold. The algorithm is depicted in Fig. 9.

Hub pages permit to discriminate between query-independent authoritative pages and pages that are authorities with respect to the query topic. The hub pages are searched within the base set B_q, and therefore they are likely to be relevant to the query topic. If the hub pages are likely to be relevant to the query topic, then they are likely to point to authorities that are relevant as well. The "hubbiness" of hub pages is related to the authority of the pointed pages, and the authority of authoritative pages is related to the "hubbiness" of the pointing pages. The circular mechanism implements a mutually reinforcing relationship

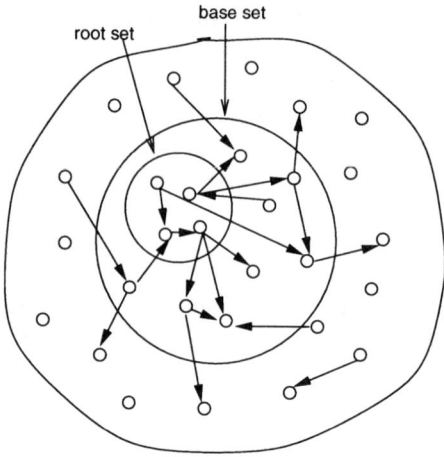

Figure 9. A Pictorial Representation of HITS [28].

between hubs and authorities: A good hub is a page that points to many good authorities, and a good authority is a page that is pointed to by many good hubs.

HITS considers the Web as a graph that can be represented in terms of nodes and links. Then, each node is connected to zero or more nodes through in- and out-links. For each query q, the algorithm aims to extract a subgraph S_q that should possess the following properties [28]:

1. small size,
2. high number of relevant pages,
3. high number of strong authorities.

Let examine the algorithm as regards to the three requirements. The starting point is a broad-topic search query q. The first step of the algorithm is the retrieval of the root set R_q which satisfies the first two properties. Indeed, R_q is quite small because the maximum number of retrieved number can be kept low. R_q is likely to be rich of relevant pages because the current "traditional" retrieval algorithms can reach a good precision.

The small size of S_q allows for applying HITS, which is computationally expensive because it needs some iterations before reaching a stable solution. The requirement of having a high number of relevant pages is related to the availability of many strong authorities, which is the last, but most important requirement. The correspondence between strong authorities and relevant pages, and then between the notion of authority and that of relevance, is a quite strong hypothesis. The latter strong hypothesis may hold, for example, for topics regarding people or companies, but these topics are rather specific, while the algorithm was designed for broad topic queries.

The third property can be satisfied by expanding R_q and construct the base set B_q. Then, the algorithm works under the assumption that there is at least a link from a node of R_q to an authority, which may be outside R_q. We can then obtain B_q by expanding R_q to include any page pointed to by a page in R_q and any page that points to a page in R_q. To avoid that B_q grows exponentially, a threshold for the number of links can be set.

The base set B_q is then the input of the iterative subroutine that compute the hubs and the authorities. The underlying assumption is that B_q should contain many relevant pages and many strong authorities. The target of the algorithm is to increase the rank of authority pages so that they can be displayed within the top ranked pages. The iterative subroutine works as follows: The set of pages with the highest in-degree is extracted because that set is likely to include many relevant pages. Indeed, a relevant page is supposed to be cited by many pages matching the query q. However, the set of pages with the highest in-degree may include many authoritative, but not relevant pages which are then simply universally popular.

```
iterate(B_q, k)
B_q:            the base set with cardinality |B_q|
k:              a natural number (the number of iterations)
z:              the vector (1, ..., 1) ∈ R^|B_q|
x_(i):          authority weight vector at step i = 1, ..., k
y_(i):          hub weight vector at step i = 1, ..., k
x_(0) = z
y_(0) = z
for each i = 1, ..., k
                x_(i) = update(y_(i-1));
                y_(i) = update(x_(i));
                normalize x_(i) and y_(i)
end for
return (x_(k), y_(k))
```

Each page is associated two weight vectors—authority weight vector x hub weight vector y—that represent the degree to which the page is a "good" authority and a "good" hub, respectively. The subroutine "normalize" maintains the invariant that the weights of each type are normalized so that their squares sum to 1. The "iterate" subroutine make use of the circular relationship between hubs and authorities because it iterates and updates a vector weight using the other vector weight via the subroutine "update", which is described in the following.

```
update(v)
v':             new vector weight
for each j = 1, ..., |B_q|
```

$$v_j' \leftarrow \sum_h v_h \times I(h,j)$$
where $I(h,j) = 1$
if a in-link from page h to page j exists
$I(h,j) = 0$ otherwise

end for

return v'

After the k-th iteration, the weight vectors $(x_{(k)}, y_{(k)})$ include the hub weight and the authority weight for each page: The largest values correspond to the best hubs and to the best authorities. The subroutine "update" is depicted in Fig. 10.

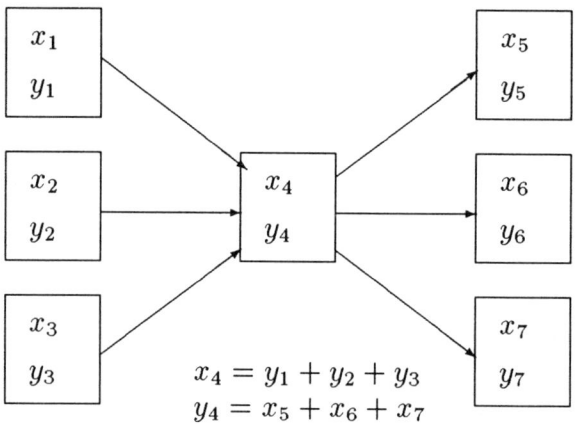

Figure 10. The operations of the Kleinberg's algorithm. The authority weight (x) is the sum of the weight (y) of the hub pointing to it. The hub weight at step is the sum of the weight of the authorities pointed to by it. For example, the authority weight of the node 4, i.e. x_4, is the sum of the hub weights y_1, y_2, y_3.

The above described algorithm has been employed to implement an automatic resource compiler, i.e. an automatic tool compiling a directory of the most important Web pages or sites for a broad topic [12]. The tool, which is called ARC (Automatic Resource Compiler), aims to produce a directory being similar to those compiled by Yahoo! or Infoseek. Differently from the latter directories, ARC is completely automatic and that paper shows that the effectiveness of ARC to compile resource directories is comparable to the effectiveness of human compilers employed to compile the Yahoo! or Infoseek directories. The same algorithm has been applied to infer Web communities [20]. A Web community is one including authoritative pages and hub pages. As above, authoritative pages are pages being relevant to a broad topic, but they are considered as the most important among all the relevant pages. The importance of authoritative pages is reinforced by hub pages, i.e. the pages citing those and other authoritative pages.

In 1998, Brin and Page wrote one of the rare scientific articles describing the architecture of a Web search engine, named Google [10]. The most important feature of Google is the ranking algorithm, which is named PageRank, that is used to compute the rank of the retrieved Web pages. Another reason of the relevance of the work reported in [10] is due to the detailed description of the architecture of Google and then of the algorithms and data structures that are needed to implement a search engine. One of the main issues of search engine implementation is that the designed algorithms and data structures should be scalable with the size of Web, without degrading retrieval effectiveness.

The rationale of the PageRank algorithm is based on the simulation of the end user's behaviour during Web browsing. The process of initial page selection and of following a link to a subsequent page is modelled within a simple probabilistic framework. The end user who is visiting an arbitrary Web page can decide to stop visiting the page and request another page with probability p. For sake of simplicity, the probability that the end user "gets bored" and chooses another page is constant over all the Web pages. Let us assume that page X has pages $Y_1, \ldots, Y_n$ pointing to it, i.e. has n in-links, and that each page Y_i has C_i out-links. The probability that the end user's visits the Web page X at a given time is given by the probability that X is still visited at that time or that the end user's stops visiting one of the n pages that point to it and follows the in-link to X. The formula has been expressed as [10]:

$$Pr(X) = (1 - d) + d \left(\frac{Pr(Y_1)}{C_1} + \cdots + \frac{Pr(Y_n)}{C_n} \right)$$

The PageRank is directly correlated with the number of pages pointing to it and with the PageRank value of the citing pages—the more the page X is pointed to by high PageRank pages, the higher its PageRank.

Bharat and Henzinger addressed topic distillation [6], which is an extension of the Kleinberg's and PageRank algorithms coping with three specific drawbacks of the latter algorithms [20]. The authors of the work reported in [6] carried out an information visualization-based experimental analysis and realized that the Kleinberg's algorithm works less well than traditional IR retrieval algorithms for some queries. There are three cases in which that algorithm is less effective:

1. *Mutual Reinforcement*: The hub-authority relationships between pages are mutually reinforced because of the presence of one-to-many or many-to-one links made by different people with contrasting reasons.
   Let consider two Web sites, and a document of the first site pointing to a set of documents of the second site. After some iterations of the Kleinberg's algorithm, the document of the first site has a very high hub weight and the documents of the second site have a very high authority weight. Something similar happens whether there are some documents of the first site pointing to one document of the second site.

The problem is that the computation of hub and authority weights is done assuming that there is one person that judges the relevance of a page as regards to the page pointing to it. On the contrary, the reality is that there are potentially as many people as the pages and therefore an authority page is considered as such because of different, and maybe contrasting opinions made by the different people.

That problem is also related to the very frequent presence of well-known pages or Web sites, yet they are irrelevant to a given query topic—examples are the Web sites by AltaVista or Yahoo! [20]. The problem is that these pages are so frequently pointed to that they are likely to be computed as authorities independently the query topic.

2. *Automatic and Ambiguous Links*: HITS and the PageRank hinge their own effectiveness on the assumption that links starting from a page are expressions of authority of the pages pointed to by it. That assumption holds for links that are inserted manually by the page's author.

   The problem is that that assumption is likely to not hold for links that are automatically generated by tools, such as search engines or Web authoring tools. There are then many links, and then many authorities and hubs that do not correspond to a human judgment about the importance of a page as regards to a query topic.

   Note that a similar problem is due to the ambiguous reasons why a link is placed to point an "authority" page. Indeed, different pages can point to an authority because of many, and maybe contrasting reasons; thus, the effectiveness of HITS and PageRank may be lower than one could imagine.

3. *Topic Drift*. HITS and PageRank algorithms aim to find special kinds of subgraph out of the Web representing authorities and hubs as regards to broad query topic. So, one may wonder what if the query topic is rather specific. There are two possible results: The algorithm is either unable to detect authorities and hubs as regards the query topic, or it produces authorities and hubs as regards a generalization of the query topic. This phenomenon is called "topic drift" [6] because the algorithm automatically moves the computation on a different topic.

   Let consider, as example, the query topic "jaguar and car" [6]: There are two possible generalizations of the topic, which can be expressed as "jaguar" and "car", respectively. Then, if the algorithms is unable to detect authorities and hubs as regards "jaguar and car", it may produces authorities and hubs as regards "jaguar" or "car", which are likely to be irrelevant to the more specific topic.

   Topic drift can sometimes be a positive side-effect if communities, instead of relevant pages are searched. Indeed, if the algorithm is unable to find authorities and hubs as regards a narrow query topic, it is able to find authorities and hubs as regards broader query topics. Thus, the algorithm succeeded to find authorities and hubs for broader query topics if they hold for the starting topic as well. This result can be accepted because relevance is a less strong constraint than pertinence of a page to a topic.

The three problems, which have been described above, can be addressed by embedding some heuristics in HITS and PageRank. In the following, we illustrate how these heuristic solutions to the three problems can be implemented within HITS.

1. *Mutual Reinforcement.* The problem caused by mutually reinforcing relationships between Web site can be solved by considering the number of documents of the first site pointing to the document of the second site, and the number of documents of the second site pointed to by the document of the first site. We call the former out-degree d_O, and the latter in-degree d_I. Then, we can give an authority weight $1/d_O$ to the document of the second site that is pointed to by the documents of the first site. In similar way, we can give a hub weight $1/d_I$ to the document of the first site pointing the documents of the second site. The subroutine "update" can then be modified as follows:

update(v)
v':   new vector weight
for each $j = 1, \ldots, |B_q|$
$\qquad\qquad v'_j \leftarrow \sum_h v_h \times W(h, j) \times I(h, j)$
$\qquad\qquad$ where $I(h, j) = 1$
$\qquad\qquad$ if a in-link from page h to page j exists
$\qquad\qquad I(h, j) = 0$ otherwise
$\qquad\qquad W(h, j)$ is the authority or the hub weight
end for
return v'

2. *Automatic and Ambiguous Links.* The detection of automatically generated links, and then understanding whether a link has been authored manually or automatically, is a difficult task. Moreover, the effectiveness of this detection is unclear because there are manually authored links that are useless for IR purposes, and automatically generated links that are useful for the same purposes. Similarly, link disambiguation is also a difficult task. No specific technique have been proposed to detect automatically generated links, yet the technique designed for the "topic drift" problem might help detect automatically generated links since they assume that those links are likely to be irrelevant to the query topic.

3. *Topic Drift.* The solution to the topic drift problem that has been proposed in [6] exploit classical IR techniques to assess the similarity of the document content with the query content. The employed method is in two steps:

   (a) the starting query is expanded, or a new query is generated, using the terms occurring within the pages of the root set,
   (b) the similarity between the content of the expanded, or generated, query and of pages is computed to select the most similar.

The modified query, either expanded or generated, is more specific than the starting query and topic drift is less likely to occur with the new query, because it is longer than with the starting query. Most similar pages are selected under the assumption that they include a high proportion of relevant pages. The latter assumption is consistent with that made when "blind" or implicit feedback is exploited to improve precision and recall [23].

The cosine of the angle between the vectors representing the document and the modified query is an assessment of the content similarity between the two objects. If x and q are the vectors representing the Web page and the query, respectively, the cosine of angle can be expressed as follows [38]:

$$\cos(x, y) = \frac{\sum_{i=1}^{K} x_i q_i}{\sqrt{\sum_{i=1}^{K} x_i^2} \sqrt{\sum_{i=1}^{K} q_i^2}}$$

where, $x_i = f_{x_i} \times d_i$ is the classical $tf \times idf$ weighing scheme, K is the total number of unique terms, f_{x_i} is the frequency of term i in the page represented by x, $d_i = \log N/n_i$, and n_i is the number of pages containing term i out of the total number N. In [37], different weighing approaches are described to implement the $tf \times idf$ weighing scheme. If the documents are Web pages, the similarity can be assessed using the same technique because Web pages can be represented as vectors. If one needs to compute the similarity between two documents, one can apply the same technique using the vectors representing the two documents. The subroutine "update" can then be modified as follows:

```
update(v)
v′:              new vector weight
for each j = 1, …, |Bq|
            v′j ←  ∑h vh × W(h, j) × S(j) × I(h, j)
                 where I(h, j) = 1
                 if a in-link from page h to page j exists
                 I(h, j) = 0 otherwise
                 W(h, j) is the authority or the hub weight
                 S(j) is the similarity between page j
                 and the modified query
end for
return v′
```

As concluding remarks, we would stress some issues about the representativeness of the authority and hub pages, yet calculated applying the changes proposed to address mutual reinforcement and topic drift.

Search agents and engines indexes a small proportion of the whole Web and are unable to update the indexes at the same speed at which the Web evolves.

As consequence, the base set being used to compute authorities and hubs is a small sample, which is very unlikely to contain a significantly large proportion of the set of relevant pages. Thus, the algorithms that use in- and out-links aim to rank authorities and hubs on top the lists of retrieved pages, but they are unable to increase the quantity of retrieved relevant pages.

The use of HITS or PageRank, or their modifications, allows to cite find authoritative and relevant pages out of large sets of retrieved pages. Once an authoritative and relevant page is found, it can be cited in a paper or another Web page. Such a citation can increase the authority of the cited page and the "hubbiness" of the citing pages. As corollary, a relevant, but non-authoritative page is not cited, and the chance of becoming an authoritative gets lower. Therefore, a subset of the set of relevant pages can be built and can consist of authoritative and popular pages, while all the other less popular are outside that set.

These algorithms have to cope with the dynamicity and the heterogeneity of the Web, which make connectivity analysis difficult, since the analysis being made at a give time period gives results that are different from those given by an analysis made at a different time period. Moreover, the analysis about a Web site, which is made considering a given part of the Web, gives results that are different from those given by an analysis about the same Web site that is considering a different part of the Web.

The effectiveness of these algorithms could be improved if the semantics of Web links is exploited. The number of in- and out-links is counted regardless what a link means, while it is likely that a link has a semantics that sometimes corresponds to the one being between a page and a relevant page, but sometimes it does not. Thus, the identification and exploitation of the Web link semantics would be matter of future research. This is one of the reasons why we introduce some notions of automatic link generation in next section.

5.4   Algorithms for Automatic Web Link Generation

In the previous sections, we have described some of the most important algorithms that are used to analyze the connectivity of parts of the Web. These algorithms rely on the presence of Web links among Web pages, either inserted in the page by the author manually, or generated by a tool automatically. In a sense, the connectivity analysis algorithms process Web pages and links passively, and try to extract the most useful information from, for example, the topology of the graphs being induced the available pages and links. These algorithms do not affect the structure of the Web because they are "read-only" and do not insert or delete links. Since late eighties, there is an interest of IR researchers in the use of hypertext to design IR systems, and, since nineties, in the automatic hypertext construction and evaluation [3, 7, 15, 34].

Automatic link generation algorithms aim to generate links among nodes in a fully automatic procedure; "fully" means that no human intervention is usually planned. The construction process result is an automatic hypertext, that is an automatically constructed hypertext. In case of the Web, we speak about automatic construction of Web links. In other terms, links can be computed among Web pages, or parts of them, and they can be implemented as Web links. Note that the newly inserted links update the Web pages implicitly because they are rather inserted in auxiliary data structures, such indices or matrices. In contrast to the connectivity analysis algorithms, the algorithms for the automatic hypertext construction aim to actively intervene in the topology to insert new links. Thus, we can create a specific topology, instead of analyzing the topology of a given subgraph of the Web.

The automatic generation of *associative* links is the core step of the whole process of automatic hypertext construction since it is what does rapidly transform a "flat" page collection into a powerful interactive retrieval tool. Associative links represent implicit associative connections between pages. They are built making use of *content*-based connections between fragments of text of the same page or pages of the same collection. Automatic link construction allows to navigate the Web pages across links being previously undefined. Once constructed, the new links can be used to navigate the hypertext or to apply connectivity analysis algorithms.

Most of the methods for the automatic construction of associative links try to catch the similarity relationship between the nodes of the hypertext to be built. Similarity is one of semantic relationships occurring between nodes. Similarity computation is then the most used IR technique to assess whether an object has a semantic content similar to the another object semantic content. Since links between nodes express a semantic relationship between nodes, similarity computation can be used to automatically build this type of links. Similarity computation is performed on *descriptions* of the pages to be linked, and page descriptions are computed using automatic indexing.

In its simplest form, the algorithm for similarity computation can be formulated as follows, provided a model, the similarity function used to compute similarity values, and a threshold value:

1. compute the descriptions of two textual node content using the model;
2. compute the similarity score between the descriptions using the function; similarity of a text with respect another text can be either global or local— local similarity is calculated for a fragment of the text, and global similarity is calculated for the whole.
3. if the score is over the given threshold, then insert the link between the nodes.

Starting from that simplest form, much more complex and effective methods for the automatic construction of links can be defined:

1. the use of text similarity to generate links;
2. the automatic detection of links and of different link types;
3. the automatic construction of links of different types between different types of node.

Text content-based methods for the automatic construction of links have been studied by different authors and with different approaches, among them: [1, 2, 2, 5, 34, 36]. We describe these methods into detail in the following.

Use of Text Similarity to Generate Links. The method can be used to create links between text segments to practically builds up a hypertext at retrieval time. At retrieval time means that the generated hypertexts is given as response and is dependent a query. The technique proposed here is an attempt to use vector similarity to produce a network of text segments that are semantically related. The basic idea is to use the vector space model to evaluate the similarity between two text segments. The normalised $tf \times idf$ weighting scheme is employed to evaluate the vector elements.

The algorithm to build similarity hyperlinks automatically starts from a query and then subsequently generates the nodes computing the similarity between a node and the query or another node. Nodes can be full-text documents, Web pages or text fragments. The algorithms can be described as the following sequence of steps:

1. Retrieve, in response to a query, a set of m text segments using local similarity with respect to the query.
2. Refine the retrieved set by rejecting all but k text segments. This can also be done in two ways—by setting the value of k first, or by employing a local similarity threshold and accept the k segments that are over that threshold. Decreasing levels of similarity can be used to control the size and the structure of hypertext. The number of accepted documents is variable since it is determined by a similarity threshold, the threshold is then progressively increased to produce a self contained map.
3. For each retrieved text segment, do the first step in a recursive way.
   The retrieved set of k segments is used as a new set of queries and for each of them restart the process. The process can be repeated n times. At each iteration link the k segments (queries) with each of the k new text segments accepted in response of each query.
   At this stage of the algorithm, clustering algorithms can be applied to text segments if they are too small or very similar one to each other. The clustered text segments are represented by a centroid which can be used as query.

The application of this algorithm produce a graph resembling a tree rooted at the query, but text segments can reappear at different levels. Depth and breadth of the "tree" can be controlled by carefully choosing respectively m, n, and k. In the following, we depict an example hypertext and code the algorithm.

```
retrieve(x, n, k)
if(n > 0) then
      extract top k text segments matching x
      for each segment y_i, i = 1, ..., k
            retrieve(y_i, n − 1, k)
end retrieve

Let n, k be natural numbers
and q be the starting query
and retrieve(q, n, k);
```

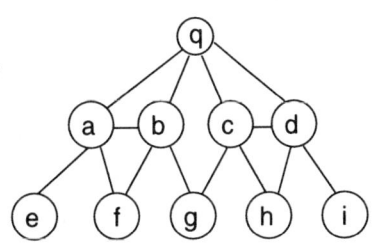

A visual representation that resembles very much a hypertext can be used. The most natural way is to draw a graph whose nodes can be pages, documents or textual fragments (paragraphs, sentences) extracted from documents. A global measure of similarity is used to measure closeness among nodes. This is based on the inner product of the weighted vectors representing the documents in the vector space model, or is an average of local similarities. In both cases, term weights are computed using the normalised $tf \times idf$ weighing scheme. Similarly, when nodes represent text segments, the same inner product is used to measure their similarity. However, in this case non-normalised term weights are used, to give preference to longer matching sentences that are more indicative of coincidences in text meaning.

An accurate analysis of the structure of a document can be obtained by putting the nodes representing text fragments along a circle and drawing a line whenever the similarity of two text fragments is over a predetermined threshold. Using this technique is possible to decompose documents by identifying homogeneous parts (sets of text segments) of the document. The same technique could be used to link parts of the document that have strong relationships between them. Local similarity is proposed as a precision filter used to discard documents that may have a high global similarity with the query due to language ambiguities, but that have a low local similarity with the query.

The Automatic Detection of Links of Different Link Types. The main aim of this technique is to automatically describe the nature of the link, i.e. to assign a type to each link, other that to construct the link itself. This is done for arbitrary collection of unrestricted subject and of any size. One assumes that one has an existing "flat" collection of "flat" documents and the following classification of link types to be automatically detected [5]:

- *revision* links are those representing versions of the same text segment;
- *summary* links are those connecting a set of text segments to the one that summaries them;
- *expansion* is the inverse of the summary link type;
- *equivalence* links connect segments that are about the same subject or very close subjects;
- *comparison* links connect fairly close contents of text segments;
- *contrast* is the inverse of comparison link type;
- *tangent* links connect segments that are marginally relevant to a segment;
- *aggregate* links are between text segments grouped together to form a new segment.

The output is a type label for each link and a graph representation of the resulting hypertext. The graph representation helps the final user understand the nature of links. The technique to detect link types is based on the combination of clustering, local and global similarities as described in previous paragraph. What makes this technique different is the algorithm for automatically typing links. Let consider two large documents from which parts can be automatically extracted using the text structure. The algorithm performed on the documents is in the following steps:

1. compute global and local similarities between documents, between documents and parts, and between parts;
2. combine global and local similarity values to classify similarities as different degree of strength, such as strong, good and weak similarities;
3. collapse strong links and merge linked parts to obtain a simplified set of links and parts;
4. split text segments linked by weak links and look for subsegments that are linked by stronger links.

The resulting set of links and parts is a hypertext which nodes are document parts or aggregation of document parts, and links between nodes are the result of collapsing strong similarity-based links or splitting segments into smaller, but more similar segments. Let us describe link collapse with an example. Let us consider two documents x and y, and two parts A and B of each of them: (A_x, B_x) and (A_y, B_y) respectively such that B does sequentially follow A. If there are two strong links between the As and between the Bs, and if A is physically near B within each document, then A and B are merged to create a new aggregate part, and a collapsed link is created between the two aggregate parts. Link types are assigned by analyzing the pattern of the merged parts and of the collapsed links. Type labels are assigned to the collapsed links of the resulting hypertext accordingly to the following rules:

- a link is of *revision* type if the two documents organize their own subjects in the same order and if corresponding parts are connected through strong similarity-based links. For example, the collapsed link between the above mentioned documents x and y is a revision one;
- a link is of *summary* or *expansion* type if the quantity of unlinked text of a document is higher than of the quantity of unlinked text of the other document; the link from the former to the latter is of type "summary", the reverse one is of type "expansion";
- a link is of *equivalence* or *comparison* type if it is neither a revision, nor is it a summary/expansion link; the choice between "equivalence" and "comparison" depends on the degree of strength of merged links, i.e. strong and good links;
- a link is of *contrast* type if the quantity of unlinked text of both documents is significantly high;
- a link is of *tangent* type if few links starts from, or ends to a node;
- a link is of *aggregate* type if it is between two nodes consisting of parts that form a cluster (see above about "hypertext structure" and related measure such as "compactness" and "stratum").

The Automatic Construction of Links of Different Types between Different Types of Node. The complexity of data modelling in classical IR is mainly due to the complex nature of the relationships between the different IR objects – documents and auxiliary data, where by auxiliary data are meant all those objects, such as index terms or thesaurus entries, which are used to represent the semantics of the documents of the collection of interest. Similarly to IR, we could, at least in principle, distinguish between two types of objects involved in IR on the Web—Web pages and Web auxiliary data.

The main aim of this technique is to automatically generate links of different types. Differently from the previously described technique, in this case, the link type is predefined by the type of the nodes to be linked. Also this technique is done for arbitrary collection of unrestricted subject and of any size. Starting from an existing "flat" collection of "flat" documents, two node types are given— pages (P) and terms (T). Assuming that there is one link type between a pair of node types, four types of link can be constructed between the two types of nodes (Fig. 11):

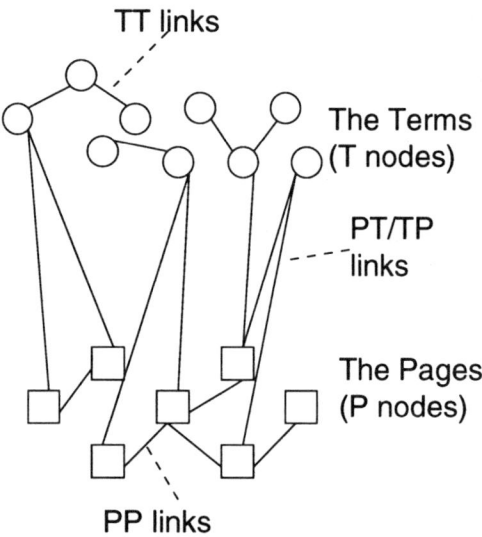

Figure 11. The Conceptual Architecture of a Two-Levels Hypertext

- PP (TT) links are between documents (phrases). A numerical measure of similarity is computed between documents (terms) i and j to estimate the closeness between the respective semantic content. If the vector-space model is employed, the measure is the cosine of the angle between the document (terms) vectors. For each document (phrase) i, a ranked list of similar documents (terms) can then be computed. A PP (TT) link is inserted between documents (term) i and j if the measure of similarity, or the rank of document (term) is over a stated threshold.

- PT links are between a document and terms, while TP links are between a term and documents. The weight of term within document can be used as numerical measure of link strength. The measure can vary according with the adopted weighting scheme. For example, if the $tf \times idf$ scheme is adopted, the term j occurring within document i is weighted with $tf_{ij} \log N/n_j$, where tf_{ij} is the frequency of term j within document i, n_j is the number of documents indexed by term j, and N is the total number of documents. A PT (TP) link is inserted between documents and terms if the weight, or the rank of document (term) is over a stated threshold.

In the following, we report a simple example of construction of a two-levels hypertext from a three-document collection. Links are computed and weighed using $\left|\frac{X \cap Y}{X \cup Y}\right|$, where X, Y are either sets of keyword stems or sets of documents. Underlined strings are keyword stems. Links are depicted as heavy lines (strong, high similarity links) or as light lines (weak, low similarity links).

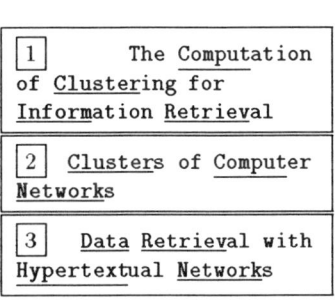

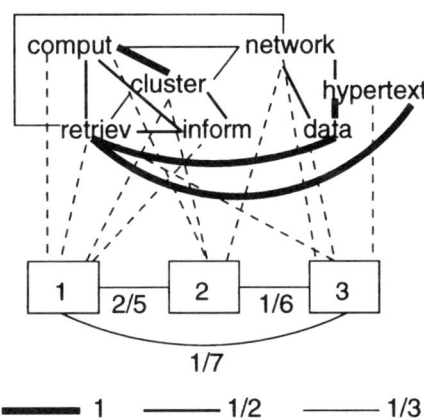

6   Evaluation of Information Retrieval on the Web

As reported in [42], the aim of evaluation in IR is to test hypotheses about one or more component of a IR system, such as the system as a whole, characteristics of the data or of the end user, or the effectiveness of a retrieval or indexing technique. As IR is a science, it is important experiments are valid and reliable to clear report all the details of the experiment and to allow the reproduction of the experiments, if results have to be confirmed, or to avoid the reproduction of the experiments, if they are the starting point of further experiments. There are two broad categories of approaches to evaluation, which correspond to two types of experiments – laboratory experiments and operational experiments. Laboratory experiments are often performed in an artificial environment using test collections and without users. Operational experiments are performed using a real operational IR system, with real end users and real databases; all of these are variables to controlled to carry the experiment out.

To a certain extent, the two types of experiments can be applied to evaluation of IR on the Web as well and the literature reports operational experiments, which test real search engine working on the Web, and laboratory experiments, which test algorithms using test collections. The object of evaluation of IR on the Web can vary because the environment is quite various. Experiments, both laboratory or operational, can regard the whole Web, one or more search engines that are seen as a "black box", or a specific technique implemented by search engines. Experiments regarding the whole Web have for example consisted of the estimation of the total number of pages or sites, the analysis of the geographical or categorical distribution of Web sites, the overlap between the sets of pages indexed by different search engines, or the computation Web impact factors. The experiments regarding the search engines seen as "black box" have consisted in comparing two or more engines processing the same set of queries; note that the conclusions that can be drawn from these comparisons are strongly time dependent. The experiments regarding a given technique are similar to those carried out in traditional IR evaluation settings. In this section, we choose to not review all the research work in evaluation of search engines and IR on the Web, but to describe the main issues of the subject, providing references to some surveys

6.1   Issues of Evaluation of IR on the Web

The issues of evaluation of IR on the Web differ from the issues of evaluation of IR because the Web, and then the processes of indexing and retrieval of Web pages, are very different from those of classical information retrieval systems. We describe in the following some of the issues that make IR on the Web, and then evaluation, different from more difficult than classical IR. Many are the issues that could be listed, but we have chosen the ones that are considered in the literature the most important. These issues are listed below and described in the rest of this section:

- *dynamicity* of the Web and of search engines;
- *heterogeneity* of documents and queries;
- *hyperlinking* among Web pages.

The Cranfield model can be applied to IR on the Web to evaluate the effectiveness of information retrieval processes performed by search engines. The Cranfield model is based on test collections; a test collection is a triplet (D, Q, R) where D is a set of test documents, Q is a set of test queries, and R is a set of judgments about the relevance of each document w.r.t each query. The assumption is that D is a representative sample of the universe of documents, Q is is a representative sample of the universe of queries, and R can, at least potentially, be compiled for each pair made of one document and one query.

In general, as Web search engines are a particular kind of IR system, the procedure of evaluating search engines is a more complex task than for IR systems. For example, the Web, and then the set of Web pages that are retrieved by search engines, are networks of documents. Evaluation must take into account the fact that Web links may represent semantic relationships between documents and that therefore the relevance of a page with respect to a query depends on directly- and indirectly-linked pages. Specifically, the issues of dynamicity, heterogeneity, and hyperlinking affect significantly the components of the Cranfield evaluation model in terms of representativeness, notion of relevance, and measures of effectiveness.

The issue of the *representativeness* of a test collection: representativeness occur as regards the three components of a test collection—D, Q, and R. The degree of heterogeneity and the size of the Web make the construction of a representative test collection, and specifically of D, very difficult, or much more difficult than in the past. If the size of the universe to be represented increases, then the sample being used to represent the universe should increase as well. The size of D would increase significantly because the size of the Web is increasing rapidly. Moreover, the size and the degree of heterogeneity of the sample should increase because the degree of heterogeneity of the Web is high and is increasing. Thus, the construction of a representative sample is difficult because has to be carried out using complex statistical techniques, which guarantee that the constructed sample is the best as possible, after considering the cost of the computational resources being necessary for its management. The situation is made worse because of the presence of many Web pages that are produced automatically by various tools, and because of the mortality of many Web which disappear from the Web by thus making the sample even less representative.

The popularity of the Web and of the search engines correspond to increase of the size of the universe of end users, and then of the queries submitted to the search engines. The widespread diffusion of the search engines and the variety of the end users means that the search engines are employed for IR purposes and for non-IR purposes, such as question answering or resource location. On the other hand, the search engines are basically designed and implemented using different IR algorithms, but search engines differ for the specific algorithms they use. Therefore, some search engines are well suited to answer to queries of a given type, but they answer to queries of other types with low effectiveness. The representativeness of Q is then related to the extent to which it is able to capture the variety of types of queries submitted to the search engines. The representativeness of Q does then affect the bias being introduced when search engines are evaluated because the choice of a set of queries may make experimental results different from those obtained if another set of queries is chosen.

Since TREC has started, the use of large test collections, in terms of D size, has become more common in the past. The Cranfield model is widely used in IR experimentation and it is the model adopted in TREC. The assumption regarding R could not be made for the TREC test collections because of the large size of D. Instead, a pooling method is adopted to compute an estimate of R. Similarly, if a representative sample D of the Web is used, the assessment of each Web page is impossible. Therefore, only a small subset of the sample D can be considered for relevance assessment. The impossibility of assessing a subset of D that is "large enough" makes the computation of recall impossible, and only an estimation can be computed. From a statistical point of view, the issue of estimation of recall introduces some requirements about unbiasedness, efficiency and consistency of the employed recall estimator.[1]

The *notion of relevance* has to be reconsidered if it is applied to Web pages, instead of traditional documents, such as those stored in the TREC test collections. Beside the controversial discussions on the notion of relevance, the pervasive presence of links among Web pages forces to change the notion of relevance: A Web page may be more ore less relevant to a query depending on its in-degree or out-degree, and not only depending on its own content. As Web pages can be browsed, other that retrieved, the dependence between relevance judgements collected at browsing-time is stronger than those during querying-time, as (i) Web pages are linked directly, (ii) users do necessarily see pages one after another, and (iii) their judgements about the relevance of a page does strongly depend on the judgements given on the previously seen pages. This means that, when using classical test collections, one has to consider that the judgements collected in a test collection are given with respect to a query representing an information requirement formulated before retrieving documents. On the contrary, users browsing the Web, or an its subset, formulate their own information requests at navigation-time and therefore judgment regarding the relevance of a visited document is given on the grounds of a partial representation of the request itself. This means that the judgements collected in a test collection for IR on the Web evaluation should represent these relationships.

For an operative point of view, we could assign different degrees of relevance to Web pages. If a Web page p is relevant and has a given in-degree, and the number of relevant pages pointing to p is positive, then a page pointing to p can be considered as relevant to a certain extent, because following the link to p permits the end user to retrieve relevant data. Similarly, if a Web page q is relevant, and has a positive out-degree, and the number of relevant pages pointed to by q is positive, then q can be considered more relevant than p, because following the link from q permits the end user to retrieve additional relevant data. We can give to Web pages different types of assessment, depending on whether they link, or are linked by, relevant or irrelevant pages. The following table illustrates a simple example of how the relevance of a Web can be tuned depending on the relevance of the page being pointed to.

---

[1] An estimator is biased if it over or underestimates the parameter it is estimating; an estimator X is more efficient than another estimator Y if the mean square error of X is less than the mean square error of Y; an estimator is consistent if it tends to get closer to the parameter it is estimating as the sample size increases.

Linking Page	Linked Page	
	relevant	non-relevant
relevant	relevant,useful	relevant
non-relevant	useful	non-relevant, useless

The rationale is that the relevance of a page should be coupled with the notion of usefulness, depending on the relevance of the page that is pointed to it. A relevant linking page can as well be useful, if it links to another different relevant page. If the linking page is non-relevant, then it is useless, because it links to a non-relevant page. Similarly, a non-relevant page can be useful, and then may be more useful than a relevant page, if it links to a relevant one.

The *measures of effectiveness* used in IR in a laboratory setting (i.e. precision and recall) are only partially usable when evaluating the characteristics of Web search engines, as these measures are based on the assumption of unlinked documents. New measures should be defined to take into account the presence of a network of nodes. There are three specific issues related to the problem of identifying adequate measures of Web IR effectiveness: The estimation of recall, the measurement of Web link navigation, and the measurement of other factors affecting IR on the Web.

To estimate recall, different approaches can be taken [31]:

– estimate recall for very specific topics of which the complete set of relevant pages is known in advance—for example, if the query is about a person, the set of pages being relevant to that query is easily computed; such an approach do not solve the problem of the more common broad topic queries;
– estimate recall computing relative recall—relative recall of a search engine is the proportion of a set of relevant pages out of the cumulative set of relevant pages that is computed through a series of different searches; the cumulative set of relevant pages is the union of all the subsets of relevant pages found at each search, which can be carried out with different search engines.

The measurement of Web link navigation can be implemented defining novel measures that take into account the increment and decrement of relevant pages at each navigation step. Precision and recall give biased estimates of navigation performance as they ignore the way the sets of relevant and non-relevant nodes vary as navigation truly proceeds. For example, let sets $B(q)$ and $B(q,i)$ be sets of pages retrieved after submitting query q and following a link from page i in $B(q)$, respectively; $B(q)$ and $B(q,i)$ can produce the same, or lower, levels of precision and recall by giving the impression that no improvements were obtained, even if the subset of retrieved relevant pages included in $B(q,i)$ were different from the one included in $B(q)$. In contrast, the end users are more interested in increments of relevant pages being non-retrieved or unseen before, rather than in permutations of the set of already retrieved pages. Analogously, the end user is more annoyed for new retrieved non-relevant pages than for the already retrieved ones, because she/he has to examine them to realize that these pages are really non-relevant to his/her information needs. It is, therefore, necessary to consider measures taking into account the variations of retrieved pages.

We can define two novel measures, called use *novelty* (V) and *noise* (S), instead of recall and precision, respectively. Novelty is the proportion of relevant pages retrieved at a given step, but missed in the preceding steps. Noise is the proportion of pages that are non-relevant and are retrieved at a given step, but that have been missed in the preceding steps. Novelty was proposed in [35] and can be used as measure of navigation effectiveness, while noise can be used as measure of navigation cost. Recall can be considered as a special case of novelty because it is the proportion of relevant pages retrieved at path $P = (q)$. Similarly, the complement of precision can be considered as a special case of noise because it is the proportion of non-relevant pages retrieved at path $P = (q)$. Novelty and noise are better suited to describe navigation-based searches than traditional precision and recall because they measure the degree to which effectiveness and cost change during navigation. Figure 12 gives a pictorial description of the retrieved page sets and their interrelationships.

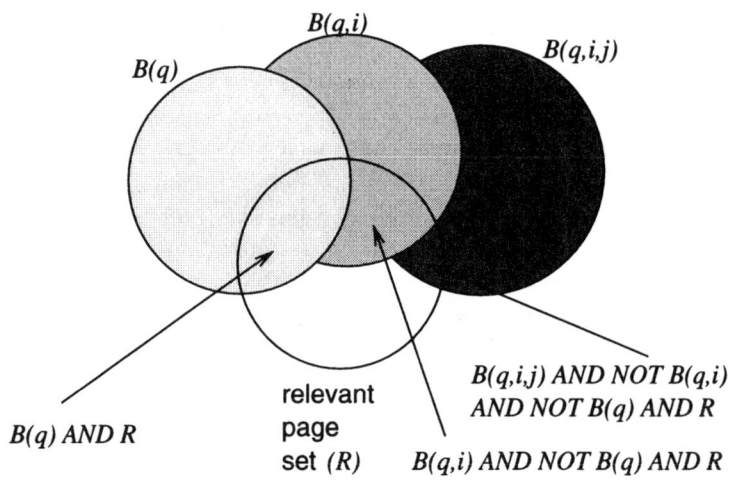

Figure 12. The pictorial representation of the relationship between subsequent retrieved page sets. The intersection between R, which is the set of relevant pages, and one or more sets $B(P)$ of retrieved pages is used to compute the novelty and noise values.

Let $P = (q, i_1, \ldots i_n)$, $n > 0$ be a navigation path starting from the list of pages matching query q; $i_s \geq 1$ identifies the i_s-th page selected as entry point at the s-th step. Let $B^*(P) = B(q) \cup (\cup_{s=1}^{n} B(q, i_1, \ldots i_s))$ be the cumulative set of retrieved documents by following path $(q, i_1, \ldots i_n)$.

Novelty V at path $P = (q, i_1, \ldots i_n), i_n \geq 1$ is the increase of *relevant* pages with respect those stored in $B^*(q, i_1, \ldots i_{n-1})$. Of course, recall $V(q)$ is the proportion of relevant pages found in $B(q)$:

$$V(P) = \frac{|R \cap B(P) \cap \neg B^*(q, i_1, \ldots i_{n-1})|}{|R|}$$

where R is the set of relevant pages. Noise S at path $P = (q, i_1, \ldots i_n), i_n \geq 1$ can be defined as the the increase of *non-relevant* pages, which are included in the newly retrieved pages, that the user has to visit by moving from path $(q, i_1, \ldots i_{n-1})$ to $(q, i_1, \ldots i_n)$.

$$S(P) = \frac{|\neg R \cap B(P) \cap \neg B^*(q, i_1, \ldots i_{n-1})|}{|B(P) \cap \neg B^*(q, i_1, \ldots i_{n-1})|}$$

In the following, we give an example of computation of novelty and noise.

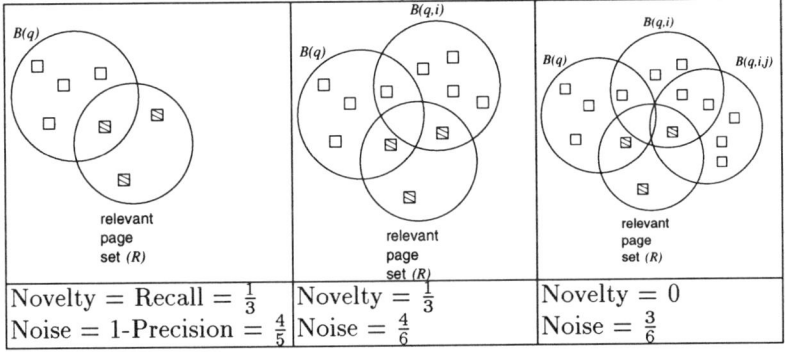

Novelty = Recall = $\frac{1}{3}$	Novelty = $\frac{1}{3}$	Novelty = 0
Noise = 1-Precision = $\frac{4}{5}$	Noise = $\frac{4}{6}$	Noise = $\frac{3}{6}$

At the first step, novelty equals recall and noise is directly related with precision. At the subsequent steps, novelty and noise are related with the values computed at the precedent steps. As regards to the alternative measures, we report some of those proposed in [31] and we suggest the reader to refer to that paper for further details and bibliographic references.

The *coverage* of a search engine can be a factor affecting its retrieval effectiveness. Note that the overlap among the databases of different search engines is rather low; a search engine indexes a small proportion of pages that are indexed by other search engines. The size and the internal structure of the indexed subset of the Web has a considerable impact on retrieval effectiveness because the quality of results, e.g. recall and precision, depends on how good the retrievable pages are. It is likely that the larger the indexed subset of the Web, the higher the recall and the lower the precision, for a given query. Viceversa, small indexed subset of the Web should correspond to higher precision and lower recall. The issue of coverage is related to the issue of search agent effectiveness. Note that search engines work tightly with a search agent that collect the pages to be indexed and retrieved. Thus, the effectiveness of page retrieval is related to the effectiveness of page collection. As consequence, an evaluation issue that need to be addressed is that of search agent evaluation together with the evaluation of search engines.

Query subject may affect search engine effectiveness because a search engine may work more effectively than another search engine if it processes a given type of queries. For example, a search engine may be more effective to retrieve personal home pages, rather that pages containing scientific content. This means that the same query can be answered with different and little overlapping result sets. ¿From an evaluation point of view, the choice of a given type of query is crucial as regards to the test results. The set of test queries should be more unbiased as possible to allow a unbiased evaluation of the tested search engine or technique.

The *interface* issues have been addressed because it is well known from the field of evaluation of IR that the interaction between system and end user is crucial for retrieval effectiveness. In case of IR on the Web, there are some additional issues that make evaluation an important aspect. These issues are basically related with (*i*) the widespread distribution of the Internet and then of search engine "terminals", and (*ii*) the distinction between the interface and system that is implied by the client-server Internet architecture. The widespread distribution of the Internet and then of search engine "terminals" means that the search engines are potentially accessible by a very large number of end users of different types, each of which with specific information needs, background, language and culture. Thus, the interface should as much correspond to any end user as possible. The client-server architecture of the Internet means that browsers, which implement the interface on the client-side, and information providers, which implement the server-side, must agree on standard protocols. Therefore, the interface must be implemented using standard protocols so that it can be rendered and effectively usable independent on what is placed on the server-side. As consequence, two important aspects of interface, which should be evaluated together with other aspects, are the capability of adaptation to different types of end user and the adequacy to the standard protocols.

6.2   The Web Track of TREC

The Web Track of TREC, which is one of the tracks of TREC, aims to provide experimental results about the performance of IR on the Web [24–26]. The Web track has evolved from the Very Large Collection (VLC) track since they are based on the same document set, but the Web track has concentrated on specific aspects of IR on the Web. The structure of the Web track is similar to that of the Ad-Hoc track because the Ad-Hoc topics were used for the Web track runs. The structure of the latest Web track, i.e. TREC-9 Web track, will be reported in [43].

At TREC-8, the Web track consists of two main tasks—the Small Web task and the Large Web task. The Small Web task required to process 2GB of Web data, which corresponds to 250,000 documents. The Large Web task requires to process 100GB of Web data, which correspond to 18.5 million documents. While the focus of the Large Web track is to investigate the issues relating to scale and efficiency of Web data retrieval, the focus of the Small Web task is to:

- test whether the IR technique developed for the traditional Ad-Hoc track work sufficiently well for Web data, at least for the test collection being compiled;
- test whether more or less sophisticated link-based techniques, such as the Kleinberg's or PageRank algorithm, work as effectively as content-only based techniques.

The results from TREC-8 have shown that the retrieval and indexing algorithms that are based on both links and content performed at the same level of effectiveness as those based on content only. A reason of that can be the small proportion of links across different Web servers in the test collection used. The evaluation criteria were the same being used for the Ad-Hoc track, and thus links were not considered to assess the relevance of linked pages. Indeed, the quantity of retrieved relevant documents increases if one considers indirectly relevant documents, i.e. relevant documents that are linked by retrieved documents.

Some reflections can be made from the TREC-8 results [24]:

- the visual rendition and position of anchors may be important to determine the relevance of linked pages; for example, the end user is more likely to follow the links starting from anchors placed on top the page or rendered with color or larger sizes;
- the context of the anchor may play an important role to suggest the end user to follow the link because the context can provide information about the linked page;
- the notion of relevance should be modified to take the links into account when the relevance of a page, either linking or linked, is evaluated;
- the test collection used for the Web track should include a significant number of links to allow to evaluate the effectiveness of link-based algorithms;
- TREC-8 experiments employed Ad-Hoc topic, but Web queries are very often different from TREC topics, not only in terms of number of keywords, but also in terms of type of query (question answering, resource location, etc.).

References

1. M. Agosti and J. Allan, editors. *Special issue on methods and tools for the automatic construction of hypertexts*, volume 33(2) of *Information Processing & Management*, 1997.
2. M. Agosti, F. Crestani, and M. Melucci. Design and implementation of a tool for the automatic construction of hypertexts for Information Retrieval. *Information Processing & Management*, 32(4):459–476, July 1996.
3. M. Agosti and M. Melucci. Information retrieval techniques for the automatic construction of hypertext. In A. Kent, editor, *Encyclopedia of Information Science*, volume 66, pages 139–172. Marcel Dekker, New York, 2000.

4. M. Agosti and A.F. Smeaton, editors. *Information Retrieval and Hypertext*. Kluwer Academic Publishers, Boston, USA, 1996.
5. J. Allan. Building hypertexts using information retrieval. *Information Processing & Management*, 33(2):145–159, 1997.
6. K. Bharat and M.R. Henzinger. Improved algorithms for topic distillation in a hyperlinked environment. In *Proceedings of the ACM International Conference on Research and Development in Information Retrieval (SIGIR)*, pages 104–111, Melbourne, Australia, August 1998. ACM Press, New York.
7. J. Blustein, R.E. Webber, and J. Tague-Sutcliffe. Methods for evaluating the quality of hypertext links. *Information Processing & Management*, 33(2):255–271, 1997.
8. R.A. Botafogo. Cluster analysis for hypertext systems. In *Proceedings of the ACM International Conference on Research and Development in Information Retrieval (SIGIR)*, pages 116–125, Pittsburgh, PA, June 1993.
9. R.A. Botafogo, E. Rivlin, and B. Shneiderman. Structural analysis of hypertext: identifying hierarchies and useful metrics. *ACM Transactions on Information Systems*, 10(2):142–180, 1992.
10. S. Brin and L. Page. The anatomy of a large-scale hypertextual Web search engine. *Computer Networks and ISDN Systems*, 30(1–7):107–117, 1998. Reprinted from [11].
11. S. Brin and L. Page. The anatomy of a large-scale hypertextual web search engine. In *Proceedings of the World Wide Web Conference*, 1998. http://www7.scu.edu.au/programme/fullpapers/1921/com1921.htm.
12. S. Chakrabarti, B.E. Dom, D. Gibson, J. Kleinberg, P. Raghavan, and S. Rajagopalan. Automatic resource compilation by analyzing hyperlink structure and associated text. In *Proceedings of the World Wide Web Conference*, 1998. http://www7.scu.edu.au/programme/fullpapers/1898/com1898.html.
13. W.B. Croft and H.R. Turtle. Retrieval strategies for hypertext. *Information Processing & Management*, 29(3):313–324, 1993.
14. S. Davis Herring. The value of interdisciplinarity: A study based on the design of Internet search engines. *Journal of the American Society for Information Science*, 50(4):358–365, 1999.
15. D. Ellis, N. Ford, and J. Furner. In search of the unknown user: indexing, hypertext and the World Wide Web. *Journal of Documentation*, 54(1):28–47, 1998.
16. AltaVista Search Engine. http://www.altavista.com/, July 2000.
17. E. A. Fox. Characterization of two new experimental collections in computer and information science containing textual and bibliographic concepts. Technical Report TR83-561, Cornell University, Computer Science Department, September 1983.
18. J. Furner, D. Ellis, and P. Willett. The representation and comparison of hypertext structures using graphs. In M. Agosti and A. Smeaton, editors, *Information retrieval and hypertext*, chapter 4, pages 75–96. Kluwer Academic, 1996.
19. E. Garfield. Citation analysis as a tool in journal evaluation. *Science*, 178:471–479, 1972.
20. D. Gibson, J. Kleinberg, and P. Raghavan. Inferring Web communities from link topology. In *Proceedings of ACM Hypertext Conference*, pages 225–234, 1998.
21. M. Gordon and P. Pathak. Finding information on the World Wide Web: the retrieval effectiveness of search engines. *Information Processing & Management*, 35(2):141–180, 1999.
22. V.N. Gudivada, V.V. Raghavan, W.I. Grosky, and R. Kasanagottu. Information Retrieval on the World Wide Web. *IEEE Internet Computing*, 1(5):58–68, 1997.

23. D. Harman. Relevance feedback and other query modification techniques. In W.B. Frakes and R. Baeza-Yates, editors, *Information Retrieval: data structures and algorithms*, chapter 11. Prentice Hall, Englewood Cliffs, NJ, 1992.

24. D. Hawking, N. Craswell, and P. Thistlewaite. Overview of TREC-7 Very Large Collection track. In *Proceedings of TREC*, 1999.

25. D. Hawking, N. Craswell, P. Thistlewaite, and D. Harman. Results and challenges in Web search evaluation. In *Proceedings of the World Wide Web Conference*, Toronto, Canada, April 1999.

26. D. Hawking, E. Voorhees, N. Craswell, and P. Bailey. Overview of TREC-8 Web track. In *Proceedings of TREC*, 2000.

27. P. Ingwersen. Web impact factors. *Journal of Documentation*, 54(2):236–243, 1998.

28. J. Kleinberg. Authorative sources in a hyperlinked environment. *Journal of the ACM*, 46(5):604–632, September 1999.

29. M. Klusch, editor. *Intelligent Information Agents: Agent-Based Information Discovery and Management on the Internet*. Springer-Verlag, Berlin, Germany, 1999.

30. S. Lawrence and C.L. Giles. Accessibility of information on the Web. *Nature*, 400:107–109, July 1999.

31. S. Lowley. The evaluation of WWW search engines. *Journal of Documentation*, 56(2):190–211, 2000.

32. Thelwall. M. Web impact factors and search engine coverage. *Journal of Documentation*, 56(2):185–189, 2000.

33. M. Maudlin. A history of search engines. (visited 4 August 2000), 1998. http://www.wiley.com/compbooks/sonnenreich/history.html,

34. M. Melucci. An evaluation of automatically constructed hypertexts for information retrieval. *Information Retrieval*, 1(1):57–80, 1999.

35. G. Salton. Evaluation problems in interactive information retrieval. Technical Report 69–39, Department of Computer Science, Cornell University, Ithaca, NY, August 1969.

36. G. Salton, J. Allan, C. Buckley, and A. Singhal. Automatic analysis, theme generation, and summarization of machine-readable texts. In M. Agosti and A. Smeaton, editors, *Information retrieval and hypertext*, pages 51–73, 1996.

37. G. Salton and C. Buckley. Term weighting approaches in automatic text retrieval. *Information Processing & Management*, 24(5):513–523, 1988.

38. G. Salton and M.J. McGill. *Introduction to modern Information Retrieval*. McGraw-Hill, New York, NY, 1983.

39. J. Savoy. Citation schemes in hypertext information retrieval. In M. Agosti and A. Smeaton, editors, *Information retrieval and hypertext*, pages 99–116. Kluwer Academic, 1996.

40. A. Smith. A tale of two web spaces: comparing sites using web impact factors. *Journal of Documentation*, 55(5):577–592, 1999.

41. H. Snyder and H. Rosenbaum. Can the search engines be used as tools for web-link analysis? A critical view. *Journal of Documentation*, 55(4):375–384, 1999.

42. J. Tague-Sutcliffe. The pragmatics of Information Retrieval experimentation, revisited. *Information Processing & Management*, 28(4):467–490, 1992.

43. *Proceedings of TREC-9*, 2000. Forthcoming.

44. C.J. van Rijsbergen. *Information Retrieval*. Butterworths, London, second edition, 1979.

Information Retrieval and Structured Documents

Yves Chiaramella

CLIPS Laboratory
BP 53. 38041 Grenoble Cedex 6—France
chiara@imag.fr

Abstract Standard Information Retrieval considers documents as *atomic* units of information that are indexed and retrieved as a whole. Modern evolution of document design and storage have since a long time introduced more elaborate representations of documents; standards such as SGML, then HTML and now XML are of course major contributions in this domain. These standards underly today evolutions towards modern electronic documents. In this context, retrieving structured documents refers to index and retrieve information according to a given structure of documents. This means that documents are no longer considered as atomic entities, but as aggregates of interrelated objects that can be retrieved separately: given a retrieval query, one may retrieve the set of document *components* that are most relevant to this query.

In this chapter we shall first emphasise some aspects which, in our opinion, relate explicit use of document structure to interactive retrieval performances, such as efficiency while browsing or querying information. In a second step we shall investigate two classes of implementation approaches dealing with indexing and retrieving structured documents: passage retrieval and explicit use of hierarchical structures of documents.

1 Introduction

Information Retrieval is by now mainly based on man-machine interaction, and this aspect has grown more and more important, following the extraordinary fast development of network communication. Even being a domain expert, one cannot pretend to solve an information retrieval problem in a single step of issuing a query and observing the corresponding system response; most probably, one will have to enter an iterative process which can be described as in Fig. 1 below, where tasks in shadowed boxes correspond to users tasks, and the others to system tasks. This simplified schema illustrates how main user and system tasks are intertwinned while retrieving information. Depending on the user's expertise this often results in a (possibly) long interactive process called a *retrieval session* delimited in Fig. 1 by the "begin" and "end" symbols. Every step in this iterative process involves defining a command, issuing it to the system, and evaluating its result in terms of document relevance.

M. Agosti, F. Crestani, and G. Pasi (Eds.): ESSIR 2000, LNCS 1980, pp. 286–309, 2000.

However, in our opinion, the essence of "interactive retrieval" lies in the constant adjustment between the "answer evaluation" and the "command reformulation" tasks to achieve user satisfaction. Answer evaluation occurs when the user learns from the system about existing documents and their indexing (or content). This operation directly confronts *standard* system relevance with *particular* user relevance. Command reformulation occurs when the system is redirected from user's relevance assessments; this may be extended to system learning when using *relevance feedback* techniques which enable automatic reformulation of queries from relevance assessments.

Then talking about "interactive information retrieval" seems somewhat redundant; surprisingly enough, and with the noticeable exception of the many studies on relevance feedback, research in the domain of IR has mainly concentrated on retrieval and indexing models, and has comparatively paid marginal attention to its interactive nature.

In the following discussion we shall discuss some about retrieval performances and structured documents or, said in other words, why indexing and accessing document components may help improving retrieval performances. In section 2 we briefly elaborate on querying and browsing, as basic retrieval techniques, and we emphasise on their dual advantages and limitations. Section 3 shows why ignoring the underlying structure of electronic documents leads to less efficient retrieval performances because of less efficient interaction and negative impact on document ranking.

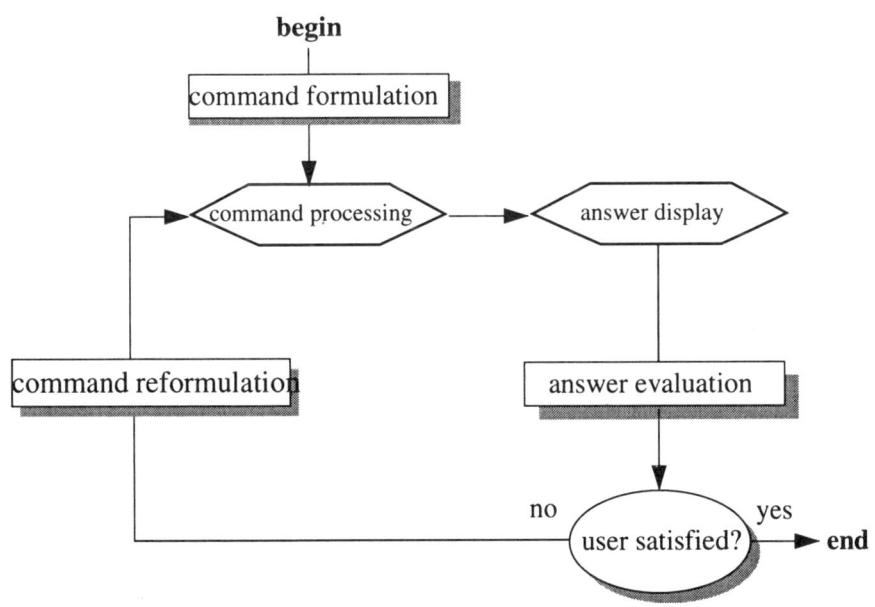

Figure 1. The Iterative Process of Information Retrieval.

The three remaining sections present models for indexing and retrieving structured documents. Section 4 describes a first class of approaches which views documents (mainly textual documents at the moment) as sequences of *passages* related to various topics. Section 5 presents the main aspects of a model integrating IR querying systems and hypermedia browsing. (for more details one can see [5, 6, 17]). This approach is based on a unified view of knowledge (see [16]) which puts an explicit emphasis on the notion of structured document, and investigates its impact on retrieval processes and effectiveness.

In section 6 we present some strategies for indexing structured documents, based on their hierarchical logical structure. As a natural complement the section also describes an algorithms which makes full use of this indexing strategy for retrieving document components which are most specific to queries.

2   Querying vs Browsing: Two Interaction Modes

Starting from a previous study [7] our goal here is to address some aspects of interactive retrieval which we think are much important considering retrieval performances.

Most standard Information Retrieval systems (IRS) provide powerful and effective access-by-content processes based on *queries*, a feature which bounds users to a specific way to interact with the computer. In terms of interaction, querying requires a specific kind of expertise from the users who have to master the index language which describes the content of the stored documents, and the query languages of the systems. More important, and going back to the iterative schema of Fig. 1, commands in this case are queries only. This is a strong feature which in turn implies properties in terms of man-machine interaction: for each query Q_i the system provides as an answer a set of documents R_i, and the user cannot "see" anything else than this set of documents. Said in other words, each system response R_i is like a "window" opened by the query on the document space. Acquiring new documents may be done only by issuing a new query Q_{i+1} which in turn defines a new "window" R_{i+1} on the corpus, as illustrated by the white circle in Fig. 2.

At time t_i the user can only view documents in R_i while at time t_{i+1} he/she again can only view documents in R_{i+1}, the other documents (shown in the gray area) remaining not accessible. The interactive search may then be viewed as a process of moving a variable size window around the document space. In terms of interaction, one see then that the main problem is about how to formulate Q_{i+1} from Q_i to improve the answer in an expected way.

Depending on user's expertise and on the complexity of his information problem, there may be a considerable cognitive effort required to properly infer Q_{i+1} from Q_i and relevance judgements on R_i. Reducing this effort is the goal of *relevance feedback* techniques. On the other hand there is almost nothing like disorientation problems in a querying session, mostly because the user is permanently asked to make explicit his information need via queries: querying can hardly be random searching.

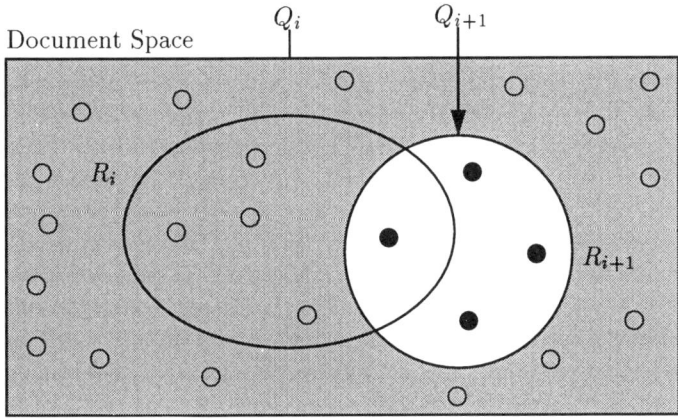

Figure 2. Querying Opens "windows" in the Document Space.

However, a certain form of disorientation may occur in situations where users do not understand why certain documents appear in query responses: the users then lose the relationship they have established in their mind between the query semantic and the semantic content of retrieved documents. Such situations occur mostly when users have not enough expertise about the system (its query language, its index language and indexing process), or when they face some system limitations such as bad handling of keyword polysemy. This type of disorientation makes the task "query reformulation" much harder because one have first to diagnose why the system response was unexpected, and second to solve the problem by choosing other terms for his query. This may also include the redesign of complex query structures whenever the query language has this feature, like for example Boolean expressions. This added difficulty obviously increases the cognitive load of the user and hence decreases the interactive qualities of the system.

This particular problem may be solved by incorporating *explanatory capabilities* in IR systems: the systems should be able to explain, at any moment, *why* a particular document has been retrieved as a relevant answer to the user's query.

This is an important aspect in the improvement of interactive information retrieval. Despite all possible improvements of index languages and indexing processes, misleading data ambiguities will never be completely eliminated. This somehow pessimistic assertion is even enforced when considering the volume, complexity and heterogeneity of currently accessed information (particularly on the Web) which all together make such an ideal even more remote at practical level.

Thus, if studies have to be developed towards enhanced index languages and corresponding indexing techniques, efforts must also be aimed towards much better explanatory capabilities for IR systems. Improved visualisation interfaces are proposed as possible contributions to solve this problem (see [14, 22, 30] for example).

Hypermedia environments, and particularly the Web, have widely demonstrated their ability for organising, storing and accessing multimedia information. Users of such systems can browse across several predefined paths (links) to access information which is organised into storage units (browsing nodes). These environments are user-friendly, provide nice interfaces and require no *a priori* particular system expertise from the user. In terms of interaction, a pure browsing session lets the user access virtually any document (node), based on a set of predefined access links: at any step t_i of the retrieval session, the user may see the content of the current node d_i. Transition to step t_{i+1} from d_i is based on the choice of a proper existing link starting from d_i. Thus, considering again Fig. 1, the command here is basically a click on an anchor, and a retrieval session is an access path followed by the user in a complex graph of hyperbase links. There is virtually no notion of "window" here, as we had in querying systems; the only potential limitation of a browsing session is, from a given starting point in the hyperbase, the connective component of the hyperbase to which this starting node belongs (represented by the white area in Fig. 3 below).

Experience has demonstrated since a long time that, in general, extensive browsing has its own limitations: in the context of large, complex hyperbases this approach for retrieving information supposes a lot of time-consuming search by try-and-error, and users often have to face problem of *disorientation* [13, 28]. After a while they may be lost in the network and need to know where they are, where to go to resume an effective browsing, and how to be properly relocated in the hyperbase. Orientation problems may be worsened by cycles and multiple access paths to nodes.

Users are also prone to face the problem of *cognitive overload*. Figure 3 below illustrates the browsing process: moving from d_i to d_{i+1} requires a selection among n anchors that are offered in d_i. Whenever $n > 1$ choices seem relevant, the user has to stack in his memory the $n - 1$ promising choices not tried at this time, and proceed further with the current choice.

Note that not only the alternate paths have to be memorised, but also the reason why these particular paths were considered of potential interest during some previous steps of the retrieval session. This amount of knowledge grows exponentially with the length of the browsing path and the average arity of the nodes (i.e. their average number of starting links).

When considering browsing and querying as interactive processes, one can see that their mutual advantages and drawbacks are quite complementary: in terms of orientation and cognitive load problems, and in terms of bound or free access to documents. This advocates for the integration of such environments: whenever the user feels uncomfortable using one modality of interaction, he/she may then switch to the other one and resume the search.

Of course, this idea of combining the two modalities is not new, and the numerous examples of the Web with its retrieval engines offering browsing and querying facilities is illustrative in itself. What we are underlining here with

Document Space

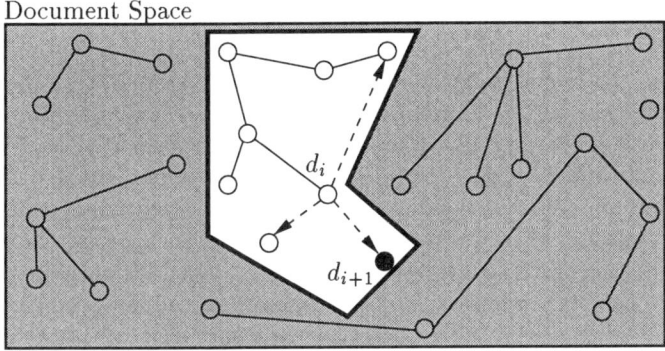

Figure 3. Browsing Gives Virtually Free Access to the Complete Graph of Linked Nodes

others (see for example [1, 9–11]) is that a real *integration* is needed, not only a *combination*. Considering again the popular example of search engines available on the Web, they all combine querying and browsing but are not based on a real integration of these two paradigms; a simple evidence of this fact lies in the extreme limitation of query languages about structural information such as links, attributes etc. In our opinion, the consideration of structured document and its impact on interaction discussed in the next section give further arguments in favour of this integration.

3   Querying and Browsing: The Impact of Structure

After considering the duality of querying and browsing one may consider as in [5, 6] the complementarities of the corresponding IR and hypermedia models considering the notion of structured information. Hypermedia systems manage highly structured information while standard IR systems deal with mostly atomic information. For example browsing structured documents is natural and easy in hypermedia environments: one can access the *logical structure* of sections, paragraphs using predefined links which implement this hierarchical structure. The user can also browse using cross-reference links, connected documents etc.

Most IR systems ignore this structure: a document is viewed as an atomic entity which is indexed and retrieved *as a whole*. There is nothing like "paragraph retrieval" for example.

This is a considerable limitation which has a direct impact on interactive performances of both querying and browsing:

1. The impact on querying: to cope with interactive retrieval on the network, available retrieval engines are mostly derived from classical IR approaches (i.e. often avatars of the Boolean retrieval model). Except for some specific features related to filtering URLs, these engines mostly ignore the notion of structure, and know only about Web pages as atomic documents. HTML also

ignores the notion of abstraction level and consequently does not allow to define abstract document types. Then, a set of linked pages which, as a whole, constitutes an hypermedia document (e.g. the NASA Web site), cannot be handled at this level of abstraction: it basically remains a set of linked pages which are indexed and retrieved completely independently, as if they were semantically independent documents. This has a number of consequences which virtually all of us have more or less experienced while using retrieval engines. Suppose that given a query Q, and given a proper indexation of web pages, the system retrieves pages p and s that are considered relevant for Q. Then what happens if p is "logically included" in s (i.e. if p is a "subpage" of page s in the abstract logical structure)? The system response presents p and s without mentioning their relationship. Moreover the ranking method of the retrieval engine will rank p and s completely independently, and these pages will most probably be displayed at distant locations in the ordered list of retrieved pages. Then when the user consults this list, two things happen: while consulting page p first (for example), and this page being relevant, he will be tempted to browse also its parent page which is s. Then resuming the consultation of the list of references, he will sometime later be presented again page s. This is purely due to the non consideration of any logical structure linking the Web site, and has a negative impact on cognitive overload, disorientation and consequently on search efficiency.

2. The impact on browsing: the effect of ignoring logical dependence such as the one described above between pages p and s on browsing is mostly about cognitive overload. Whenever a logical structure virtually exists in a hyperbase, it should be made explicit and accessible to the user. This would allow him to quickly master it and hence to understand faster what the "document" is alike and what in its content is most relevant to his information needs. In the contrary, he/she has to somehow re-engineer this structure, which is a quite complex and time consuming task, and has a negative impact on cognitive overload. Other aspects related to "structure" are of importance while browsing. The basic support for browsing being links and anchors, the informative properties of these elements considering *orientation* are obviously important. The availability of link types or anchor types is important for improving browsing performances. Said otherwise, links and anchors are too often misleading compared to user's needs: an anchor word "moon" in a page may either point to a page containing a picture of the moon, or a text about the moon, or both. If the user wants only images of the moon, he has then about a 1/3 chance to get a relevant answer while clicking on this anchor.

3. The impact on document ranking: an important factor of retrieval efficiency is the way the retrieval system displays relevant documents. The most popular way to do so is the linear list of references where retrieved documents are ranked in decreasing order of system relevance. Many such evaluation techniques include term frequency (often noted as tf). Considering atomic documents means that tf_{ij}, accounts for the total number of occurrences of term t_i, in document D_j. Actual definitions of tf (see [26] for example) take

into account the possible differences in document sizes, and include a normalisation that smoothens the impact of document size on values of tf. This in turn helps in computing system relevance values (for example one of the popular $tf.idf$ weighting methods) that are not too distorted by document sizes. Since users are supposed to perform the "evaluation task" of Fig. 1 from top to bottom of the ranked list, rank correctness is of great importance regarding retrieval performance. As an example, one have to remind that rank of retrieved documents is an explicit element when computing recall/precision points (a much standard way of evaluating retrieval performances). One may also add that interactive retrieval is also very sensitive to correct ranking, because rank is directly tied to cognitive effort: the lowest the rank, the lowest the probability that the user will examine the document for relevance assessment, due to cognitive load. One may remember here the classical average of 1 to 2 top-ranked web pages that are effectively considered for examination by web users. Going back to structured documents, let us consider a term t_i having n_{ij} occurrences in document D_j, and tf_{ij} its corresponding (normalised) term frequency. Suppose now that we observe that occurrences of t_i are more concentrated in section (or passage) D_{jk} of D_j. Then computing the term frequency of t_i in D_{jk}, noted tf_{ijk}, based on the same method used for computing tf_{ij}, will most certainly produce values such as $tf_{ijk} > tf_{ij}$ because for (about) the same rough number of occurrences of t_i, the size of D_j is much larger than the size of its section D_{jk}. The consequence is that if a user issues a query using t_i, and if the system was able to retrieve separately D_j and its section D_{jk}, the later (which is probably most relevant because of the higher value of tf_{ijk}) would be ranked first, and the former ranked behind. It should be clear now that whenever relevant information are *located within document components* (as opposed to spread through whole documents), these documents, while relevant, will suffer comparatively lower ranking. This in turn will lead to poorer retrieval performances by any standard.

4. The impact of concentration: whatever the considered access method, and referring to the search session of Fig. 1, one have also to consider the user task of "evaluating the system answer" which is about manual examination of retrieved documents and making decisions about their relevance to the current information need. Efficiency (and sometimes effectiveness) of this critical process depends on the *specificity* of retrieved documents compared to the information need: if a document presents a low concentration of relevant information, it will be much longer and tedious for the user to make the relevance decision (he may in fact abort the process and hence implicitly decide that it is not relevant). On the contrary, a document presenting a high proportion of relevant information will be more quickly and more reliably selected as relevant. Clearly this notion of "concentration" may be related to the notion of document structure, whether it refers to single images, or to sets of web pages like sites, or to upper-level textual structures like chapter or sections. The relationship between document structure and document semantic content is usually significant because one usually structure a doc-

ument according to a given "discourse scheme" (for texts) or "presentation scheme" (for web sites). Then given an information need, one would be tempted to integrate the notion of structure as in improvement both in evaluating system relevance (as considered in the previous section), and in organising system answers: instead of returning document references, the system would return references of *document component*, select and rank them according to concentration of relevant information (i.e. according to their specificity to the information need).

As a consequence of these four aspects (not a limitative list) of human interaction, we may consider that taking into account structure is important for improving overall performance of interactive information retrieval. In the following sections we present some approaches dealing with this problem of retrieving structured documents.

4   Passage Retrieval

The idea of retrieving document components is not at all new, though the motivation and approaches could have been rather different in the past. Retrieving only relevant parts called "passages" of embedding documents is certainly the oldest approach in the domain (see for example papers from John O'Connor [23, 24], some of them dating back to 1972). The underlying principle of passage retrieval is fairly simple: within textual documents, passages are textual sequences of consecutive words presenting some homogeneity about topicality. By "consecutive words" one mean a sequence of words according to the "reading order" of the textual document (i.e. from the first page to the last). Once isolated, passages are then considered as separate documents and indexed and retrieved in much the classical way, based on standard indexing and retrieval models (Boolean, vector space, probabilistic etc.).

According to this approach, documents are viewed as linear sequences of (most often non-overlapping) passages that may or may not exactly coincide with structural units such as paragraphs, chapters or sections. This is for example the case of a model developed by E. Mittendorf and P. Schaüble in 1994 [19]. Because they *a priori* ignore the underlying logical structure of the documents, the main problem here is to find a "good" segmentation of the documents in a sequence of sound passages. Starting from the first word to the latest in every given document, the main questions then are: into how many passages to split the document, and what would be their boundaries within the text?

One may recognise here a problem alike the well-known case of indexing video data: being also basically sequential (one say "continuous") data, and usually not (or loosely) structured at the moment, video data has first to be cut down— or segmented—in segments of so-called "sequences" in the terminology.of video. If finding proper sequencing in videos is still somewhat challenging and a hot topic, the problem of sequencing textual data in passages seems less complex, if not easy, thanks to the fact that natural language is far less ambiguous and complex than pixel areas found in video images.

A classical method for finding passages consists in defining a fixed-length window of n consecutive words, position it at the beginning of a given text, analyse the distribution of words within the window, and then repeat this process at various positions of the window, down to the end of the document. At each step, the window is shifted by a fixed number of s words; most algorithms use slightly overlapping positions of the shifting window to improve performances in detecting passages.

Boundaries of passages are found when, at a given position of the window, a significant change in the distribution of the local vocabulary (as compared to what it was a the previous steps) is observed. Again, this approach reminds of the methods used for segmenting video data; the hypothesis here is that a significant change in the word distribution denotes a change in topicality within the document, and hence that the process is leaving passage n (related to topic n) and is about to enter in passage $n + 1$ which is probably about an other topic. While simple in principle this method needs thorough tuning of key parameters such as window length n, slide step length s etc. It seems obvious that these parameters have to be adapted to various types of documents.

Approaches based on passages but closer to the notion of logical structure were also proposed in the past. As an example F. Burkowski [3] proposed to handle, for every document, multiple lists of non overlapping sequences (passages); the connection with the logical structure being that each list correspondents to a given level in the hierarchical structure (i.e. there was a list for chapters, an other for sections etc.). In the list corresponding to sections for example, segment 1 corresponded to the whole text of section 1 in the document; the principle applies for the lower levels. These lists and their segments are then indexed and segments may be retrieved using a single index of segments combining all levels. Finally it is interesting to notice that passage retrieval is also investigated in the context of interactive retrieval as for example the study from G.V Cormack et al. [8] in the framework of the TREC-6 experiments, based on the Multitext IR system.

This class of approaches clearly presents the advantage of some simplicity, which certainly leads to better efficiency of derived indexing or retrieval algorithms. It has also the advantage of a quite simple application of standard retrieval engines applied on a corpus of passages instead of a corpus of documents. The question of their effectiveness in terms of retrieval performances is still mainly open to large-scale experimentation as undertaken in [8].

On the other hand passage retrieval cannot make full use of the logical structure of documents, as they are defined by document authors. Given their definition, passages may or may not correspond to elements of the logical structure of documents; everything here depends on the ability of the segmentation model to detect proper passage boundaries. And even in this case one can understand that consecutive passage boundaries may correspond to different levels of the logical structure, some corresponding to paragraphs, others to whole chapters or sections. This heterogeneity also depends on the documents themselves, on their size and style (whether or not elements of the document structure correspond to specific discourses characterised by specific term densities). Moreover, passages correspond to sequential (i.e. non hierarchical) static pre-computed segments the size of which cannot be dynamically adapted to specific queries in terms of document specificity (see bullet 4 in section 3 above). In this sense passage retrieval is a simple—of course useful—extension of the standard notion of document corpus; we shall see in section 6 that full use of the logical structure allows a better implementation of this notion of document specificity based on dynamic adjustment of document components to user queries.

5   An Integrated Model

As stated before, a convenient (but not unique) way to tackle the document structure problem, and the need of combining querying and browsing as basic retrieval techniques is to consider the integration of hypermedia and IR models. The model detailed in [16] and more extensively in [5] considers this integration from a unifying point of view *about knowledge*: hypermedia models and IR models deal only with data and indexes, (i.e. knowledge making explicit the useful content of these documents). Domain concepts that describe the semantic content of atomic data (of whatever media) are *content knowledge*, while links connecting these document components are considered as a specific kind of knowledge, also made explicit, named *structural knowledge*. Consider for example a library corpus containing scientific papers, or an office automation corpus containing contracts and letters: in both cases the application deals with types of documents (e.g. SGML or ODA types) and cross-reference links between these documents. Document types constitute *structural knowledge*, while the set of concepts that are used to index them constitute the *content knowledge* of the retrieval system. Browsing and querying in both applications require explicit references to document types, links, index languages etc. One may now consider *system knowledge* as the union of content and structural knowledge.

5.1   The Hypermedia Component

The use of explicit knowledge in hypermedia systems is not recent [2,18,20]. Most of these approaches aimed to integrate hypermedia with database systems. Many studies were also developed to model hypermedia itself [12,25]. The hypermedia model described here is based on the classical two-level organisation of *hyperindex* and *hyperbase* [1,28]:

1. **The hyperindex** contains *structural knowledge* needed to define structures in the hyperbase (all navigation links are part of this knowledge), and *content knowledge* needed to index documents, or hyperdocuments. The main role of the hyperindex is to provide a thematic reference that users can consult to orient themselves (or reorient when they are disoriented—one say "lost"—in the hyperbase). The hyperindex is also used to help users starting (or resuming) a browsing session from relevant nodes in the hyperbase

(*beam down* function). It helps users formulating their needs in a more complete and precise way, much in the same way as in IR environments where users consult online thesaurii as a help for issuing queries (or here prior to "beam down" into the hyperbase). When users are lost in the hyperbase, they can conversely "beam up" into the hyperindex to reorient themselves in finding more relevant concepts. An advantage of the integration is that users may then use the hyperindex either in the context of a browsing session as described above, or for formulating IR queries (hyperindex nodes are then index terms).

2. **The hyperbase** contains all the hyperdocuments and links which implement their logical structure and which allow navigation among—and within—hyperdocuments. Important here is the notion of abstraction: the model includes abstraction levels ranging from single media (i.e. atomic) nodes, to structured objects, and then to hyperdocuments. This notion has already been introduced in the domain of hypermedia and is undoubtedly a powerful help for the users who may consider the highly structured data stored in the hyperbase using views ranging from atomic to highly aggregative levels. In the proposed model these abstraction levels correspond to structural knowledge; they also allow retrieval (i.e. querying) at any of these abstraction levels. This means that documents are no longer considered as atomic entities by the retrieval system: answers to a query may contain any kind of component of the logical structure of documents. As discussed later (see section 6 below), and unlike in passage retrieval (as described in section 4 above), this implies a major revision of classical indexing and retrieval strategies.

This integrated view of a hypermedia system allows users to issue queries combining *content* and *structure* as parts of the needed information. For example, one can issue a query aimed to retrieve all "medical reports" that are about "lung cancer" and which are "illustrated by images of a given type" (X-ray etc.). I this query "lung cancer" is the topic assigned to retrieve medical reports (i.e. textual information) while "X-ray images" refers to a particular type of images. The expression "illustrated by" refers to links that relate both kinds of data in the hyperbase. As a consequence the answers to such a query will be *structured objects* extracted from the hyperbase, the structure and the content of which having to match the requirements stated by the query. Following the first approach presented in [17] Sowa's Conceptual Graphs [27] were used as an unifying formalism to represent both content knowledge and structural knowledge.

5.2   The IR Component

IR models contain four major components which are: a document model, a query model, a matching function which compares queries to documents, and a knowledge base. This last component is a generic definition of the reference knowledge mentioned before, which is used for indexing the hyperbase documents. The identification and the extraction of implicit knowledge from rough information is the essential task of the *indexing process*: knowledge embedded, say within natural language sentences of a text, is said to be implicit because accessible, or usable, by the retrieval process only at a signal level (word or character string matching in this case). Implicit knowledge is low-level, ambiguous and is one on the main causes of poor retrieval performances (albeit its advantage lies in simplicity and low computing complexity). The indexing process is then said to make this knowledge explicit because it will identify, disambiguate and represent this knowledge in a way that is usable in a non ambiguous way by the user and the system.

Many knowledge representation formalisms are available; conceptual graphs for example may be used for representing structural and content knowledge. This knowledge is then entirely manageable using the four basic operators on graphs and the projection operator. This means first that the notions of "document" and of "document index" have now deeply changed from their classical definition in IR:

 – as needed, documents are no longer atomic units. One may index and retrieve entities belonging to various abstraction levels. According to this, the notion of corpus also changes: it becomes now the set of all structural units that are instances of the predefined abstraction levels.
 – "document indexes" encompass now structural and content knowledge.

Example:

This is a model of an hyperdocument #1, where both structural ("contains" relation) and content knowledge ("is-about" relation) are represented. In this simplified representation of a (hierarchical) logical structure based on conceptual graphs, the ⇒ symbol stands for the conceptual relation "is-about", and → stands for the conceptual relation "contains" (as in [5]):

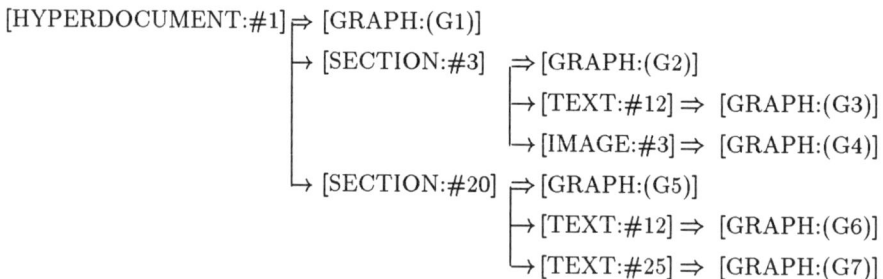

Figure 4. An Example of Hyperdocument.

In the formalism of conceptual graphs, abstraction levels of the document structure (instances of which are structural units) are represented by specific concept types like HYPERDOCUMENT, SECTION etc. All structural units of the hyperdocument may be indexed, and individual indexes are themselves represented by conceptual graphs of type GRAPH, used as referents $G1, G2, \ldots, G7$

in the right side of "is-about" relations. $G1, G2$ etc. contain index expressions describing the semantic content of the corresponding units.

The model allows to complete this representation by adding attribute values, internal references between nodes of the document, external references towards nodes of other documents, links to classes etc. There is virtually no limitation about the representation of such structural knowledge using conceptual graphs. It is worth noticing that this flexibility and expressivity in the representation of structured information is compatible with standards such as SGML, HTML, or XML: it is feasible to design structure translators (i.e. compilers) that transform the representation of a structured document from one formalism to the other.

One question arising at this step is the underlying methods, or strategies, that could be used to assign actual values to $G1, G2, \ldots, G7$. This is the problem of indexing structured information which is discussed in the next section.

6 Indexing and Retrieving the Hyperbase

6.1 Introduction

Several problems have to be solved to achieve this proper indexing of structured documents. The first one lies in the definition of index units—or structural unit types that are individually indexed and then retrieved—among the set of all component types of the structured documents. The second problem lies in the relationship between linked nodes considering their content (and hence their index). Then the third problem is the definition of the index language itself.

- We call index units structural units that are assigned an explicit representation of their semantic content, and hence are individually retrievable from
  content queries. The choice of the proper subset of such units is related to
  the notion of informative units, or units that bear self-explaining information from the users' point of view. Let us consider the case of an atomic unit
  (a terminal node) associated to a graphic. This data can be self-explaining
  for example if it consists in a histogram showing the annual gross benefit
  of a company between years 1970 and year 1995 (provided of course that
  the graphic contains the proper textual captions and title). A graphic representing a curve with label G on y coordinates axis, and f as the label of
  its x coordinate axis, and entitled "Variations of Gain with Frequency for
  solution 3" is probably not self-explaining, because one do not know what
  gain, what frequency it is about, and what is "solution 3." Clearly this unit,
  if presented to users, has to be displayed jointly with some textual node that
  explains these notions. Thus while the first example may correspond to an
  index unit, the second will most probably not. Such granularity choices are
  then directed by application requirements about the types of units to be
  managed and by the typology of users (i.e. are they knowledgeable enough
  about the application domain to properly interpret any informative node?).
  Once these choices are made, one have to remember that the user will always

be able, if needed, to browse from retrieved index units in the hyperbase using structural links starting from these nodes. This is a clear advantage of combining querying and browsing in a single model.

- Assuming that the previous problem is solved, we may now observe that the semantic content of different units may not be independent. This is particularly obvious in the case of linked nodes. What is the incidence of a referenced informative unit on the content of the referencing unit, for example? Or, for textual documents, what is the contribution of a sub-section on the content of its embedding section? This kind of problem has not been paid extensive studies, though several researches are more or less related to this problem (e.g. one can mention here the numerous investigations aimed to evaluate the impact of citations and bibliographical references on retrieval performances).

- The definition of the index language has to fulfil two main requirements: due to the explosion of the corpus size (a set of index units as defined above) it must allow the definition of precise concepts to improve precision (i.e. to avoid ambiguities in the expression of information needs, and to improve the discrimination power of index terms) but it has also to allow inferences to improve recall when needed. For these reasons we think that the indexing language has to be based on explicit knowledge representation, instead of implicit knowledge representation such as natural language. This is of course an additional justification for our choice of conceptual graphs as the basis of the index language.

6.2   Index Units

Let us consider the logical structure of a document, which is generally defined as a hierarchy of abstraction levels ranging from the notion of hyperdocument down to the level of atomic (usually single-media) components. We may define within this structure a maximal index level and a minimal index level which respectively correspond, for every document of this type, to the largest and smallest types of index units. This idea has been proposed and successfully experimented within the IOTA project [15].

The figure illustrates a general situation where the maximal level of index unit does not correspond to the document level. This means that a document as a whole will never be retrieved using content-based queries. Examples of such situations occur for highly structured documents such as an encyclopedia where one could decide that returning say, volume references as answers would not be very helpful (i.e. focused enough) for the users. On the other hand, the minimal level of index unit does not correspond here to the minimal abstraction level either. This means that, for this type of document, such units are not considered— as discussed above—enough informative from an average user's point of view. As discussed in the previous section, users getting such units as answers would almost unavoidably have to browse within their embedding subsections to understand what they are about.

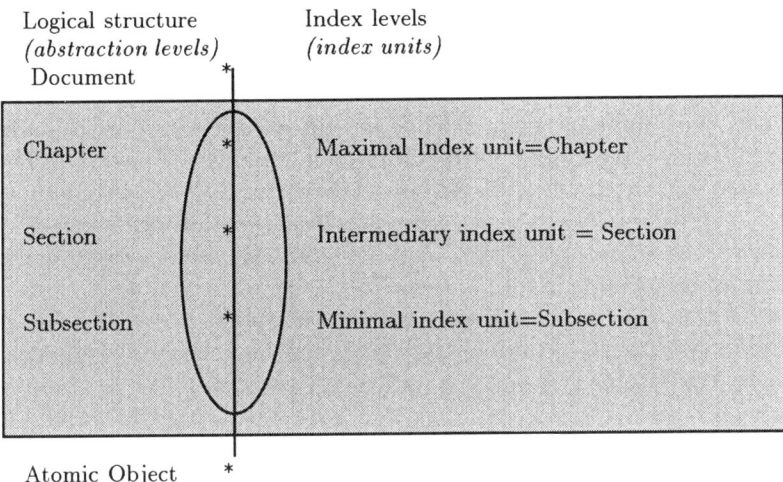

Figure 5. Hierarchy of Index Units and Structural Units.

As a consequence, one may state that the hierarchy of index units (circled in the example of Fig. 5) is isomorphic to a subset of the hierarchy of the abstraction levels.

Let us concentrate now on the problem of indexing using this schema. Like in the IOTA project the indexing strategy proposed for hierarchical structures is ascending: the process starts from the atomic objects and, from indexes assigned to these nodes, calculates the indexes of upper-level nodes. The figure below summarises the principle: once the index units have been defined according to the type of structure (maximum and minimum levels), this schema is instantiated on every document N_i of this type. Here according to the particular structure of document N1 the index units $U_{i1}, \ldots, U_{i7}$ are defined. Index values will be assigned to the corresponding nodes $N_{i1}, \ldots, N_{i7}$, and only to them. According to the definition of index units, the index relation IR associating index expressions to structural units is restricted to index units.

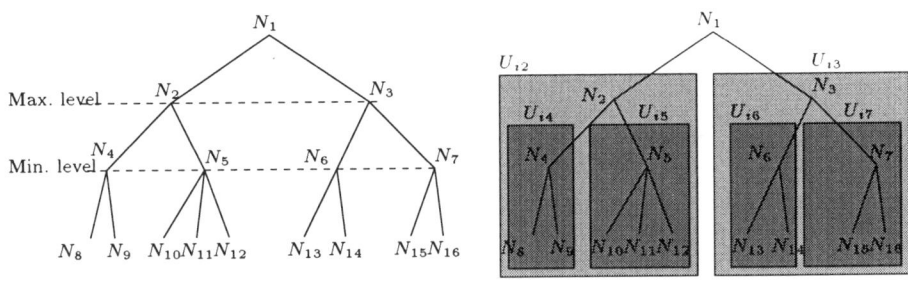

Figure 6. Indexing Structured Documents.

We suppose that a function I is available for indexing the leaf nodes (all single-media nodes) of the logical structure: $I : C_{BI} \rightarrow .I_L$ where C_{BI} is the set of minimal index units (a subset of the structural units C_B) and I_L is the index language. This function will not be detailed here; it is based on available processes used for indexing specific media such as text fragments, images etc. The assumption here is that there is a unique index language I_L. Starting from these original index expressions, the process recursively *evaluates* index expressions of parent nodes (i.e. in an ascending way), and *assigns* these values *only* to nodes corresponding to index units of $C_{BI} \subseteq C_B$.

In a general way, the index expression $g_i \in I_L$ assigned to node $N_i \in C_{BI}$ is recursively calculated as $\neg(N_i)$ from the index expressions g_{ij} of its n component nodes N_{ij} (see Fig. 7 below):

- $\neg(N_i) = \neg(N_{i1}) \oplus \neg(N_{i2}) \oplus \cdots \oplus \neg(N_{in}) = g_{i1} \oplus g_{i2} \oplus \cdots \oplus g_{in} = g_i \in I_L$
- If N_{ij} is an atomic node, then $\neg(N_{ij}) = I(N_{ij})$

Let us discuss now the definition of index expression g_i and hence the semantics of the $\oplus$ operator. Several indexing strategies can be considered here while defining this operator. We shall limitate ourselves here to the one corresponding to an aggregative interpretation of the "contains" links implementing the hierarchy of the logical structure. This corresponds to the intuitive idea that if a structural unit D_i contains n sub-units D_{ij}, then the index expression assigned to D_i must contain some aggregation of the information describing the content of all its sub-units D_{ij}.

At this step of the presentation we may notice that this aggregation function can several definitions according to the model chosen for representing document content:

1. Index expressions as sets of keywords: this may apply to many simple models where documents are modelled as sets of keywords. In this case the index expression g_i would be the union of the index expressions of all sub-units D_{ij}, and $\oplus$ would simply correspond to the set union operator.
2. Index expressions as conjunctions of keywords: this would apply to Boolean modelling of document content, an other popular model among available retrieval engines (particularly on the web). In this case, each indexing expression is considered as a conjunction of keywords, and g_i would be the Boolean conjunction of the index expressions of all sub-units Dij, and $\oplus$ would simply correspond to the "and" Boolean operator.
3. Index expressions as conceptual graphs: this approach of aggregated indexes corresponds to the construction of a new graph G_i combining the given graphs g_{ij} without loss of information. The minimal expression of this new notion is given whenever we can achieve the simultaneous join of as many as possible concepts and relations from the given CGs. This is precisely the so-called notion of *maximal join* (part of the conceptual graph algebra) which produces from these graphs their *maximal common specialisation*. Thus, given this aggregative indexing strategy, the maximal join is a good choice

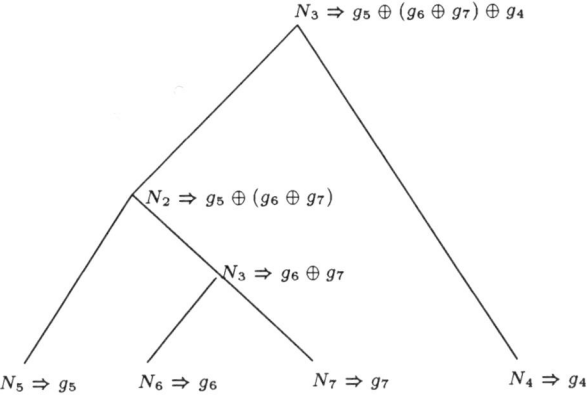

$$N_3 \Rightarrow g_5 \oplus (g_6 \oplus g_7) \oplus g_4$$

$$N_2 \Rightarrow g_5 \oplus (g_6 \oplus g_7)$$

$$N_3 \Rightarrow g_6 \oplus g_7$$

$$N_5 \Rightarrow g_5 \qquad N_6 \Rightarrow g_6 \qquad N_7 \Rightarrow g_7 \qquad N_4 \Rightarrow g_4$$

Figure 7. Ascending Aggregation of Index Expressions.

for the $\oplus$ operator applied to conceptual graphs, because optimal in terms of redundancy.

One could notice that we did not mention anything about weighting methods until now; in general terms, assignation of weights to indexing units follows the same ascending propagation strategy defined for aggregating index expressions. We may in fact consider an extended definition $\otimes$ of the aggregation function, which computes weighted index expressions noted $(g_i, w_i) \in I_L \times W$, where W stands for the set of weight values w_i:

1.

$$\neg(N_i) = \neg(N_{i1}) \otimes \neg(N_{i2}) \otimes \cdots \otimes \neg(N_{in})$$
$$= (g_{i1}, w_{i1}) \otimes (g_{i2}, w_{i2}) \otimes \cdots \otimes (g_{in}, w_{in}) = (g_i, w_i) \in I_L \times W$$
where:
$$g_i = g_{i1} \oplus g_{i2} \oplus \cdots \oplus g_{in} = g_i \in I_L \text{(as before), and}$$
$$w_i = w_{i1} \Psi w_{i2} \Psi \ldots \Psi w_{in} \in W$$
where Ψ is the aggregation function for weights

2. if N_{ij} is an atomic node, then $\neg(N_{ij}) = I(N_{ij}) = (g_i, w_i) \in I_L \in W$

We shall not elaborate much on the definition of function Ψ for aggregating weights. It seems enough to say here that it may be defined as an extension of some basic weighting function, according to the ascending propagation of content within the logical structure.

6.3   Attributes

Attributes usually correspond to properties assigned to elements of the logical structure (e.g. structural object U_i has author "Smith"). When considering structured documents, one have to address the problem of possible propagation of these properties among related structural units of the logical structure. If we consider for example the case of attribute *Author*, and given an assigned value of this attribute to a structural object U_i, an intuitive assumption is that this property applies to all component objects U_{ij} of U_i (if any). The above notion of "dynamic indexing" then seems to be extendible to the broader notion of *attribute propagation*.

Of course the reality is more complex: there are multi-author documents (e.g. conference proceedings, encyclopediae etc.), and the inheritance mechanism of attribute *Author* in the logical structure is in fact not so obvious. Because retrieval may include constraints on attribute values, it is important to integrate such capabilities in a model aimed to proper retrieval of structured document. To address this problem one may consider *attribute classes* defined by a common behaviour about *inheritance of attribute values* in the logical structure. Considering the extreme variety of attributes that can be defined in actual applications, it is of course difficult to foresee a complete classification; we shall then limitate ourselves to three broad classes which encompass most of the cases. In the following discussion we use α as a metasymbol for any attribute name.

1. Dynamic Attributes: these attributes propagate their values in the logical structure. This means that if some attribute α of this sort has a defined value v for a given structural object U_i (noted $\alpha(U_i) = v$), one may infer the values of attribute α for some other structural objects U_j related to U_i in the logical structure: $\alpha(U_j) = f(v)$, where $f(v)$ symbolises this dependency of values. Modelling this class of attributes then implies the definition of a *propagation condition* (i.e. in which condition attribute values may propagate), and an *assignation operation* (i.e. how propagated values apply to related structural objects). We consider here two subclasses of Dynamic Attributes: Descending Dynamic Attributes and Ascending Dynamic Attributes.

   (a) Descending Dynamic Attributes (DDA): considering the hierarchy of the logical structure, these attributes propagate values from top to bottom; the assignation mechanism is here an operator which computes the attribute values of component units U_{ij} of U_i; we note it $\oplus_\alpha$. An example of this type of attribute is *Publication-Date*, the value of which applies to every component of a document. In this case, the operator $\oplus_\alpha$ is simply *Copy*.

   (b) Ascending Dynamic Attributes (ADA): these attributes propagate values from bottom to the top of the logical structure. The assignation affects the attribute value of parent-components; the operator $\oplus_\alpha$ corresponds here to some aggregation the definition of which depends on the considered attribute α. An example of such attributes is *Author*: if two distinct components U_{i1} and U_{i2} of a single structural object U_i are assigned different author names $n1$ and $n2$, then the inferred value of *Author* for U_i is some aggregation of the two author names chosen to model the notion of co-authoring (for example a set: $\{n1, n2\}$).

2. Static Attributes: static attributes do not propagate their values in the logical structure; they correspond to properties that remain purely local to the structural object they are assigned to. An example of such attributes is *Title* which applies to a structural object, but neither to its possible components nor to its parents in the logical structure. Note that this does not prevent several related structural units to share the same title; this may occur if these components have been assigned the same title for some reason, but is not due to inheritance of attribute values.

As detailed in [6], this generalisation to attribute values provides a convenient way to model the indexing of structured multimedia data: indexing structural units may be viewed as the computation of a particular Dynamic Ascendant Attribute named *Content*, the values of which are expressions of the index language I_L. However this model is still limited to hierarchically structured documents; though covering a particular case of practical importance, this model has still to be extended to more general structures.

6.4   The Matching Function

The matching function is central to IR models in that it implements the notion of system relevance: given a query and a corpus, every document will be retrieved and ranked according to this definition. The model given in the previous section for indexing structured documents allows for many strategies dealing with as many definitions of indexing languages and aggregation functions to be applied to the *Content* attribute. We already mentioned the case of conceptual graphs and sets of keywords; one may see that Boolean or vector space models could also be applied to this general strategy of dynamic ascendant aggregation. As an illustration we shall consider a matching function based on Van Rijsbergen's *uncertain implication* definition for document relevance; according to this approach, relevance of document D to a query Q is related to the certainty of D logically implying Q, noted $P(D \rightarrow Q)$ [29].

Based on our previous choice about modelling queries Q and documents D by Conceptual Graphs (CGs), on may then use the semantics of CGs, which relate them to first order logic. The CG theory tells that any graph G has a unique interpretation in terms of a 1st-order logic predicate, given by $\Phi(G)$. Considering the implication $D \rightarrow Q$, on have here to rely primarily on material implication between 1st-order predicates associated to graphs D and Q; this logical implication is then equivalent to $\Phi(D) \supset \Phi(Q)$. The CG theory also tells that this implication holds whenever there exist a *projection* of Q into D or said, in other words, $D \leq Q$. This means that Q is a subgraph of D, modulo possible restrictions (according to given concept and relation type lattices) on concept and relation of D and Q [4, 27]. There is no room here to elaborate further on the various possibilities opened by CGs to implement more sophisticated matching functions, and particularly about dealing with CGs and uncertainty (hence about designing some matching function of the type $P(\Phi(D) \supset \Phi(Q))$)— see for example [31].

Returning to our main focus about retrieving structured documents, we consider now how this logic-based model can be extended to fulfil some of our previously stated goals, and particularly the notion of document *specificity* to a query. Following Nie's statement [21] about the interpretation of the direct implication between D and Q and its reciprocal, one may think at an interesting extension of the model: "given a query Q and a document D, the matching R between D and Q is determined by a function F of the *exhaustivity* of the document about the query (measured by $D \rightarrow Q$) and the *specificity* of the document about the query (measured by $Q \rightarrow D$):

$$R(D,Q) = F[P_K(D \rightarrow Q), P'_K(Q \rightarrow D)]$$

where P_K, P'_K are two functions that measure the implications uncertainty, F is a function combining the two implications and K expresses that these implications are evaluated according to knowledge K which includes domain knowledge and knowledge about the user." Exhaustivity refers to the *complete* fulfilment of a query by a document (the document satisfies any stated criteria), while Specificity refers to the fact that the document fulfils *only* these constraints. In [5] we have described an algorithm which makes use of the direct and reciprocal implications to retrieve, given a query Q, all index units U_i such that:

$U_i \rightarrow Q$ (exhaustivity of U_i) and
there is no component unit U_{ij} of U_i such as $Q \rightarrow U_{ij}$
(maximal specificity of U_i)

The algorithm proceeds in two steps:

1. **Fetch:** selection of all upper-level indexing units U_i satisfying $U_i \rightarrow Q$. This retrieval phase is much the same as those performed by standard retrieval systems: documents are selected as atomic entities, based on their complete content (as defined at the upper indexing level by the aggregation mechanism).

2. **Browse:** among the fetched documents U_i, the algorithm tries to select the indexing units U_{ij} that are most specific to the query Q. The reverse implication $Q \rightarrow U_{ij}$ is used ad a test—or filter—about document specificity. Why $Q \rightarrow U_{ij}$ may be used as a test about specificity may be better understood using an example. If we consider the case of the Boolean model, then an indexing U_{ij} unit having $t1 \wedge t2$ as its indexing expression will be considered too specific for a query such as $Q = t_1 \wedge t_2 \wedge t_3$ which corresponds to the case where $Q \supset U_{ij}$ (here the implication $\rightarrow$ is the material implication $\supset$). Hence the inverse condition $\neg(Q \supset U_{ij})$ denotes a situation where the indexing unit is not specific to the query.

1. Recursion condition: $U_{ij} \rightarrow Q$ and $\neg(Q \rightarrow U_{ij})$ this condition allows the algorithm to skip indexing units which are exhaustive to the query ($U_{ij} \rightarrow Q$) but not specific to the query ($\neg(Q \rightarrow U_{ij})$). This is the essence of browsing the logical structure, looking for a component unit which is as specific as possible to the query.

2. Stop condition: the stop condition is obtained by negating the recursion condition; this gives $\neg(U_{ij} \to Q)$ or $(U_{ij} \to Q$ and $U_{ij} \to Q)$

3. The second part of the condition $(U_{ij} \to Q$ and $U_{ij} \to Q)$ is the ideal case where and are logically equivalent. Though possible, one can understand that this condition corresponding to an exact match will occur rarely in real application.

4. The first part of the condition $(\neg(U_{ij} \to Q))$ is the most likely stop case for the browsing algorithm. It occurs when the considered indexing unit U_{ij}, component of its embedding indexing unit U_i, is too specific for Q (U_{ij} is not exhaustive for Q). Then the proposed best approximation for Q will be U_i, the embedding indexing unit, instead of U_{ij}. In this sense, the proposed answer is something alike the smallest majorant of Q, considering the specificity of indexing units.

All the retrieved U_{ij} are then the smallest indexing units of the logical structure which satisfy the query. Other strategies could have been defined in selecting what are considered as the best level of retrieved units in the logical structure; also, a different algorithm than the above described "fetch and browse" algorithm could have been designed to retrieve exactly the same units. The point here was to illustrate how indexing strategy (here the ascending aggregation of indexing expressions) may allow effective retrieval of specific document components. It has been shown that this algorithm works iff, for every U_i and for every of its component units U_{ij} the following condition holds: $\neg(U_i) \to \neg(U_{ij})$. This is an additional constraint that has to be fulfilled by the aggregation operator $\oplus$ discussed above.

This kind of approach allows to avoid the redundancies in system responses discussed in section 3, and consequently to limitate their negative impact on interaction performances.

7 Conclusion

In this paper we have discussed several issues about the impact of structured data on interaction performances while querying or browsing data. We have attempted to demonstrate how critical this issue is, and to what extent it justifies attempts to design more advanced models integrating browsing and querying facilities. We have illustrated this discussion with a brief presentation of an example of such integrated model. An important point was the use of document structure to help focusing system's responses to the best fitting document units (best fit being related to the notion of specificity of the document component to the query). In this process we have also seen that the problem of indexing strategies for structured information is critical for the design of such retrieval strategies. Through the same example have also seen that logic-based approaches (here based on conceptual graphs) allow for high-level, powerful retrieval and indexing strategies that may take full advantage of structures, based on a unified vision of structural and domain knowledge.

However, whether based on explicit use of logical structure or based on passage retrieval, retrieval models dealing with structured document are still experimental and lack extensive experimentation on large collections. In particular is remains difficult to compare them at qualitative level because one still lack experimental methodology an corresponding test collections to do so.

Further developments in the field are challenging at research level and of great practical importance; examples of this kind are the processing of uncertain data, the integration of multimedia data and the consideration of more general cases than the hierarchical structure considered here.

Despite this, the fast growing context of multimedia databases, the impact of the Web and its hundreds of millions of interlinked pages and the availability of international standards such as XML, HTML etc. make more and more valuable and urgent to fully address this problem of making full use of explicit structural knowledge to improve interactive retrieval performances.

References

1. M. Agosti, R. Colotti, and G. Gradenigo. *A Tow-Level Hypertext Retrieval Model for Legal Data*. ACM, 1991, p. 316–325.
2. B. Amann, M. Scholl. *GRAM: A graph model and query language*. ECHT'92, ACM, December 1992, p. 201–211.
3. F. Burkowski. *Retrieval activities in a database consisting of heterogeneous collections of structured text*. In Proc. 15th annual international ACM-SIGIR Conference on Research and Development in Information Retrieval. Copenhagen, 1992.
4. J. P. Chevallet. *Un modèle logique de Recherche d'Informations appliqué au formalisme des Graphes Conceptuels, le prototype ELEN et son expérimentation sur un corpus de composants logiciels*. PhD thesis in Computer Science. University Joseph Fourier, Grenoble, May 15 1992.
5. Y. Chiaramella, A. Kheirbek *An Integrated Model for Hypermedia and Information Retrieval*. Chapter in "Information Retrieval and Hypertext" (pp 139–176). Edited by Maristella Agosti and Alan Smeaton.1996. Kluwer Academic Press.
6. Y. Chiaramella, Ph. Mulhem, F. Fourel. *A model for Multimedia Information Retrieval*. Technical Report of ESPRIT Project 8134 "FERMI". University of Glasgow. Technical Report Series No. 4/96. December 1996.
7. Y. Chiaramella. *Browsing and Querying: two complementary approaches for Multimedia Information Retrieval*. In Proc. HIM'97 International Conference, Dortmund. 1997.
8. G.V. Cormak, C.L. Clarke, C.R. Palmer. *Passage-based query refinement (Multitext experiments for TREC-6)*. Information Processing & Management; 36(1). January 2000. 133–153.
9. W. B. Croft and H. Turtle. *A Retrieval Model for Incorporating Hypertext Links*. Proceedings of the second ACM conference on Hypertext, Hypertext '89, Pittsburg USA, p213–224.
10. Z. Li, H. Davis, W. Hall. *Hypermedia Links and Information Retrieval*. 14th Information Retrieval Colloquium, Lancaster 1992, p. 169–180.
11. M. D. Dunlop, C. J. Van Rijsbergen. *Hypermedia and Free Text Retrieval*. Information Processing & Management, Vol. 29, No. 3, p. 287–298, 1993.

12. P. Garg. *Abstraction mechanisms in Hypertext.* Communications of the ACM, Vol. 31, No. 7, July 1988.
13. F. G. Halasz. *Reflections on NoteCards: Seven Issues for the Next Generation of Hypermedia System.* Communication of the ACM, Vol. 31, No. 7, July 1988, p. 836–852.
14. M. A. Hearst, J. O. Pedersen. *Reexamining the cluster hypothesis: scatter/gather on retrieval results.* In Proc. 19th ACM-SIGIR International Conference on Research and Development in Information Retrieval. Zurich, 1996.
15. D. Kerkouba. *Indexation automatique et aspects structurels des textes.* In Proc. International conference RIAO 85, (version anglaise disponible), Grenoble, March 1985, pp. 227–249. (english version available).
16. A. Kheirbek. *Two-level Hypermedia Model Based on Conceptual Graph Theory.* Workshop on Intelligent Hypertext, CIKM'93, 5 Nov. 1993.
17. A. Kheirbek, Y. Chiaramella. *Integrating Hypermedia and Information Retrieval using Conceptual Graphs.* Proc. HIM'95 Conference, pp 47–60. Konstanz, Germany. April 1995.
18. D. Lucarella, S. Parisotto, A. Zanzi. *MORE: Multimedia Object Retrieval Environment.* Hypertext'93 Proc., p. 39–50, Seattle, Washington USA, Nov. 1993, ACM.
19. E. Mittendorf, P. Schaüble. *Document and passage retrieval based on Hidden Markov Models.* In Proc. ACM SIGIR International Conference on Research and Developments in Information Retrieval. 1994. p 318–327.
20. J. Nanard, M. Nanard. *Using structured Types to Incorporate Knowledge in Hypertext.* Hypertext'91, p. 329–343, San Antonio, Texas, USA, Dec. 1991, ACM.
21. J. Nie. *An Information Retrieval Model based on Modal Logic.* Information Processing & Management, Vol 25, No. 5, p.477–491, 1990.
22. L.T. Nowell, R.K. France, D. Hix, L. S. Heath, E. A. Fox. *Visualizing search results: some alternatives to query-document similarity.* In Proc. 19th ACM-SIGIR International Conference on Research and Development in Information Retrieval. Zurich, 1996.
23. J. O'Connor. *Retrieval of answer-sentences and answer-figures from papers by text searching.* Information Processing & Management; 11(5/7). 1975. p 155–164.
24. J. O'Connor. *Answer-passage retrieval by text searching.* Journal of the American Society for Information Science; 31(4). July 1980. p 227–239.
25. G. Richard, A. Rizk. *Quelques idées pour une modélisation des systemes hypertextes.* T.S.I. Technique et Science Informatique, Vol. 9, No. 6, 1990.
26. G. Salton, M.J. Mc Gill. *Introduction to Modern Information Retrieval.* McGraw Hill Book Company, 1983
27. J. F. Sowa. *Conceptual Structures: Information Processing in Mind and Machine.* Addison-Wesley publishing company, 1984.
28. T.P. Van Der Weide, P.D. Bruza. *Two level Hypermedia: An improved architecture for Hypertext.* Proc. of the Database and Expert System Applications, DEXA'90, Springer Verlag, Vienne, Autriche, September 1990.
29. C.J. Van Rijsbergen. *A New Theoretical Framework for Information Retrieval.* Proc. of the ACM Conference on Research and Development in Information Retrieval, Pisa, September 1986, p. 194–200.
30. A. Veerasamy, N.J. Belkin. *Evaluation of a tool for visualization of information retrieval results.* In Proc. 19th ACM-SIGIR International Conference on Research and Development in Information Retrieval. Zurich, 1996.
31. V. Wuwongse, M. Manzano. *Fuzzy conceptual graphs.* Proc. of ICCS'93, Quebec City, Canada, August 1993. Lecture Notes in Artificial Intelligence, 699.

Author Index

Lecture Notes in Computer Science

For information about Vols. 1–1944
please contact your bookseller or Springer-Verlag

Lecture Notes in Computer Science 1980

Edited by G. Goos, J. Hartmanis and J. van Leeuwen

Springer
Berlin
Heidelberg
New York
Barcelona
Hong Kong
London
Milan
Paris
Singapore
Tokyo